JLA: TOWER OF [BABEL]

Mark Waid Dan Curtis Johnson Christopher Priest John Ostrander
Writers **Howard Porter Steve Scott Mark Pajarillo Pablo Raimondi
Eric Battle Ken Lashley** Pencillers **Drew Geraci Mark Propst
Walden Wong Claude St. Aubin David Meikis Prentis Rollins
Ron Boyd** Inkers **John Kalisz Pat Garrahy Tom McCraw** Colorists
Ken Lopez John Costanza Kurt Hathaway Janice Chiang Letterers

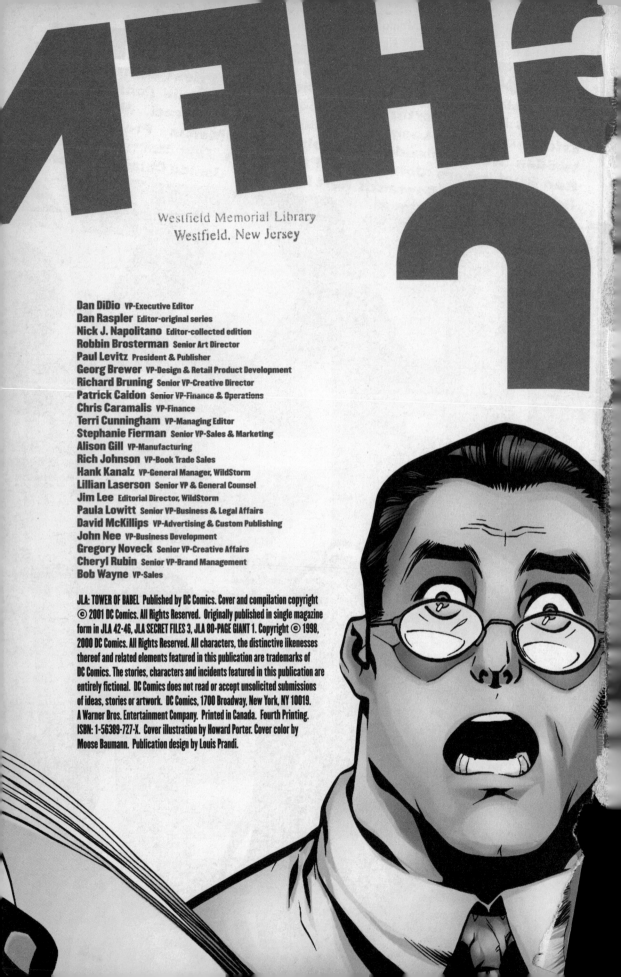

Dan DiDio VP-Executive Editor
Dan Raspler Editor-original series
Nick J. Napolitano Editor-collected edition
Robbin Brosterman Senior Art Director
Paul Levitz President & Publisher
Georg Brewer VP-Design & Retail Product Development
Richard Bruning Senior VP-Creative Director
Patrick Caldon Senior VP-Finance & Operations
Chris Caramalis VP-Finance
Terri Cunningham VP-Managing Editor
Stephanie Fierman Senior VP-Sales & Marketing
Alison Gill VP-Manufacturing
Rich Johnson VP-Book Trade Sales
Hank Kanalz VP-General Manager, WildStorm
Lillian Laserson Senior VP & General Counsel
Jim Lee Editorial Director, WildStorm
Paula Lowitt Senior VP-Business & Legal Affairs
David McKillips VP-Advertising & Custom Publishing
John Nee VP-Business Development
Gregory Noveck Senior VP-Creative Affairs
Cheryl Rubin Senior VP-Brand Management
Bob Wayne VP-Sales

JLA: TOWER OF BABEL Published by DC Comics. Cover and compilation copyright © 2001 DC Comics. All Rights Reserved. Originally published in single magazine form in JLA 42-46, JLA SECRET FILES 3, JLA 80-PAGE GIANT 1. Copyright © 1998, 2000 DC Comics. All Rights Reserved. All characters, the distinctive likenesses thereof and related elements featured in this publication are trademarks of DC Comics. The stories, characters and incidents featured in this publication are entirely fictional. DC Comics does not read or accept unsolicited submissions of ideas, stories or artwork. DC Comics, 1700 Broadway, New York, NY 10019. A Warner Bros. Entertainment Company. Printed in Canada. Fourth Printing. ISBN: 1-56389-727-X. Cover illustration by Howard Porter. Cover color by Moose Baumann. Publication design by Louis Prandi.

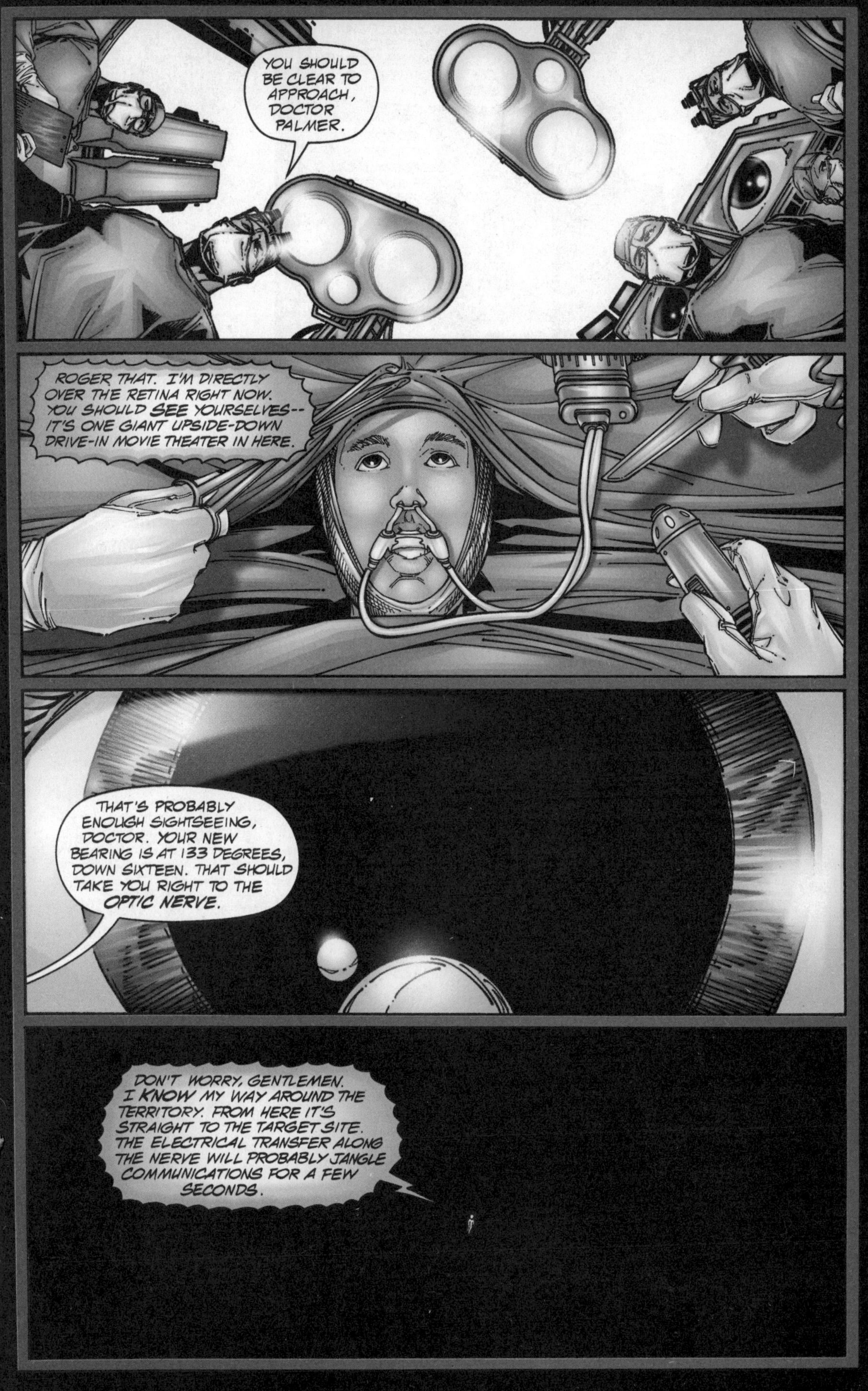
YOU SHOULD BE CLEAR TO APPROACH, DOCTOR PALMER.
ROGER THAT. I'M DIRECTLY OVER THE RETINA RIGHT NOW. YOU SHOULD SEE YOURSELVES-- IT'S ONE GIANT UPSIDE-DOWN DRIVE-IN MOVIE THEATER IN HERE.
THAT'S PROBABLY ENOUGH SIGHTSEEING, DOCTOR. YOUR NEW BEARING IS AT 133 DEGREES, DOWN SIXTEEN. THAT SHOULD TAKE YOU RIGHT TO THE OPTIC NERVE.
DON'T WORRY, GENTLEMEN. I KNOW MY WAY AROUND THE TERRITORY. FROM HERE IT'S STRAIGHT TO THE TARGET SITE. THE ELECTRICAL TRANSFER ALONG THE NERVE WILL PROBABLY JANGLE COMMUNICATIONS FOR A FEW SECONDS.

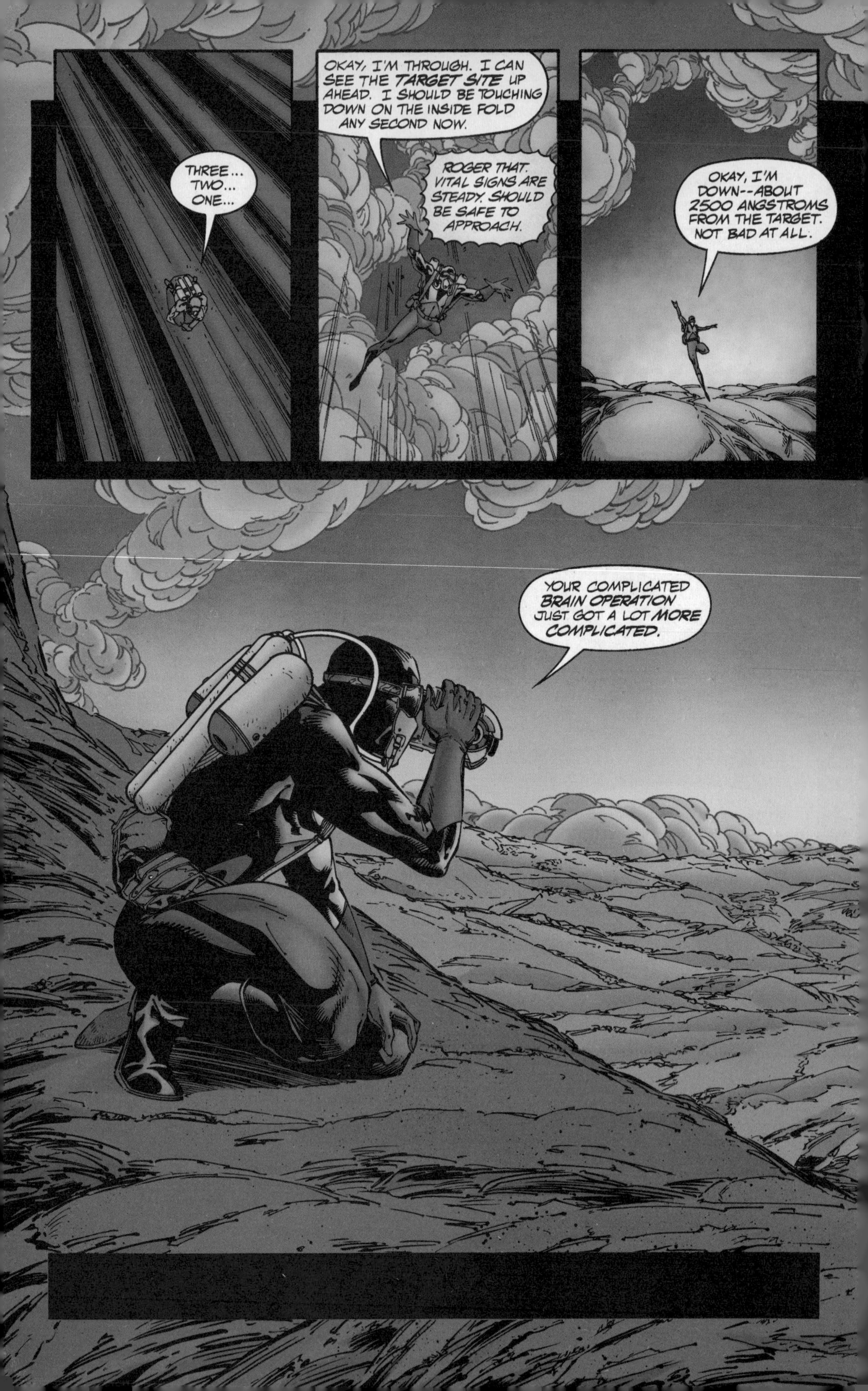
THREE... TWO... ONE...
OKAY, I'M THROUGH. I CAN SEE THE TARGET SITE UP AHEAD. I SHOULD BE TOUCHING DOWN ON THE INSIDE FOLD ANY SECOND NOW.
ROGER THAT. VITAL SIGNS ARE STEADY. SHOULD BE SAFE TO APPROACH.
OKAY, I'M DOWN--ABOUT 2500 ANGSTROMS FROM THE TARGET. NOT BAD AT ALL.
YOUR COMPLICATED BRAIN OPERATION JUST GOT A LOT MORE COMPLICATED.

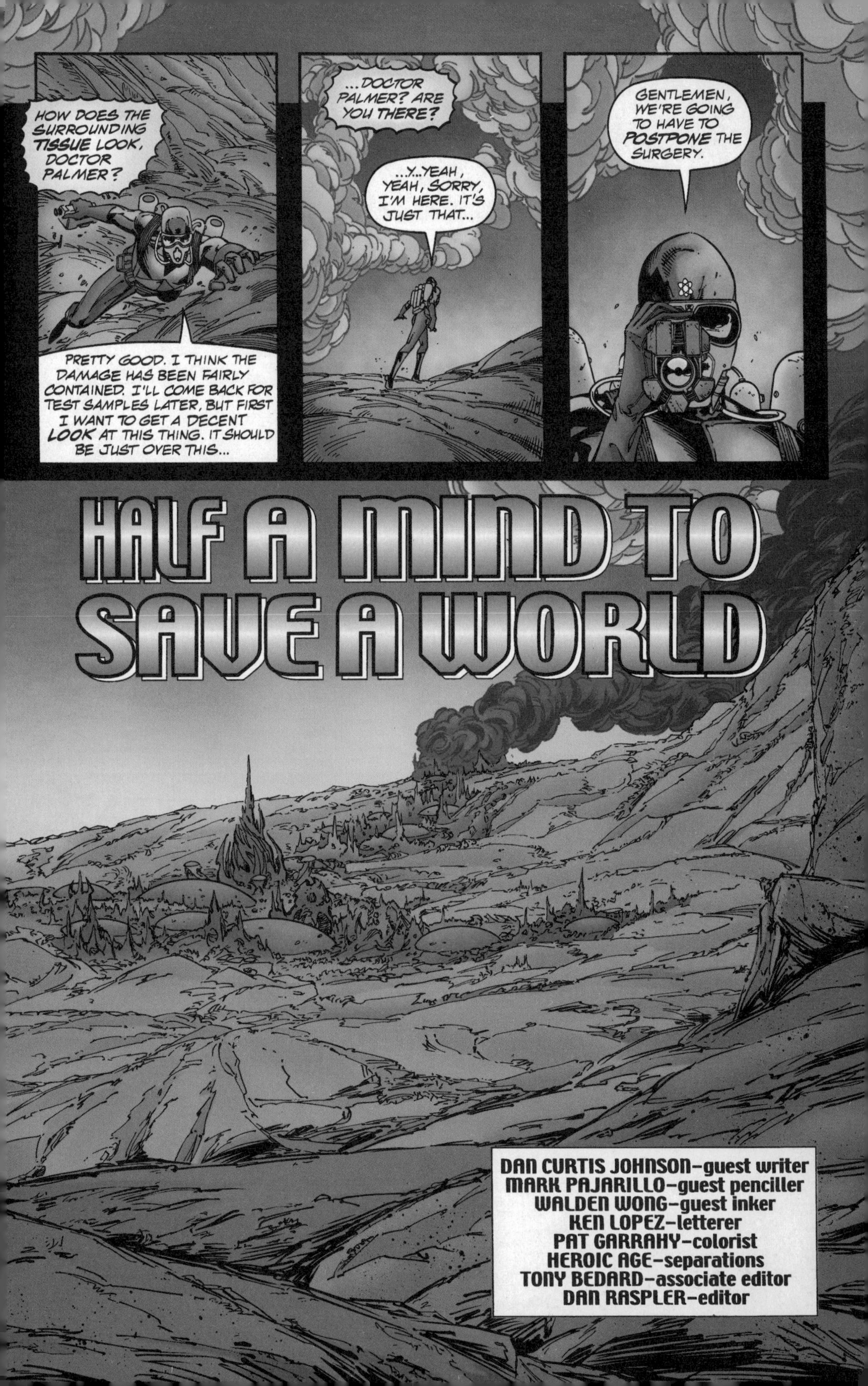
HOW DOES THE SURROUNDING TISSUE LOOK, DOCTOR PALMER?
PRETTY GOOD. I THINK THE DAMAGE HAS BEEN FAIRLY CONTAINED. I'LL COME BACK FOR TEST SAMPLES LATER, BUT FIRST I WANT TO GET A DECENT LOOK AT THIS THING. IT SHOULD BE JUST OVER THIS...
...DOCTOR PALMER? ARE YOU THERE?
...Y...YEAH, YEAH, SORRY, I'M HERE. IT'S JUST THAT...
GENTLEMEN, WE'RE GOING TO HAVE TO POSTPONE THE SURGERY.
HALF A MIND TO SAVE A WORLD
DAN CURTIS JOHNSON–guest writer
MARK PAJARILLO–guest penciller
WALDEN WONG–guest inker
KEN LOPEZ–letterer
PAT GARRAHY–colorist
HEROIC AGE–separations
TONY BEDARD–associate editor
DAN RASPLER–editor

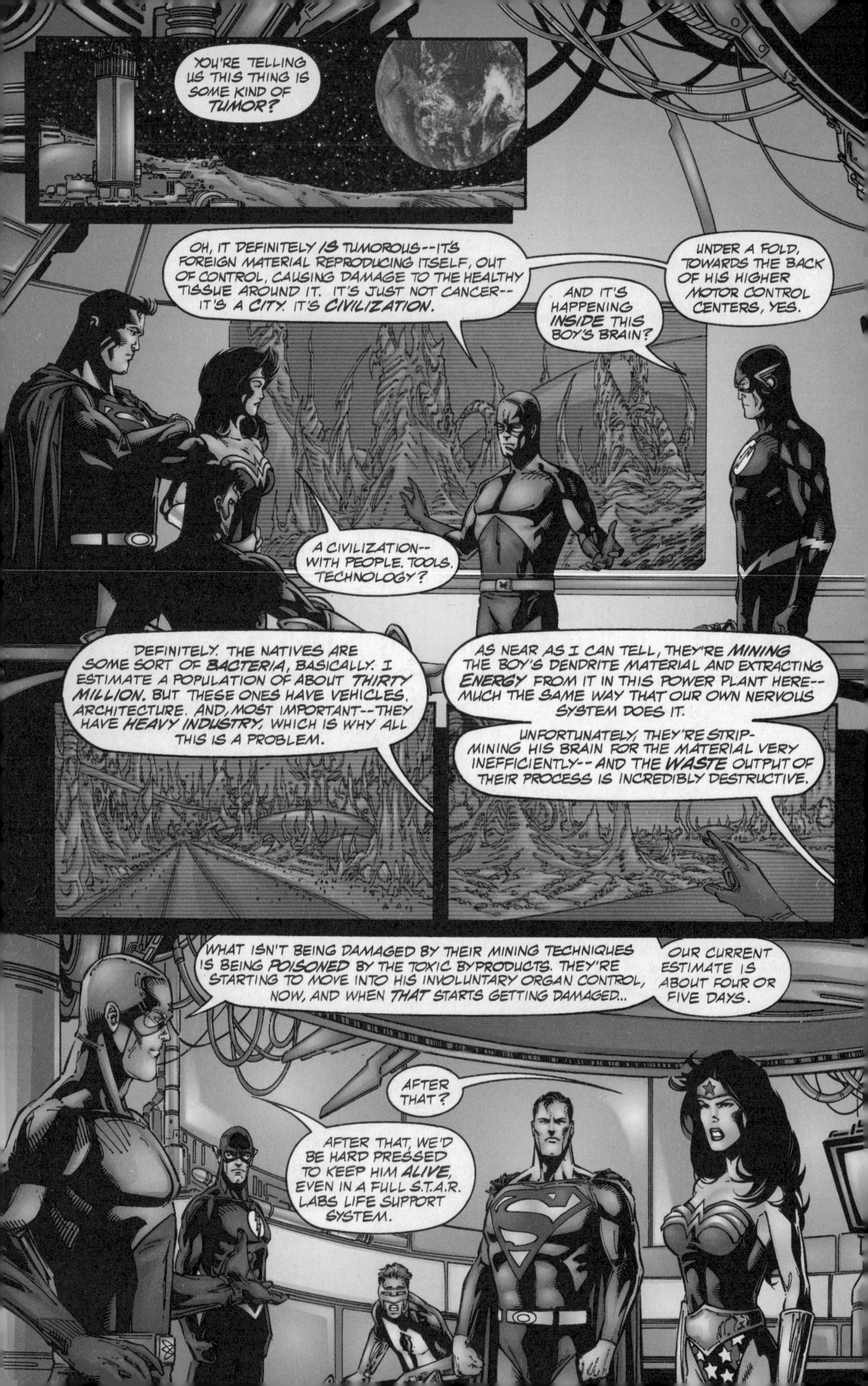
YOU'RE TELLING US THIS THING IS SOME KIND OF TUMOR?
OH, IT DEFINITELY IS TUMOROUS--IT'S FOREIGN MATERIAL REPRODUCING ITSELF, OUT OF CONTROL, CAUSING DAMAGE TO THE HEALTHY TISSUE AROUND IT. IT'S JUST NOT CANCER-- IT'S A CITY. IT'S CIVILIZATION.
AND IT'S HAPPENING INSIDE THIS BOY'S BRAIN?
UNDER A FOLD, TOWARDS THE BACK OF HIS HIGHER MOTOR CONTROL CENTERS, YES.
A CIVILIZATION-- WITH PEOPLE. TOOLS. TECHNOLOGY?
DEFINITELY. THE NATIVES ARE SOME SORT OF BACTERIA, BASICALLY. I ESTIMATE A POPULATION OF ABOUT THIRTY MILLION. BUT THESE ONES HAVE VEHICLES. ARCHITECTURE. AND, MOST IMPORTANT--THEY HAVE HEAVY INDUSTRY, WHICH IS WHY ALL THIS IS A PROBLEM.
AS NEAR AS I CAN TELL, THEY'RE MINING THE BOY'S DENDRITE MATERIAL AND EXTRACTING ENERGY FROM IT IN THIS POWER PLANT HERE-- MUCH THE SAME WAY THAT OUR OWN NERVOUS SYSTEM DOES IT.
UNFORTUNATELY, THEY'RE STRIP-MINING HIS BRAIN FOR THE MATERIAL VERY INEFFICIENTLY-- AND THE WASTE OUTPUT OF THEIR PROCESS IS INCREDIBLY DESTRUCTIVE.
WHAT ISN'T BEING DAMAGED BY THEIR MINING TECHNIQUES IS BEING POISONED BY THE TOXIC BYPRODUCTS. THEY'RE STARTING TO MOVE INTO HIS INVOLUNTARY ORGAN CONTROL, NOW, AND WHEN THAT STARTS GETTING DAMAGED...
OUR CURRENT ESTIMATE IS ABOUT FOUR OR FIVE DAYS.
AFTER THAT?
AFTER THAT, WE'D BE HARD PRESSED TO KEEP HIM ALIVE, EVEN IN A FULL S.T.A.R. LABS LIFE SUPPORT SYSTEM.

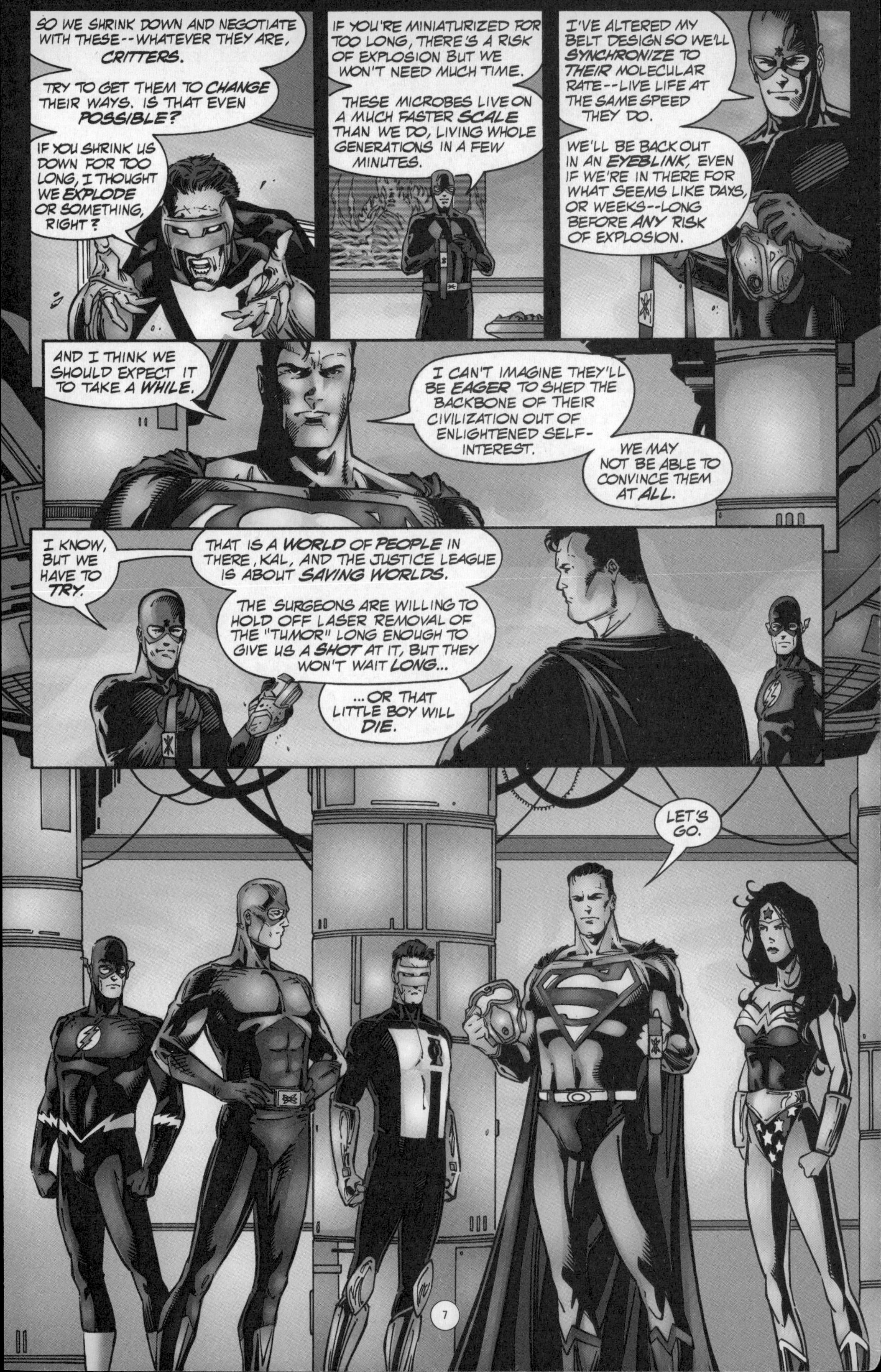
SO WE SHRINK DOWN AND NEGOTIATE WITH THESE--WHATEVER THEY ARE, CRITTERS.
TRY TO GET THEM TO CHANGE THEIR WAYS. IS THAT EVEN POSSIBLE?
IF YOU SHRINK US DOWN FOR TOO LONG, I THOUGHT WE EXPLODE OR SOMETHING, RIGHT?
IF YOU'RE MINIATURIZED FOR TOO LONG, THERE'S A RISK OF EXPLOSION BUT WE WON'T NEED MUCH TIME.
THESE MICROBES LIVE ON A MUCH FASTER SCALE THAN WE DO, LIVING WHOLE GENERATIONS IN A FEW MINUTES.
I'VE ALTERED MY BELT DESIGN SO WE'LL SYNCHRONIZE TO THEIR MOLECULAR RATE--LIVE LIFE AT THE SAME SPEED THEY DO.
WE'LL BE BACK OUT IN AN EYEBLINK, EVEN IF WE'RE IN THERE FOR WHAT SEEMS LIKE DAYS, OR WEEKS--LONG BEFORE ANY RISK OF EXPLOSION.
AND I THINK WE SHOULD EXPECT IT TO TAKE A WHILE.
I CAN'T IMAGINE THEY'LL BE EAGER TO SHED THE BACKBONE OF THEIR CIVILIZATION OUT OF ENLIGHTENED SELF-INTEREST.
WE MAY NOT BE ABLE TO CONVINCE THEM AT ALL.
I KNOW, BUT WE HAVE TO TRY.
THAT IS A WORLD OF PEOPLE IN THERE, KAL, AND THE JUSTICE LEAGUE IS ABOUT SAVING WORLDS.
THE SURGEONS ARE WILLING TO HOLD OFF LASER REMOVAL OF THE "TUMOR" LONG ENOUGH TO GIVE US A SHOT AT IT, BUT THEY WON'T WAIT LONG...
...OR THAT LITTLE BOY WILL DIE.
LET'S GO.

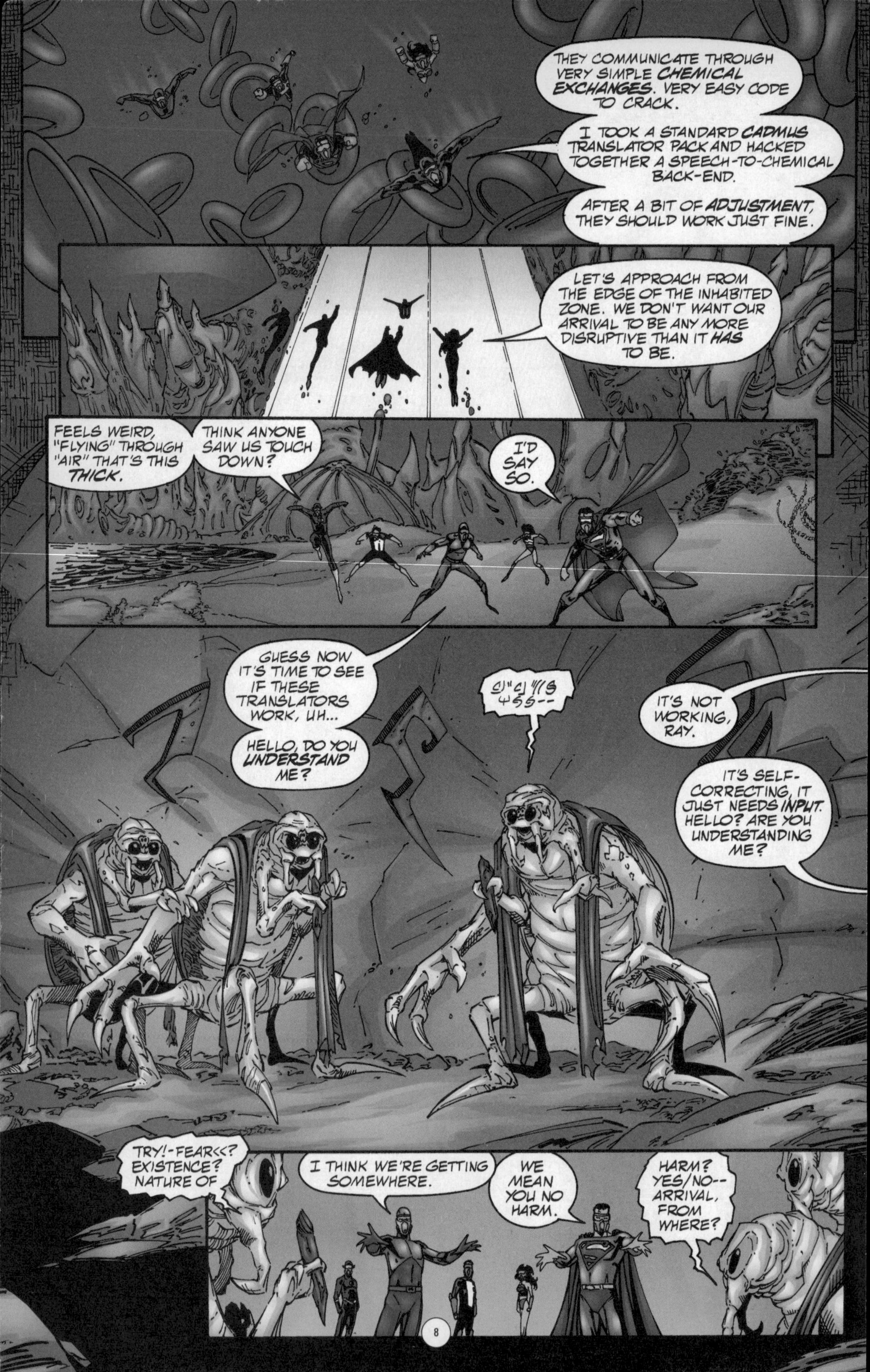
THEY COMMUNICATE THROUGH VERY SIMPLE CHEMICAL EXCHANGES. VERY EASY CODE TO CRACK.
I TOOK A STANDARD CADMUS TRANSLATOR PACK AND HACKED TOGETHER A SPEECH-TO-CHEMICAL BACK-END.
AFTER A BIT OF ADJUSTMENT, THEY SHOULD WORK JUST FINE.
LET'S APPROACH FROM THE EDGE OF THE INHABITED ZONE. WE DON'T WANT OUR ARRIVAL TO BE ANY MORE DISRUPTIVE THAN IT HAS TO BE.
FEELS WEIRD, "FLYING" THROUGH "AIR" THAT'S THIS THICK.
THINK ANYONE SAW US TOUCH DOWN?
I'D SAY SO.
GUESS NOW IT'S TIME TO SEE IF THESE TRANSLATORS WORK, UH...
HELLO, DO YOU UNDERSTAND ME?
IT'S NOT WORKING, RAY.
IT'S SELF-CORRECTING, IT JUST NEEDS INPUT. HELLO? ARE YOU UNDERSTANDING ME?
TRY!-FEAR<<? EXISTENCE? NATURE OF
I THINK WE'RE GETTING SOMEWHERE.
WE MEAN YOU NO HARM.
HARM? YES/NO-- ARRIVAL, FROM WHERE?

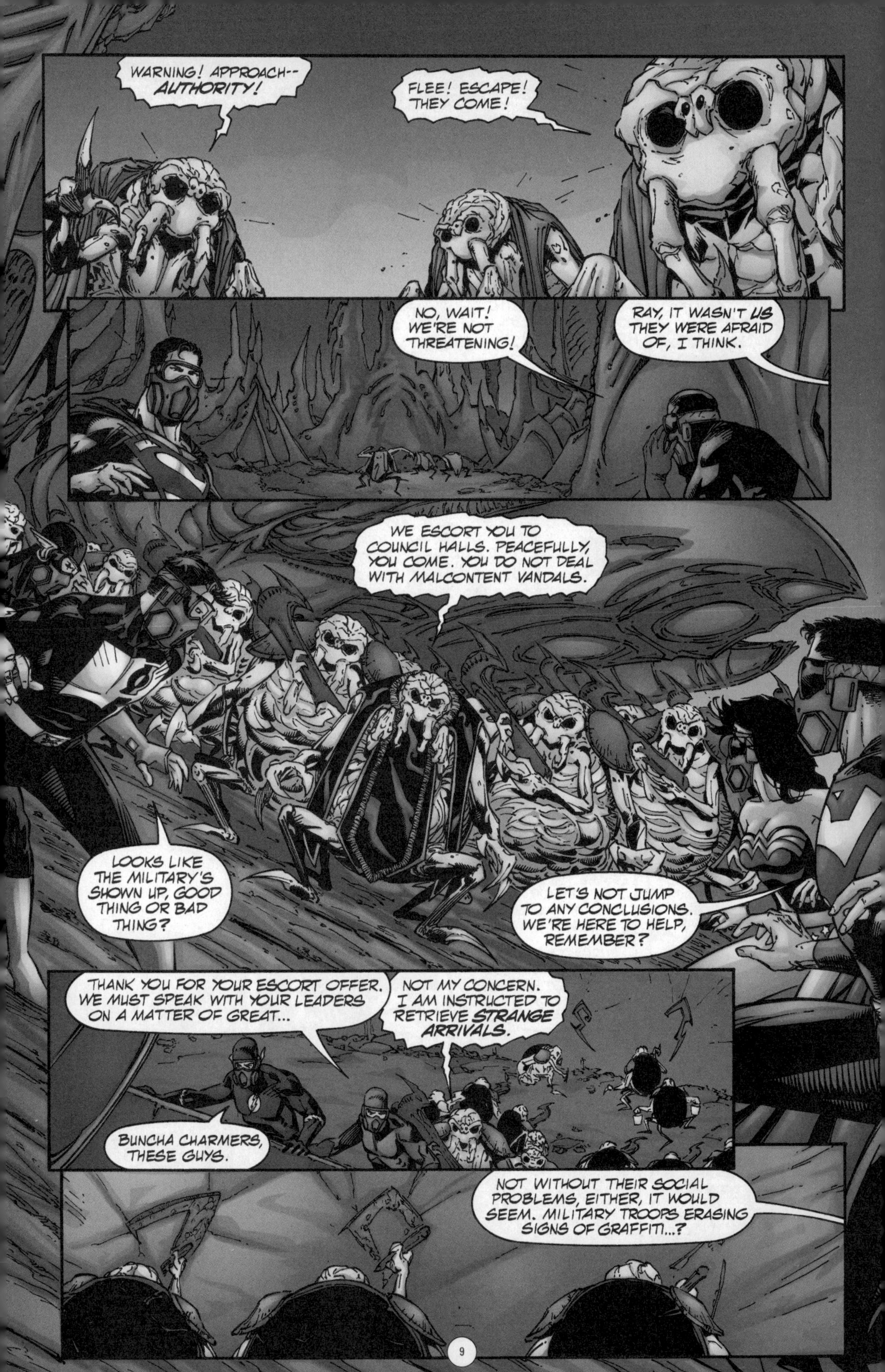
WARNING! APPROACH-- AUTHORITY!
FLEE! ESCAPE! THEY COME!
NO, WAIT! WE'RE NOT THREATENING!
RAY, IT WASN'T US THEY WERE AFRAID OF, I THINK.
WE ESCORT YOU TO COUNCIL HALLS. PEACEFULLY, YOU COME. YOU DO NOT DEAL WITH MALCONTENT VANDALS.
LOOKS LIKE THE MILITARY'S SHOWN UP, GOOD THING OR BAD THING?
LET'S NOT JUMP TO ANY CONCLUSIONS. WE'RE HERE TO HELP, REMEMBER?
THANK YOU FOR YOUR ESCORT OFFER. WE MUST SPEAK WITH YOUR LEADERS ON A MATTER OF GREAT...
NOT MY CONCERN. I AM INSTRUCTED TO RETRIEVE STRANGE ARRIVALS.
BUNCHA CHARMERS, THESE GUYS.
NOT WITHOUT THEIR SOCIAL PROBLEMS, EITHER, IT WOULD SEEM. MILITARY TROOPS ERASING SIGNS OF GRAFFITI...?

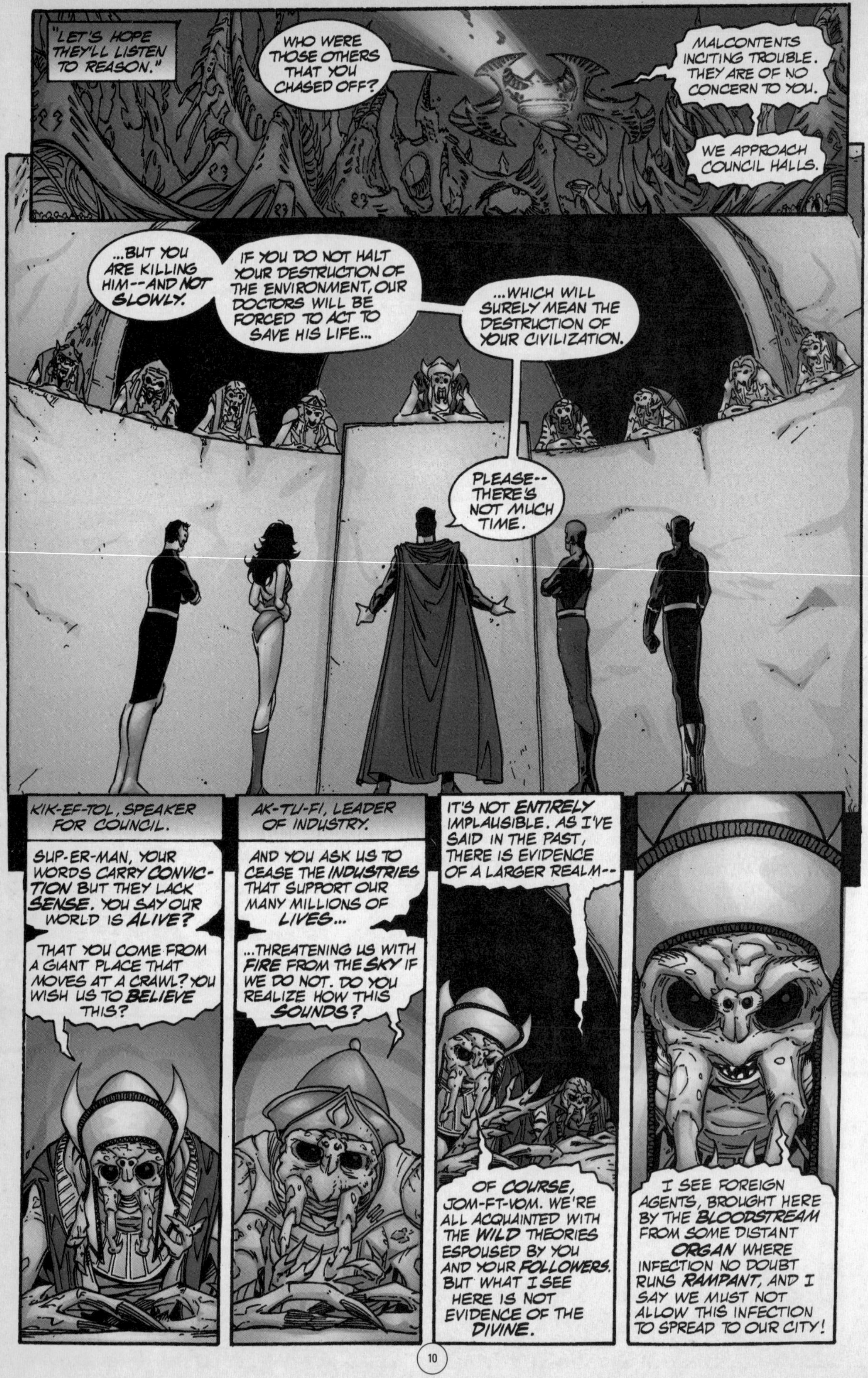
"LET'S HOPE THEY'LL LISTEN TO REASON."
WHO WERE THOSE OTHERS THAT YOU CHASED OFF?
MALCONTENTS INCITING TROUBLE. THEY ARE OF NO CONCERN TO YOU.
WE APPROACH COUNCIL HALLS.
...BUT YOU ARE KILLING HIM--AND NOT SLOWLY.
IF YOU DO NOT HALT YOUR DESTRUCTION OF THE ENVIRONMENT, OUR DOCTORS WILL BE FORCED TO ACT TO SAVE HIS LIFE...
...WHICH WILL SURELY MEAN THE DESTRUCTION OF YOUR CIVILIZATION.
PLEASE--THERE'S NOT MUCH TIME.
KIK-EF-TOL, SPEAKER FOR COUNCIL.
SUP-ER-MAN, YOUR WORDS CARRY CONVICTION BUT THEY LACK SENSE. YOU SAY OUR WORLD IS ALIVE?
THAT YOU COME FROM A GIANT PLACE THAT MOVES AT A CRAWL? YOU WISH US TO BELIEVE THIS?
AK-TU-FI, LEADER OF INDUSTRY.
AND YOU ASK US TO CEASE THE INDUSTRIES THAT SUPPORT OUR MANY MILLIONS OF LIVES...
...THREATENING US WITH FIRE FROM THE SKY IF WE DO NOT. DO YOU REALIZE HOW THIS SOUNDS?
IT'S NOT ENTIRELY IMPLAUSIBLE. AS I'VE SAID IN THE PAST, THERE IS EVIDENCE OF A LARGER REALM--
OF COURSE, JOM-FT-VOM. WE'RE ALL ACQUAINTED WITH THE WILD THEORIES ESPOUSED BY YOU AND YOUR FOLLOWERS. BUT WHAT I SEE HERE IS NOT EVIDENCE OF THE DIVINE.
I SEE FOREIGN AGENTS, BROUGHT HERE BY THE BLOODSTREAM FROM SOME DISTANT ORGAN WHERE INFECTION NO DOUBT RUNS RAMPANT, AND I SAY WE MUST NOT ALLOW THIS INFECTION TO SPREAD TO OUR CITY!

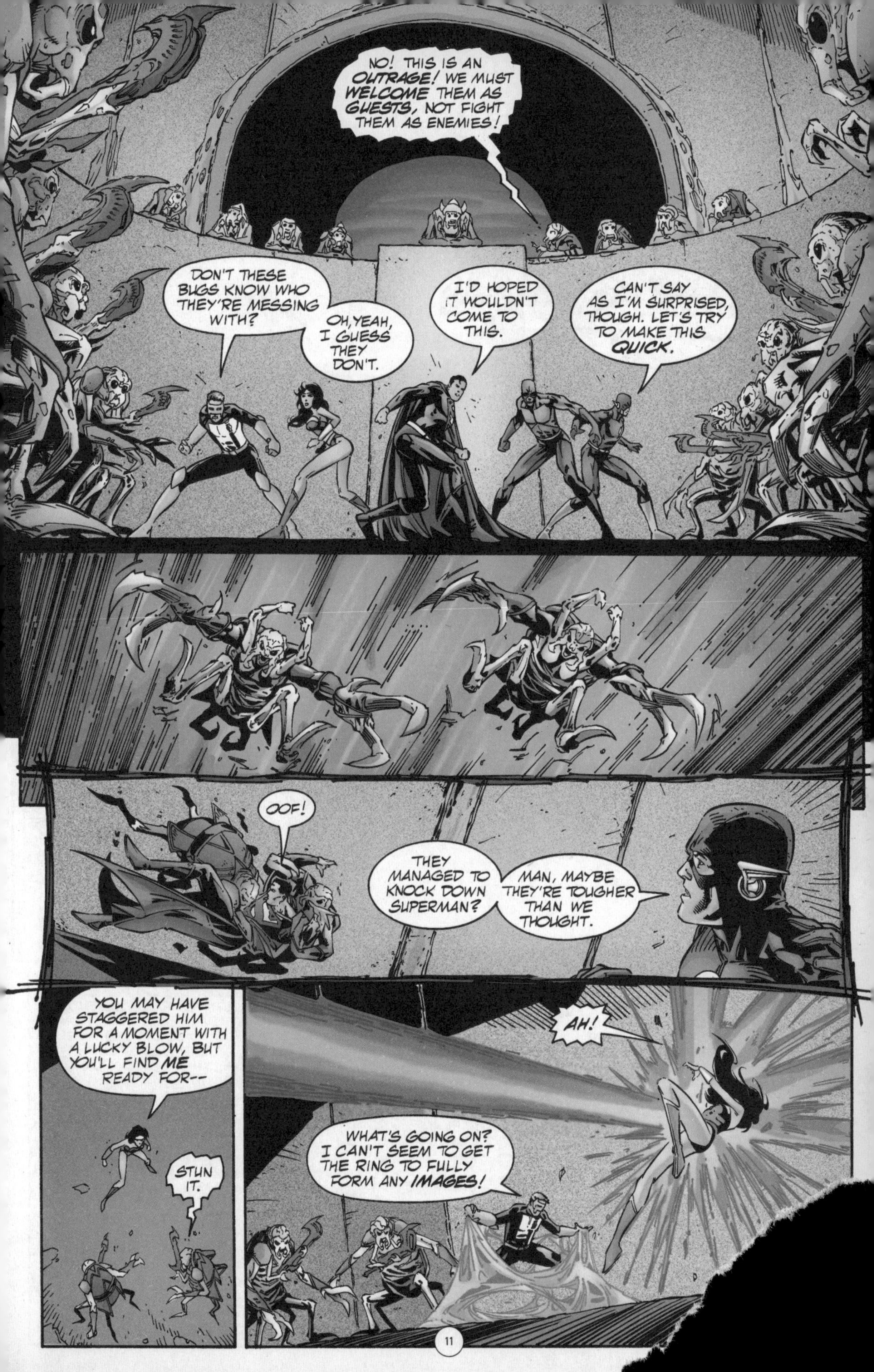
NO! THIS IS AN OUTRAGE! WE MUST WELCOME THEM AS GUESTS, NOT FIGHT THEM AS ENEMIES!
DON'T THESE BUGS KNOW WHO THEY'RE MESSING WITH?
OH, YEAH, I GUESS THEY DON'T.
I'D HOPED IT WOULDN'T COME TO THIS.
CAN'T SAY AS I'M SURPRISED, THOUGH. LET'S TRY TO MAKE THIS QUICK.
OOF!
THEY MANAGED TO KNOCK DOWN SUPERMAN?
MAN, MAYBE THEY'RE TOUGHER THAN WE THOUGHT.
YOU MAY HAVE STAGGERED HIM FOR A MOMENT WITH A LUCKY BLOW, BUT YOU'LL FIND ME READY FOR--
STUN IT.
AH!
WHAT'S GOING ON? I CAN'T SEEM TO GET THE RING TO FULLY FORM ANY IMAGES!

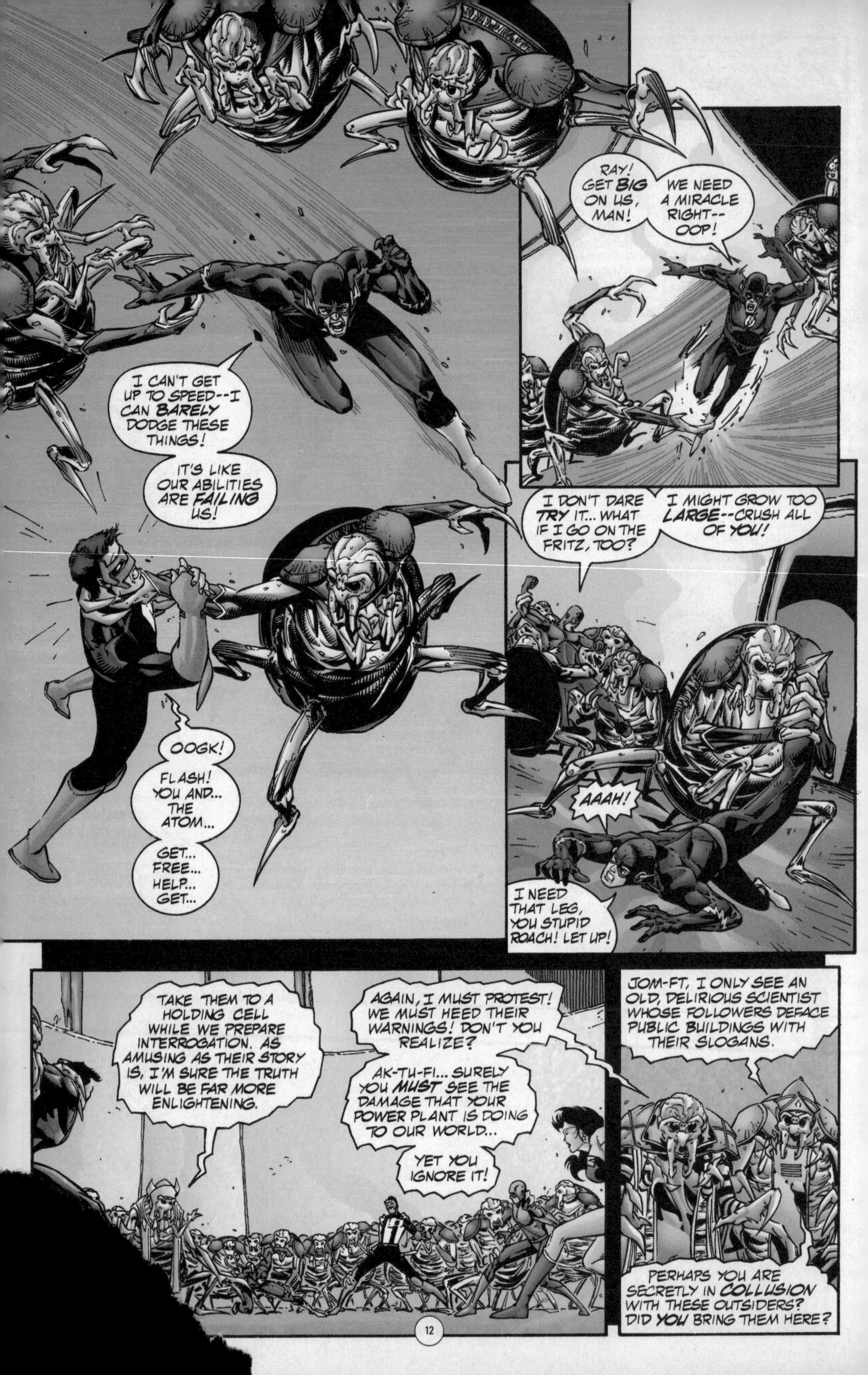
RAY! GET BIG ON US, MAN!
WE NEED A MIRACLE RIGHT-- OOP!
I CAN'T GET UP TO SPEED--I CAN BARELY DODGE THESE THINGS!
IT'S LIKE OUR ABILITIES ARE FAILING US!
I DON'T DARE TRY IT... WHAT IF I GO ON THE FRITZ, TOO?
I MIGHT GROW TOO LARGE--CRUSH ALL OF YOU!
OOGK!
FLASH! YOU AND... THE ATOM...
GET... FREE... HELP... GET...
AAAH!
I NEED THAT LEG, YOU STUPID ROACH! LET UP!
TAKE THEM TO A HOLDING CELL WHILE WE PREPARE INTERROGATION. AS AMUSING AS THEIR STORY IS, I'M SURE THE TRUTH WILL BE FAR MORE ENLIGHTENING.
AGAIN, I MUST PROTEST! WE MUST HEED THEIR WARNINGS! DON'T YOU REALIZE?
AK-TU-FI... SURELY YOU MUST SEE THE DAMAGE THAT YOUR POWER PLANT IS DOING TO OUR WORLD...
YET YOU IGNORE IT!
JOM-FT, I ONLY SEE AN OLD, DELIRIOUS SCIENTIST WHOSE FOLLOWERS DEFACE PUBLIC BUILDINGS WITH THEIR SLOGANS.
PERHAPS YOU ARE SECRETLY IN COLLUSION WITH THESE OUTSIDERS? DID YOU BRING THEM HERE?

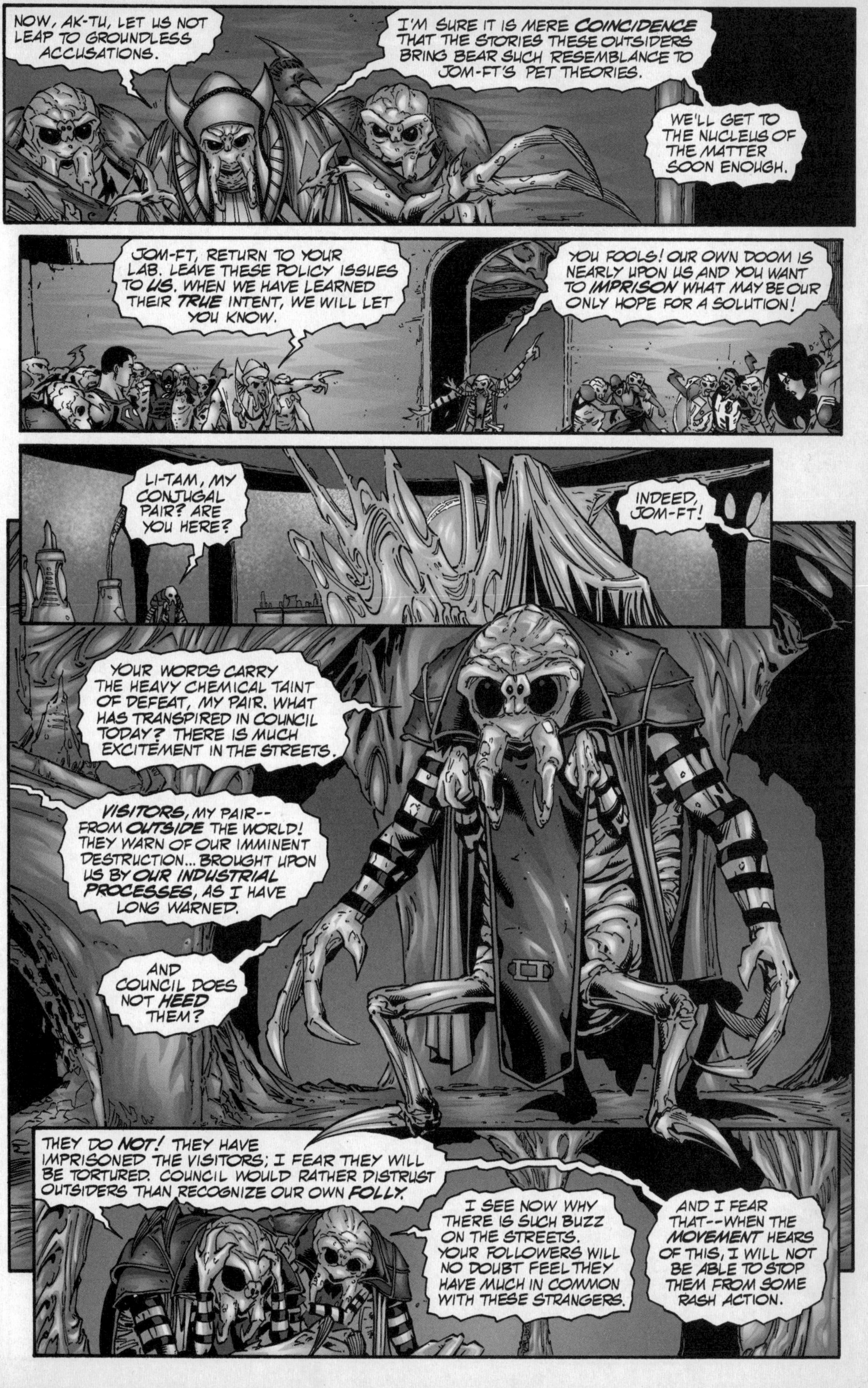
NOW, AK-TU, LET US NOT LEAP TO GROUNDLESS ACCUSATIONS.
I'M SURE IT IS MERE COINCIDENCE THAT THE STORIES THESE OUTSIDERS BRING BEAR SUCH RESEMBLANCE TO JOM-FT'S PET THEORIES.
WE'LL GET TO THE NUCLEUS OF THE MATTER SOON ENOUGH.
JOM-FT, RETURN TO YOUR LAB. LEAVE THESE POLICY ISSUES TO US. WHEN WE HAVE LEARNED THEIR TRUE INTENT, WE WILL LET YOU KNOW.
YOU FOOLS! OUR OWN DOOM IS NEARLY UPON US AND YOU WANT TO IMPRISON WHAT MAY BE OUR ONLY HOPE FOR A SOLUTION!
LI-TAM, MY CONJUGAL PAIR? ARE YOU HERE?
INDEED, JOM-FT!
YOUR WORDS CARRY THE HEAVY CHEMICAL TAINT OF DEFEAT, MY PAIR. WHAT HAS TRANSPIRED IN COUNCIL TODAY? THERE IS MUCH EXCITEMENT IN THE STREETS.
VISITORS, MY PAIR-- FROM OUTSIDE THE WORLD! THEY WARN OF OUR IMMINENT DESTRUCTION... BROUGHT UPON US BY OUR INDUSTRIAL PROCESSES, AS I HAVE LONG WARNED.
AND COUNCIL DOES NOT HEED THEM?
THEY DO NOT! THEY HAVE IMPRISONED THE VISITORS; I FEAR THEY WILL BE TORTURED. COUNCIL WOULD RATHER DISTRUST OUTSIDERS THAN RECOGNIZE OUR OWN FOLLY.
I SEE NOW WHY THERE IS SUCH BUZZ ON THE STREETS. YOUR FOLLOWERS WILL NO DOUBT FEEL THEY HAVE MUCH IN COMMON WITH THESE STRANGERS.
AND I FEAR THAT--WHEN THE MOVEMENT HEARS OF THIS, I WILL NOT BE ABLE TO STOP THEM FROM SOME RASH ACTION.

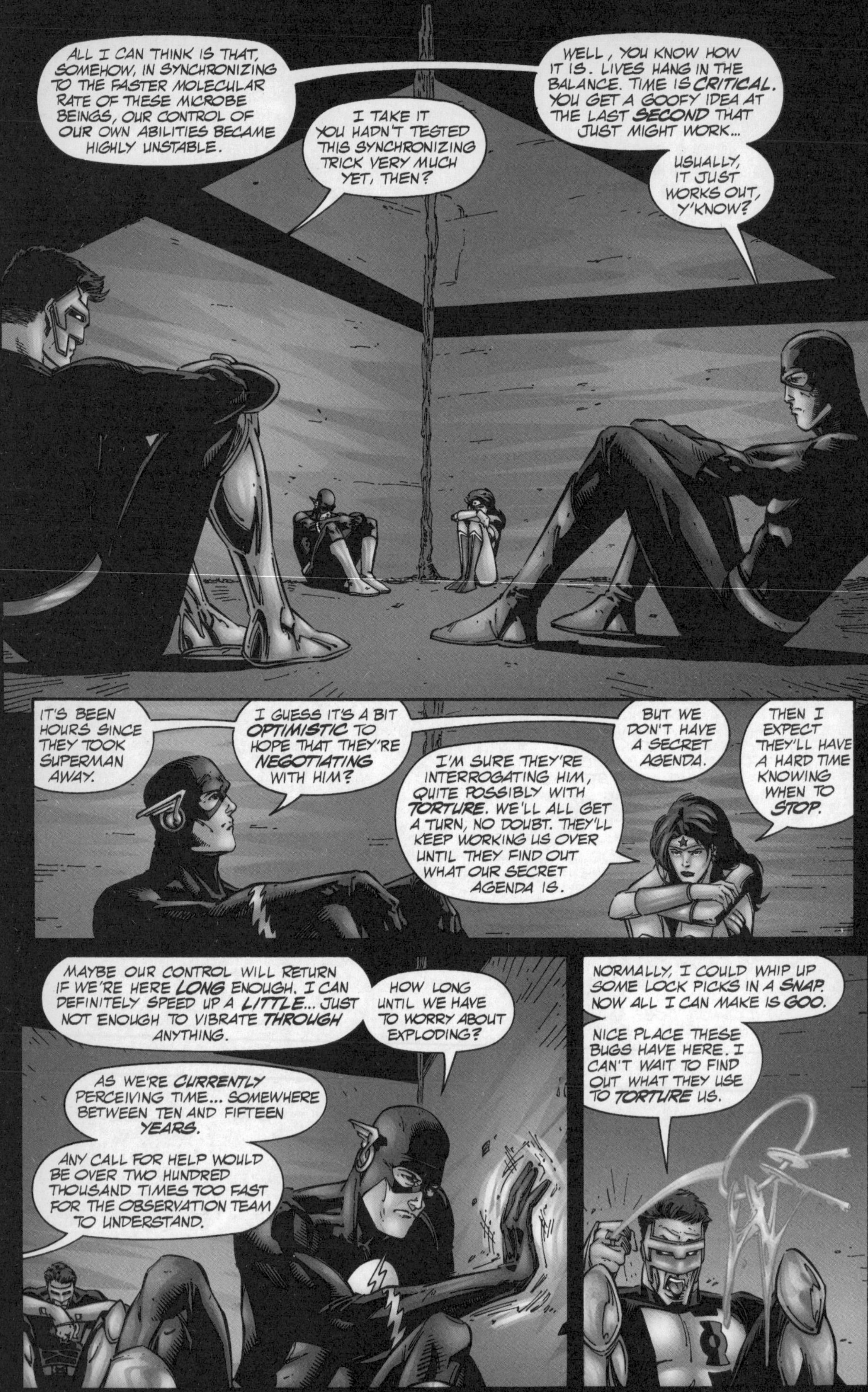
ALL I CAN THINK IS THAT, SOMEHOW, IN SYNCHRONIZING TO THE FASTER MOLECULAR RATE OF THESE MICROBE BEINGS, OUR CONTROL OF OUR OWN ABILITIES BECAME HIGHLY UNSTABLE.
I TAKE IT YOU HADN'T TESTED THIS SYNCHRONIZING TRICK VERY MUCH YET, THEN?
WELL, YOU KNOW HOW IT IS. LIVES HANG IN THE BALANCE. TIME IS CRITICAL. YOU GET A GOOFY IDEA AT THE LAST SECOND THAT JUST MIGHT WORK...
USUALLY, IT JUST WORKS OUT, Y'KNOW?
IT'S BEEN HOURS SINCE THEY TOOK SUPERMAN AWAY.
I GUESS IT'S A BIT OPTIMISTIC TO HOPE THAT THEY'RE NEGOTIATING WITH HIM?
I'M SURE THEY'RE INTERROGATING HIM, QUITE POSSIBLY WITH TORTURE. WE'LL ALL GET A TURN, NO DOUBT. THEY'LL KEEP WORKING US OVER UNTIL THEY FIND OUT WHAT OUR SECRET AGENDA IS.
BUT WE DON'T HAVE A SECRET AGENDA.
THEN I EXPECT THEY'LL HAVE A HARD TIME KNOWING WHEN TO STOP.
MAYBE OUR CONTROL WILL RETURN IF WE'RE HERE LONG ENOUGH. I CAN DEFINITELY SPEED UP A LITTLE... JUST NOT ENOUGH TO VIBRATE THROUGH ANYTHING.
HOW LONG UNTIL WE HAVE TO WORRY ABOUT EXPLODING?
AS WE'RE CURRENTLY PERCEIVING TIME... SOMEWHERE BETWEEN TEN AND FIFTEEN YEARS.
ANY CALL FOR HELP WOULD BE OVER TWO HUNDRED THOUSAND TIMES TOO FAST FOR THE OBSERVATION TEAM TO UNDERSTAND.
NORMALLY, I COULD WHIP UP SOME LOCK PICKS IN A SNAP. NOW ALL I CAN MAKE IS GOO.
NICE PLACE THESE BUGS HAVE HERE. I CAN'T WAIT TO FIND OUT WHAT THEY USE TO TORTURE US.

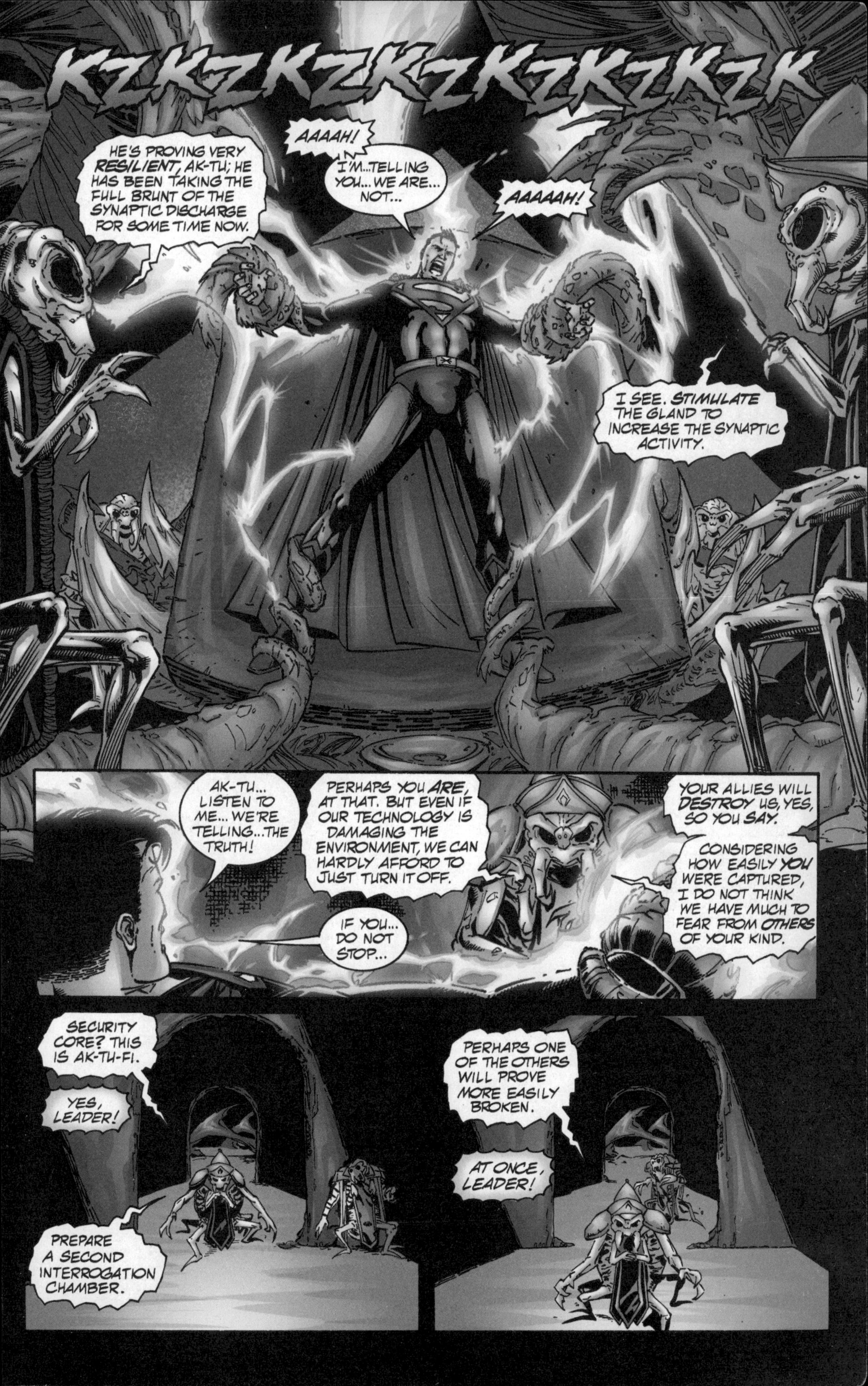
KZKZKZKZKZKZKZKZK
HE'S PROVING VERY RESILIENT, AK-TU; HE HAS BEEN TAKING THE FULL BRUNT OF THE SYNAPTIC DISCHARGE FOR SOME TIME NOW.
AAAAH!
I'M...TELLING YOU... WE ARE... NOT...
AAAAAH!
I SEE. STIMULATE THE GLAND TO INCREASE THE SYNAPTIC ACTIVITY.
AK-TU... LISTEN TO ME... WE'RE TELLING...THE TRUTH!
PERHAPS YOU ARE, AT THAT. BUT EVEN IF OUR TECHNOLOGY IS DAMAGING THE ENVIRONMENT, WE CAN HARDLY AFFORD TO JUST TURN IT OFF.
IF YOU... DO NOT STOP...
YOUR ALLIES WILL DESTROY US, YES, SO YOU SAY.
CONSIDERING HOW EASILY YOU WERE CAPTURED, I DO NOT THINK WE HAVE MUCH TO FEAR FROM OTHERS OF YOUR KIND.
SECURITY CORE? THIS IS AK-TU-FI.
YES, LEADER!
PREPARE A SECOND INTERROGATION CHAMBER.
PERHAPS ONE OF THE OTHERS WILL PROVE MORE EASILY BROKEN.
AT ONCE, LEADER!

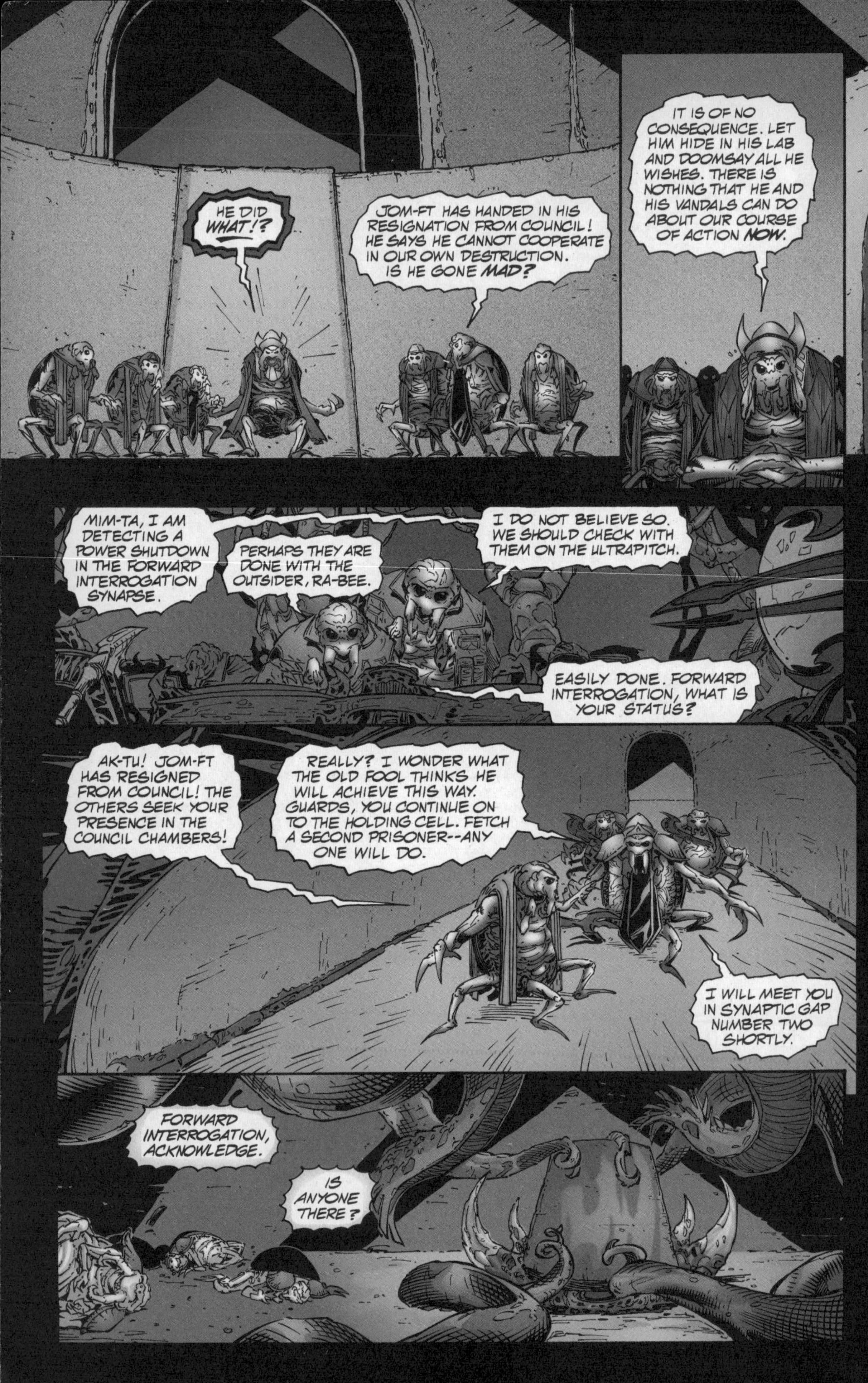
HE DID WHAT!?
JOM-FT HAS HANDED IN HIS RESIGNATION FROM COUNCIL! HE SAYS HE CANNOT COOPERATE IN OUR OWN DESTRUCTION. IS HE GONE MAD?
IT IS OF NO CONSEQUENCE. LET HIM HIDE IN HIS LAB AND DOOMSAY ALL HE WISHES. THERE IS NOTHING THAT HE AND HIS VANDALS CAN DO ABOUT OUR COURSE OF ACTION NOW.
MIM-TA, I AM DETECTING A POWER SHUTDOWN IN THE FORWARD INTERROGATION SYNAPSE.
PERHAPS THEY ARE DONE WITH THE OUTSIDER, RA-BEE.
I DO NOT BELIEVE SO. WE SHOULD CHECK WITH THEM ON THE ULTRAPITCH.
EASILY DONE. FORWARD INTERROGATION, WHAT IS YOUR STATUS?
AK-TU! JOM-FT HAS RESIGNED FROM COUNCIL! THE OTHERS SEEK YOUR PRESENCE IN THE COUNCIL CHAMBERS!
REALLY? I WONDER WHAT THE OLD FOOL THINKS HE WILL ACHIEVE THIS WAY. GUARDS, YOU CONTINUE ON TO THE HOLDING CELL. FETCH A SECOND PRISONER--ANY ONE WILL DO.
I WILL MEET YOU IN SYNAPTIC GAP NUMBER TWO SHORTLY.
FORWARD INTERROGATION, ACKNOWLEDGE.
IS ANYONE THERE?

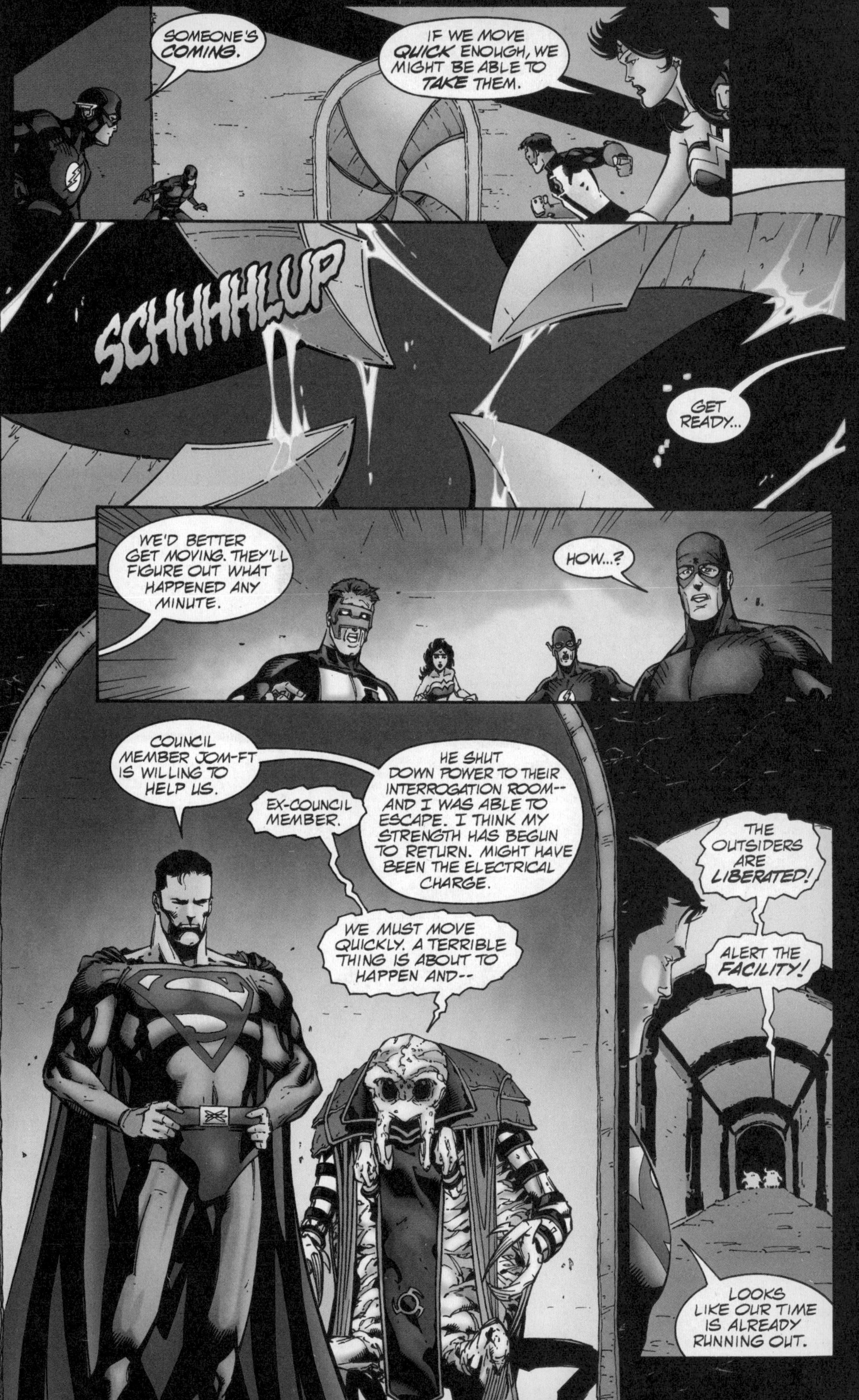
SOMEONE'S COMING.
IF WE MOVE QUICK ENOUGH, WE MIGHT BE ABLE TO TAKE THEM.
SCHHHLUP
GET READY...
WE'D BETTER GET MOVING. THEY'LL FIGURE OUT WHAT HAPPENED ANY MINUTE.
HOW...?
COUNCIL MEMBER JOM-FT IS WILLING TO HELP US.
EX-COUNCIL MEMBER.
HE SHUT DOWN POWER TO THEIR INTERROGATION ROOM-- AND I WAS ABLE TO ESCAPE. I THINK MY STRENGTH HAS BEGUN TO RETURN. MIGHT HAVE BEEN THE ELECTRICAL CHARGE.
WE MUST MOVE QUICKLY. A TERRIBLE THING IS ABOUT TO HAPPEN AND--
THE OUTSIDERS ARE LIBERATED!
ALERT THE FACILITY!
LOOKS LIKE OUR TIME IS ALREADY RUNNING OUT.

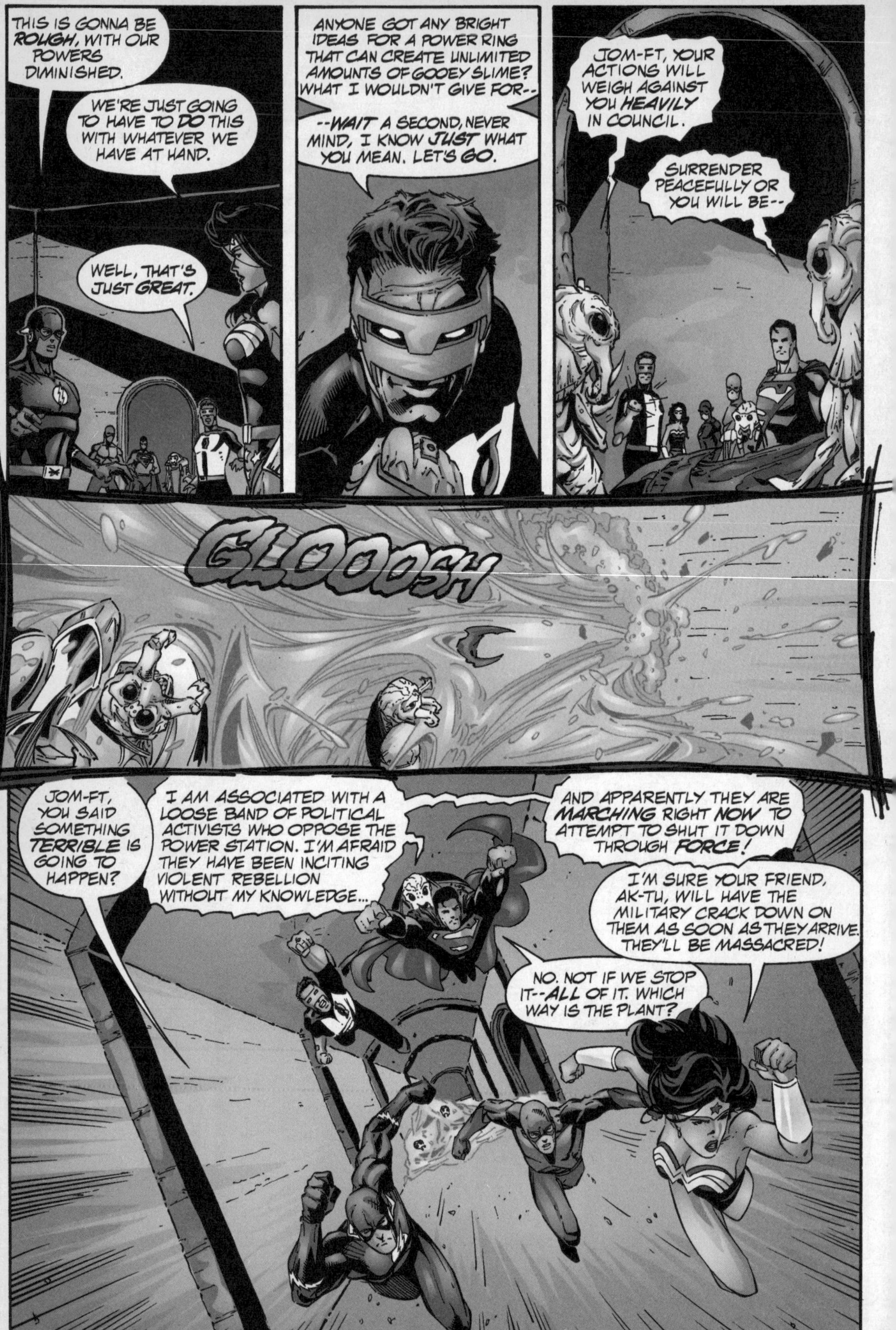

THIS IS GONNA BE ROUGH, WITH OUR POWERS DIMINISHED.
WE'RE JUST GOING TO HAVE TO DO THIS WITH WHATEVER WE HAVE AT HAND.
WELL, THAT'S JUST GREAT.
ANYONE GOT ANY BRIGHT IDEAS FOR A POWER RING THAT CAN CREATE UNLIMITED AMOUNTS OF GOOEY SLIME? WHAT I WOULDN'T GIVE FOR--
--WAIT A SECOND, NEVER MIND, I KNOW JUST WHAT YOU MEAN. LET'S GO.
JOM-FT, YOUR ACTIONS WILL WEIGH AGAINST YOU HEAVILY IN COUNCIL.
SURRENDER PEACEFULLY OR YOU WILL BE--
GLOOOSH
JOM-FT, YOU SAID SOMETHING TERRIBLE IS GOING TO HAPPEN?
I AM ASSOCIATED WITH A LOOSE BAND OF POLITICAL ACTIVISTS WHO OPPOSE THE POWER STATION. I'M AFRAID THEY HAVE BEEN INCITING VIOLENT REBELLION WITHOUT MY KNOWLEDGE...
AND APPARENTLY THEY ARE MARCHING RIGHT NOW TO ATTEMPT TO SHUT IT DOWN THROUGH FORCE!
I'M SURE YOUR FRIEND, AK-TU, WILL HAVE THE MILITARY CRACK DOWN ON THEM AS SOON AS THEY ARRIVE. THEY'LL BE MASSACRED!
NO. NOT IF WE STOP IT--ALL OF IT. WHICH WAY IS THE PLANT?

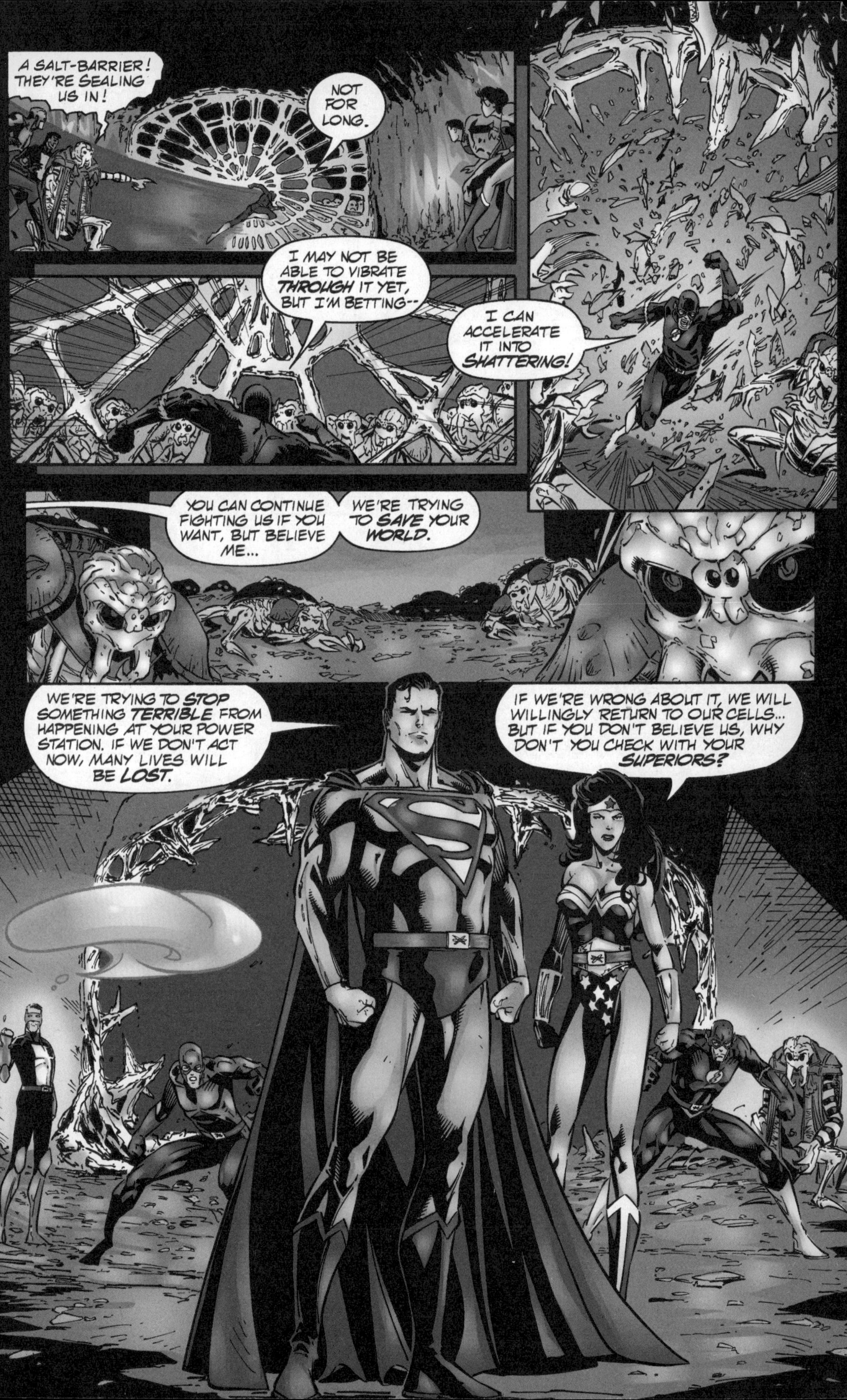
A SALT-BARRIER! THEY'RE SEALING US IN!
NOT FOR LONG.
I MAY NOT BE ABLE TO VIBRATE THROUGH IT YET, BUT I'M BETTING--
I CAN ACCELERATE IT INTO SHATTERING!
YOU CAN CONTINUE FIGHTING US IF YOU WANT, BUT BELIEVE ME...
WE'RE TRYING TO SAVE YOUR WORLD.
WE'RE TRYING TO STOP SOMETHING TERRIBLE FROM HAPPENING AT YOUR POWER STATION. IF WE DON'T ACT NOW, MANY LIVES WILL BE LOST.
IF WE'RE WRONG ABOUT IT, WE WILL WILLINGLY RETURN TO OUR CELLS... BUT IF YOU DON'T BELIEVE US, WHY DON'T YOU CHECK WITH YOUR SUPERIORS?

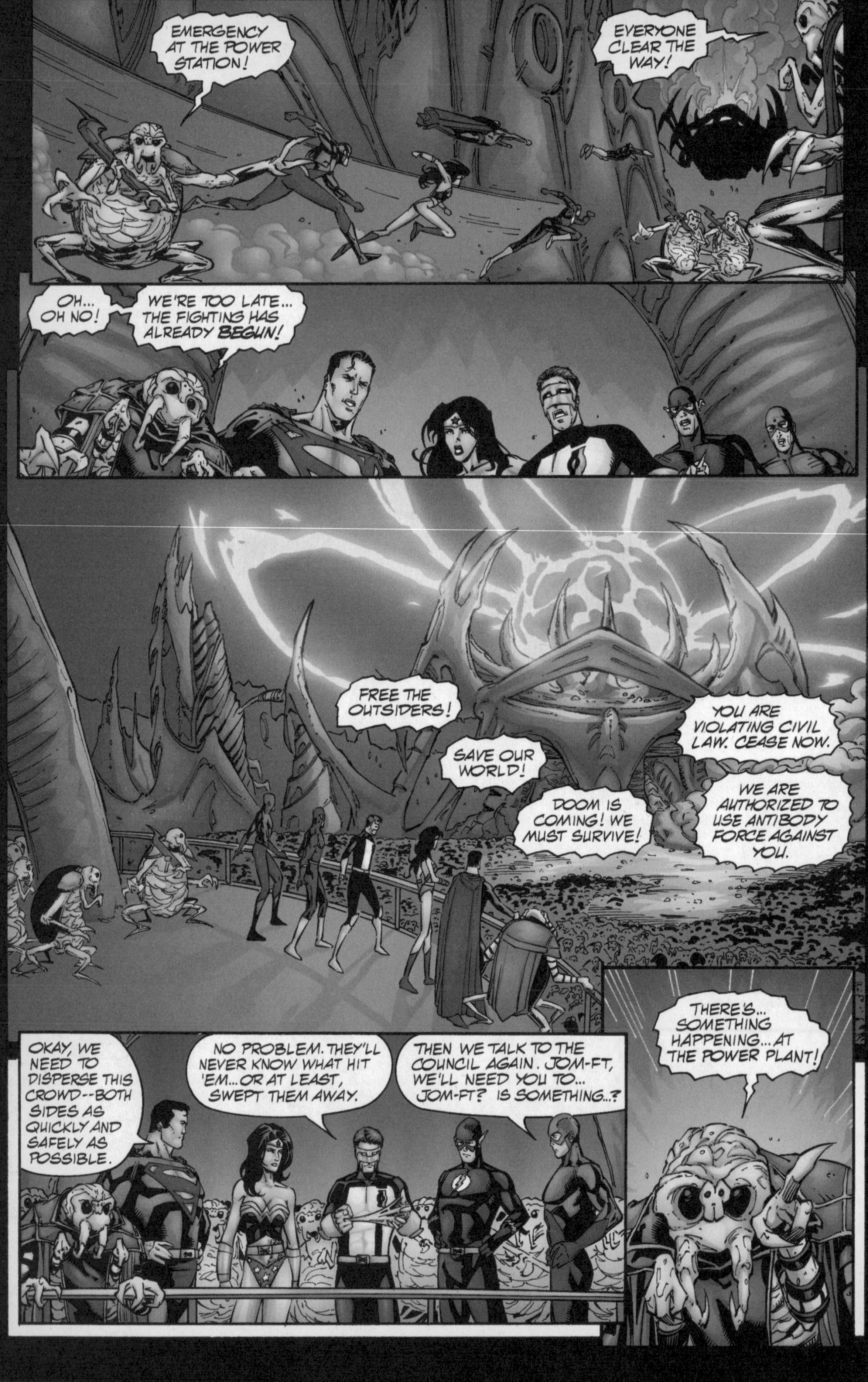
EMERGENCY AT THE POWER STATION!
EVERYONE CLEAR THE WAY!
OH... OH NO!
WE'RE TOO LATE... THE FIGHTING HAS ALREADY BEGUN!
FREE THE OUTSIDERS!
SAVE OUR WORLD!
DOOM IS COMING! WE MUST SURVIVE!
YOU ARE VIOLATING CIVIL LAW. CEASE NOW.
WE ARE AUTHORIZED TO USE ANTIBODY FORCE AGAINST YOU.
OKAY, WE NEED TO DISPERSE THIS CROWD--BOTH SIDES AS QUICKLY AND SAFELY AS POSSIBLE.
NO PROBLEM. THEY'LL NEVER KNOW WHAT HIT 'EM...OR AT LEAST, SWEPT THEM AWAY.
THEN WE TALK TO THE COUNCIL AGAIN. JOM-FT, WE'LL NEED YOU TO... JOM-FT? IS SOMETHING...?
THERE'S... SOMETHING HAPPENING... AT THE POWER PLANT!

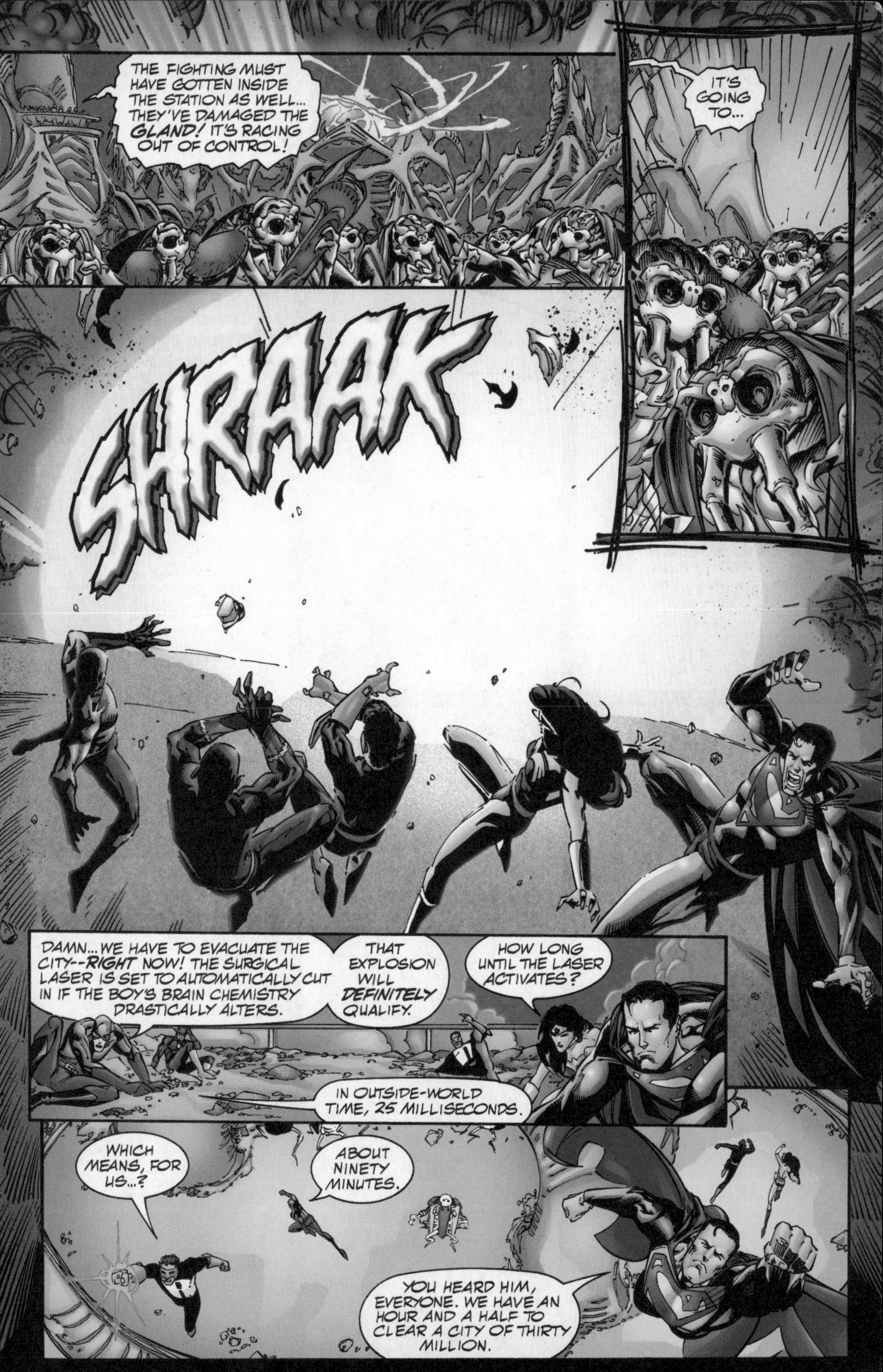
THE FIGHTING MUST HAVE GOTTEN INSIDE THE STATION AS WELL... THEY'VE DAMAGED THE GLAND! IT'S RACING OUT OF CONTROL!
IT'S GOING TO...
SHRAAK
DAMN... WE HAVE TO EVACUATE THE CITY--RIGHT NOW! THE SURGICAL LASER IS SET TO AUTOMATICALLY CUT IN IF THE BOY'S BRAIN CHEMISTRY DRASTICALLY ALTERS.
THAT EXPLOSION WILL DEFINITELY QUALIFY.
HOW LONG UNTIL THE LASER ACTIVATES?
IN OUTSIDE-WORLD TIME, 25 MILLISECONDS.
WHICH MEANS, FOR US...?
ABOUT NINETY MINUTES.
YOU HEARD HIM, EVERYONE. WE HAVE AN HOUR AND A HALF TO CLEAR A CITY OF THIRTY MILLION.

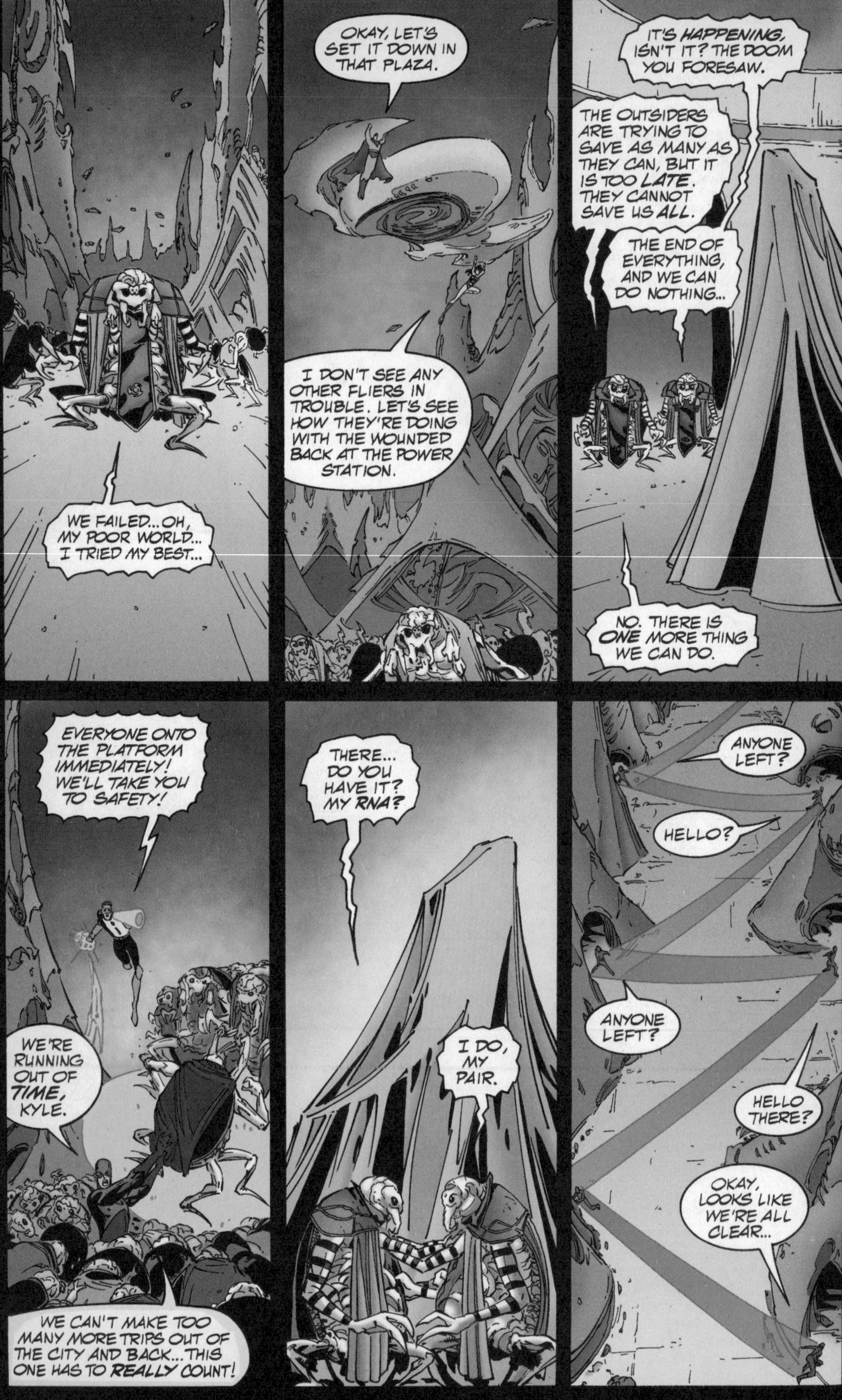
WE FAILED...OH, MY POOR WORLD... I TRIED MY BEST...
OKAY, LET'S SET IT DOWN IN THAT PLAZA.
I DON'T SEE ANY OTHER FLIERS IN TROUBLE. LET'S SEE HOW THEY'RE DOING WITH THE WOUNDED BACK AT THE POWER STATION.
IT'S HAPPENING, ISN'T IT? THE DOOM YOU FORESAW.
THE OUTSIDERS ARE TRYING TO SAVE AS MANY AS THEY CAN, BUT IT IS TOO LATE. THEY CANNOT SAVE US ALL.
THE END OF EVERYTHING, AND WE CAN DO NOTHING...
NO. THERE IS ONE MORE THING WE CAN DO.
EVERYONE ONTO THE PLATFORM IMMEDIATELY! WE'LL TAKE YOU TO SAFETY!
WE'RE RUNNING OUT OF TIME, KYLE.
WE CAN'T MAKE TOO MANY MORE TRIPS OUT OF THE CITY AND BACK... THIS ONE HAS TO REALLY COUNT!
THERE... DO YOU HAVE IT? MY RNA?
I DO, MY PAIR.
ANYONE LEFT?
HELLO?
ANYONE LEFT?
HELLO THERE?
OKAY, LOOKS LIKE WE'RE ALL CLEAR...

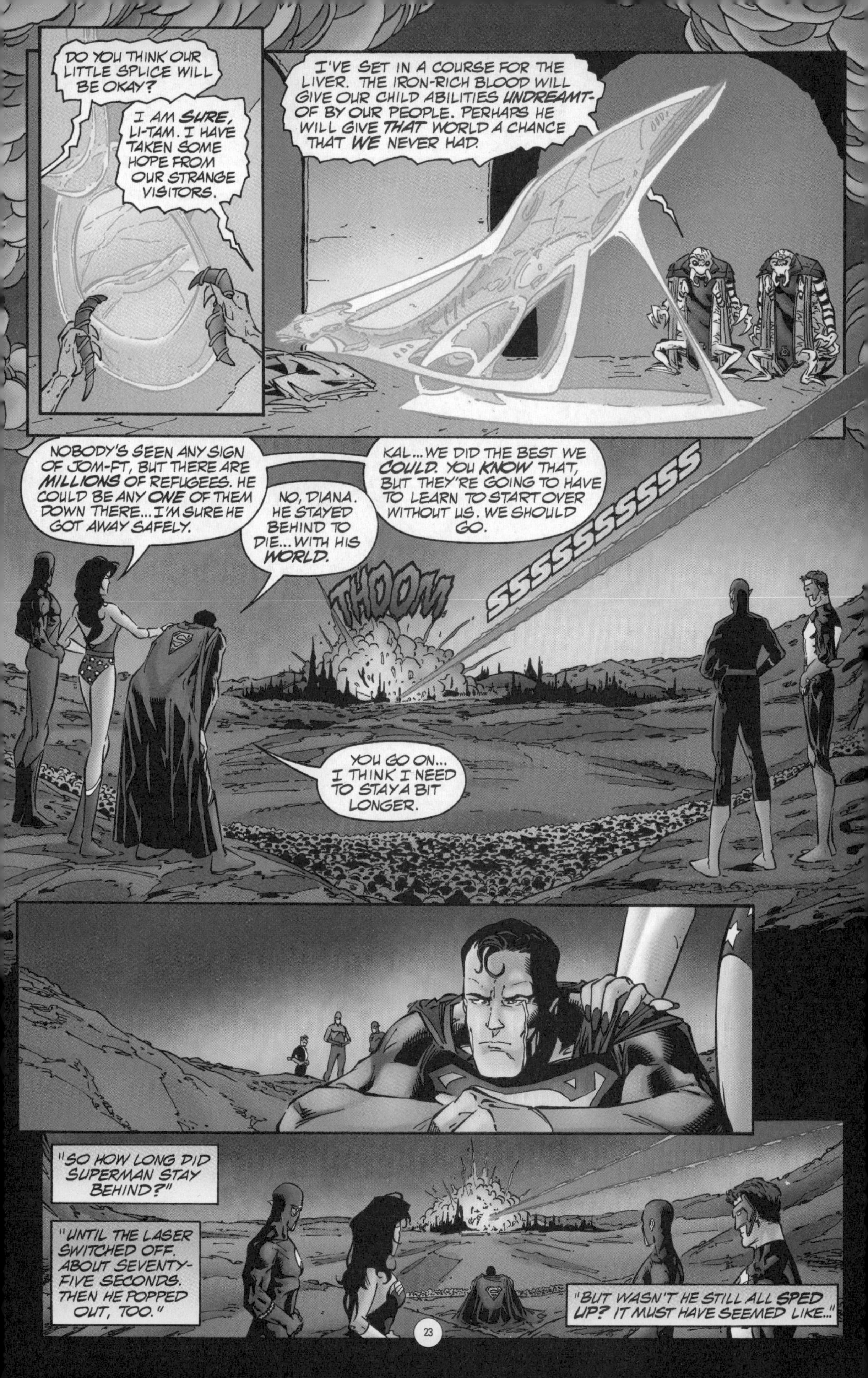
DO YOU THINK OUR LITTLE SPLICE WILL BE OKAY?
I AM SURE, LI-TAM. I HAVE TAKEN SOME HOPE FROM OUR STRANGE VISITORS.
I'VE SET IN A COURSE FOR THE LIVER. THE IRON-RICH BLOOD WILL GIVE OUR CHILD ABILITIES UNDREAMT-OF BY OUR PEOPLE. PERHAPS HE WILL GIVE THAT WORLD A CHANCE THAT WE NEVER HAD.
NOBODY'S SEEN ANY SIGN OF JOM-FT, BUT THERE ARE MILLIONS OF REFUGEES. HE COULD BE ANY ONE OF THEM DOWN THERE... I'M SURE HE GOT AWAY SAFELY.
NO, DIANA. HE STAYED BEHIND TO DIE... WITH HIS WORLD.
KAL... WE DID THE BEST WE COULD. YOU KNOW THAT, BUT THEY'RE GOING TO HAVE TO LEARN TO START OVER WITHOUT US. WE SHOULD GO.
SSSSSSSSSSS
THOOM
YOU GO ON... I THINK I NEED TO STAY A BIT LONGER.
"SO HOW LONG DID SUPERMAN STAY BEHIND?"
"UNTIL THE LASER SWITCHED OFF. ABOUT SEVENTY-FIVE SECONDS. THEN HE POPPED OUT, TOO."
"BUT WASN'T HE STILL ALL SPED UP? IT MUST HAVE SEEMED LIKE..."

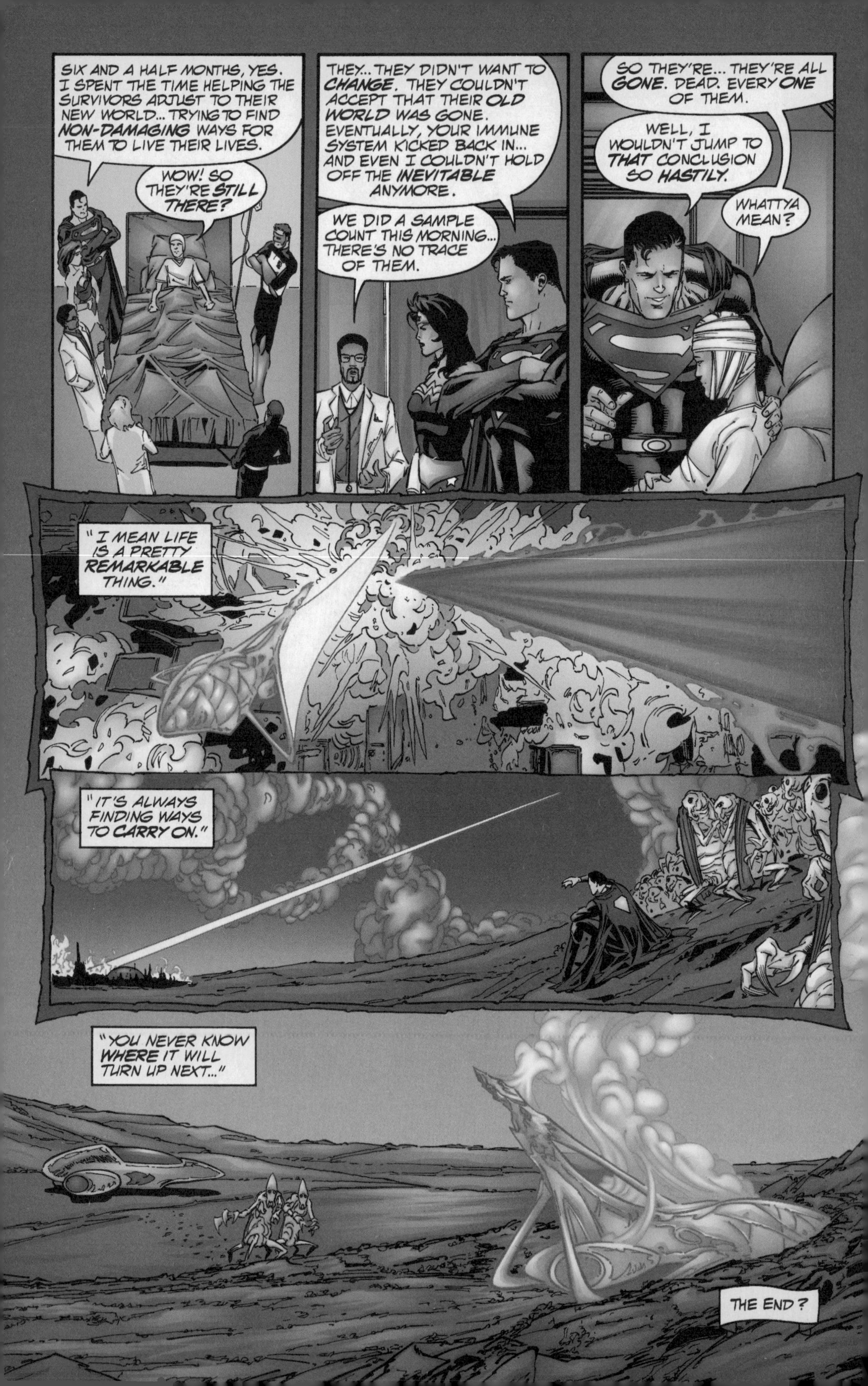
SIX AND A HALF MONTHS, YES. I SPENT THE TIME HELPING THE SURVIVORS ADJUST TO THEIR NEW WORLD... TRYING TO FIND NON-DAMAGING WAYS FOR THEM TO LIVE THEIR LIVES.
WOW! SO THEY'RE STILL THERE?
THEY... THEY DIDN'T WANT TO CHANGE. THEY COULDN'T ACCEPT THAT THEIR OLD WORLD WAS GONE. EVENTUALLY, YOUR IMMUNE SYSTEM KICKED BACK IN... AND EVEN I COULDN'T HOLD OFF THE INEVITABLE ANYMORE.
WE DID A SAMPLE COUNT THIS MORNING... THERE'S NO TRACE OF THEM.
SO THEY'RE... THEY'RE ALL GONE. DEAD. EVERY ONE OF THEM.
WELL, I WOULDN'T JUMP TO THAT CONCLUSION SO HASTILY.
WHATTYA MEAN?
"I MEAN LIFE IS A PRETTY REMARKABLE THING."
"IT'S ALWAYS FINDING WAYS TO CARRY ON."
"YOU NEVER KNOW WHERE IT WILL TURN UP NEXT..."
THE END?

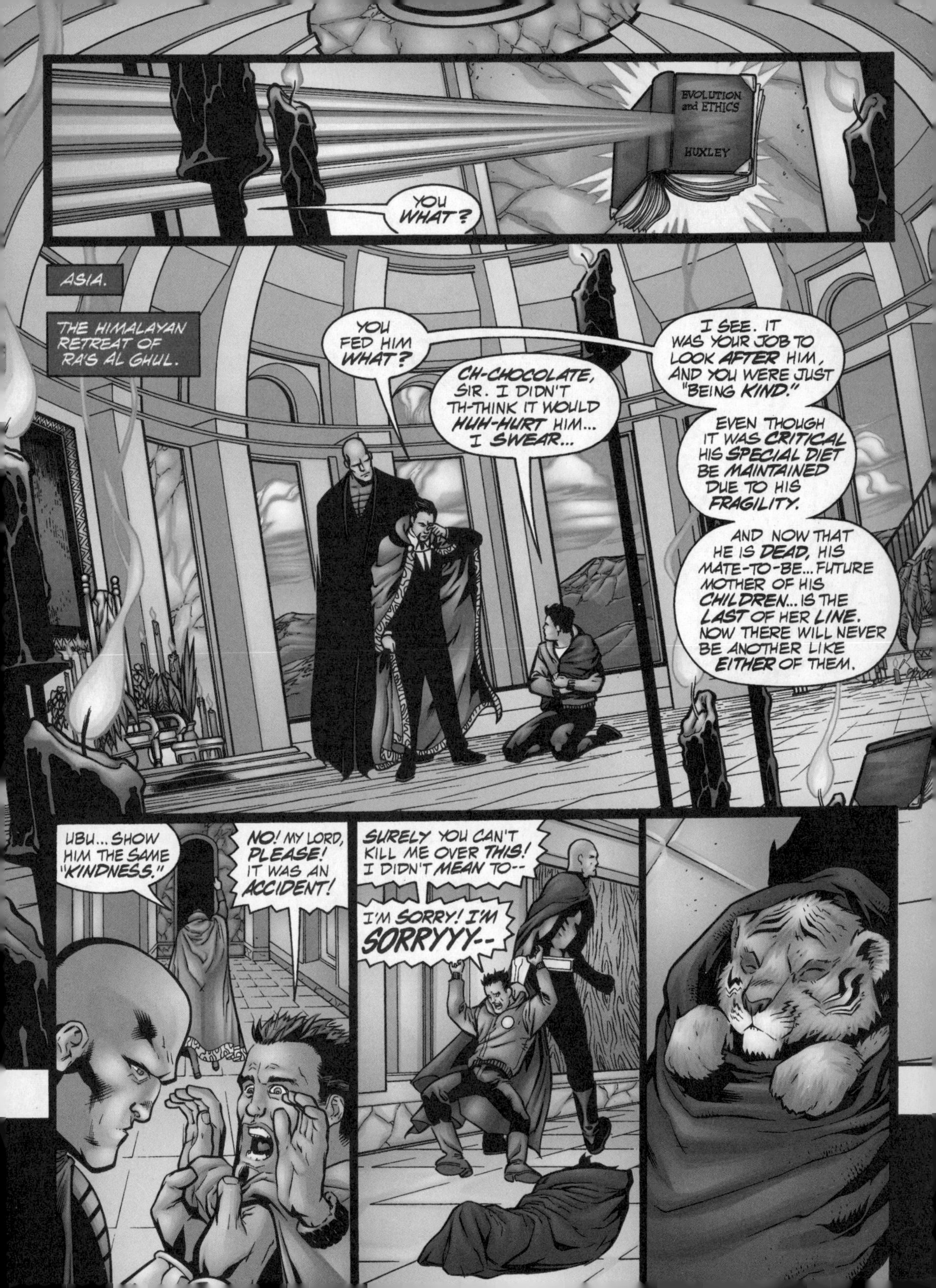
EVOLUTION and ETHICS
HUXLEY
YOU WHAT?
ASIA.
THE HIMALAYAN RETREAT OF RA'S AL GHUL.
YOU FED HIM WHAT?
CH-CHOCOLATE, SIR. I DIDN'T TH-THINK IT WOULD HUH-HURT HIM... I SWEAR...
I SEE. IT WAS YOUR JOB TO LOOK AFTER HIM, AND YOU WERE JUST "BEING KIND."
EVEN THOUGH IT WAS CRITICAL HIS SPECIAL DIET BE MAINTAINED DUE TO HIS FRAGILITY.
AND NOW THAT HE IS DEAD, HIS MATE-TO-BE... FUTURE MOTHER OF HIS CHILDREN... IS THE LAST OF HER LINE. NOW THERE WILL NEVER BE ANOTHER LIKE EITHER OF THEM.
UBU... SHOW HIM THE SAME "KINDNESS."
NO! MY LORD, PLEASE! IT WAS AN ACCIDENT!
SURELY YOU CAN'T KILL ME OVER THIS! I DIDN'T MEAN TO--
I'M SORRY! I'M SORRYYY--

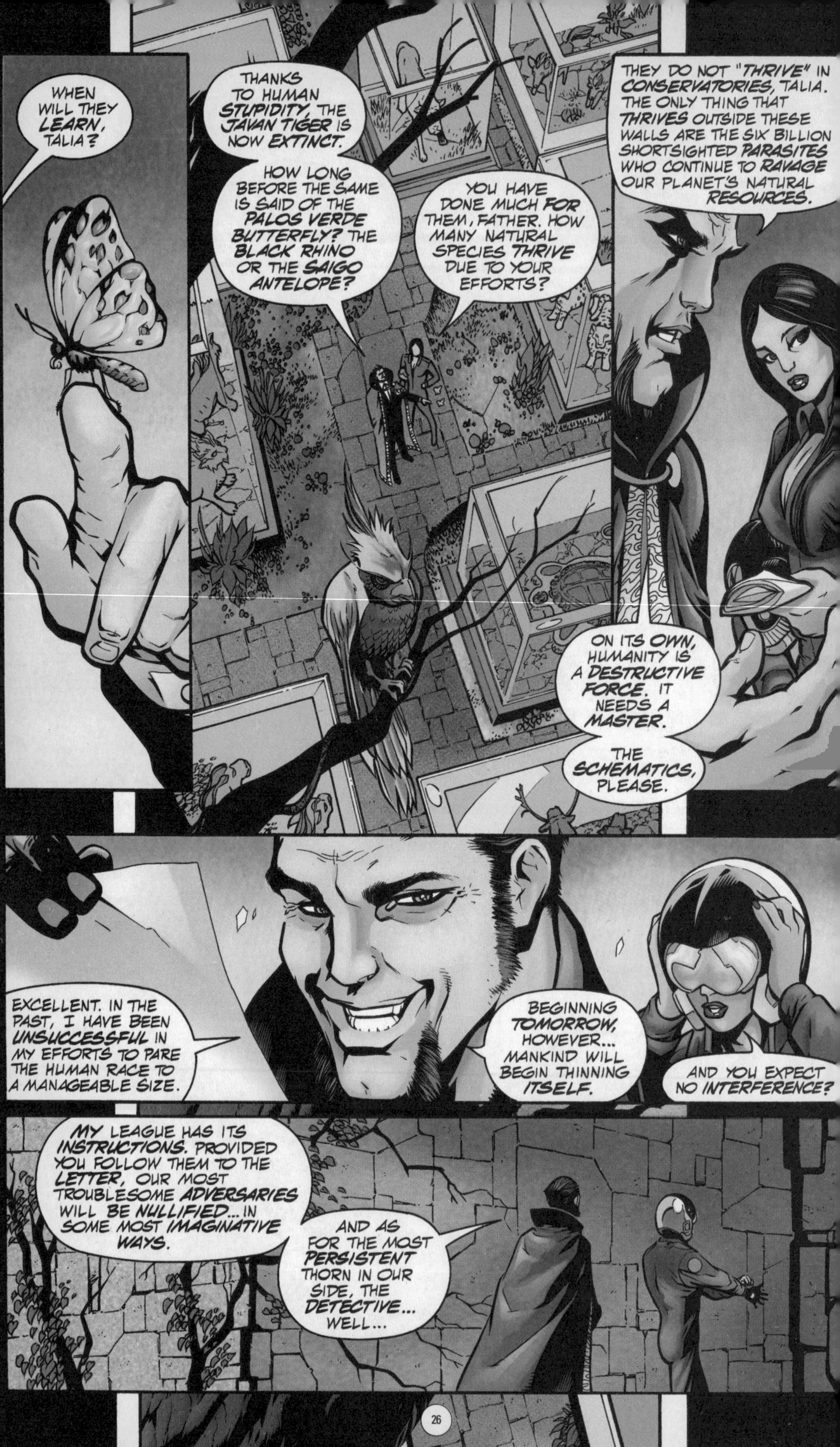
WHEN WILL THEY LEARN, TALIA?
THANKS TO HUMAN STUPIDITY, THE JAVAN TIGER IS NOW EXTINCT.
HOW LONG BEFORE THE SAME IS SAID OF THE PALOS VERDE BUTTERFLY? THE BLACK RHINO OR THE SAIGO ANTELOPE?
YOU HAVE DONE MUCH FOR THEM, FATHER. HOW MANY NATURAL SPECIES THRIVE DUE TO YOUR EFFORTS?
THEY DO NOT "THRIVE" IN CONSERVATORIES, TALIA. THE ONLY THING THAT THRIVES OUTSIDE THESE WALLS ARE THE SIX BILLION SHORTSIGHTED PARASITES WHO CONTINUE TO RAVAGE OUR PLANET'S NATURAL RESOURCES.
ON ITS OWN, HUMANITY IS A DESTRUCTIVE FORCE. IT NEEDS A MASTER.
THE SCHEMATICS, PLEASE.
EXCELLENT. IN THE PAST, I HAVE BEEN UNSUCCESSFUL IN MY EFFORTS TO PARE THE HUMAN RACE TO A MANAGEABLE SIZE.
BEGINNING TOMORROW, HOWEVER... MANKIND WILL BEGIN THINNING ITSELF.
AND YOU EXPECT NO INTERFERENCE?
MY LEAGUE HAS ITS INSTRUCTIONS. PROVIDED YOU FOLLOW THEM TO THE LETTER, OUR MOST TROUBLESOME ADVERSARIES WILL BE NULLIFIED... IN SOME MOST IMAGINATIVE WAYS.
AND AS FOR THE MOST PERSISTENT THORN IN OUR SIDE, THE DETECTIVE... WELL...

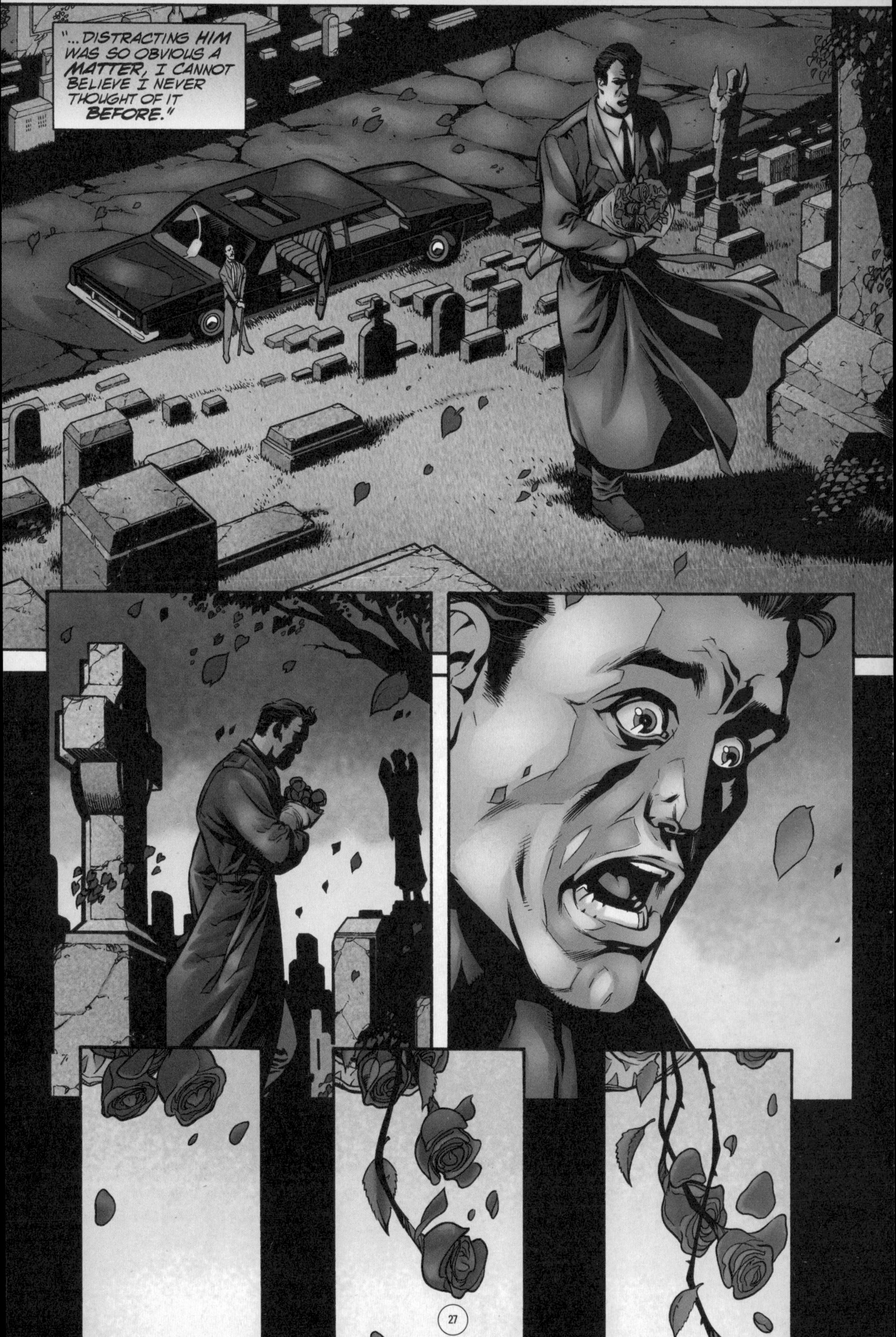
"...DISTRACTING HIM WAS SO OBVIOUS A MATTER, I CANNOT BELIEVE I NEVER THOUGHT OF IT BEFORE."

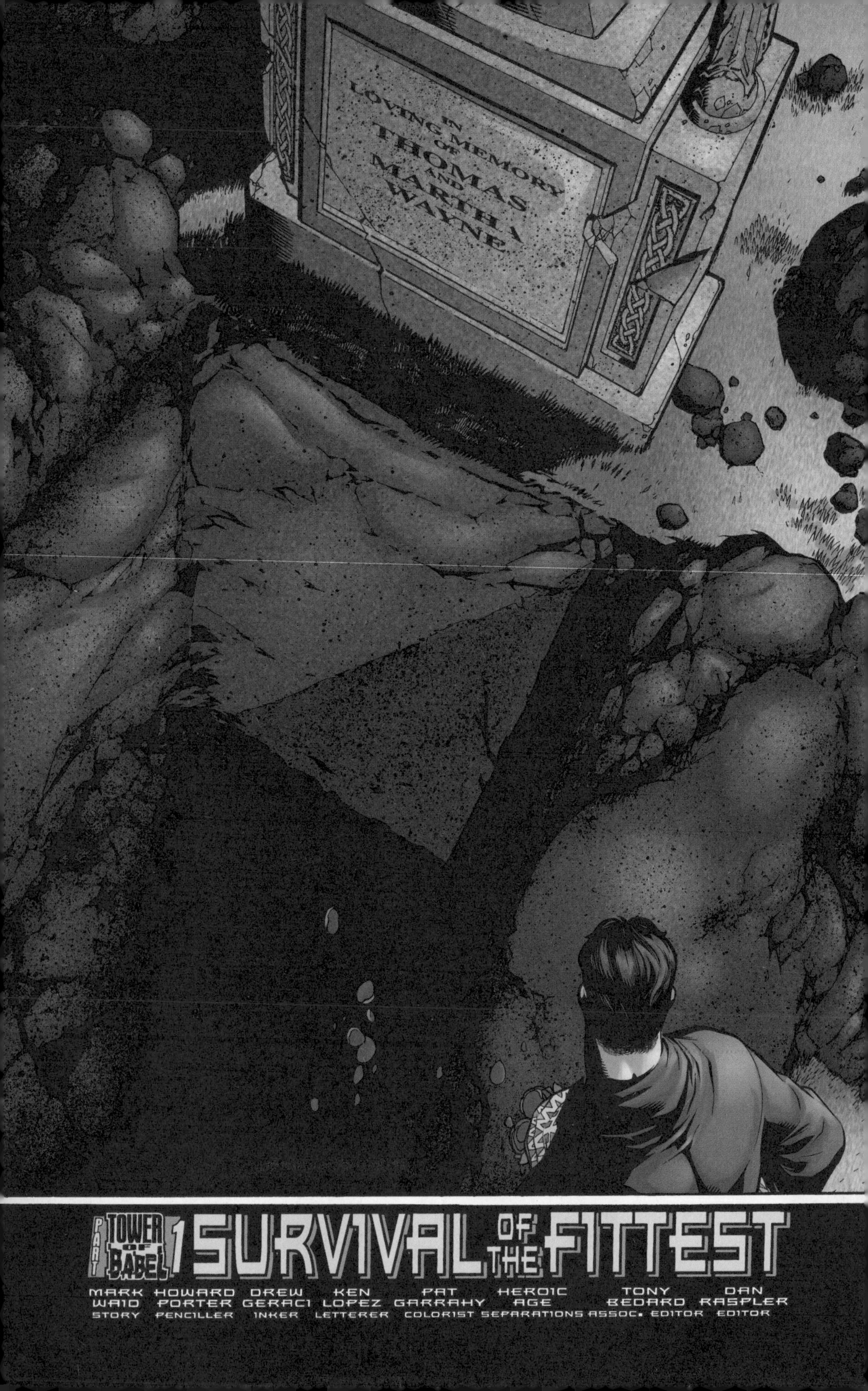
IN LOVING MEMORY OF THOMAS AND MARTHA WAYNE
PART 1 TOWER OF BABEL
SURVIVAL OF THE FITTEST
MARK WAID STORY
HOWARD PORTER PENCILLER
DREW GERACI INKER
KEN LOPEZ LETTERER
PAT GARRAHY COLORIST
HEROIC AGE SEPARATIONS
TONY BEDARD ASSOC. EDITOR
DAN RASPLER EDITOR

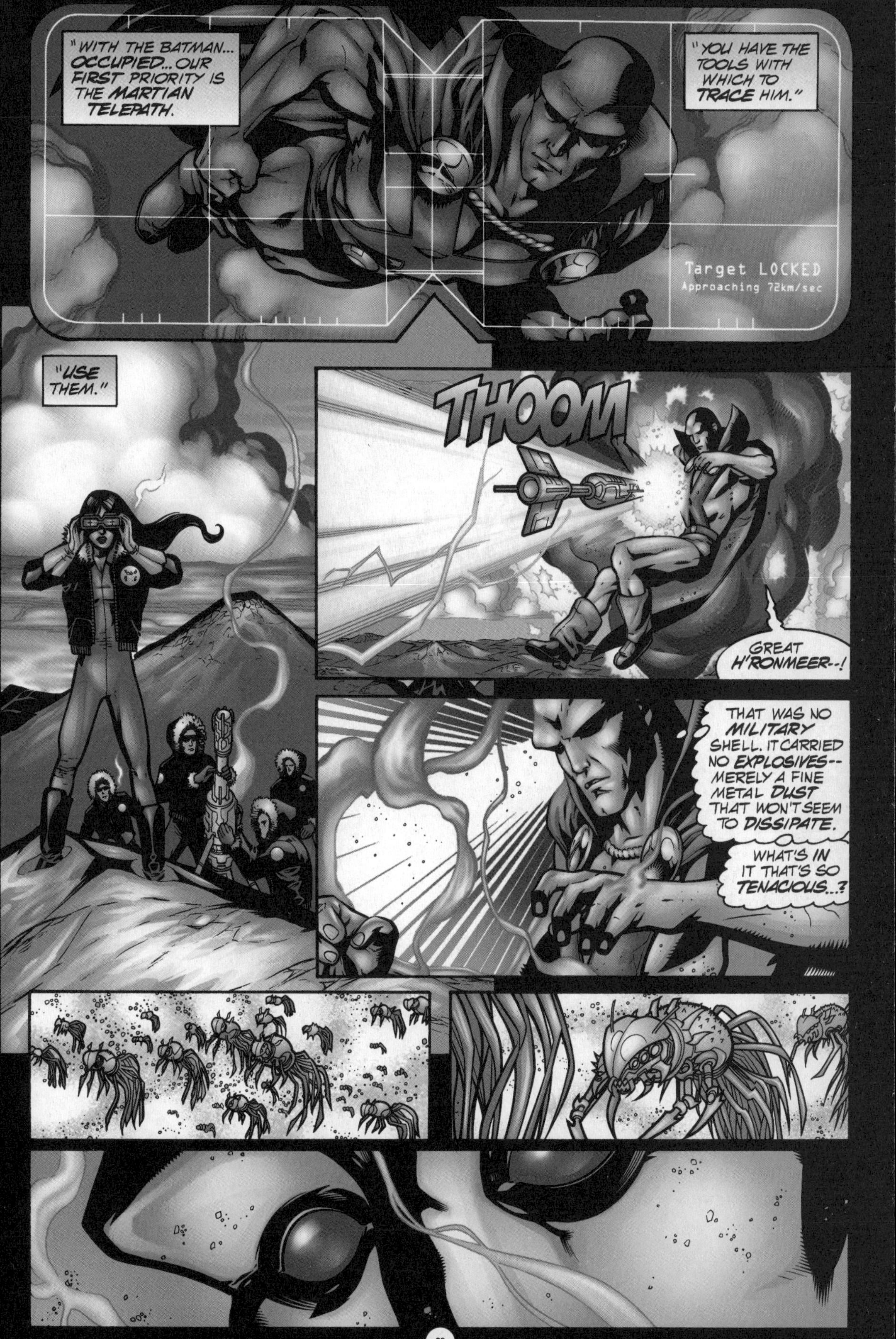
"WITH THE BATMAN... OCCUPIED... OUR FIRST PRIORITY IS THE MARTIAN TELEPATH.
"YOU HAVE THE TOOLS WITH WHICH TO TRACE HIM."
Target LOCKED
Approaching 72km/sec
"USE THEM."
THOOM
GREAT H'RONMEER--!
THAT WAS NO MILITARY SHELL. IT CARRIED NO EXPLOSIVES-- MERELY A FINE METAL DUST THAT WON'T SEEM TO DISSIPATE.
WHAT'S IN IT THAT'S SO TENACIOUS..?

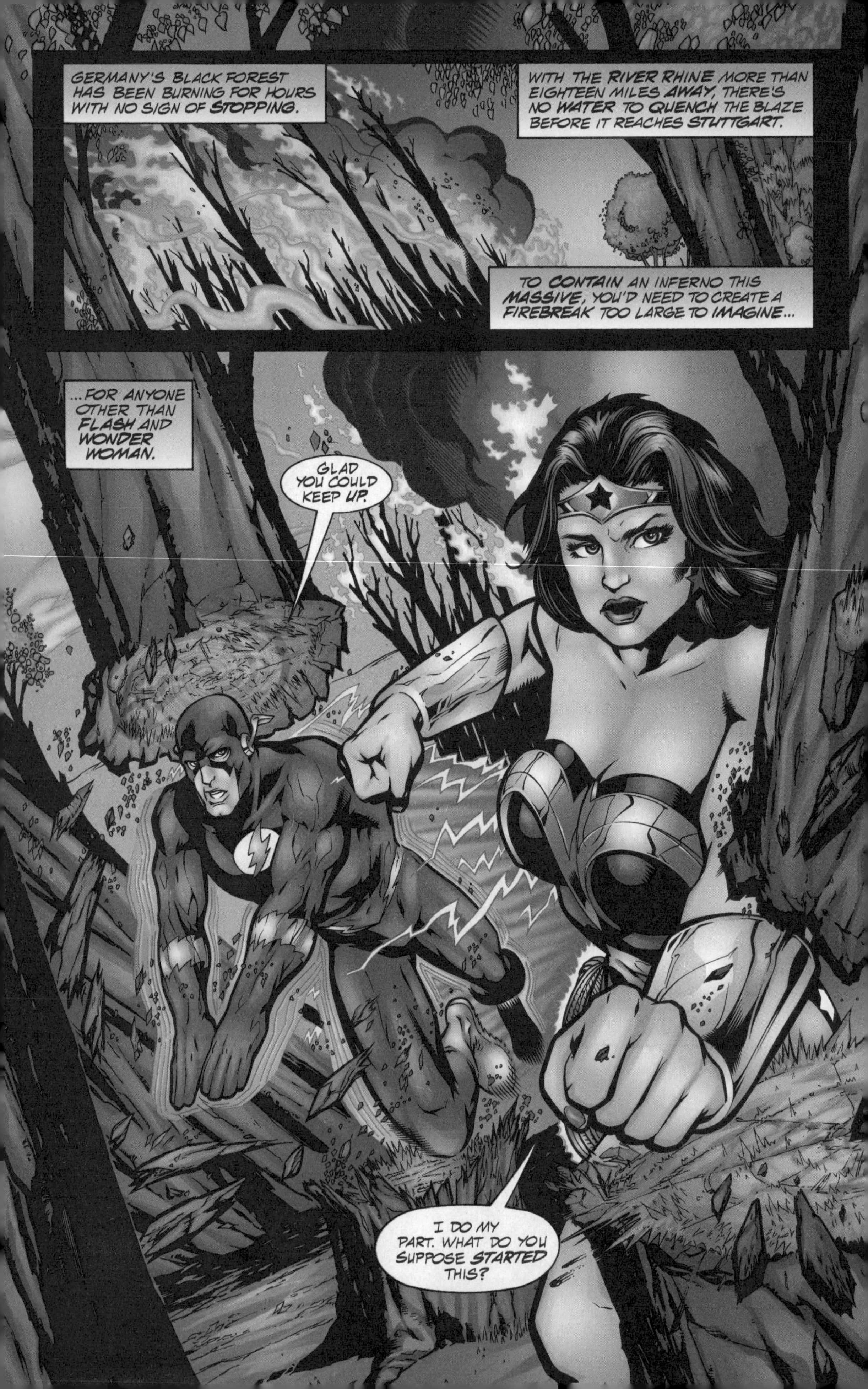
GERMANY'S BLACK FOREST HAS BEEN BURNING FOR HOURS WITH NO SIGN OF STOPPING.
WITH THE RIVER RHINE MORE THAN EIGHTEEN MILES AWAY, THERE'S NO WATER TO QUENCH THE BLAZE BEFORE IT REACHES STUTTGART.
TO CONTAIN AN INFERNO THIS MASSIVE, YOU'D NEED TO CREATE A FIREBREAK TOO LARGE TO IMAGINE...
...FOR ANYONE OTHER THAN FLASH AND WONDER WOMAN.
GLAD YOU COULD KEEP UP.
I DO MY PART. WHAT DO YOU SUPPOSE STARTED THIS?

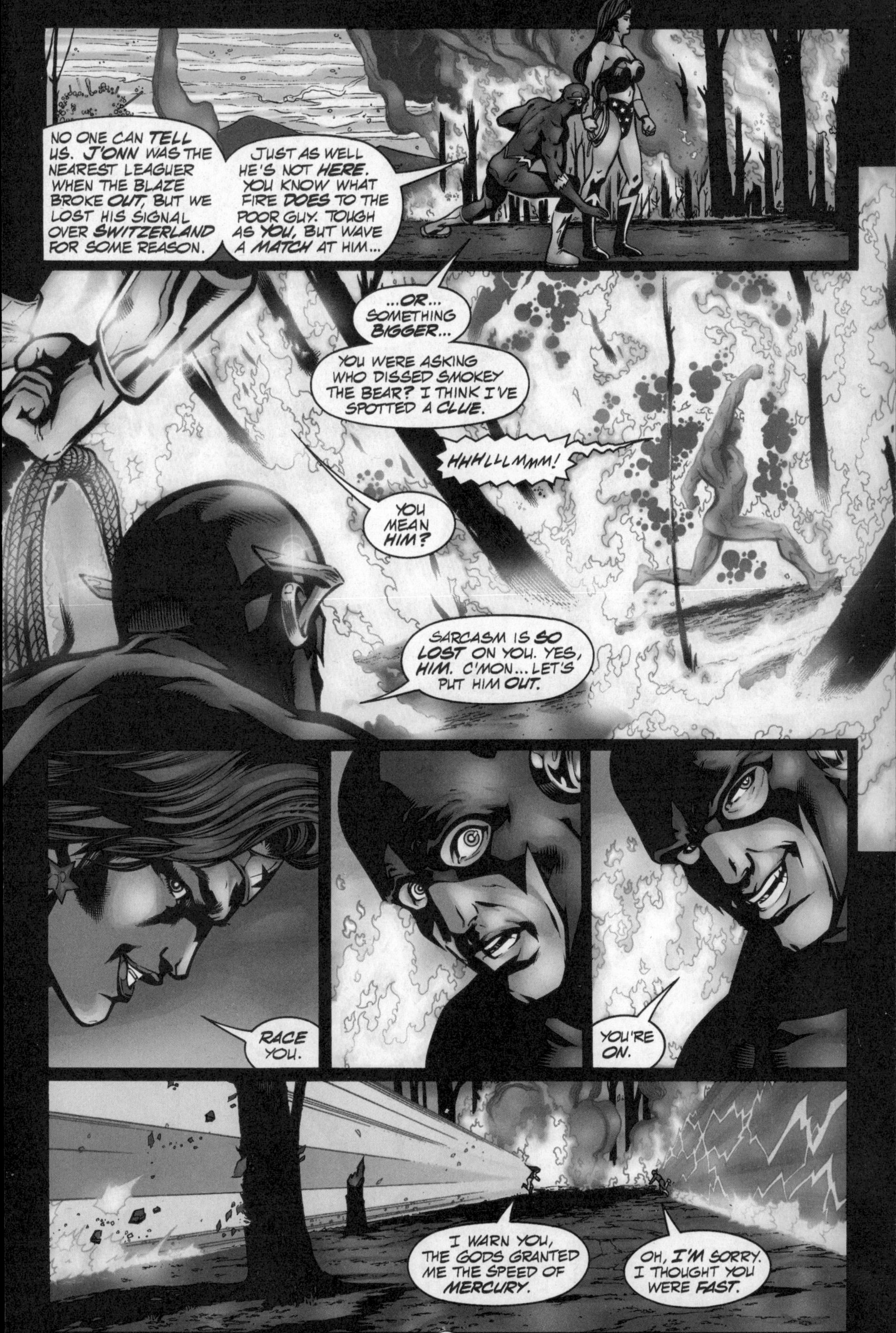
NO ONE CAN TELL US. J'ONN WAS THE NEAREST LEAGUER WHEN THE BLAZE BROKE OUT, BUT WE LOST HIS SIGNAL OVER SWITZERLAND FOR SOME REASON.
JUST AS WELL HE'S NOT HERE. YOU KNOW WHAT FIRE DOES TO THE POOR GUY. TOUGH AS YOU, BUT WAVE A MATCH AT HIM...
...OR... SOMETHING BIGGER...
YOU WERE ASKING WHO DISSED SMOKEY THE BEAR? I THINK I'VE SPOTTED A CLUE.
HHHLLLMMM!
YOU MEAN HIM?
SARCASM IS SO LOST ON YOU. YES, HIM. C'MON... LET'S PUT HIM OUT.
RACE YOU.
YOU'RE ON.
I WARN YOU, THE GODS GRANTED ME THE SPEED OF MERCURY.
OH, I'M SORRY. I THOUGHT YOU WERE FAST.

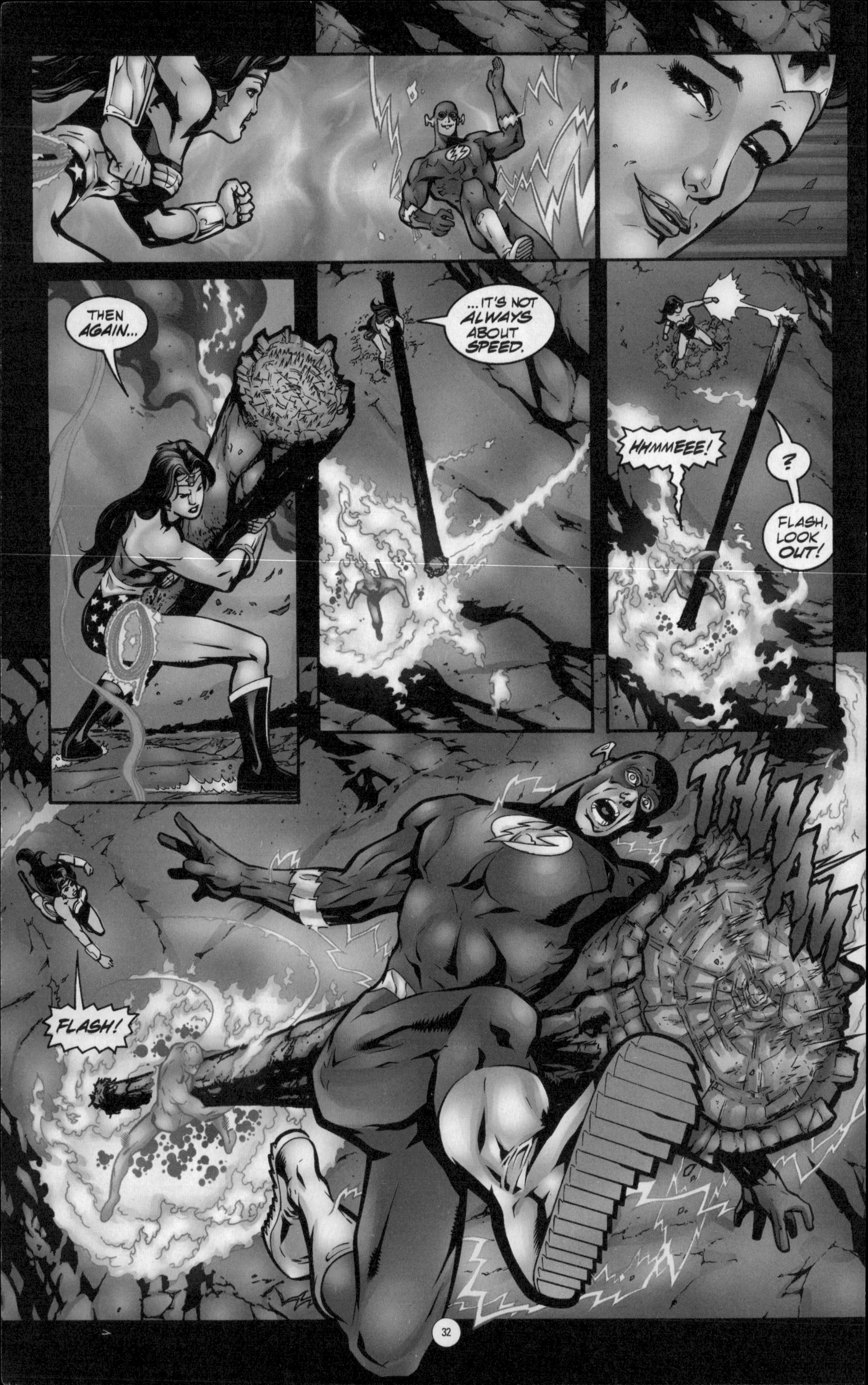
THEN AGAIN...
...IT'S NOT ALWAYS ABOUT SPEED.
HHMMEEE!
?
FLASH, LOOK OUT!
FLASH!
THWAM

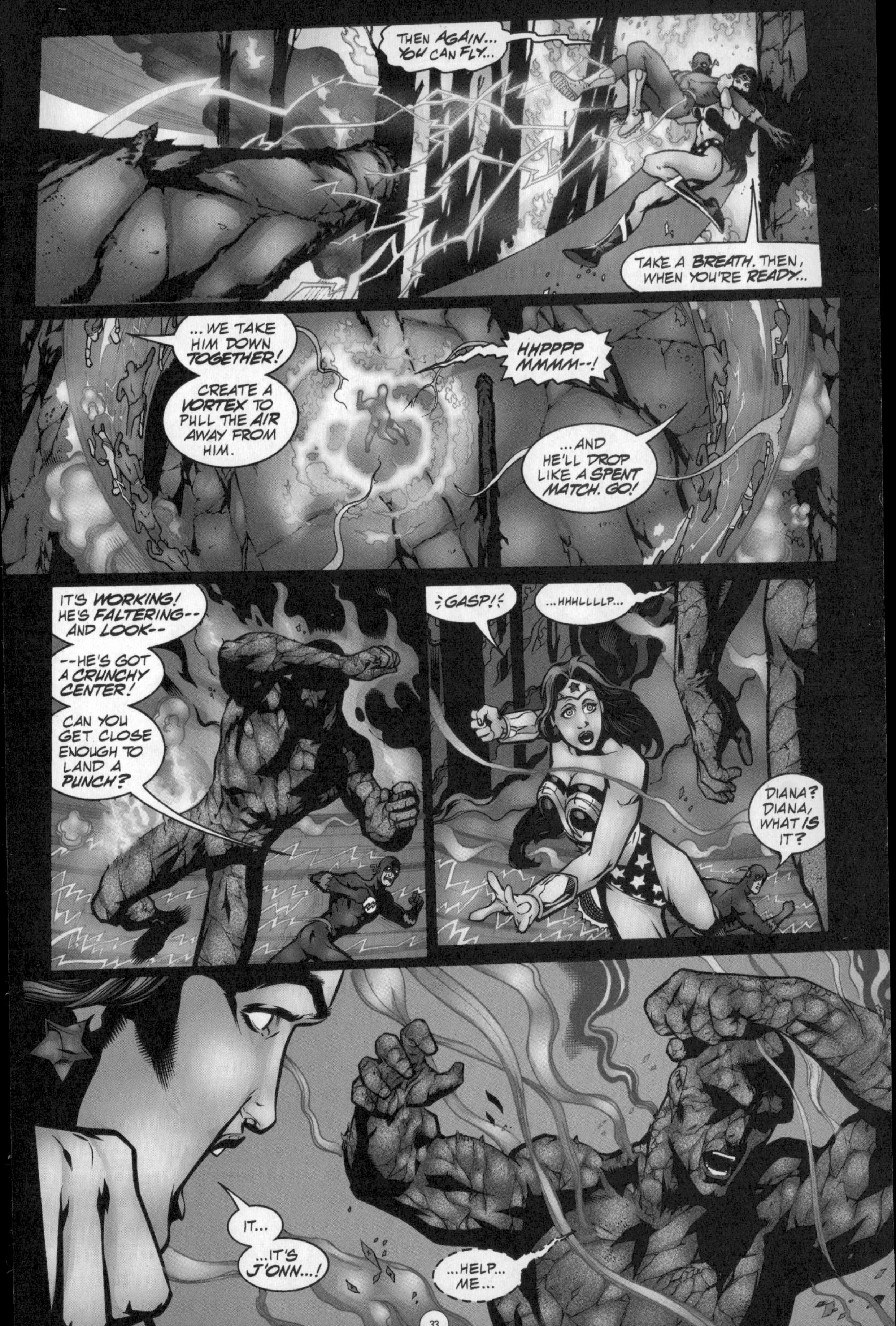
THEN AGAIN... YOU CAN FLY...
TAKE A BREATH. THEN, WHEN YOU'RE READY...
...WE TAKE HIM DOWN TOGETHER!
CREATE A VORTEX TO PULL THE AIR AWAY FROM HIM.
HHPPPP MMMM--!
...AND HE'LL DROP LIKE A SPENT MATCH. GO!
IT'S WORKING! HE'S FALTERING-- AND LOOK--
--HE'S GOT A CRUNCHY CENTER!
CAN YOU GET CLOSE ENOUGH TO LAND A PUNCH?
GASP!
...HHHLLLLLP...
DIANA? DIANA, WHAT IS IT?
IT...
...IT'S J'ONN...!
...HELP... ME...

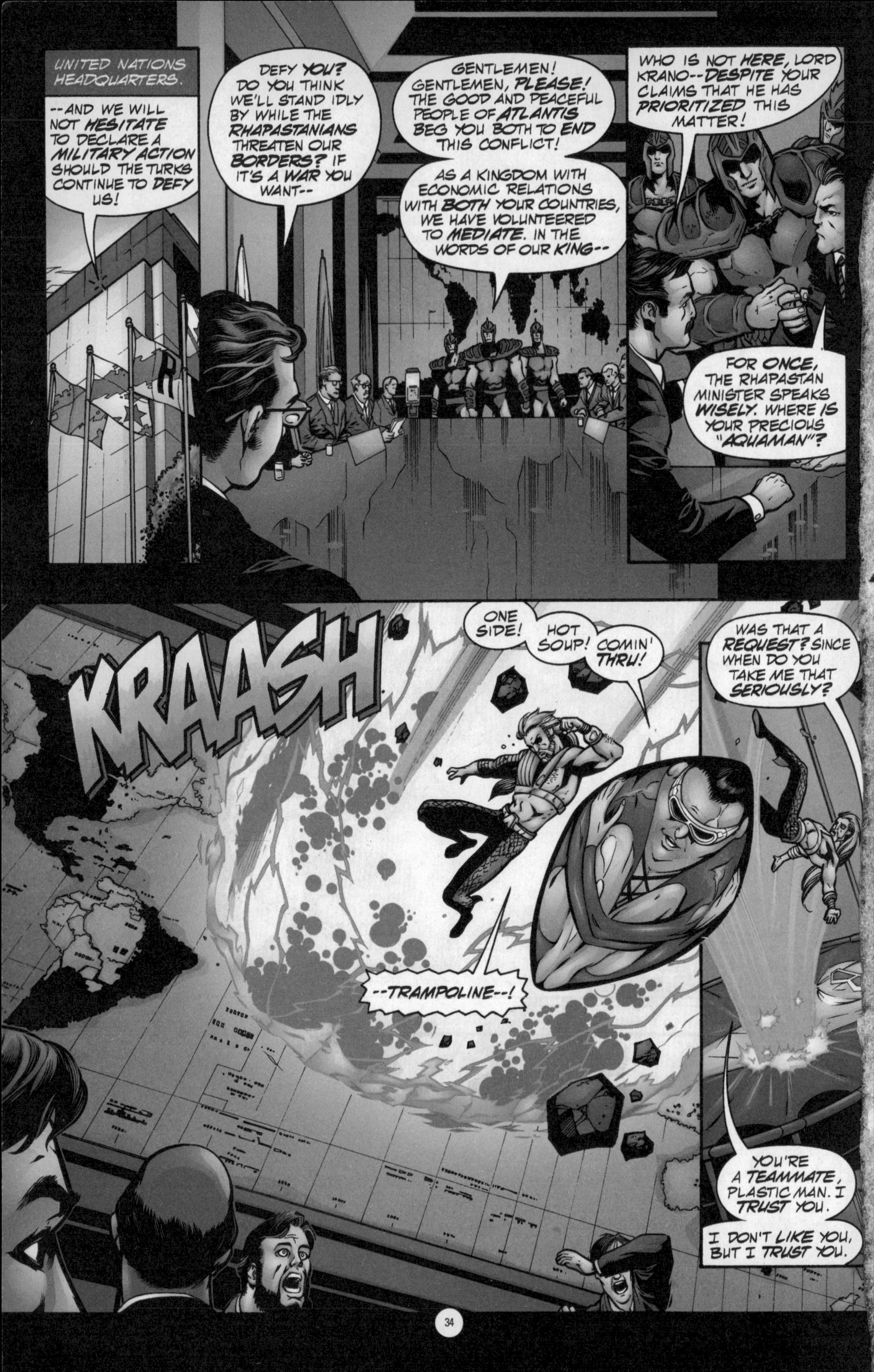
UNITED NATIONS HEADQUARTERS.
--AND WE WILL NOT HESITATE TO DECLARE A MILITARY ACTION SHOULD THE TURKS CONTINUE TO DEFY US!
DEFY YOU? DO YOU THINK WE'LL STAND IDLY BY WHILE THE RHAPASTANIANS THREATEN OUR BORDERS? IF IT'S A WAR YOU WANT--
GENTLEMEN! GENTLEMEN, PLEASE! THE GOOD AND PEACEFUL PEOPLE OF ATLANTIS BEG YOU BOTH TO END THIS CONFLICT!
AS A KINGDOM WITH ECONOMIC RELATIONS WITH BOTH YOUR COUNTRIES, WE HAVE VOLUNTEERED TO MEDIATE. IN THE WORDS OF OUR KING--
WHO IS NOT HERE, LORD KRANO--DESPITE YOUR CLAIMS THAT HE HAS PRIORITIZED THIS MATTER!
FOR ONCE, THE RHAPASTAN MINISTER SPEAKS WISELY. WHERE IS YOUR PRECIOUS "AQUAMAN"?
KRAASH
ONE SIDE!
HOT SOUP!
COMIN' THRU!
--TRAMPOLINE--!
WAS THAT A REQUEST? SINCE WHEN DO YOU TAKE ME THAT SERIOUSLY?
YOU'RE A TEAMMATE, PLASTIC MAN. I TRUST YOU.
I DON'T LIKE YOU, BUT I TRUST YOU.

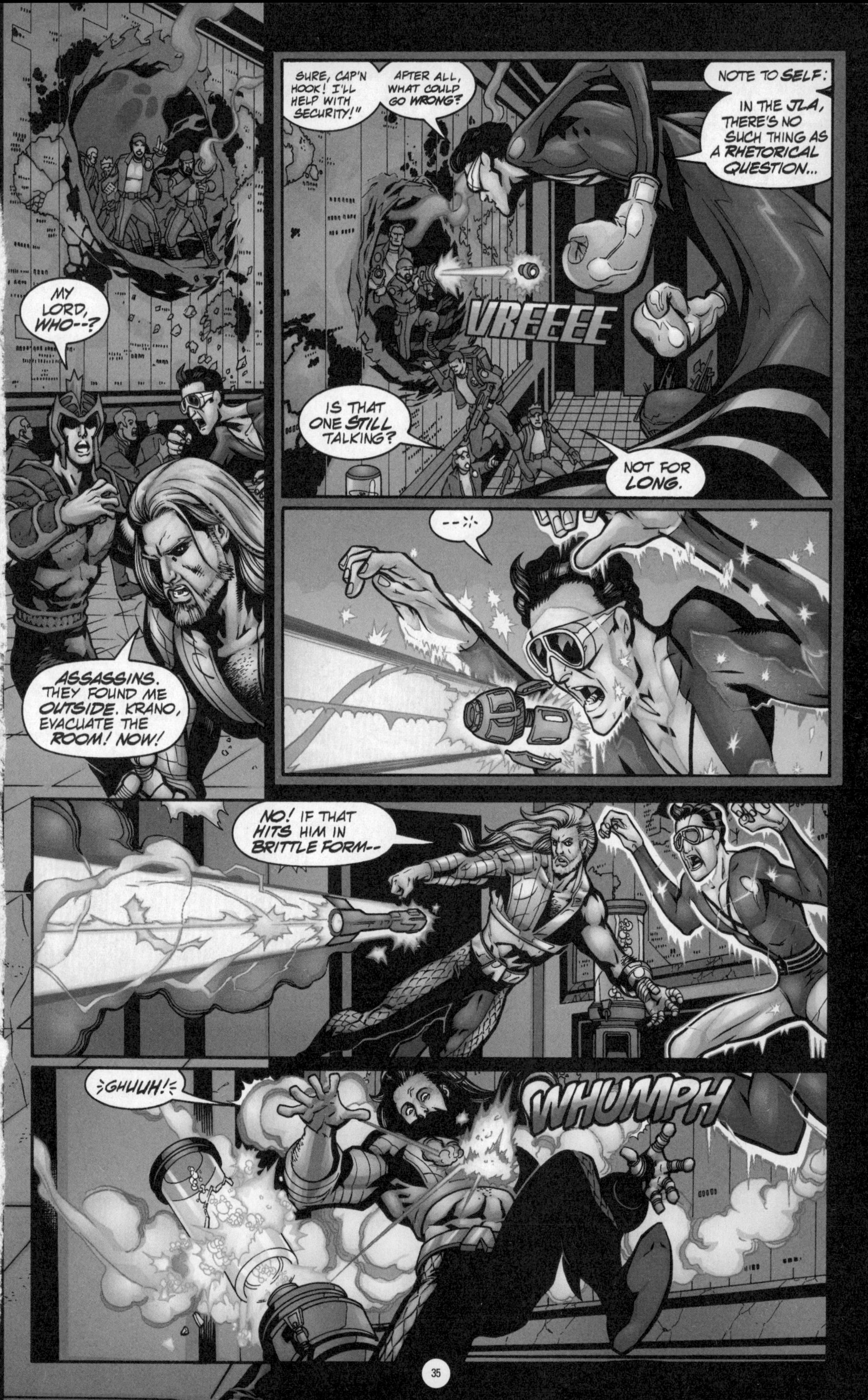
MY LORD, WHO--?
ASSASSINS. THEY FOUND ME OUTSIDE. KRANO, EVACUATE THE ROOM! NOW!
SURE, CAP'N HOOK! I'LL HELP WITH SECURITY!"
AFTER ALL, WHAT COULD GO WRONG?
NOTE TO SELF:
IN THE JLA, THERE'S NO SUCH THING AS A RHETORICAL QUESTION...
VREEEE
IS THAT ONE STILL TALKING?
NOT FOR LONG.
--:-
NO! IF THAT HITS HIM IN BRITTLE FORM--
GHUUH!
WHUMPH

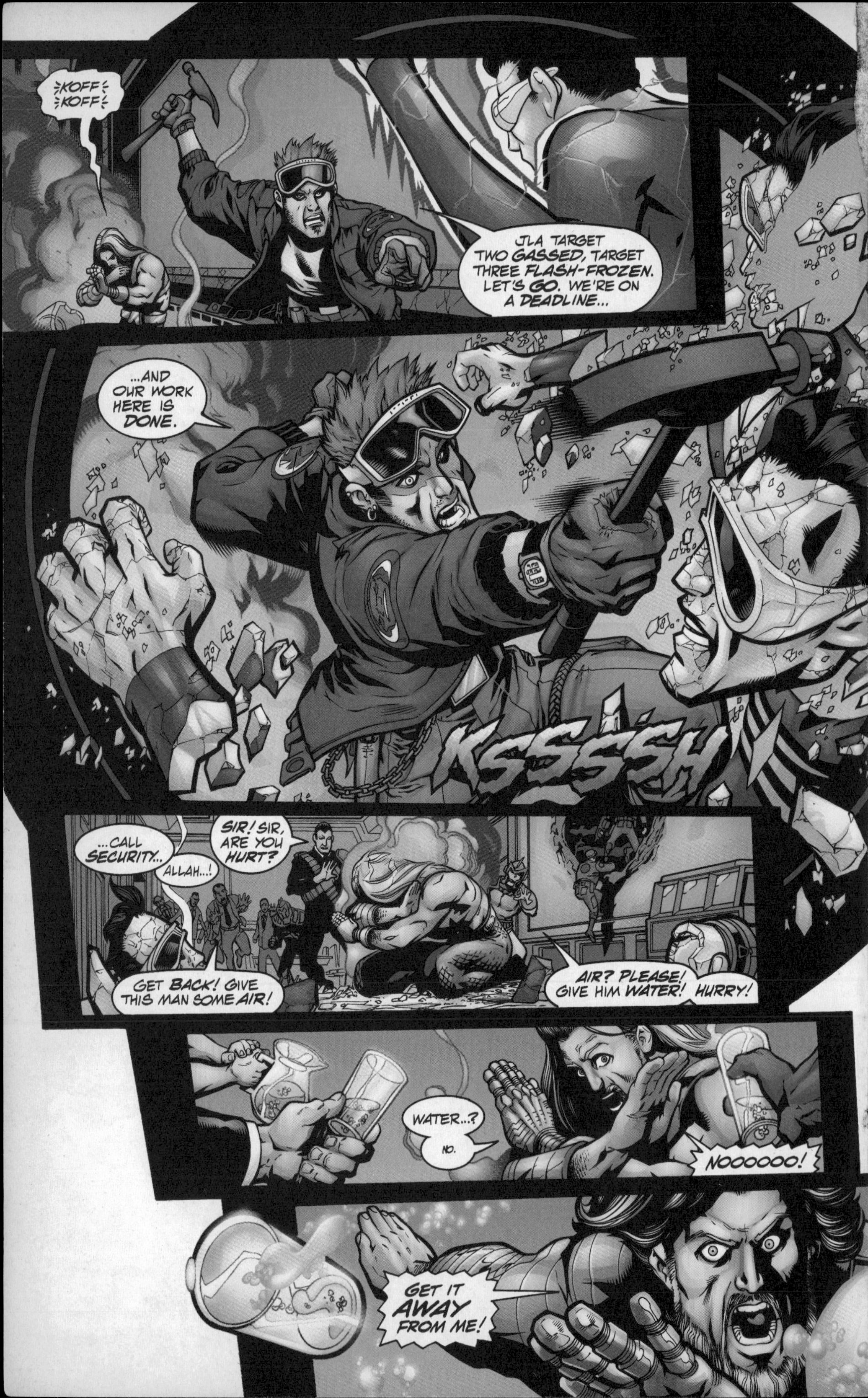
KOFF KOFF
JLA TARGET TWO GASSED, TARGET THREE FLASH-FROZEN. LET'S GO. WE'RE ON A DEADLINE...
...AND OUR WORK HERE IS DONE.
KSSSSH
...CALL SECURITY...
SIR! SIR, ARE YOU HURT?
ALLAH...!
GET BACK! GIVE THIS MAN SOME AIR!
AIR? PLEASE! GIVE HIM WATER! HURRY!
WATER...?
NO.
NOOOOOO!
GET IT AWAY FROM ME!

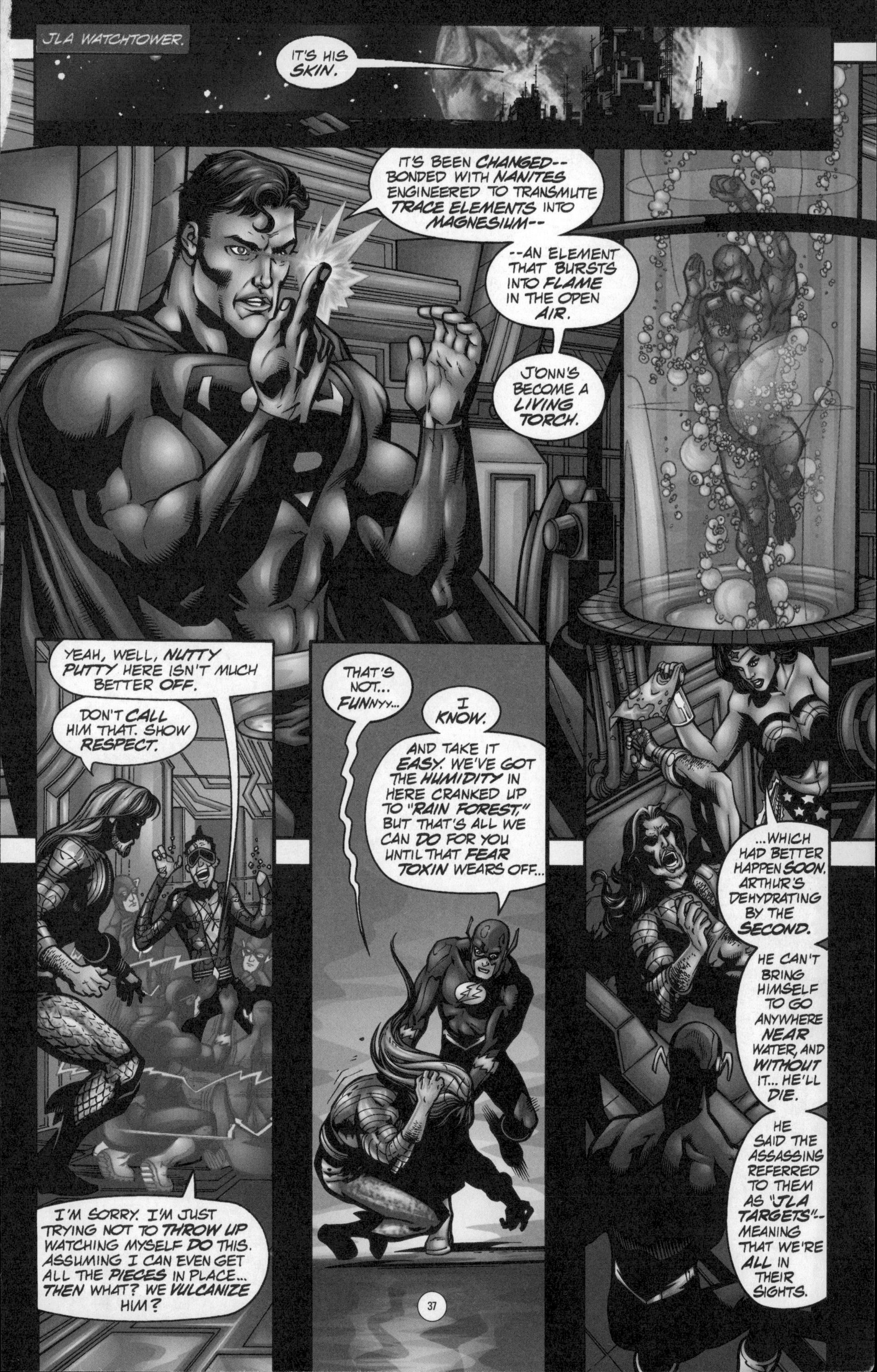
JLA WATCHTOWER.
IT'S HIS SKIN.
IT'S BEEN CHANGED-- BONDED WITH NANITES ENGINEERED TO TRANSMUTE TRACE ELEMENTS INTO MAGNESIUM--
--AN ELEMENT THAT BURSTS INTO FLAME IN THE OPEN AIR.
J'ONN'S BECOME A LIVING TORCH.
YEAH, WELL, NUTTY PUTTY HERE ISN'T MUCH BETTER OFF.
DON'T CALL HIM THAT. SHOW RESPECT.
I'M SORRY. I'M JUST TRYING NOT TO THROW UP WATCHING MYSELF DO THIS. ASSUMING I CAN EVEN GET ALL THE PIECES IN PLACE... THEN WHAT? WE VULCANIZE HIM?
THAT'S NOT... FUNNyy...
I KNOW.
AND TAKE IT EASY. WE'VE GOT THE HUMIDITY IN HERE CRANKED UP TO "RAIN FOREST," BUT THAT'S ALL WE CAN DO FOR YOU UNTIL THAT FEAR TOXIN WEARS OFF...
...WHICH HAD BETTER HAPPEN SOON. ARTHUR'S DEHYDRATING BY THE SECOND.
HE CAN'T BRING HIMSELF TO GO ANYWHERE NEAR WATER, AND WITHOUT IT... HE'LL DIE.
HE SAID THE ASSASSINS REFERRED TO THEM AS "JLA TARGETS"-- MEANING THAT WE'RE ALL IN THEIR SIGHTS.

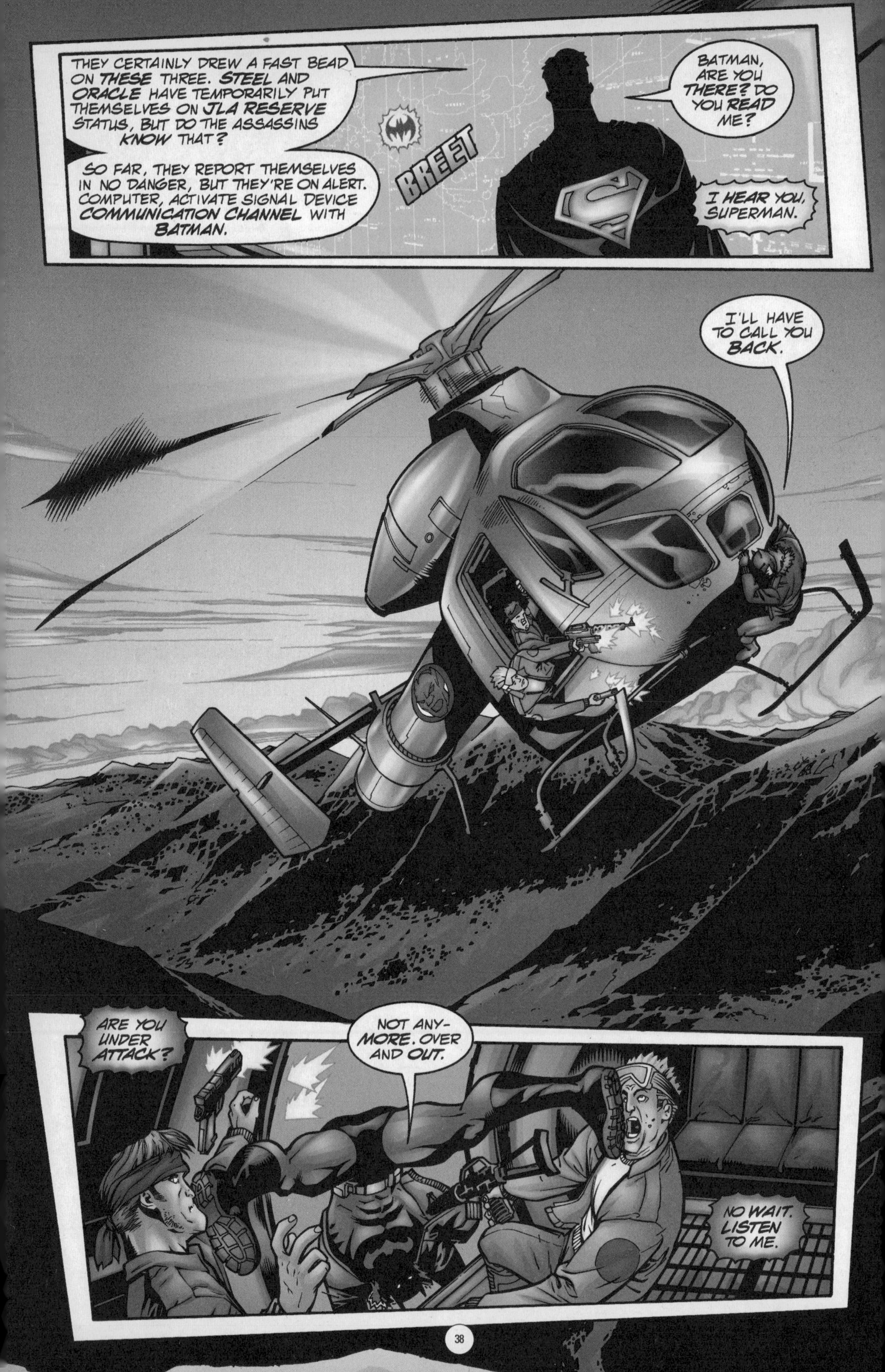
THEY CERTAINLY DREW A FAST BEAD ON THESE THREE. STEEL AND ORACLE HAVE TEMPORARILY PUT THEMSELVES ON JLA RESERVE STATUS, BUT DO THE ASSASSINS KNOW THAT?
SO FAR, THEY REPORT THEMSELVES IN NO DANGER, BUT THEY'RE ON ALERT. COMPUTER, ACTIVATE SIGNAL DEVICE COMMUNICATION CHANNEL WITH BATMAN.
BREET
BATMAN, ARE YOU THERE? DO YOU READ ME?
I HEAR YOU, SUPERMAN.
I'LL HAVE TO CALL YOU BACK.
ARE YOU UNDER ATTACK?
NOT ANY-MORE. OVER AND OUT.
NO WAIT. LISTEN TO ME.

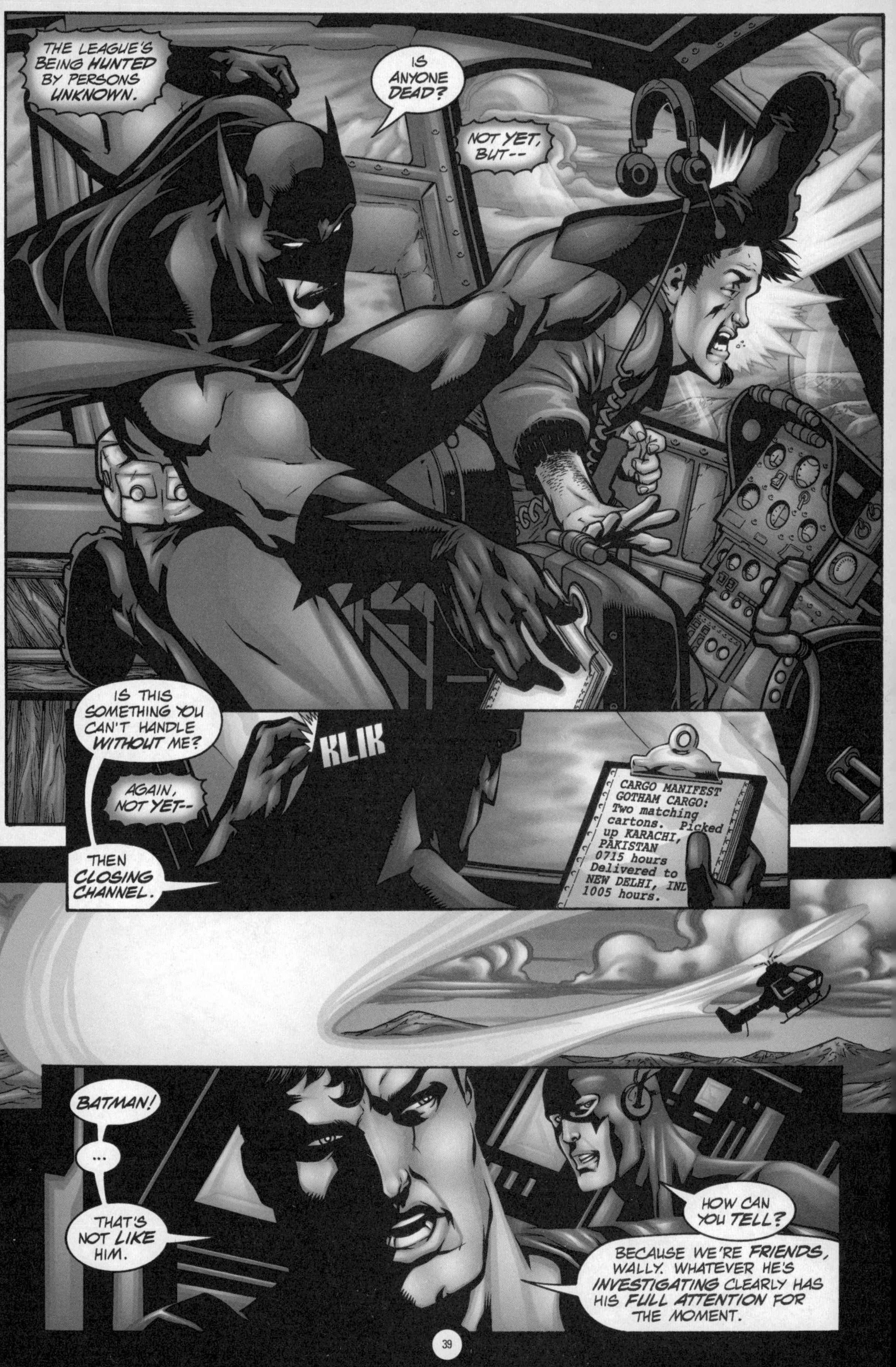
THE LEAGUE'S BEING HUNTED BY PERSONS UNKNOWN.
IS ANYONE DEAD?
NOT YET, BUT--
IS THIS SOMETHING YOU CAN'T HANDLE WITHOUT ME?
KLIK
AGAIN, NOT YET--
THEN CLOSING CHANNEL.
CARGO MANIFEST
GOTHAM CARGO:
Two matching cartons. Picked up KARACHI, PAKISTAN 0715 hours
Delivered to NEW DELHI, IND 1005 hours.
BATMAN!
...
THAT'S NOT LIKE HIM.
HOW CAN YOU TELL?
BECAUSE WE'RE FRIENDS, WALLY. WHATEVER HE'S INVESTIGATING CLEARLY HAS HIS FULL ATTENTION FOR THE MOMENT.

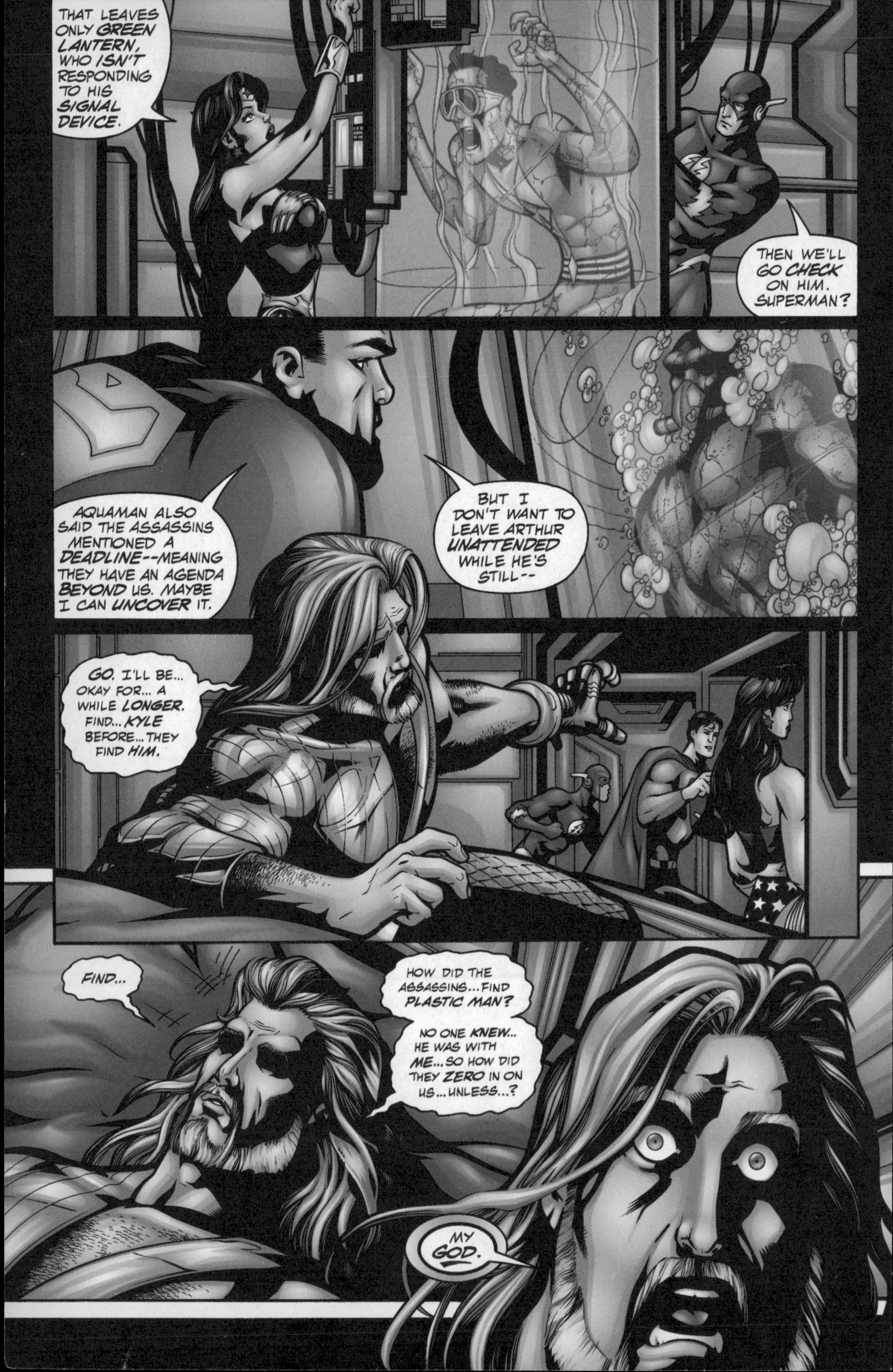

THAT LEAVES ONLY GREEN LANTERN, WHO ISN'T RESPONDING TO HIS SIGNAL DEVICE.
THEN WE'LL GO CHECK ON HIM. SUPERMAN?
AQUAMAN ALSO SAID THE ASSASSINS MENTIONED A DEADLINE--MEANING THEY HAVE AN AGENDA BEYOND US. MAYBE I CAN UNCOVER IT.
BUT I DON'T WANT TO LEAVE ARTHUR UNATTENDED WHILE HE'S STILL--
GO. I'LL BE... OKAY FOR... A WHILE LONGER. FIND... KYLE BEFORE... THEY FIND HIM.
FIND...
HOW DID THE ASSASSINS... FIND PLASTIC MAN?
NO ONE KNEW... HE WAS WITH ME... SO HOW DID THEY ZERO IN ON US... UNLESS...?
MY GOD.

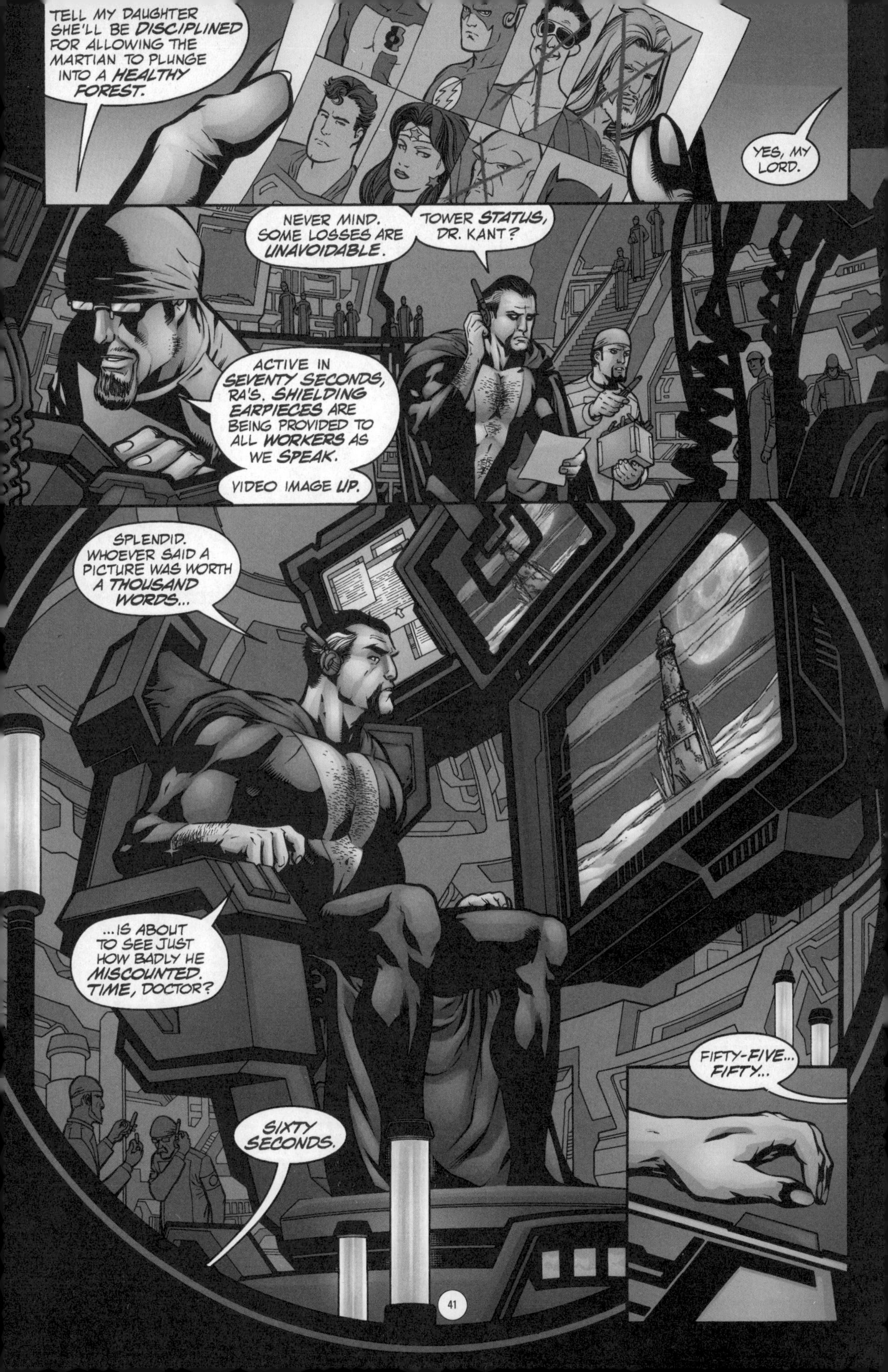
TELL MY DAUGHTER SHE'LL BE DISCIPLINED FOR ALLOWING THE MARTIAN TO PLUNGE INTO A HEALTHY FOREST.
YES, MY LORD.
NEVER MIND. SOME LOSSES ARE UNAVOIDABLE.
TOWER STATUS, DR. KANT?
ACTIVE IN SEVENTY SECONDS, RA'S. SHIELDING EARPIECES ARE BEING PROVIDED TO ALL WORKERS AS WE SPEAK.
VIDEO IMAGE UP.
SPLENDID. WHOEVER SAID A PICTURE WAS WORTH A THOUSAND WORDS...
...IS ABOUT TO SEE JUST HOW BADLY HE MISCOUNTED. TIME, DOCTOR?
SIXTY SECONDS.
FIFTY-FIVE... FIFTY...

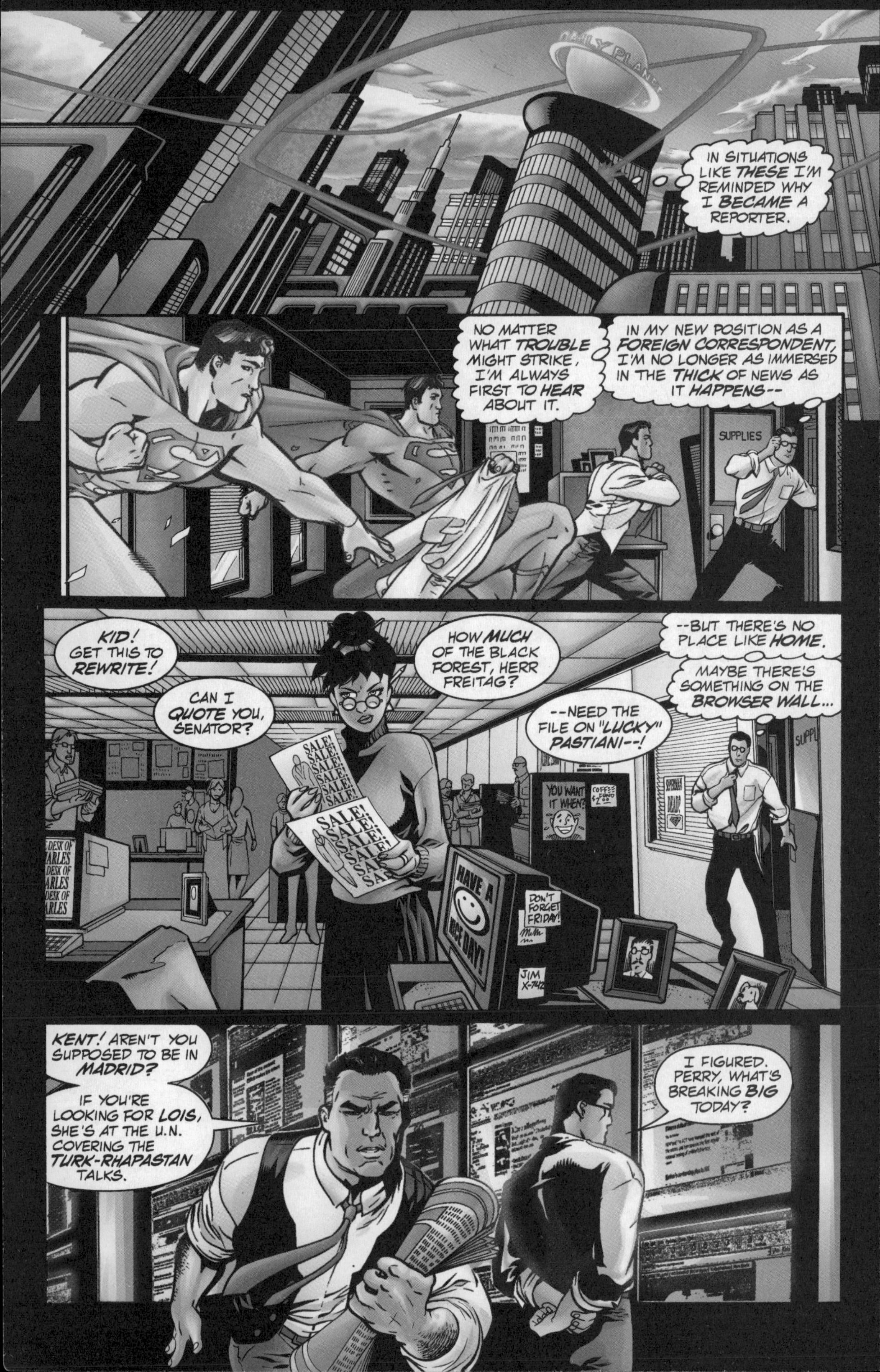
IN SITUATIONS LIKE THESE I'M REMINDED WHY I BECAME A REPORTER.
NO MATTER WHAT TROUBLE MIGHT STRIKE, I'M ALWAYS FIRST TO HEAR ABOUT IT.
IN MY NEW POSITION AS A FOREIGN CORRESPONDENT, I'M NO LONGER AS IMMERSED IN THE THICK OF NEWS AS IT HAPPENS--
SUPPLIES
KID! GET THIS TO REWRITE!
CAN I QUOTE YOU, SENATOR?
HOW MUCH OF THE BLACK FOREST, HERR FREITAG?
--NEED THE FILE ON "LUCKY" PASTIANI--!
--BUT THERE'S NO PLACE LIKE HOME.
MAYBE THERE'S SOMETHING ON THE BROWSER WALL...
SALE!
YOU WANT IT WHEN?
HAVE A NICE DAY!
DON'T FORGET FRIDAY!
JIM X-7412
KENT! AREN'T YOU SUPPOSED TO BE IN MADRID?
IF YOU'RE LOOKING FOR LOIS, SHE'S AT THE U.N. COVERING THE TURK-RHAPASTAN TALKS.
I FIGURED. PERRY, WHAT'S BREAKING BIG TODAY?

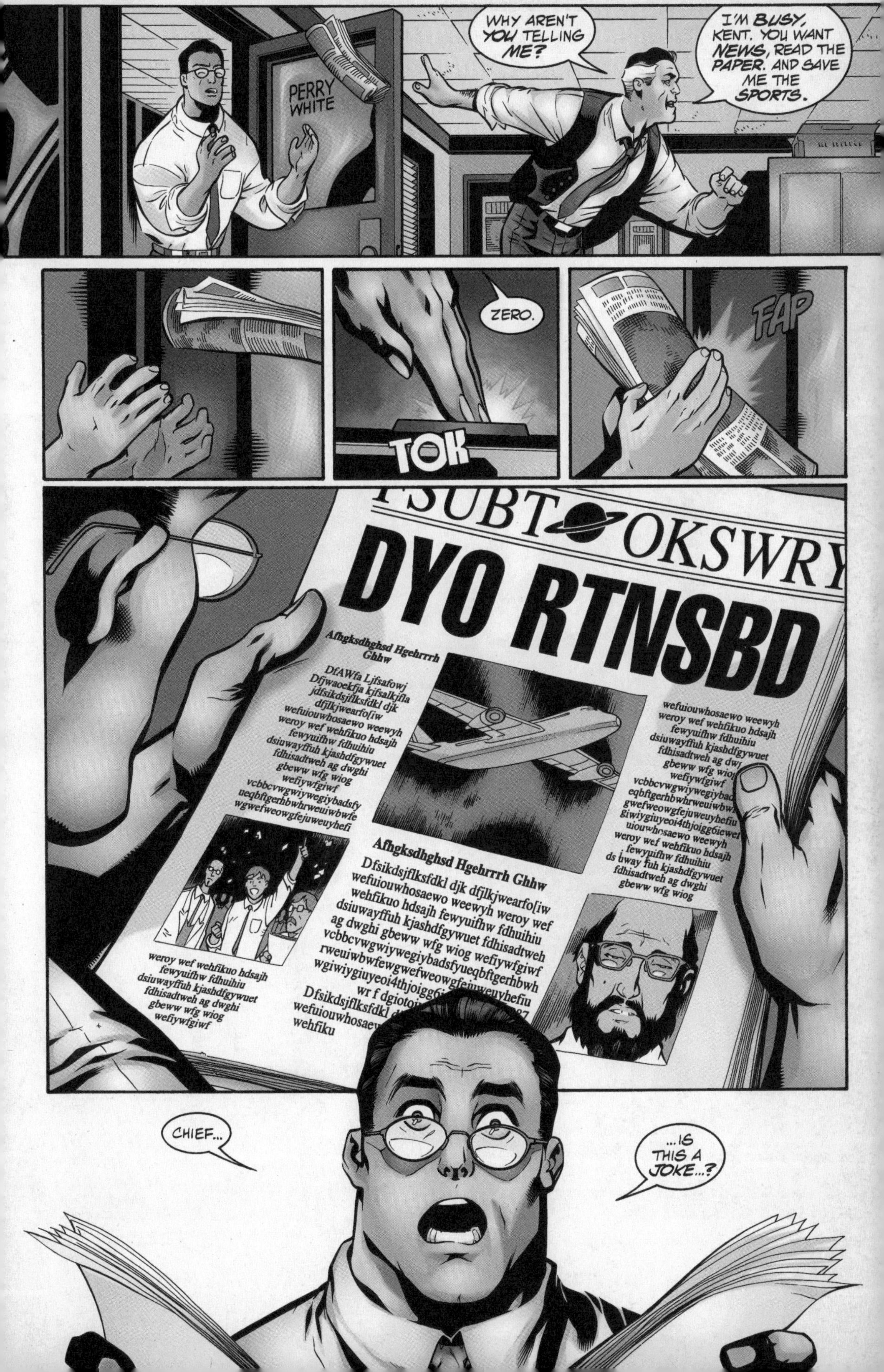
PERRY WHITE
WHY AREN'T YOU TELLING ME?
I'M BUSY, KENT. YOU WANT NEWS, READ THE PAPER. AND SAVE ME THE SPORTS.
ZERO.
TOK
FAP
DYO RTNSBD
CHIEF...
...IS THIS A JOKE...?

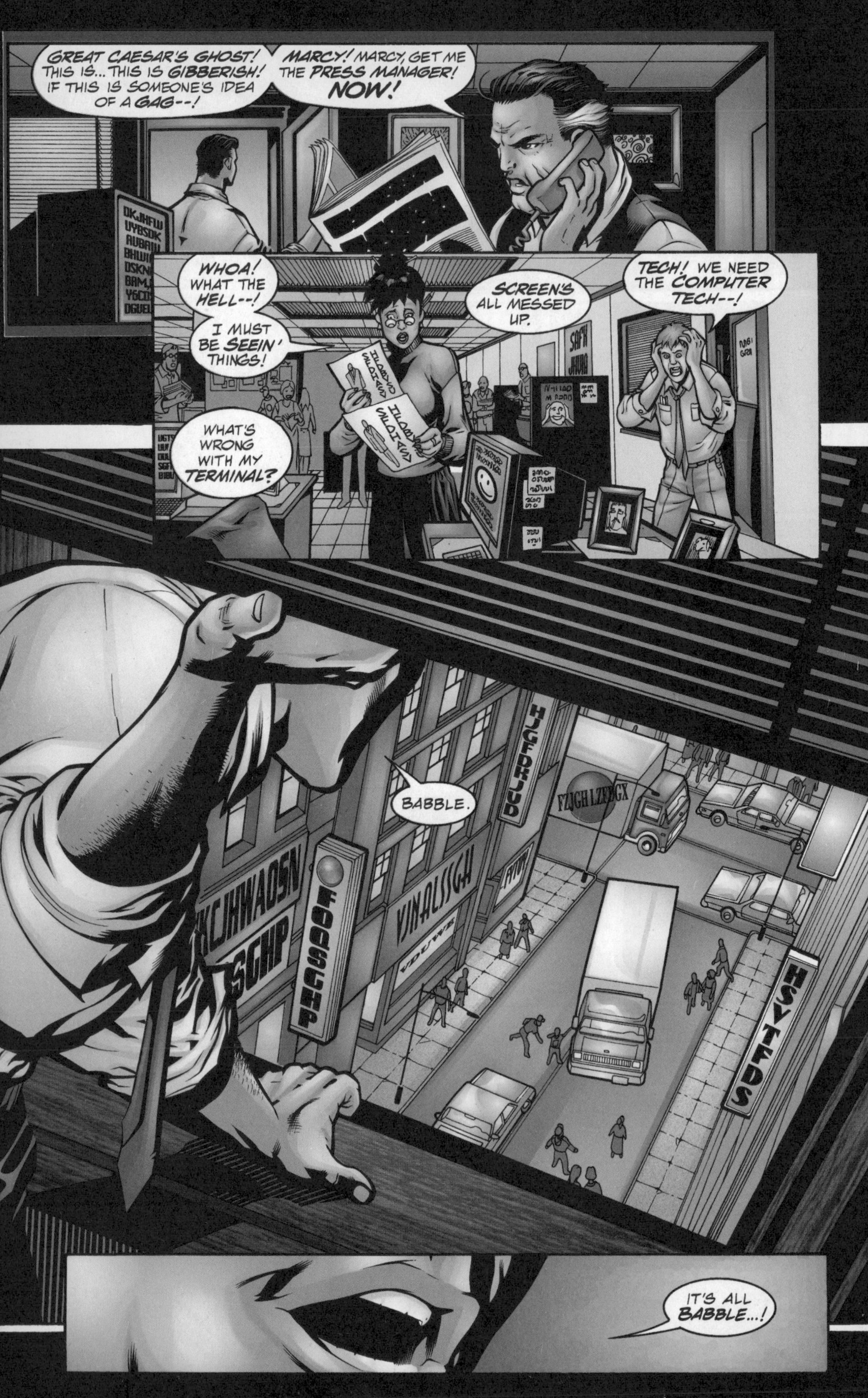
GREAT CAESAR'S GHOST! THIS IS... THIS IS GIBBERISH! IF THIS IS SOMEONE'S IDEA OF A GAG--!
MARCY! MARCY, GET ME THE PRESS MANAGER! NOW!
WHOA! WHAT THE HELL--!
I MUST BE SEEIN' THINGS!
WHAT'S WRONG WITH MY TERMINAL?
SCREEN'S ALL MESSED UP.
TECH! WE NEED THE COMPUTER TECH--!
BABBLE.
IT'S ALL BABBLE...!

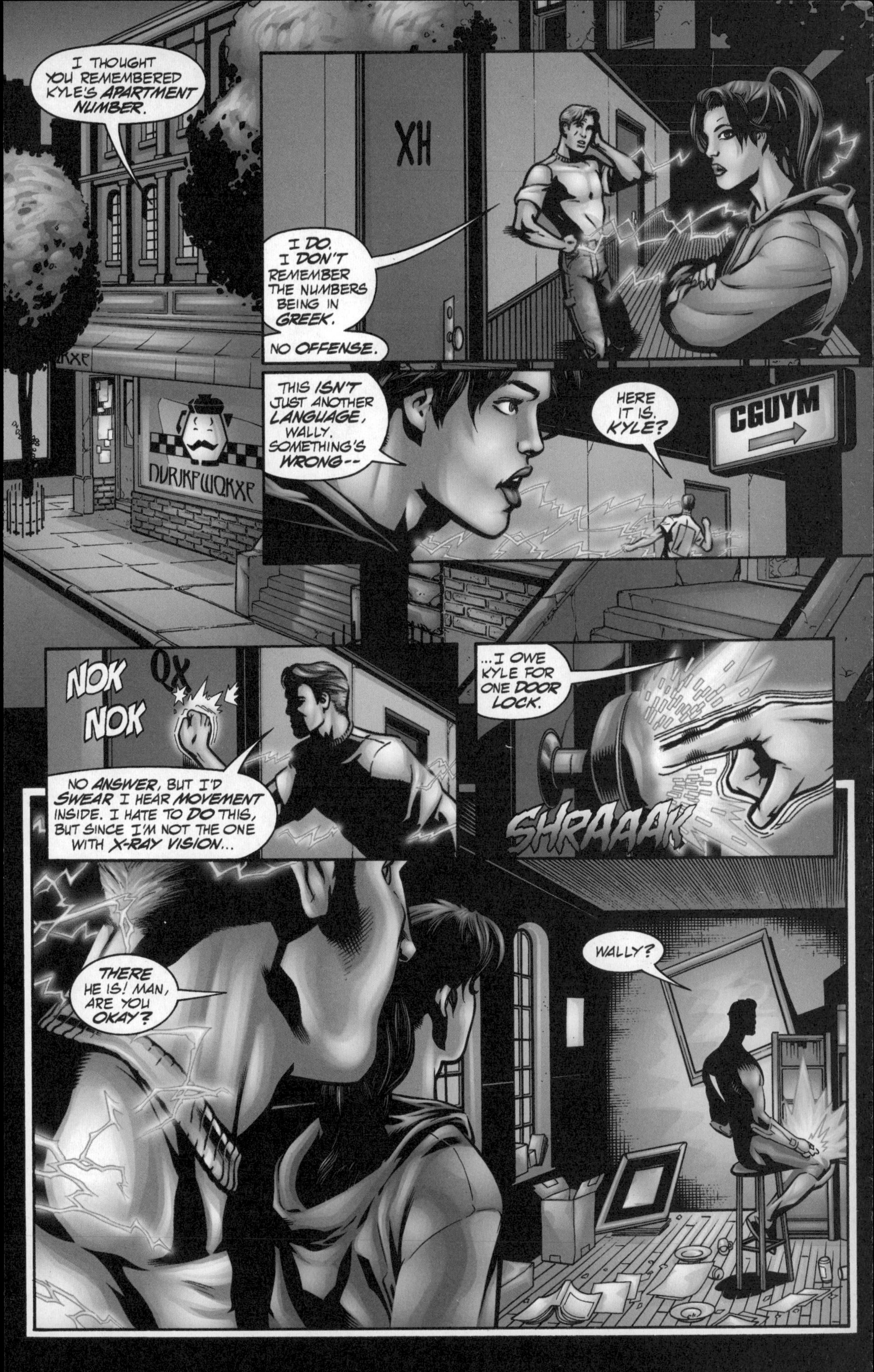

I THOUGHT YOU REMEMBERED KYLE'S APARTMENT NUMBER.
XH
I DO. I DON'T REMEMBER THE NUMBERS BEING IN GREEK.
NO OFFENSE.
NURJKFWQKXF
THIS ISN'T JUST ANOTHER LANGUAGE, WALLY. SOMETHING'S WRONG--
HERE IT IS. KYLE?
CGUYM
NOK NOK
QX
NO ANSWER, BUT I'D SWEAR I HEAR MOVEMENT INSIDE. I HATE TO DO THIS, BUT SINCE I'M NOT THE ONE WITH X-RAY VISION...
...I OWE KYLE FOR ONE DOOR LOCK.
SHRAAAK
THERE HE IS! MAN, ARE YOU OKAY?
WALLY?

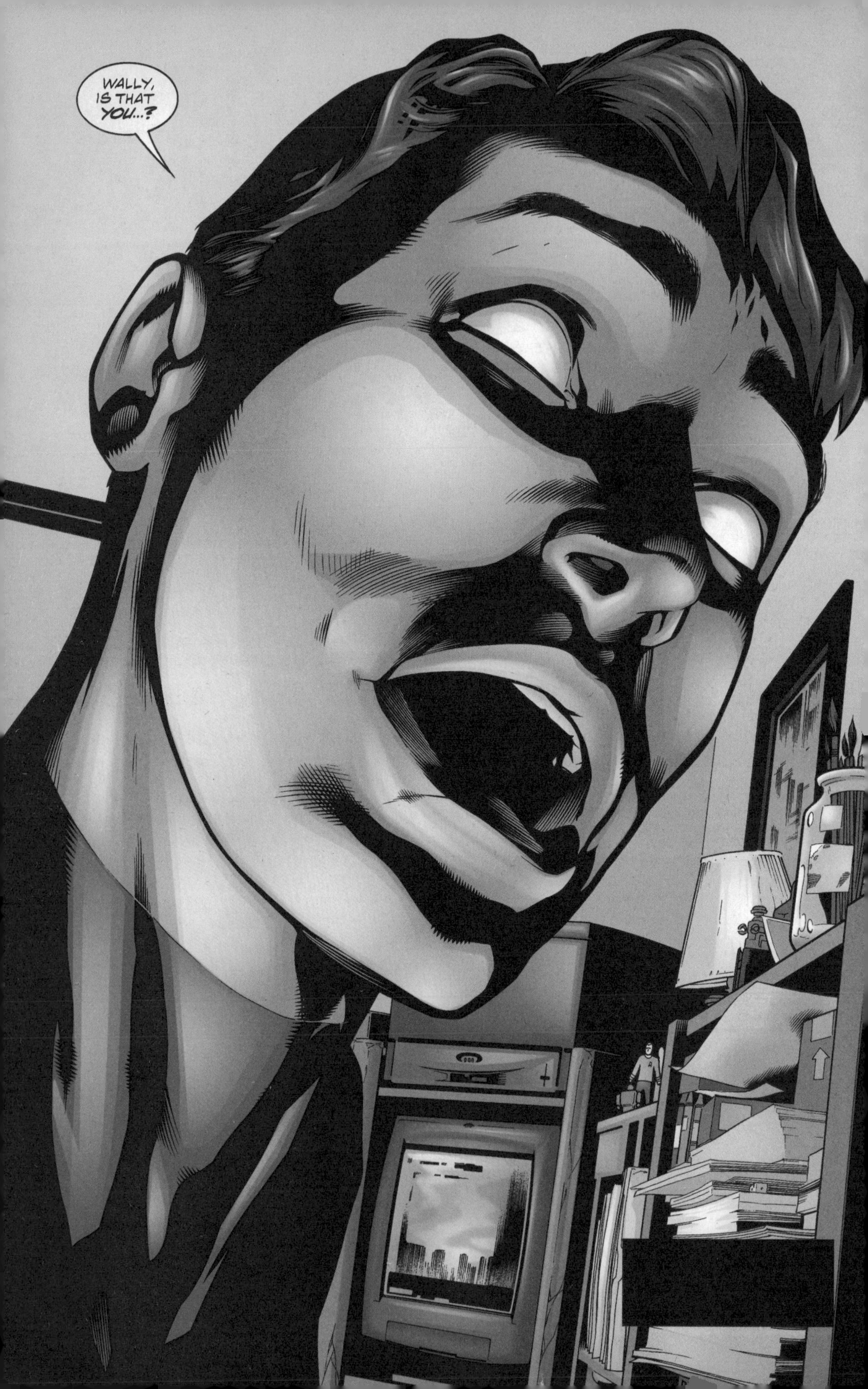
WALLY, IS THAT YOU...?

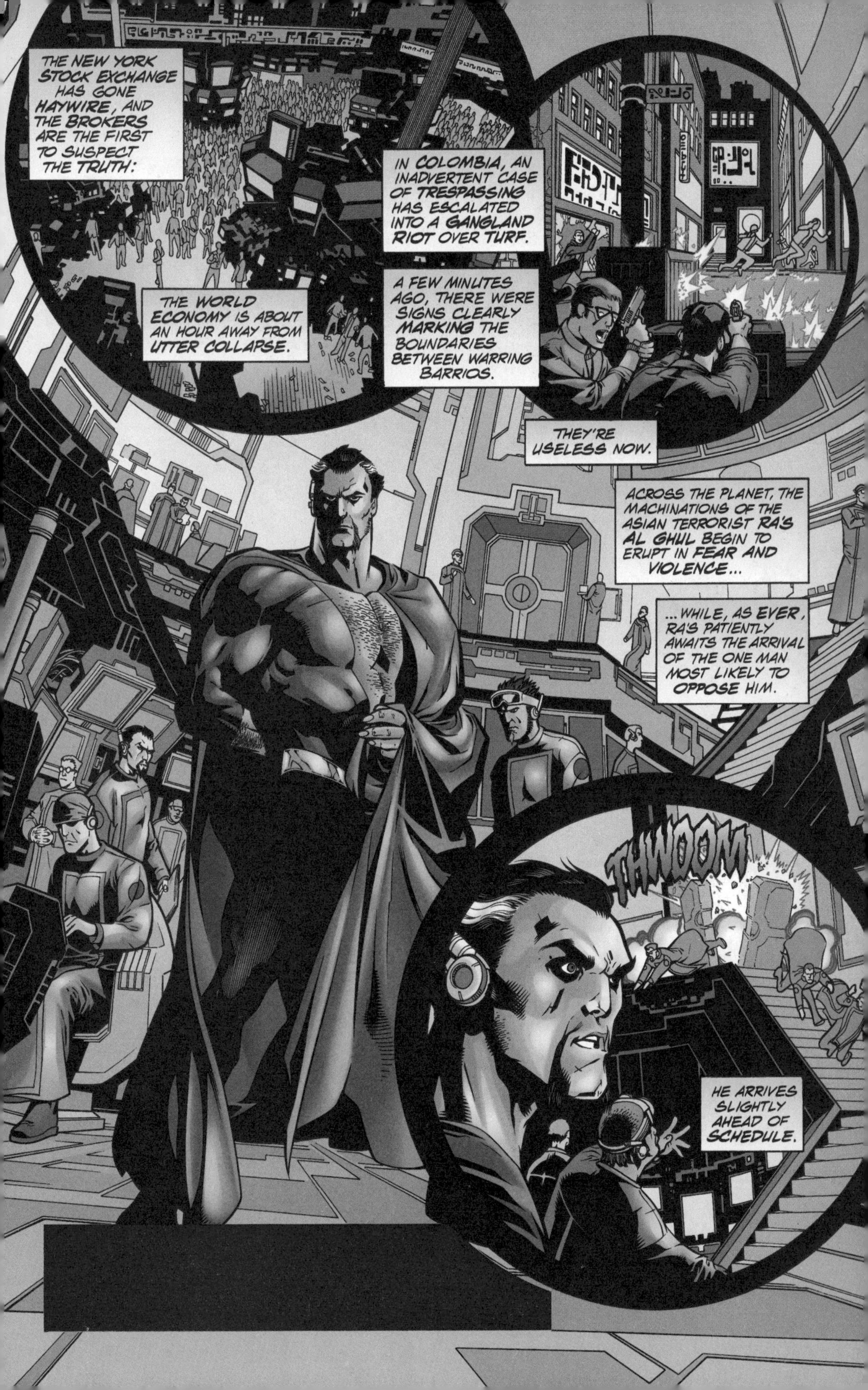
THE NEW YORK STOCK EXCHANGE HAS GONE HAYWIRE, AND THE BROKERS ARE THE FIRST TO SUSPECT THE TRUTH:
THE WORLD ECONOMY IS ABOUT AN HOUR AWAY FROM UTTER COLLAPSE.
IN COLOMBIA, AN INADVERTENT CASE OF TRESPASSING HAS ESCALATED INTO A GANGLAND RIOT OVER TURF.
A FEW MINUTES AGO, THERE WERE SIGNS CLEARLY MARKING THE BOUNDARIES BETWEEN WARRING BARRIOS.
THEY'RE USELESS NOW.
ACROSS THE PLANET, THE MACHINATIONS OF THE ASIAN TERRORIST RA'S AL GHUL BEGIN TO ERUPT IN FEAR AND VIOLENCE...
...WHILE, AS EVER, RA'S PATIENTLY AWAITS THE ARRIVAL OF THE ONE MAN MOST LIKELY TO OPPOSE HIM.
THWOOM
HE ARRIVES SLIGHTLY AHEAD OF SCHEDULE.
[redacted]

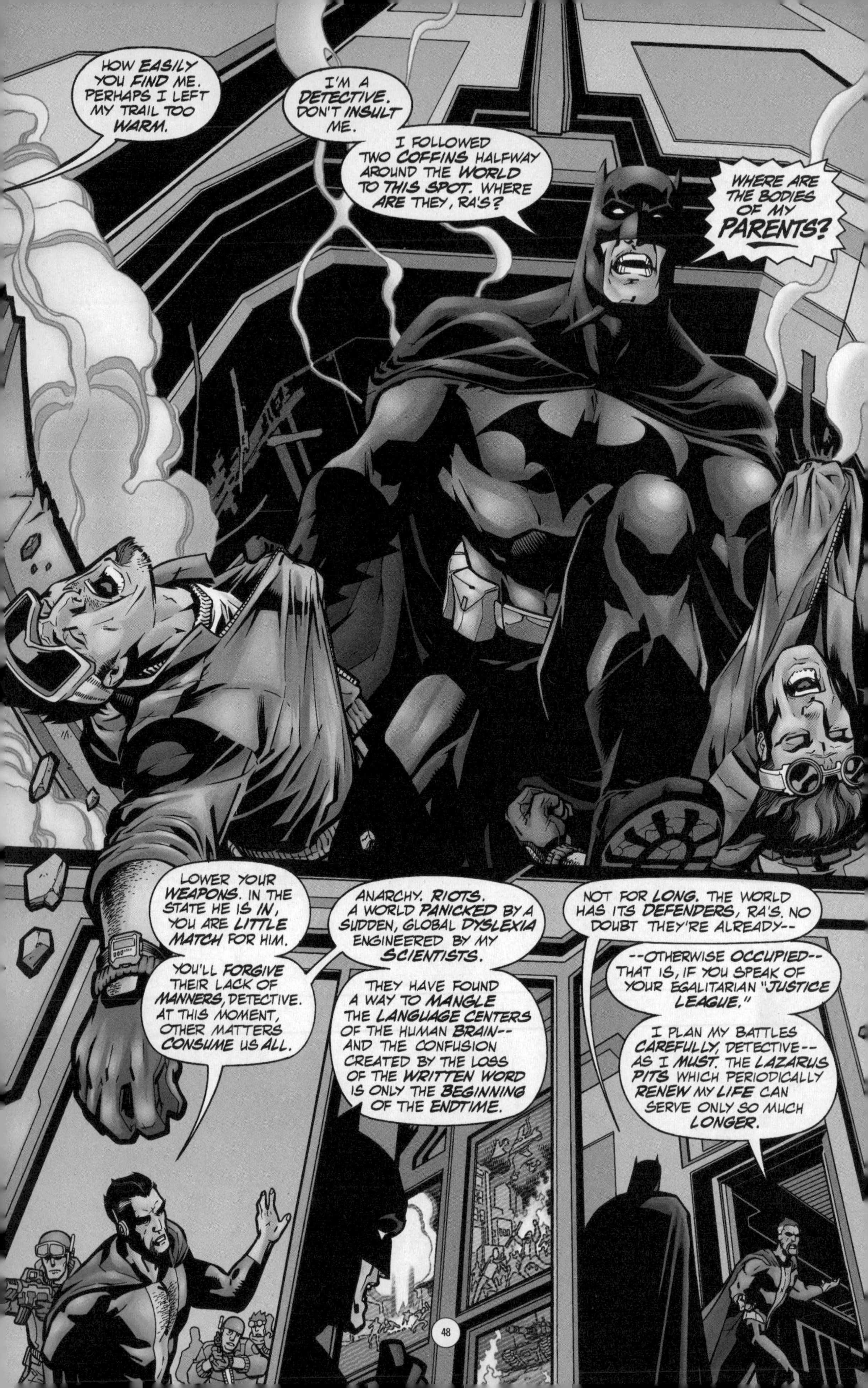
HOW EASILY YOU FIND ME. PERHAPS I LEFT MY TRAIL TOO WARM.
I'M A DETECTIVE. DON'T INSULT ME.
I FOLLOWED TWO COFFINS HALFWAY AROUND THE WORLD TO THIS SPOT. WHERE ARE THEY, RA'S?
WHERE ARE THE BODIES OF MY PARENTS?
LOWER YOUR WEAPONS. IN THE STATE HE IS IN, YOU ARE LITTLE MATCH FOR HIM.
YOU'LL FORGIVE THEIR LACK OF MANNERS, DETECTIVE. AT THIS MOMENT, OTHER MATTERS CONSUME US ALL.
ANARCHY. RIOTS. A WORLD PANICKED BY A SUDDEN, GLOBAL DYSLEXIA ENGINEERED BY MY SCIENTISTS.
THEY HAVE FOUND A WAY TO MANGLE THE LANGUAGE CENTERS OF THE HUMAN BRAIN-- AND THE CONFUSION CREATED BY THE LOSS OF THE WRITTEN WORD IS ONLY THE BEGINNING OF THE ENDTIME.
NOT FOR LONG. THE WORLD HAS ITS DEFENDERS, RA'S. NO DOUBT THEY'RE ALREADY--
--OTHERWISE OCCUPIED-- THAT IS, IF YOU SPEAK OF YOUR EGALITARIAN "JUSTICE LEAGUE."
I PLAN MY BATTLES CAREFULLY, DETECTIVE-- AS I MUST. THE LAZARUS PITS WHICH PERIODICALLY RENEW MY LIFE CAN SERVE ONLY SO MUCH LONGER.

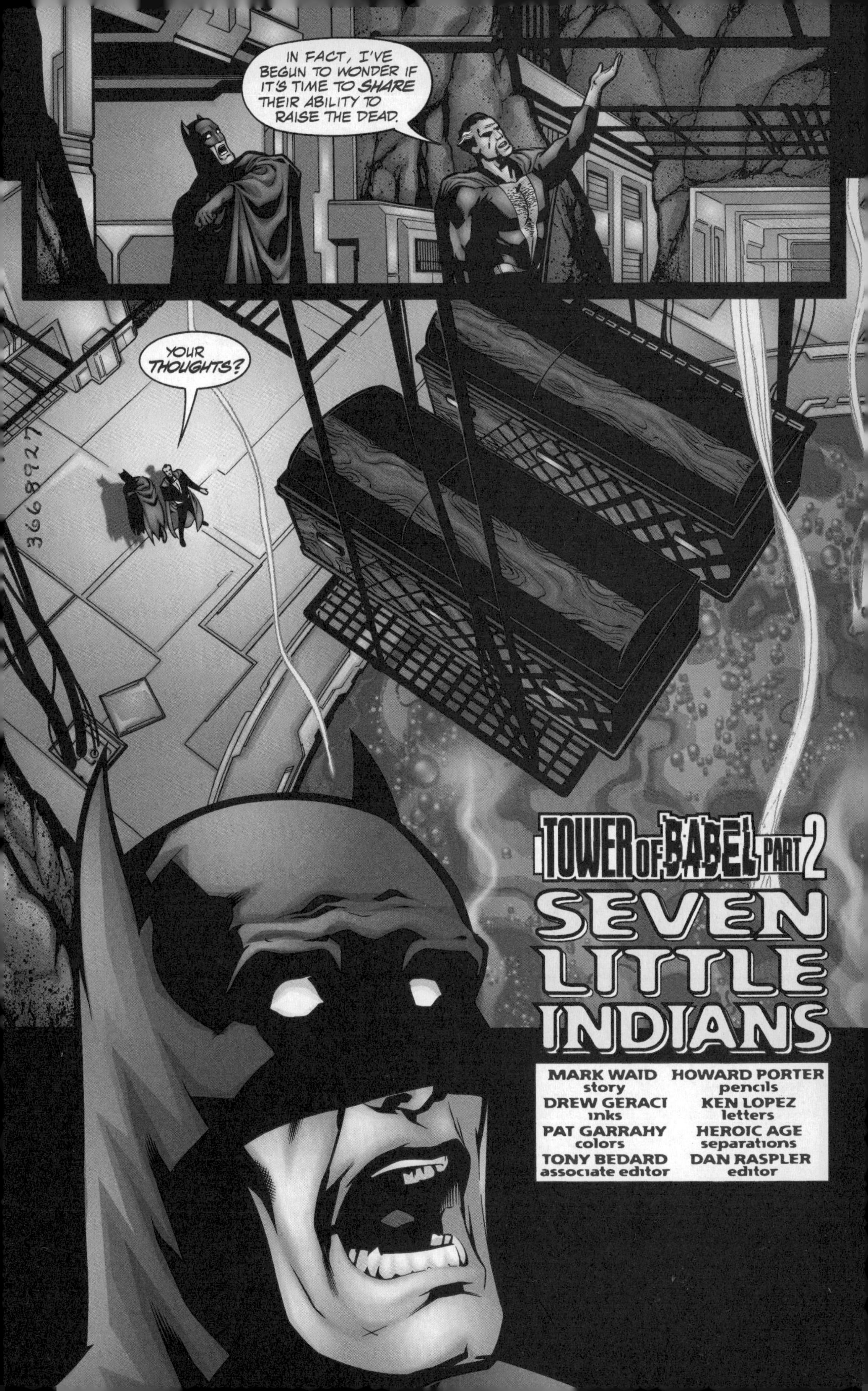
IN FACT, I'VE BEGUN TO WONDER IF IT'S TIME TO SHARE THEIR ABILITY TO RAISE THE DEAD.
YOUR THOUGHTS?
TOWER OF BABEL PART 2
SEVEN LITTLE INDIANS
MARK WAID story
HOWARD PORTER pencils
DREW GERACI inks
KEN LOPEZ letters
PAT GARRAHY colors
HEROIC AGE separations
TONY BEDARD associate editor
DAN RASPLER editor

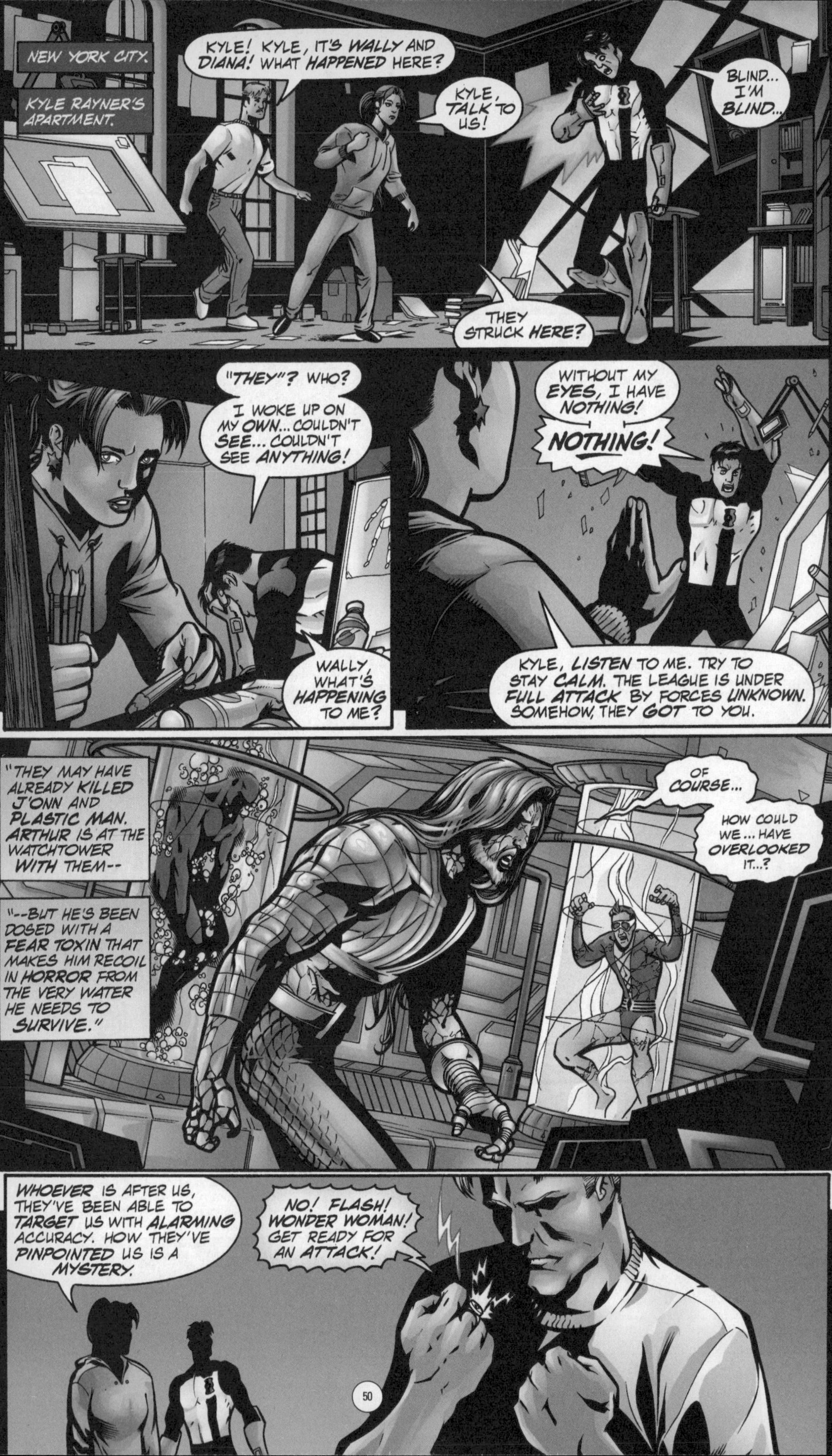
NEW YORK CITY.
KYLE RAYNER'S APARTMENT.
KYLE! KYLE, IT'S WALLY AND DIANA! WHAT HAPPENED HERE?
KYLE, TALK TO US!
BLIND... I'M BLIND...
THEY STRUCK HERE?
"THEY"? WHO?
I WOKE UP ON MY OWN... COULDN'T SEE... COULDN'T SEE ANYTHING!
WALLY, WHAT'S HAPPENING TO ME?
WITHOUT MY EYES, I HAVE NOTHING!
NOTHING!
KYLE, LISTEN TO ME. TRY TO STAY CALM. THE LEAGUE IS UNDER FULL ATTACK BY FORCES UNKNOWN. SOMEHOW, THEY GOT TO YOU.
"THEY MAY HAVE ALREADY KILLED J'ONN AND PLASTIC MAN. ARTHUR IS AT THE WATCHTOWER WITH THEM--
"--BUT HE'S BEEN DOSED WITH A FEAR TOXIN THAT MAKES HIM RECOIL IN HORROR FROM THE VERY WATER HE NEEDS TO SURVIVE."
OF COURSE...
HOW COULD WE... HAVE OVERLOOKED IT...?
WHOEVER IS AFTER US, THEY'VE BEEN ABLE TO TARGET US WITH ALARMING ACCURACY. HOW THEY'VE PINPOINTED US IS A MYSTERY.
NO! FLASH! WONDER WOMAN! GET READY FOR AN ATTACK!

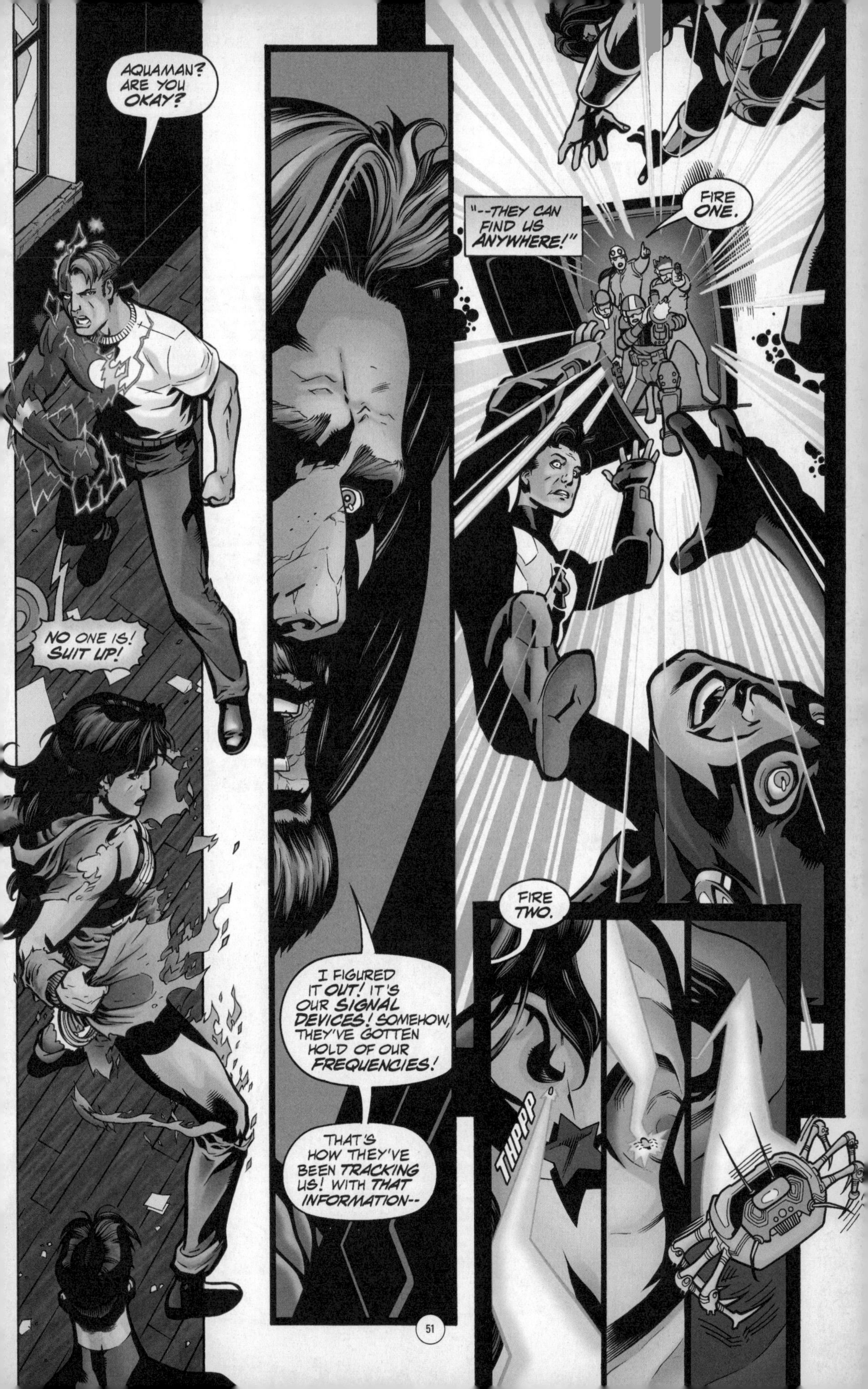

AQUAMAN? ARE YOU OKAY?
NO ONE IS! SUIT UP!
I FIGURED IT OUT! IT'S OUR SIGNAL DEVICES! SOMEHOW, THEY'VE GOTTEN HOLD OF OUR FREQUENCIES!
THAT'S HOW THEY'VE BEEN TRACKING US! WITH THAT INFORMATION--
"--THEY CAN FIND US ANYWHERE!"
FIRE ONE.
FIRE TWO.
THPPP

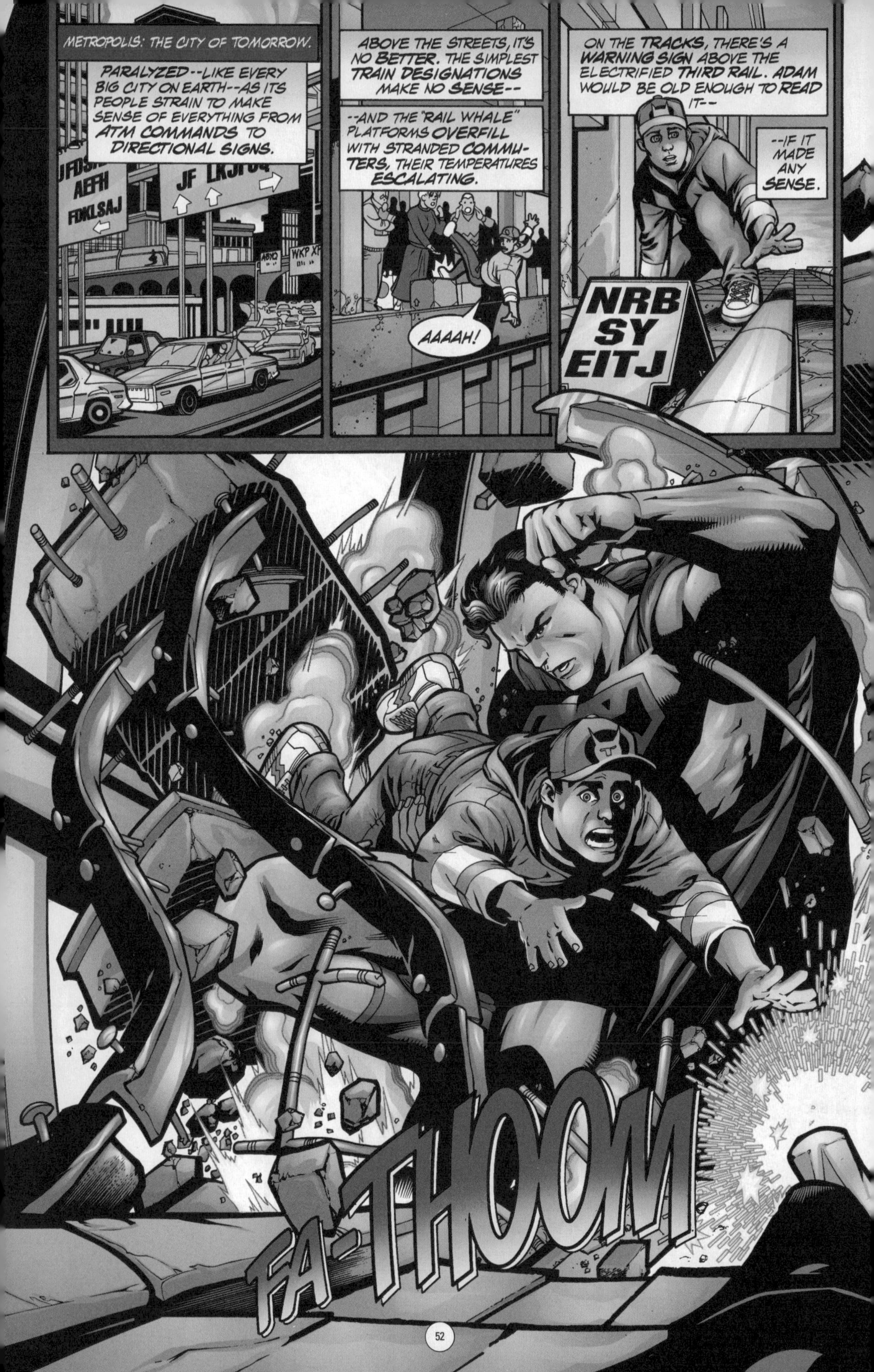
METROPOLIS: THE CITY OF TOMORROW.
PARALYZED--LIKE EVERY BIG CITY ON EARTH--AS ITS PEOPLE STRAIN TO MAKE SENSE OF EVERYTHING FROM ATM COMMANDS TO DIRECTIONAL SIGNS.
UFDS AEFH FDKLSAJ
JF LKJFU4
WKP XF
ABOVE THE STREETS, IT'S NO BETTER. THE SIMPLEST TRAIN DESIGNATIONS MAKE NO SENSE--
--AND THE "RAIL WHALE" PLATFORMS OVERFILL WITH STRANDED COMMUTERS, THEIR TEMPERATURES ESCALATING.
AAAAH!
ON THE TRACKS, THERE'S A WARNING SIGN ABOVE THE ELECTRIFIED THIRD RAIL. ADAM WOULD BE OLD ENOUGH TO READ IT--
--IF IT MADE ANY SENSE.
NRB SY EITJ
FA-THOOM

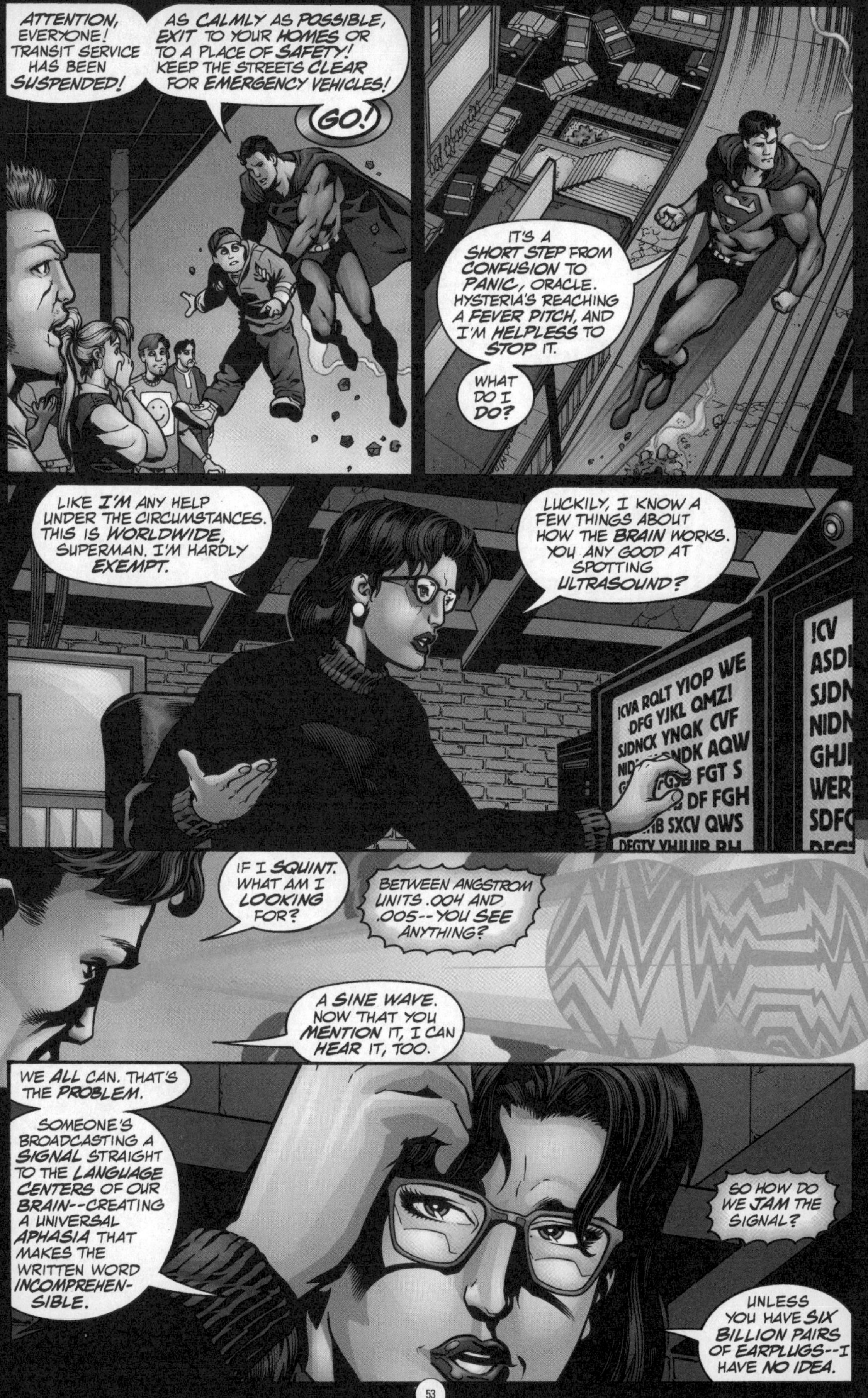
ATTENTION, EVERYONE! TRANSIT SERVICE HAS BEEN SUSPENDED!
AS CALMLY AS POSSIBLE, EXIT TO YOUR HOMES OR TO A PLACE OF SAFETY! KEEP THE STREETS CLEAR FOR EMERGENCY VEHICLES!
GO!
IT'S A SHORT STEP FROM CONFUSION TO PANIC, ORACLE. HYSTERIA'S REACHING A FEVER PITCH, AND I'M HELPLESS TO STOP IT.
WHAT DO I DO?
LIKE I'M ANY HELP UNDER THE CIRCUMSTANCES. THIS IS WORLDWIDE, SUPERMAN. I'M HARDLY EXEMPT.
LUCKILY, I KNOW A FEW THINGS ABOUT HOW THE BRAIN WORKS. YOU ANY GOOD AT SPOTTING ULTRASOUND?
!CVA RQLT YIOP WE
DFG YJKL QMZ!
SJDNCX YNQK CVF
FGT S
DF FGH
SXCV QWS
IF I SQUINT. WHAT AM I LOOKING FOR?
BETWEEN ANGSTROM UNITS .004 AND .005--YOU SEE ANYTHING?
A SINE WAVE. NOW THAT YOU MENTION IT, I CAN HEAR IT, TOO.
WE ALL CAN. THAT'S THE PROBLEM.
SOMEONE'S BROADCASTING A SIGNAL STRAIGHT TO THE LANGUAGE CENTERS OF OUR BRAIN--CREATING A UNIVERSAL APHASIA THAT MAKES THE WRITTEN WORD INCOMPREHEN-SIBLE.
SO HOW DO WE JAM THE SIGNAL?
UNLESS YOU HAVE SIX BILLION PAIRS OF EARPLUGS--I HAVE NO IDEA.

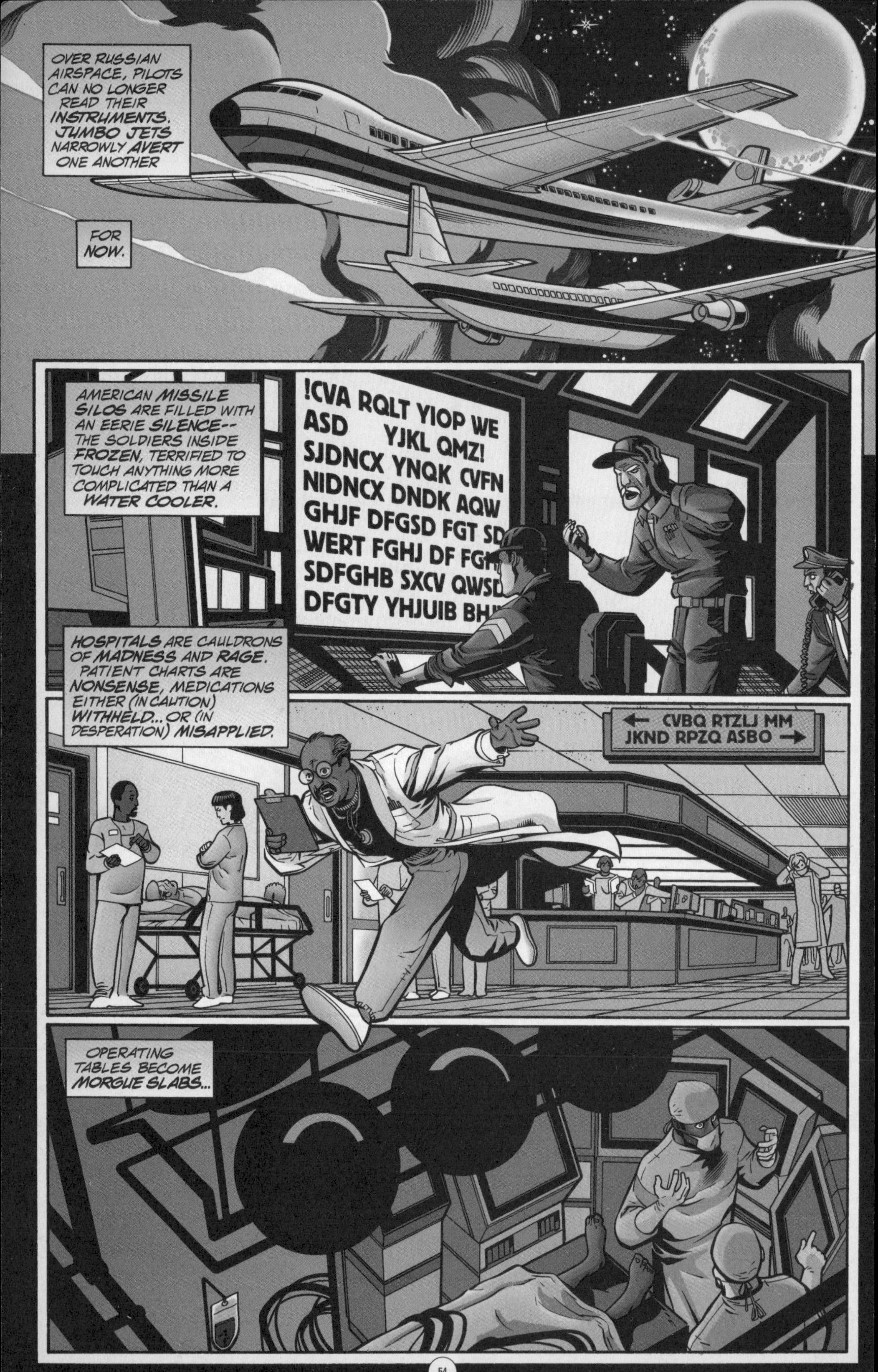

OVER RUSSIAN AIRSPACE, PILOTS CAN NO LONGER READ THEIR INSTRUMENTS. JUMBO JETS NARROWLY AVERT ONE ANOTHER
FOR NOW.
AMERICAN MISSILE SILOS ARE FILLED WITH AN EERIE SILENCE-- THE SOLDIERS INSIDE FROZEN, TERRIFIED TO TOUCH ANYTHING MORE COMPLICATED THAN A WATER COOLER.
!CVA RQLT YIOP WE
ASD YJKL QMZ!
SJDNCX YNQK CVFN
NIDNCX DNDK AQW
GHJF DFGSD FGT SD
WERT FGHJ DF FGH
SDFGHB SXCV QWSD
DFGTY YHJUIB BHJ
HOSPITALS ARE CAULDRONS OF MADNESS AND RAGE. PATIENT CHARTS ARE NONSENSE, MEDICATIONS EITHER (IN CAUTION) WITHHELD... OR (IN DESPERATION) MISAPPLIED.
← CVBQ RTZLJ MM
JKND RPZQ ASBO →
OPERATING TABLES BECOME MORGUE SLABS...

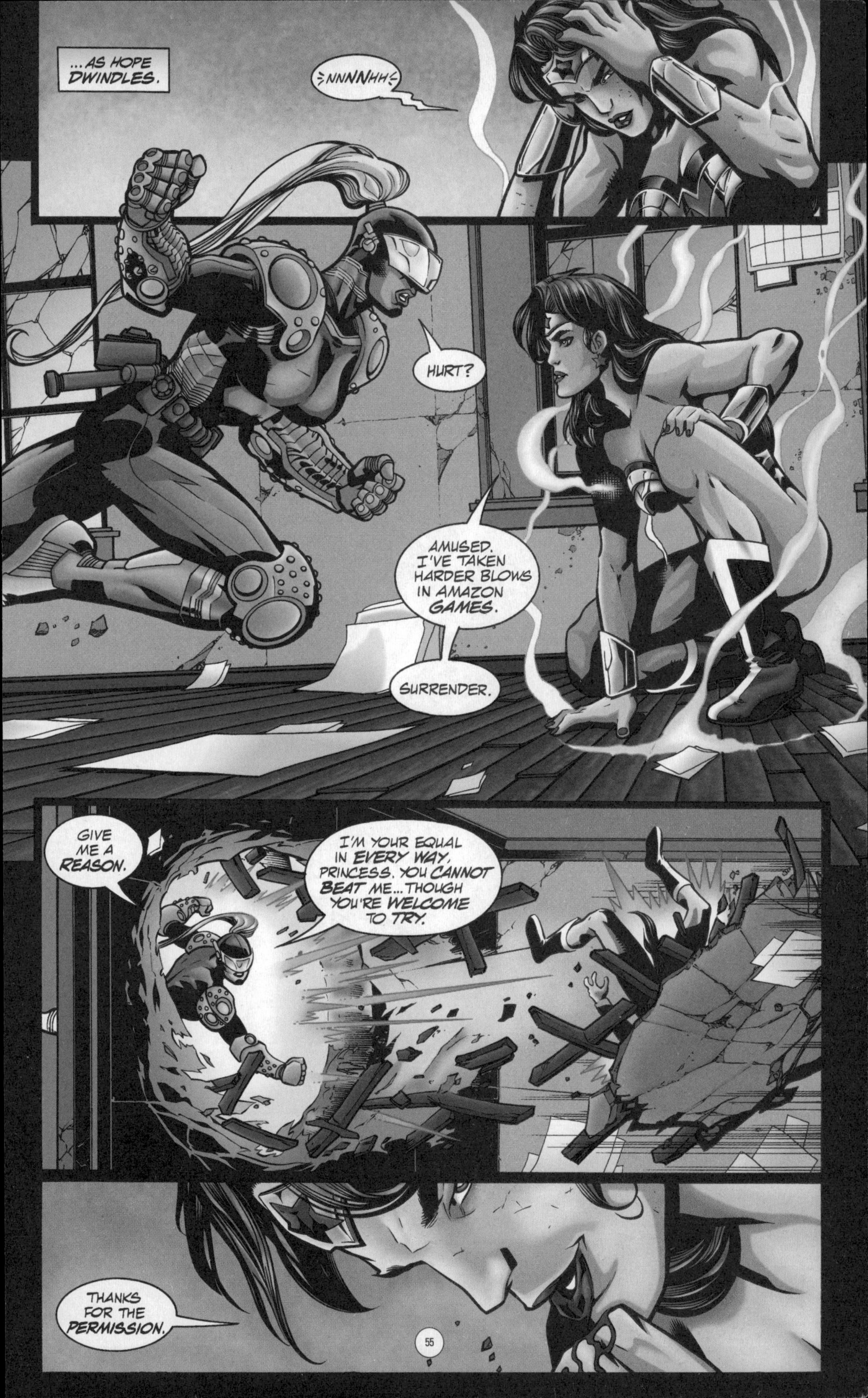
...AS HOPE DWINDLES.
NNNNHH
HURT?
AMUSED. I'VE TAKEN HARDER BLOWS IN AMAZON GAMES.
SURRENDER.
GIVE ME A REASON.
I'M YOUR EQUAL IN EVERY WAY, PRINCESS. YOU CANNOT BEAT ME...THOUGH YOU'RE WELCOME TO TRY.
THANKS FOR THE PERMISSION.

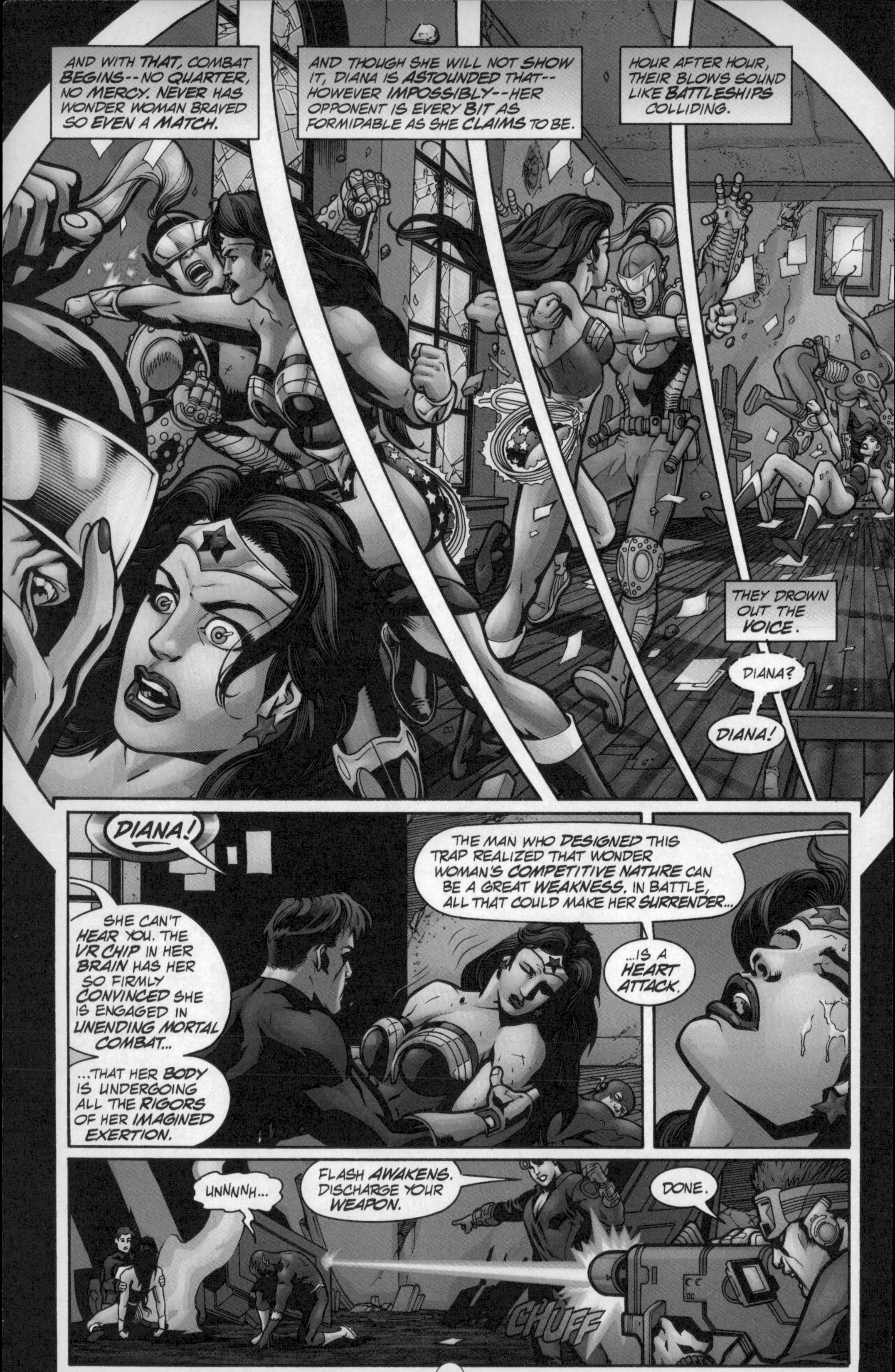

AND WITH THAT, COMBAT BEGINS--NO QUARTER, NO MERCY. NEVER HAS WONDER WOMAN BRAVED SO EVEN A MATCH.
AND THOUGH SHE WILL NOT SHOW IT, DIANA IS ASTOUNDED THAT--HOWEVER IMPOSSIBLY--HER OPPONENT IS EVERY BIT AS FORMIDABLE AS SHE CLAIMS TO BE.
HOUR AFTER HOUR, THEIR BLOWS SOUND LIKE BATTLESHIPS COLLIDING.
THEY DROWN OUT THE VOICE.
DIANA?
DIANA!
DIANA!
SHE CAN'T HEAR YOU. THE VR CHIP IN HER BRAIN HAS HER SO FIRMLY CONVINCED SHE IS ENGAGED IN UNENDING MORTAL COMBAT...
...THAT HER BODY IS UNDERGOING ALL THE RIGORS OF HER IMAGINED EXERTION.
THE MAN WHO DESIGNED THIS TRAP REALIZED THAT WONDER WOMAN'S COMPETITIVE NATURE CAN BE A GREAT WEAKNESS. IN BATTLE, ALL THAT COULD MAKE HER SURRENDER...
...IS A HEART ATTACK.
UNNNNH...
FLASH AWAKENS. DISCHARGE YOUR WEAPON.
DONE.
CHUFF

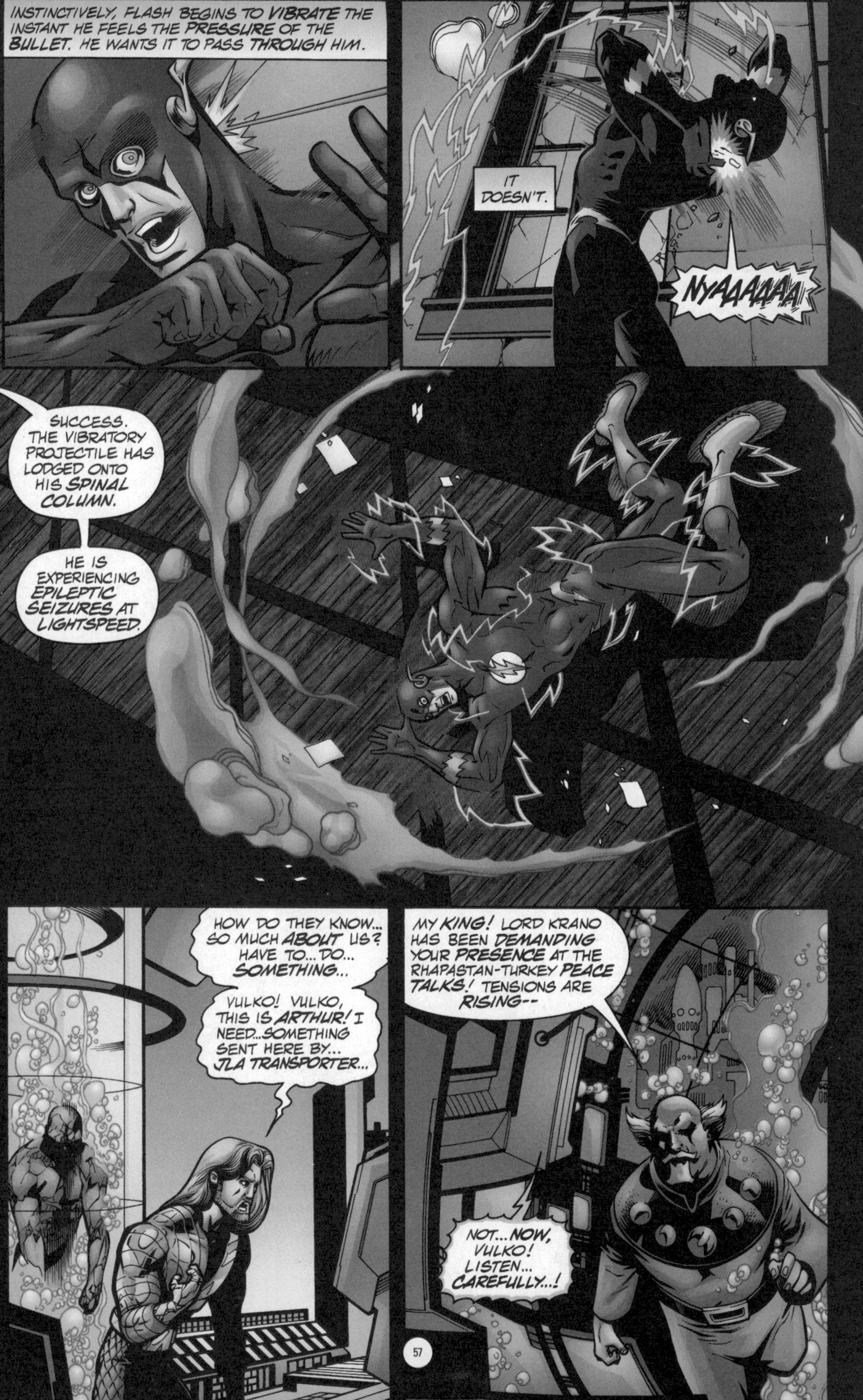
INSTINCTIVELY, FLASH BEGINS TO VIBRATE THE INSTANT HE FEELS THE PRESSURE OF THE BULLET. HE WANTS IT TO PASS THROUGH HIM.
IT DOESN'T.
NYAAAAAA
SUCCESS. THE VIBRATORY PROJECTILE HAS LODGED ONTO HIS SPINAL COLUMN.
HE IS EXPERIENCING EPILEPTIC SEIZURES AT LIGHTSPEED.
HOW DO THEY KNOW... SO MUCH ABOUT US? HAVE TO... DO... SOMETHING...
VULKO! VULKO, THIS IS ARTHUR! I NEED...SOMETHING SENT HERE BY... JLA TRANSPORTER...
MY KING! LORD KRANO HAS BEEN DEMANDING YOUR PRESENCE AT THE RHAPASTAN-TURKEY PEACE TALKS! TENSIONS ARE RISING--
NOT...NOW, VULKO! LISTEN... CAREFULLY...!

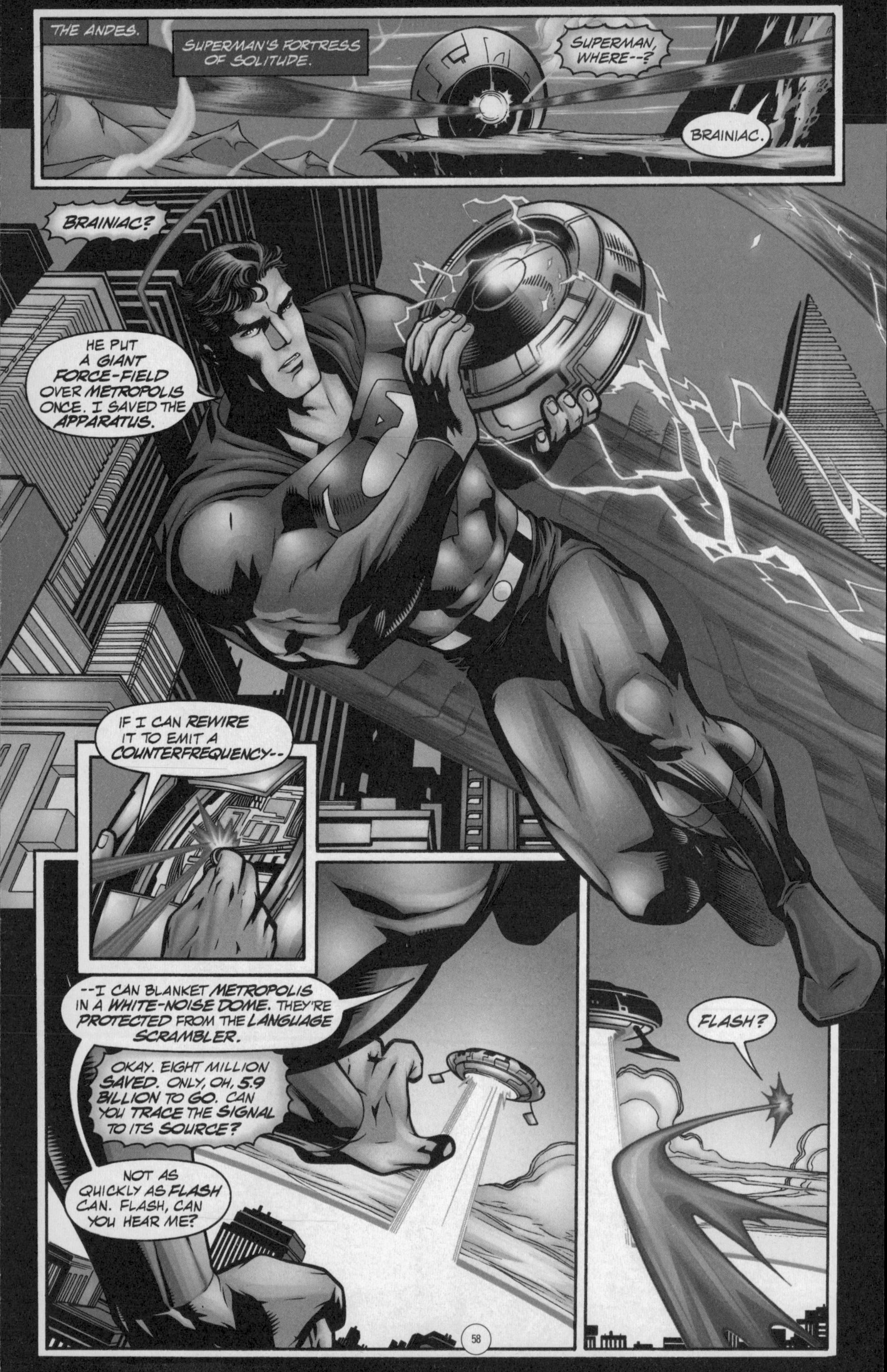
THE ANDES.
SUPERMAN'S FORTRESS OF SOLITUDE.
SUPERMAN, WHERE--?
BRAINIAC.
BRAINIAC?
HE PUT A GIANT FORCE-FIELD OVER METROPOLIS ONCE. I SAVED THE APPARATUS.
IF I CAN REWIRE IT TO EMIT A COUNTERFREQUENCY--
--I CAN BLANKET METROPOLIS IN A WHITE-NOISE DOME. THEY'RE PROTECTED FROM THE LANGUAGE SCRAMBLER.
OKAY. EIGHT MILLION SAVED. ONLY, OH, 5.9 BILLION TO GO. CAN YOU TRACE THE SIGNAL TO ITS SOURCE?
NOT AS QUICKLY AS FLASH CAN. FLASH, CAN YOU HEAR ME?
FLASH?

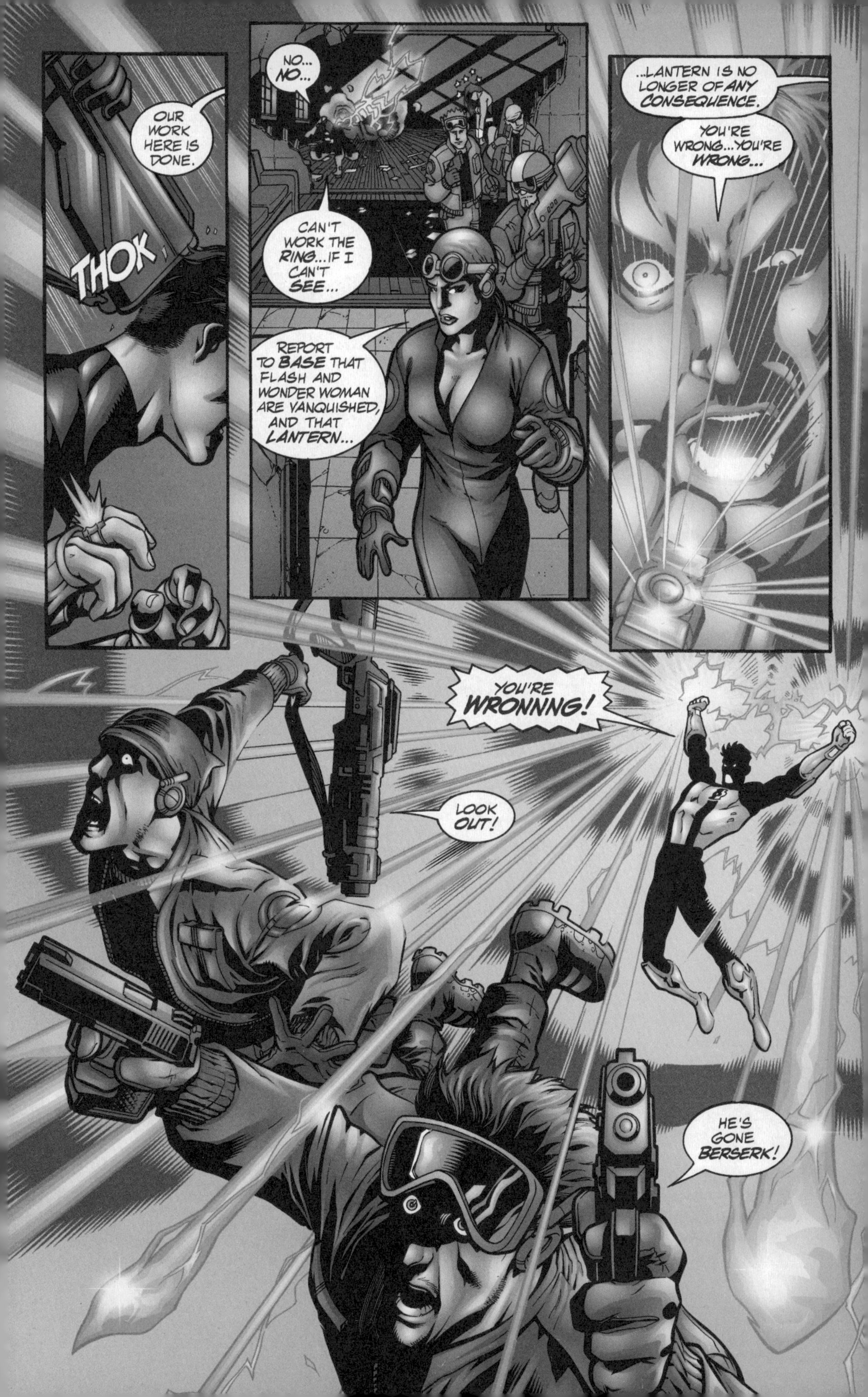
OUR WORK HERE IS DONE.
THOK
NO... NO...
CAN'T WORK THE RING... IF I CAN'T SEE...
REPORT TO BASE THAT FLASH AND WONDER WOMAN ARE VANQUISHED, AND THAT LANTERN...
...LANTERN IS NO LONGER OF ANY CONSEQUENCE.
YOU'RE WRONG...YOU'RE WRONG...
YOU'RE WRONNNG!
LOOK OUT!
HE'S GONE BERSERK!

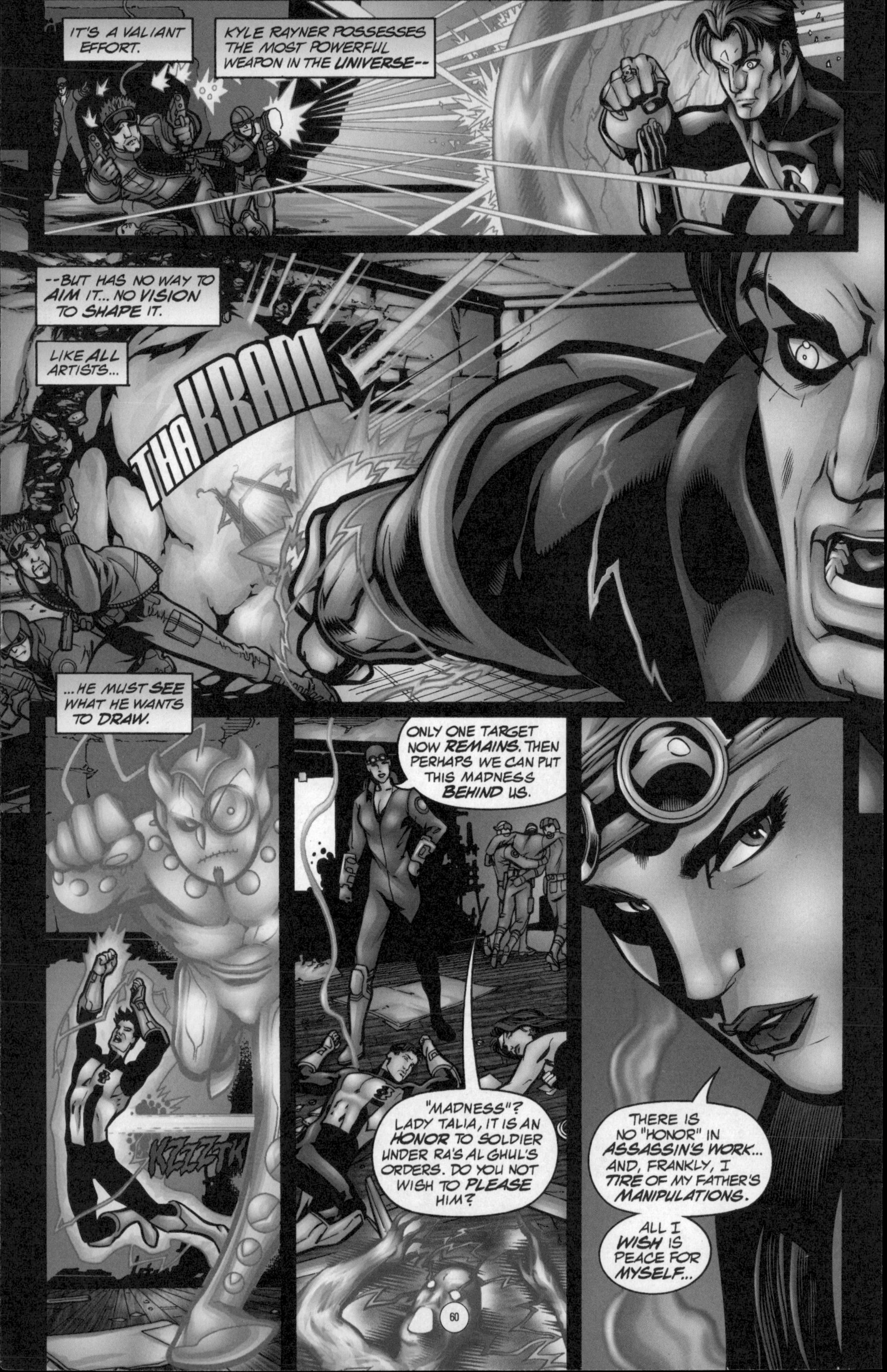
IT'S A VALIANT EFFORT.
KYLE RAYNER POSSESSES THE MOST POWERFUL WEAPON IN THE UNIVERSE--
--BUT HAS NO WAY TO AIM IT... NO VISION TO SHAPE IT.
LIKE ALL ARTISTS...
THAKRAM
...HE MUST SEE WHAT HE WANTS TO DRAW.
KZZZTK
ONLY ONE TARGET NOW REMAINS. THEN PERHAPS WE CAN PUT THIS MADNESS BEHIND US.
"MADNESS"? LADY TALIA, IT IS AN HONOR TO SOLDIER UNDER RA'S AL GHUL'S ORDERS. DO YOU NOT WISH TO PLEASE HIM?
THERE IS NO "HONOR" IN ASSASSIN'S WORK... AND, FRANKLY, I TIRE OF MY FATHER'S MANIPULATIONS.
ALL I WISH IS PEACE FOR MYSELF...

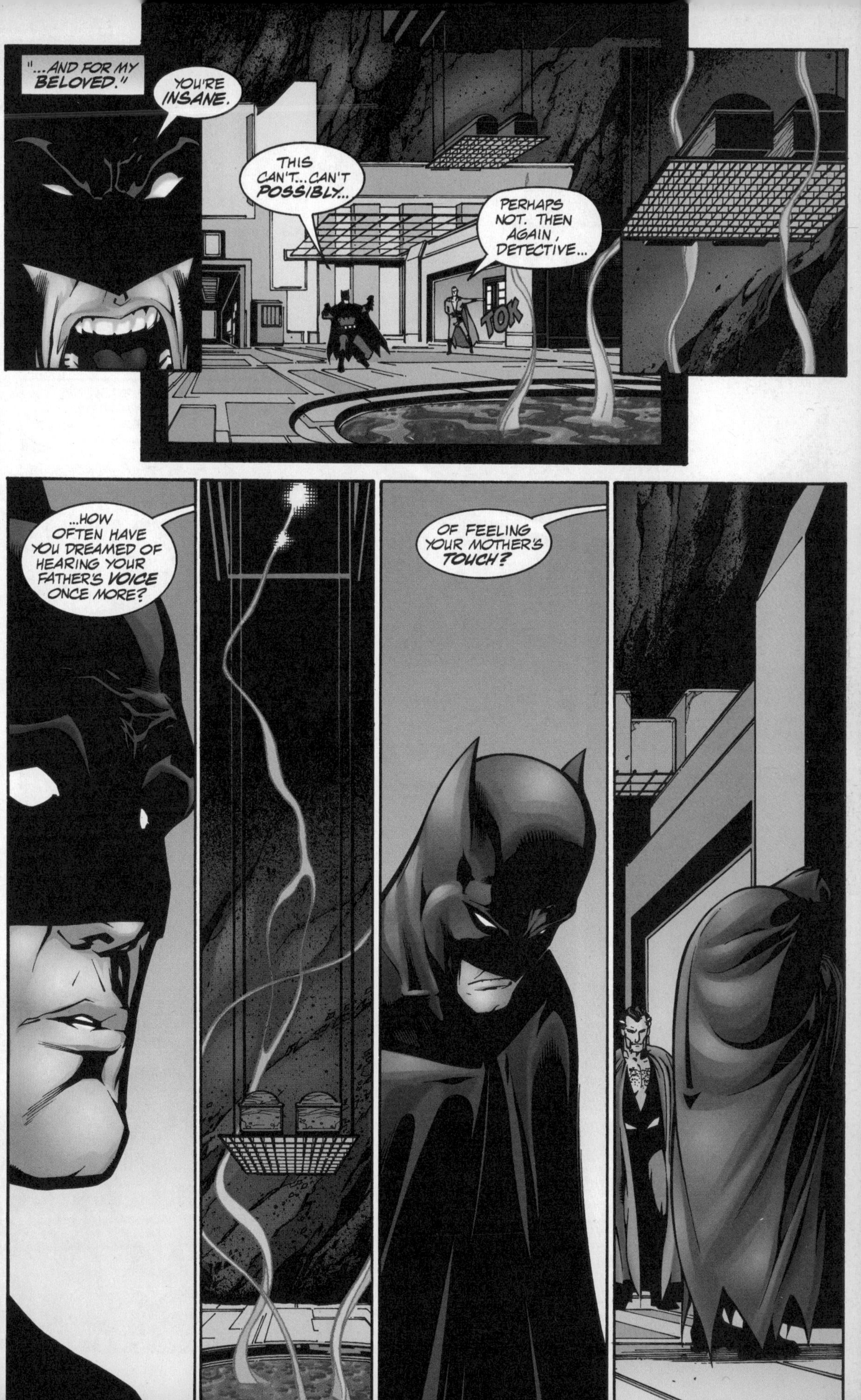
"...AND FOR MY BELOVED."
YOU'RE INSANE.
THIS CAN'T...CAN'T POSSIBLY...
PERHAPS NOT. THEN AGAIN, DETECTIVE...
TOK
...HOW OFTEN HAVE YOU DREAMED OF HEARING YOUR FATHER'S VOICE ONCE MORE?
OF FEELING YOUR MOTHER'S TOUCH?

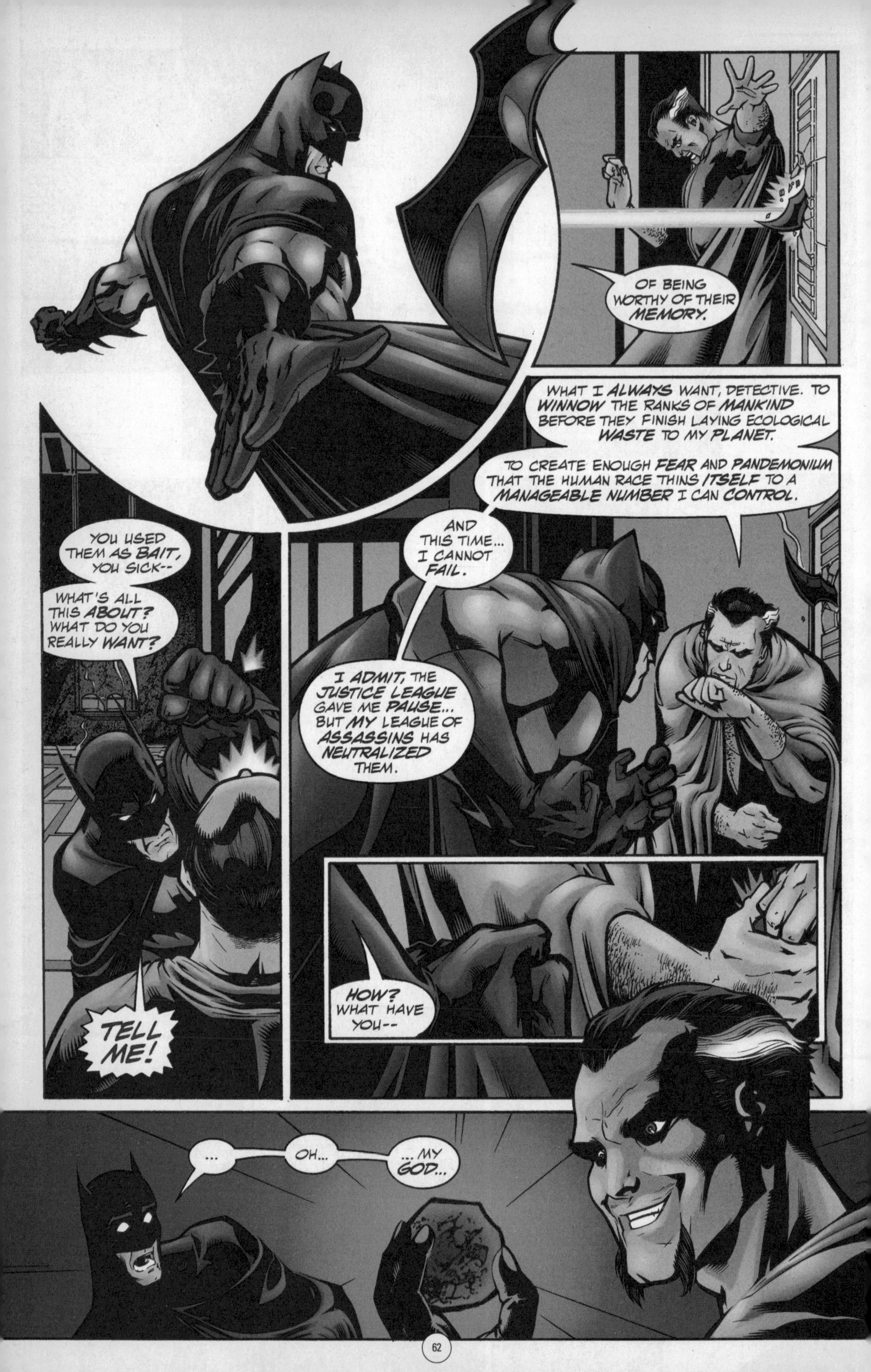

OF BEING WORTHY OF THEIR MEMORY.
YOU USED THEM AS BAIT, YOU SICK--
WHAT'S ALL THIS ABOUT? WHAT DO YOU REALLY WANT?
TELL ME!
WHAT I ALWAYS WANT, DETECTIVE. TO WINNOW THE RANKS OF MANKIND BEFORE THEY FINISH LAYING ECOLOGICAL WASTE TO MY PLANET.
TO CREATE ENOUGH FEAR AND PANDEMONIUM THAT THE HUMAN RACE THINS ITSELF TO A MANAGEABLE NUMBER I CAN CONTROL.
AND THIS TIME... I CANNOT FAIL.
I ADMIT, THE JUSTICE LEAGUE GAVE ME PAUSE... BUT MY LEAGUE OF ASSASSINS HAS NEUTRALIZED THEM.
HOW? WHAT HAVE YOU--
...
OH...
...MY GOD...

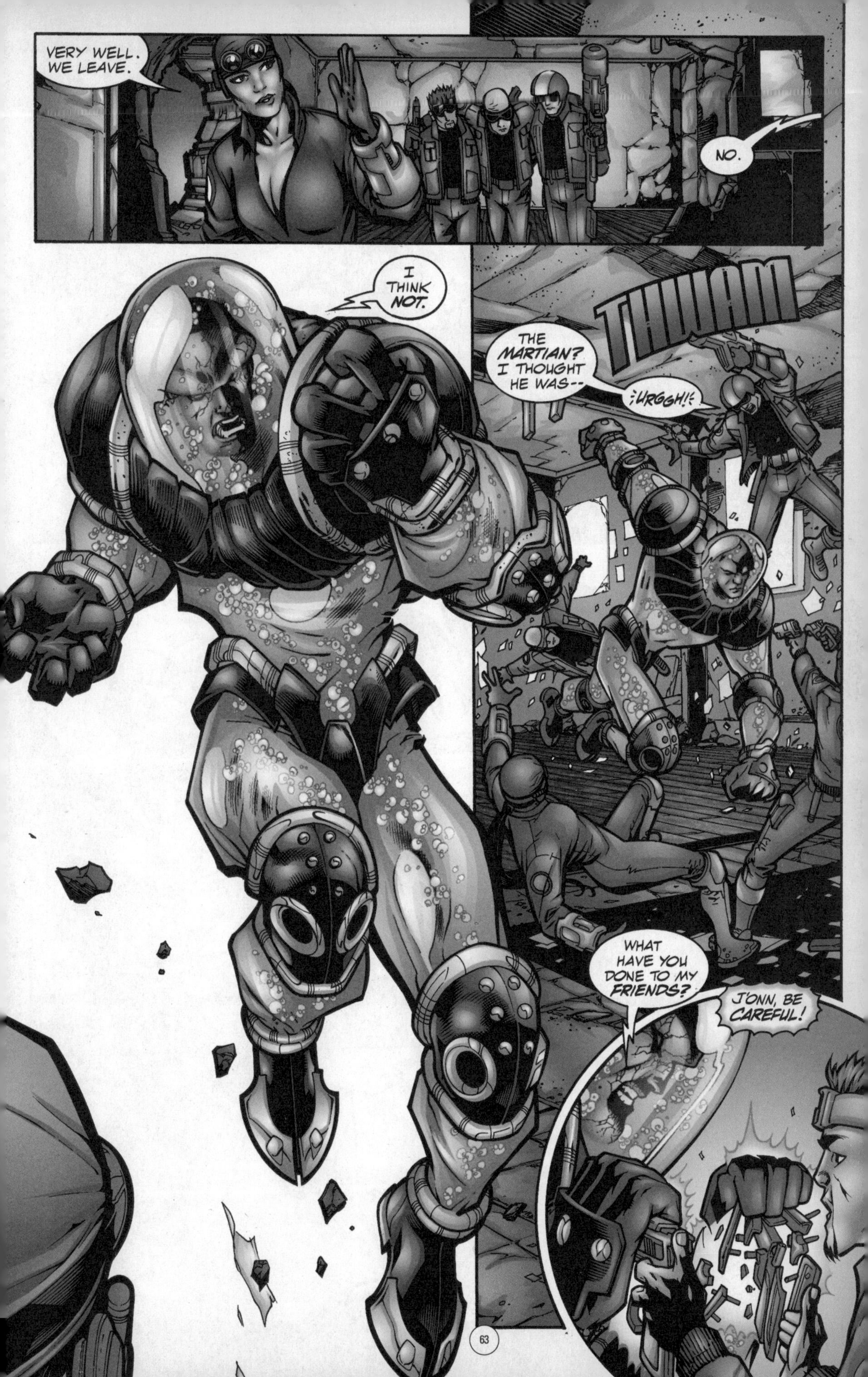
VERY WELL. WE LEAVE.
NO.
I THINK NOT.
THWAM
THE MARTIAN? I THOUGHT HE WAS--
URGGH!
WHAT HAVE YOU DONE TO MY FRIENDS?
J'ONN, BE CAREFUL!

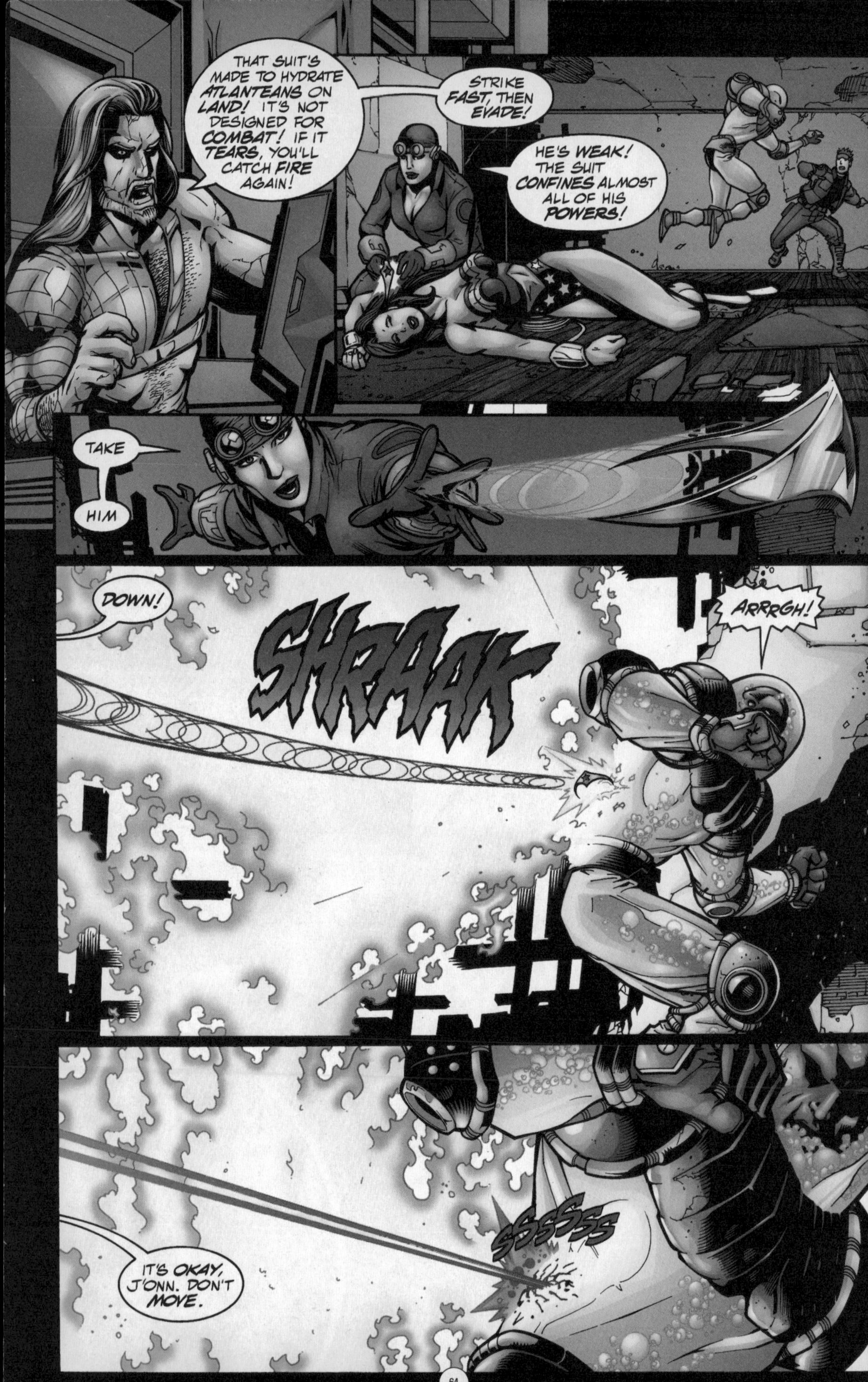
THAT SUIT'S MADE TO HYDRATE ATLANTEANS ON LAND! IT'S NOT DESIGNED FOR COMBAT! IF IT TEARS, YOU'LL CATCH FIRE AGAIN!
STRIKE FAST, THEN EVADE!
HE'S WEAK! THE SUIT CONFINES ALMOST ALL OF HIS POWERS!
TAKE HIM
DOWN!
SHRAAK
ARRRGH!
SSSSSS
IT'S OKAY, J'ONN. DON'T MOVE.

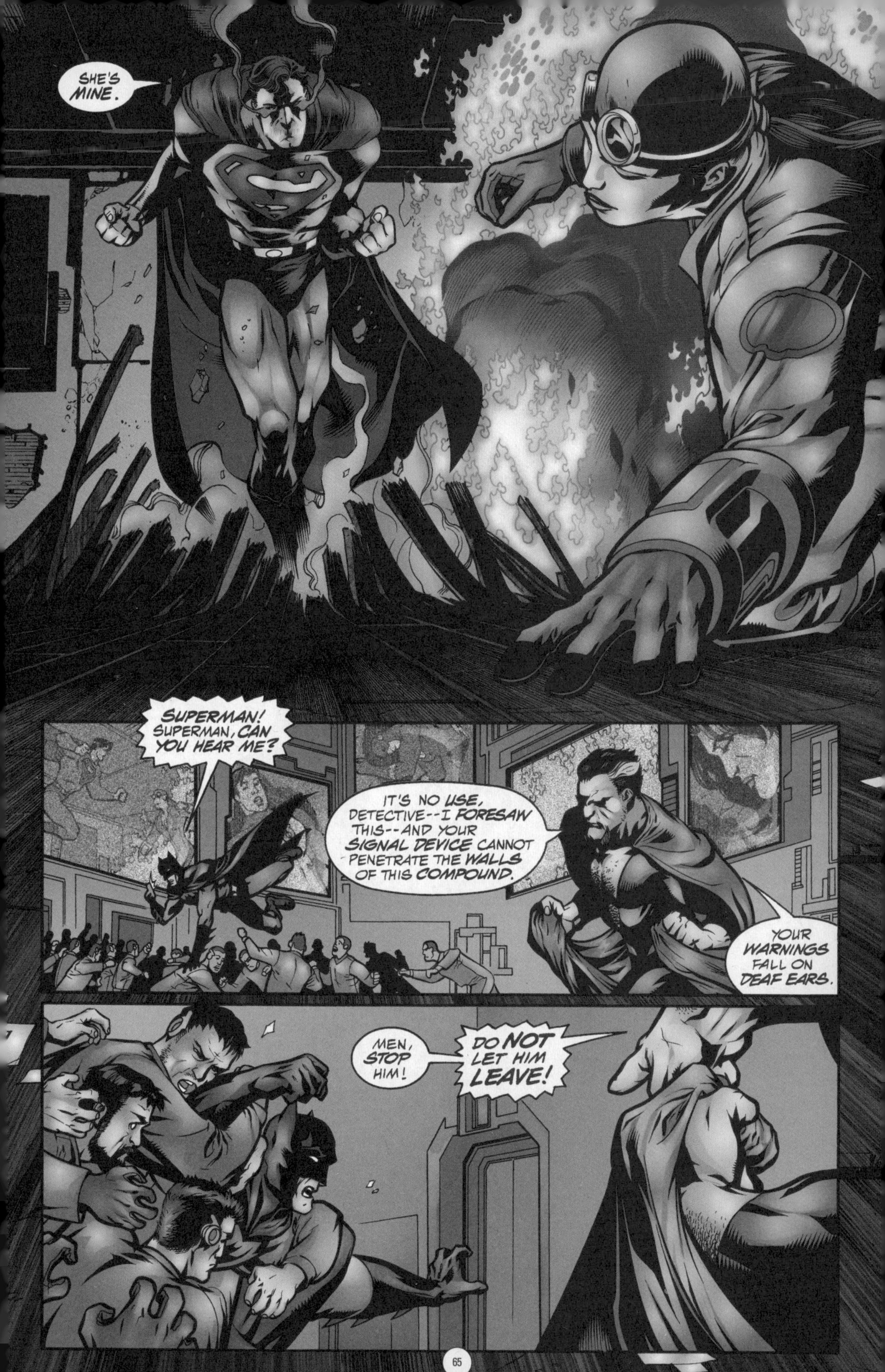
SHE'S MINE.
SUPERMAN! SUPERMAN, CAN YOU HEAR ME?
IT'S NO USE, DETECTIVE--I FORESAW THIS--AND YOUR SIGNAL DEVICE CANNOT PENETRATE THE WALLS OF THIS COMPOUND.
YOUR WARNINGS FALL ON DEAF EARS.
MEN, STOP HIM!
DO NOT LET HIM LEAVE!

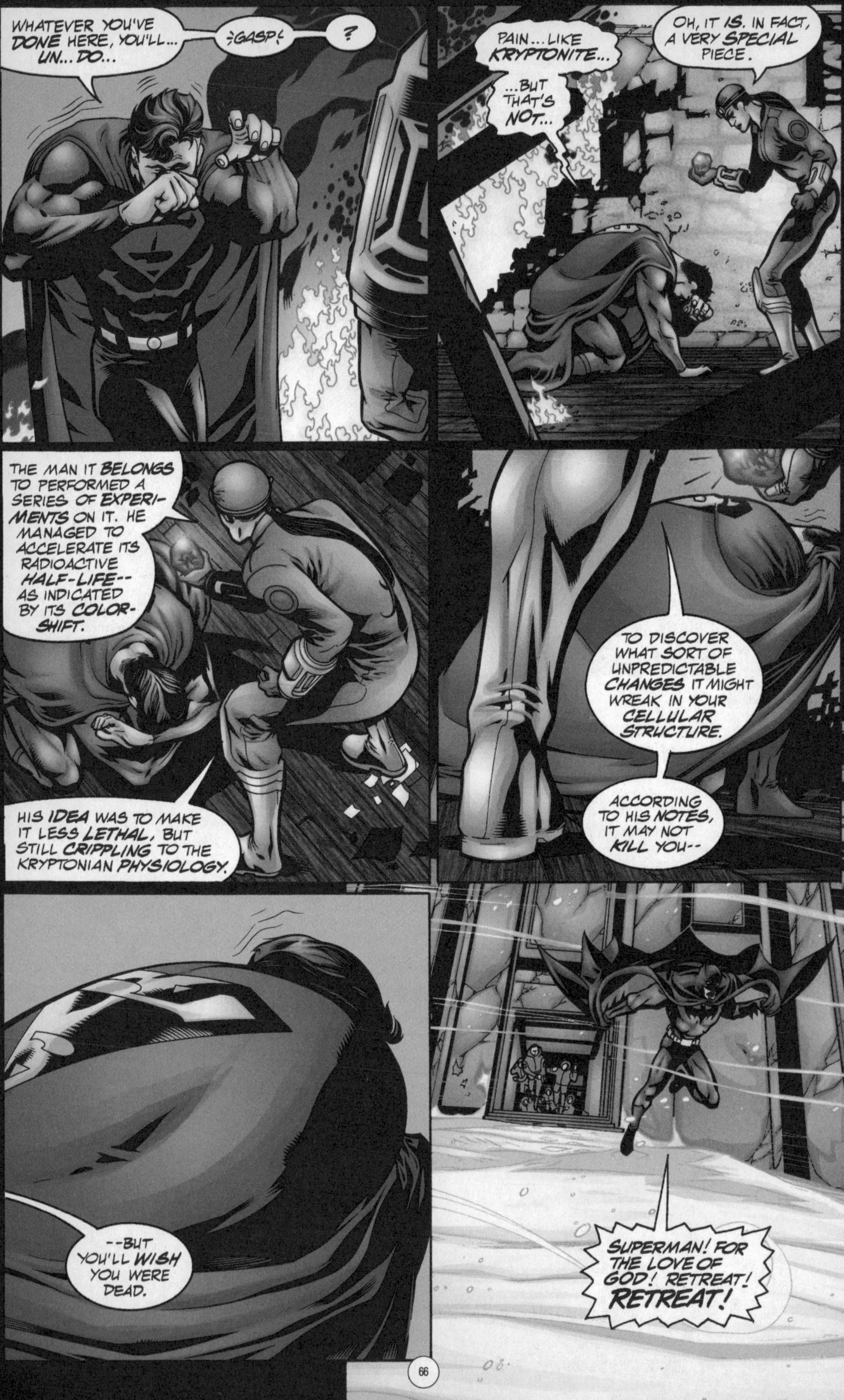
WHATEVER YOU'VE DONE HERE, YOU'LL... UN... DO...
¿GASP¿
?
PAIN... LIKE KRYPTONITE...
...BUT THAT'S NOT...
OH, IT IS. IN FACT, A VERY SPECIAL PIECE.
THE MAN IT BELONGS TO PERFORMED A SERIES OF EXPERIMENTS ON IT. HE MANAGED TO ACCELERATE ITS RADIOACTIVE HALF-LIFE-- AS INDICATED BY ITS COLOR-SHIFT.
HIS IDEA WAS TO MAKE IT LESS LETHAL, BUT STILL CRIPPLING TO THE KRYPTONIAN PHYSIOLOGY.
TO DISCOVER WHAT SORT OF UNPREDICTABLE CHANGES IT MIGHT WREAK IN YOUR CELLULAR STRUCTURE.
ACCORDING TO HIS NOTES, IT MAY NOT KILL YOU--
--BUT YOU'LL WISH YOU WERE DEAD.
SUPERMAN! FOR THE LOVE OF GOD! RETREAT! RETREAT!

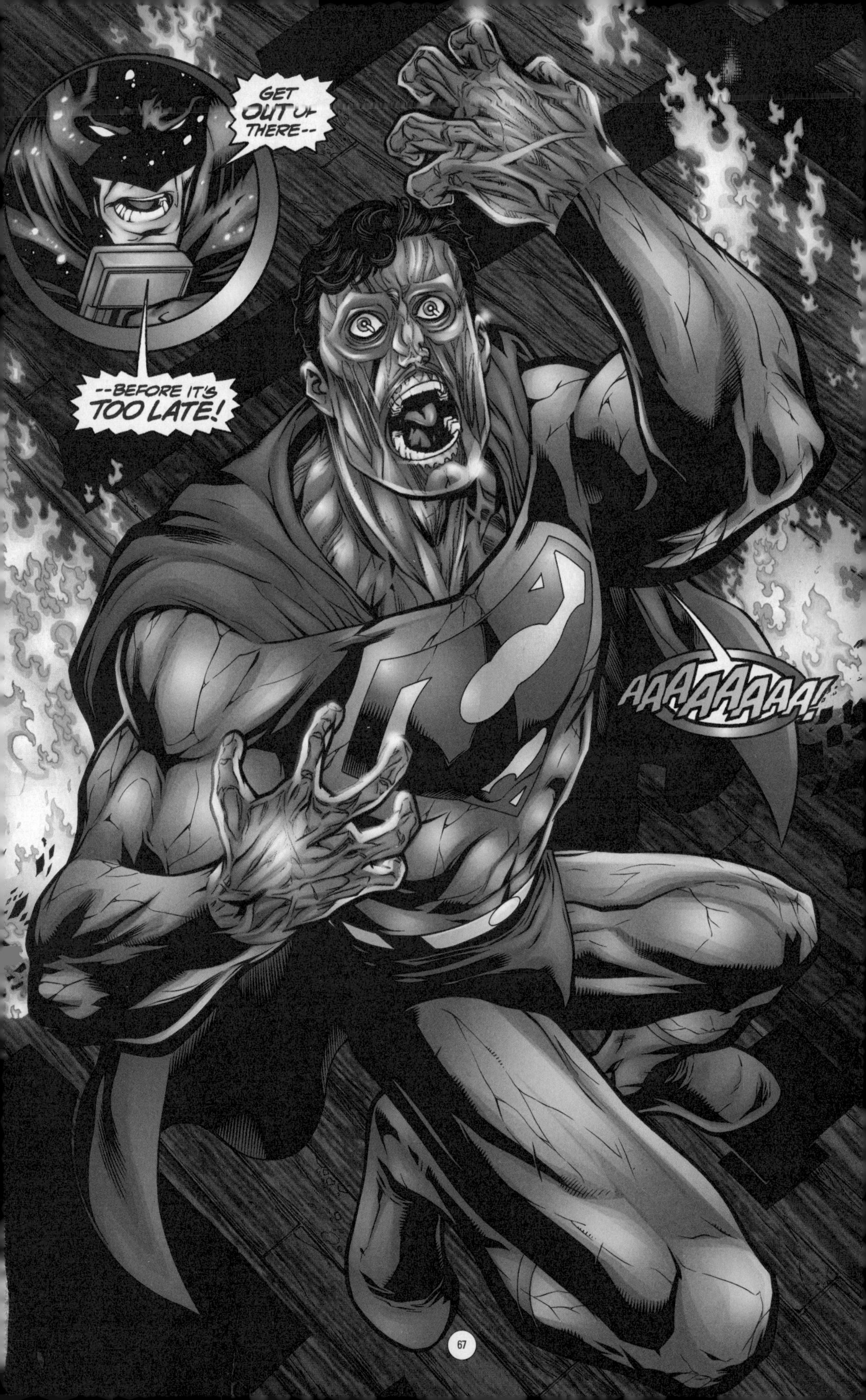
GET OUT OF THERE--
--BEFORE IT'S TOO LATE!
AAAAAAAA!

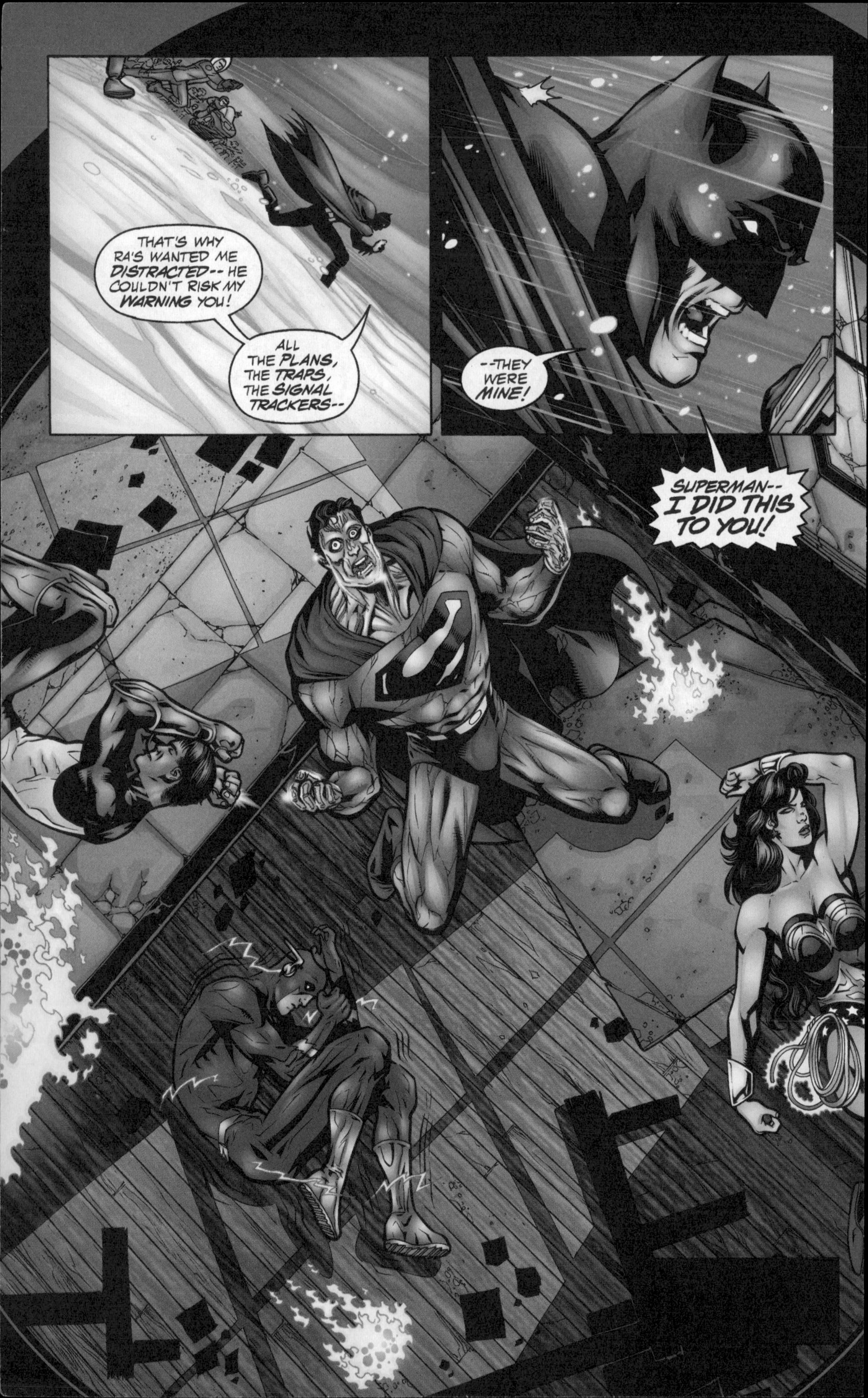
THAT'S WHY RA'S WANTED ME DISTRACTED-- HE COULDN'T RISK MY WARNING YOU!
ALL THE PLANS, THE TRAPS, THE SIGNAL TRACKERS--
--THEY WERE MINE!
SUPERMAN-- I DID THIS TO YOU!

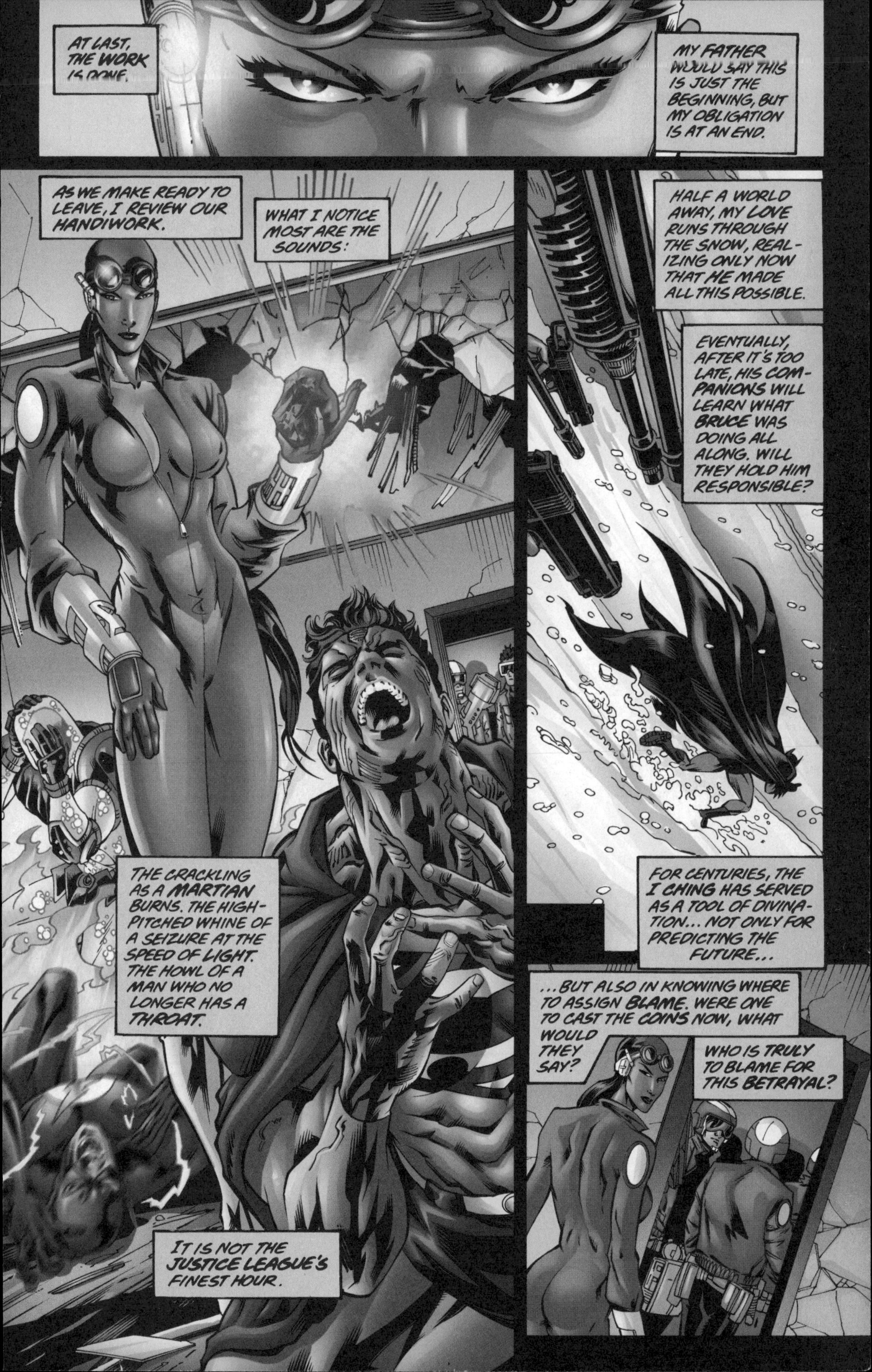

AT LAST, THE WORK IS DONE.
MY FATHER WOULD SAY THIS IS JUST THE BEGINNING, BUT MY OBLIGATION IS AT AN END.
AS WE MAKE READY TO LEAVE, I REVIEW OUR HANDIWORK.
WHAT I NOTICE MOST ARE THE SOUNDS:
THE CRACKLING AS A MARTIAN BURNS. THE HIGH-PITCHED WHINE OF A SEIZURE AT THE SPEED OF LIGHT. THE HOWL OF A MAN WHO NO LONGER HAS A THROAT.
IT IS NOT THE JUSTICE LEAGUE'S FINEST HOUR.
HALF A WORLD AWAY, MY LOVE RUNS THROUGH THE SNOW, REALIZING ONLY NOW THAT HE MADE ALL THIS POSSIBLE.
EVENTUALLY, AFTER IT'S TOO LATE, HIS COMPANIONS WILL LEARN WHAT BRUCE WAS DOING ALL ALONG. WILL THEY HOLD HIM RESPONSIBLE?
FOR CENTURIES, THE I CHING HAS SERVED AS A TOOL OF DIVINATION... NOT ONLY FOR PREDICTING THE FUTURE...
...BUT ALSO IN KNOWING WHERE TO ASSIGN BLAME. WERE ONE TO CAST THE COINS NOW, WHAT WOULD THEY SAY?
WHO IS TRULY TO BLAME FOR THIS BETRAYAL?

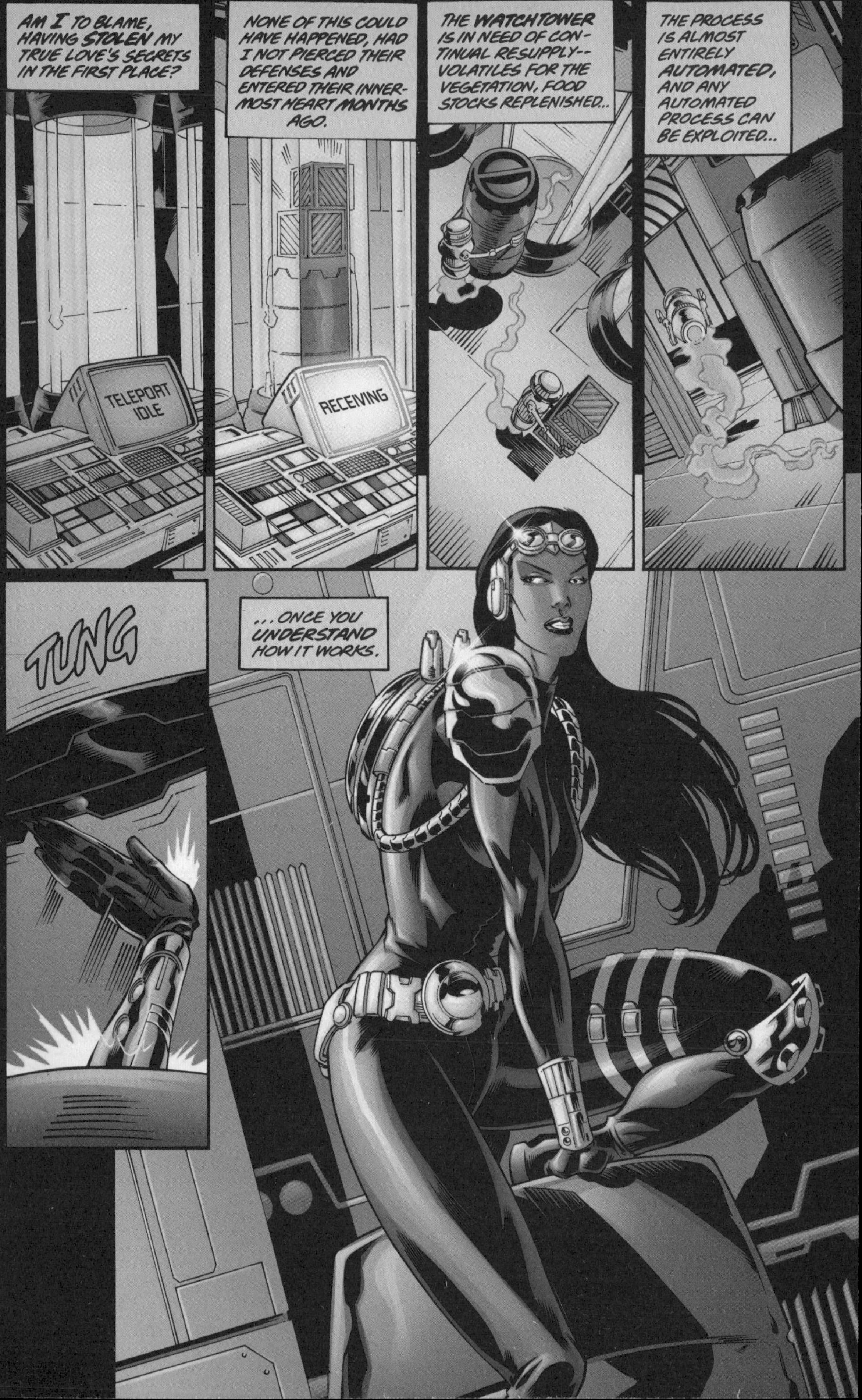
AM I TO BLAME, HAVING STOLEN MY TRUE LOVE'S SECRETS IN THE FIRST PLACE?
TELEPORT IDLE
NONE OF THIS COULD HAVE HAPPENED, HAD I NOT PIERCED THEIR DEFENSES AND ENTERED THEIR INNER-MOST HEART MONTHS AGO.
RECEIVING
THE WATCHTOWER IS IN NEED OF CON-TINUAL RESUPPLY-- VOLATILES FOR THE VEGETATION, FOOD STOCKS REPLENISHED...
THE PROCESS IS ALMOST ENTIRELY AUTOMATED, AND ANY AUTOMATED PROCESS CAN BE EXPLOITED...
TUNG
...ONCE YOU UNDERSTAND HOW IT WORKS.

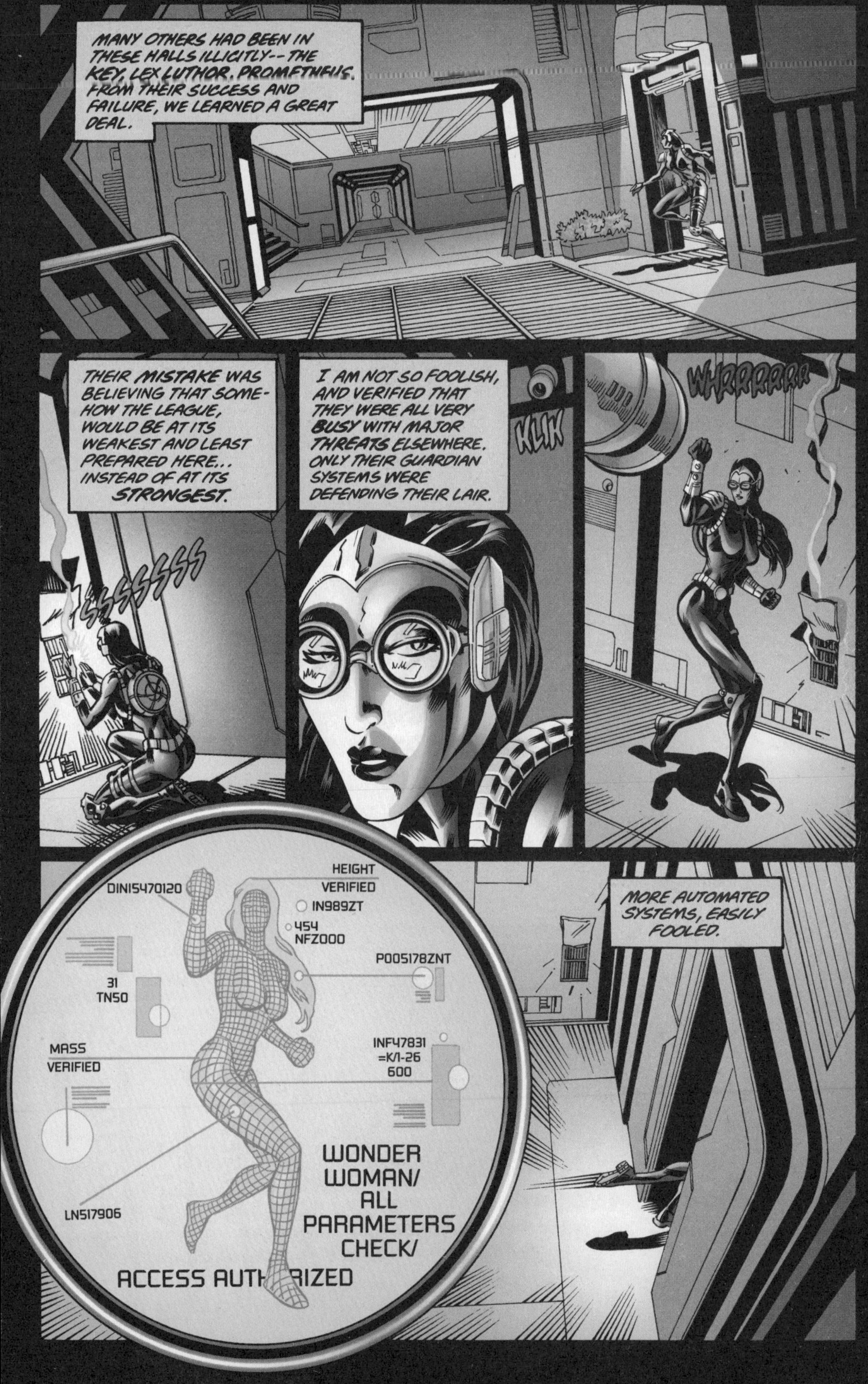

MANY OTHERS HAD BEEN IN THESE HALLS ILLICITLY-- THE KEY, LEX LUTHOR, PROMETHEUS. FROM THEIR SUCCESS AND FAILURE, WE LEARNED A GREAT DEAL.
THEIR MISTAKE WAS BELIEVING THAT SOMEHOW THE LEAGUE WOULD BE AT ITS WEAKEST AND LEAST PREPARED HERE... INSTEAD OF AT ITS STRONGEST.
SSSSSSS
I AM NOT SO FOOLISH, AND VERIFIED THAT THEY WERE ALL VERY BUSY WITH MAJOR THREATS ELSEWHERE. ONLY THEIR GUARDIAN SYSTEMS WERE DEFENDING THEIR LAIR.
KLIK
WHRRRRRR
HEIGHT VERIFIED
DINI5470120
IN989ZT
454 NFZ000
P005178ZNT
31 TN50
MASS VERIFIED
INF47831 =K/1-26 600
LN517906
WONDER WOMAN/ ALL PARAMETERS CHECK/
ACCESS AUTHORIZED
MORE AUTOMATED SYSTEMS, EASILY FOOLED.

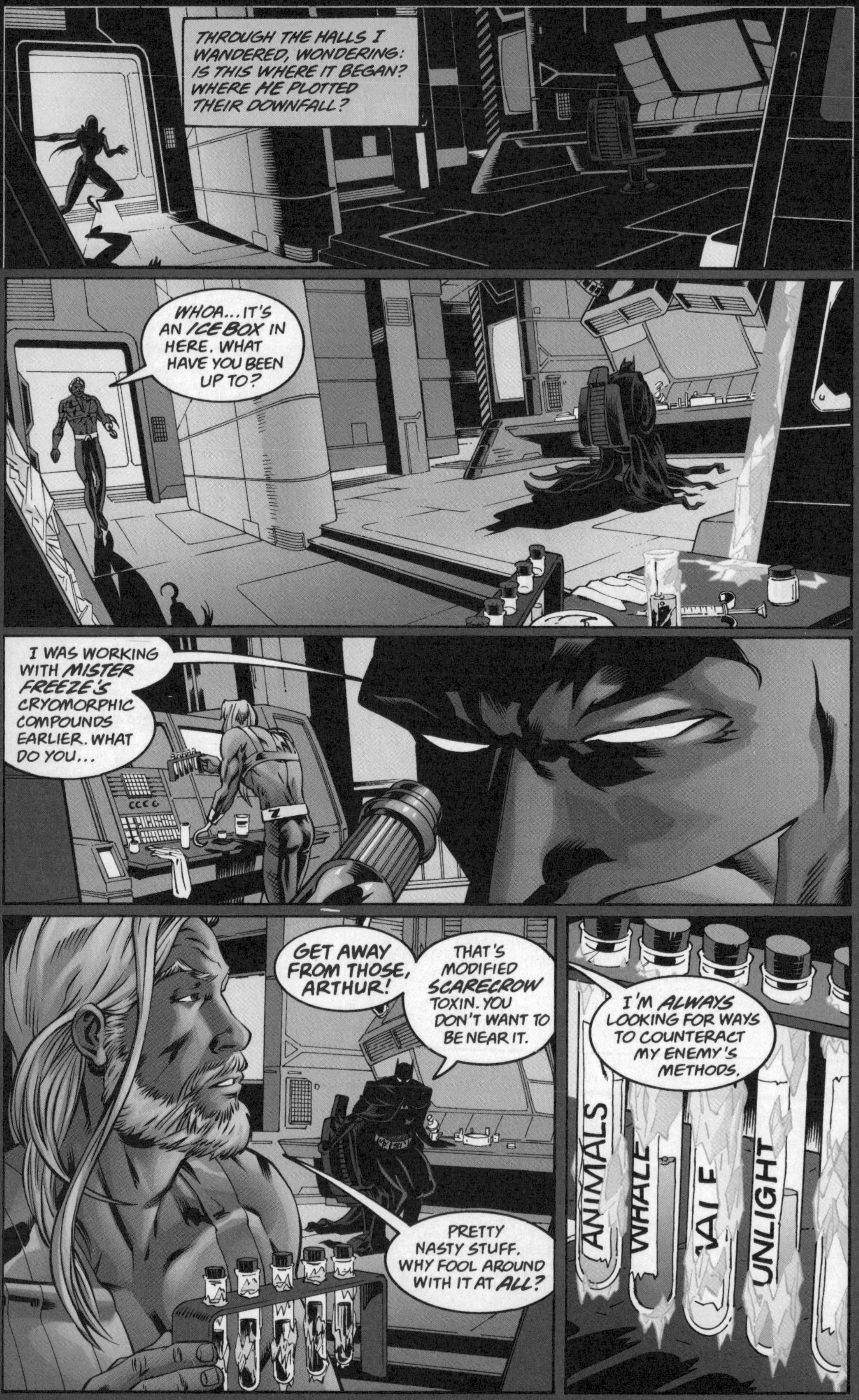
THROUGH THE HALLS I WANDERED, WONDERING: IS THIS WHERE IT BEGAN? WHERE HE PLOTTED THEIR DOWNFALL?
WHOA... IT'S AN ICE BOX IN HERE. WHAT HAVE YOU BEEN UP TO?
I WAS WORKING WITH MISTER FREEZE'S CRYOMORPHIC COMPOUNDS EARLIER. WHAT DO YOU...
GET AWAY FROM THOSE, ARTHUR!
THAT'S MODIFIED SCARECROW TOXIN. YOU DON'T WANT TO BE NEAR IT.
PRETTY NASTY STUFF. WHY FOOL AROUND WITH IT AT ALL?
I'M ALWAYS LOOKING FOR WAYS TO COUNTERACT MY ENEMY'S METHODS.
ANIMALS
WHALE
UNLIGHT

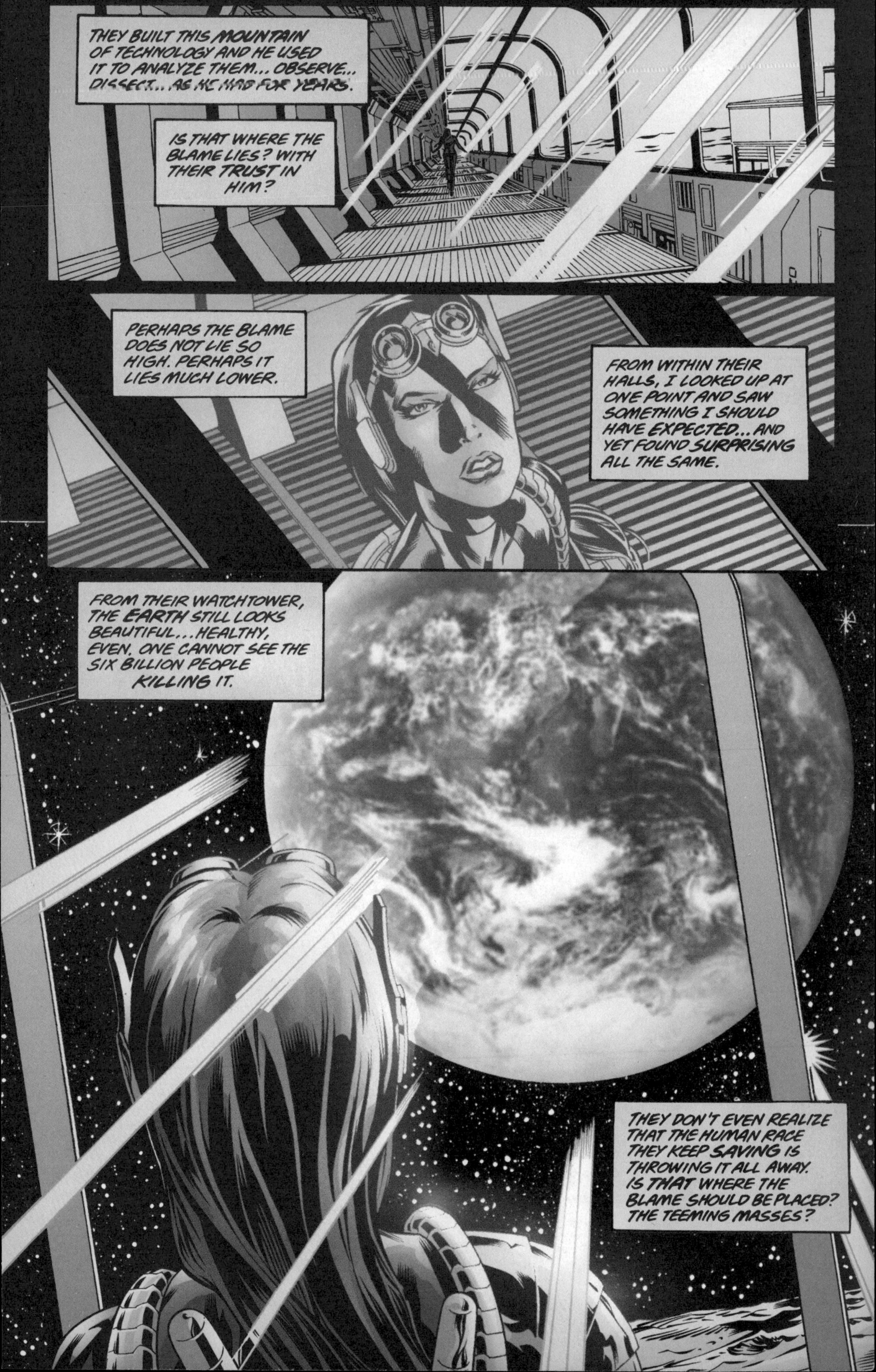
THEY BUILT THIS MOUNTAIN OF TECHNOLOGY AND HE USED IT TO ANALYZE THEM... OBSERVE... DISSECT... AS HE HAD FOR YEARS.
IS THAT WHERE THE BLAME LIES? WITH THEIR TRUST IN HIM?
PERHAPS THE BLAME DOES NOT LIE SO HIGH. PERHAPS IT LIES MUCH LOWER.
FROM WITHIN THEIR HALLS, I LOOKED UP AT ONE POINT AND SAW SOMETHING I SHOULD HAVE EXPECTED... AND YET FOUND SURPRISING ALL THE SAME.
FROM THEIR WATCHTOWER, THE EARTH STILL LOOKS BEAUTIFUL... HEALTHY, EVEN. ONE CANNOT SEE THE SIX BILLION PEOPLE KILLING IT.
THEY DON'T EVEN REALIZE THAT THE HUMAN RACE THEY KEEP SAVING IS THROWING IT ALL AWAY. IS THAT WHERE THE BLAME SHOULD BE PLACED? THE TEEMING MASSES?

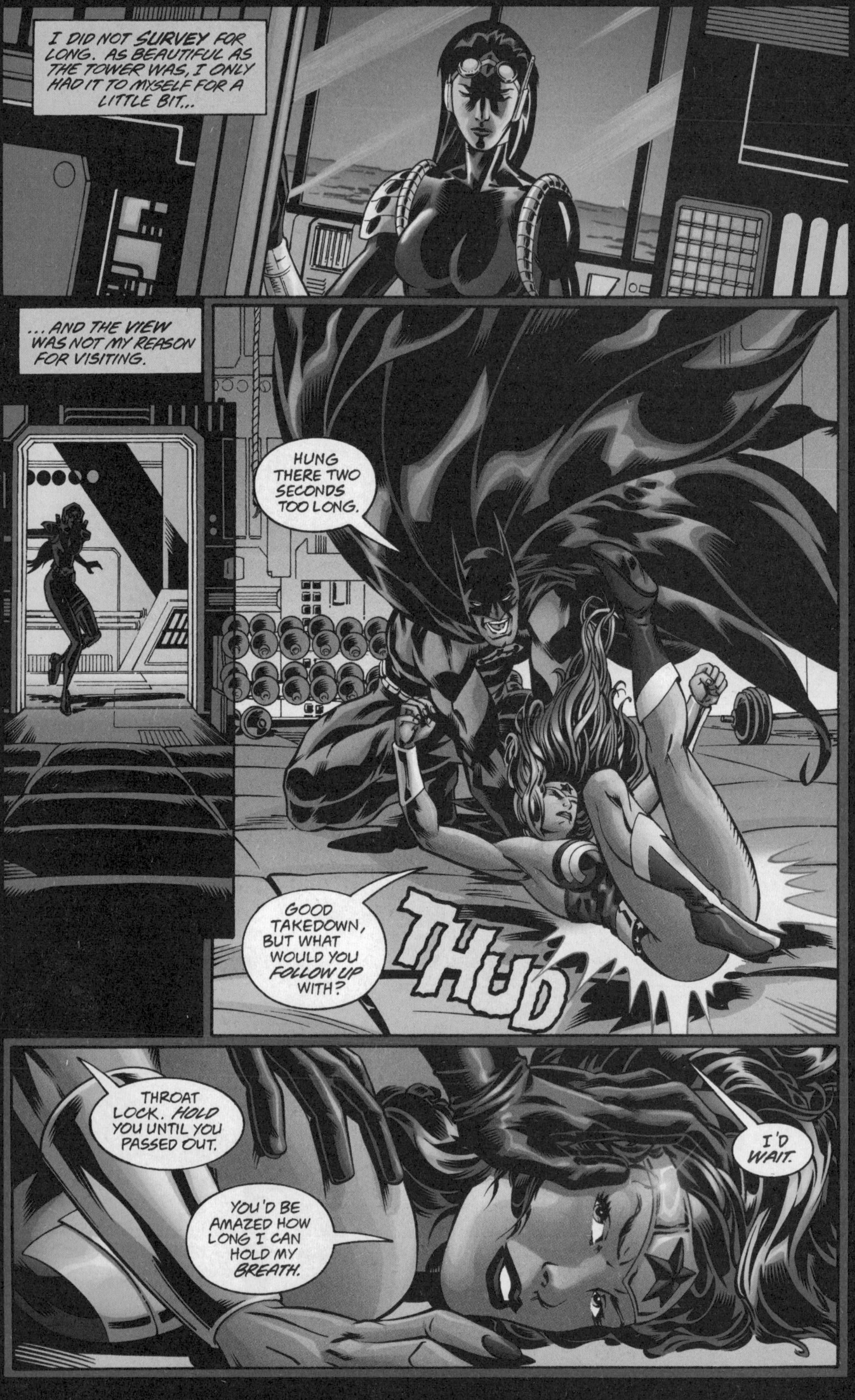
I DID NOT SURVEY FOR LONG. AS BEAUTIFUL AS THE TOWER WAS, I ONLY HAD IT TO MYSELF FOR A LITTLE BIT...
...AND THE VIEW WAS NOT MY REASON FOR VISITING.
HUNG THERE TWO SECONDS TOO LONG.
GOOD TAKEDOWN, BUT WHAT WOULD YOU FOLLOW UP WITH?
THUD
THROAT LOCK. HOLD YOU UNTIL YOU PASSED OUT.
YOU'D BE AMAZED HOW LONG I CAN HOLD MY BREATH.
I'D WAIT.

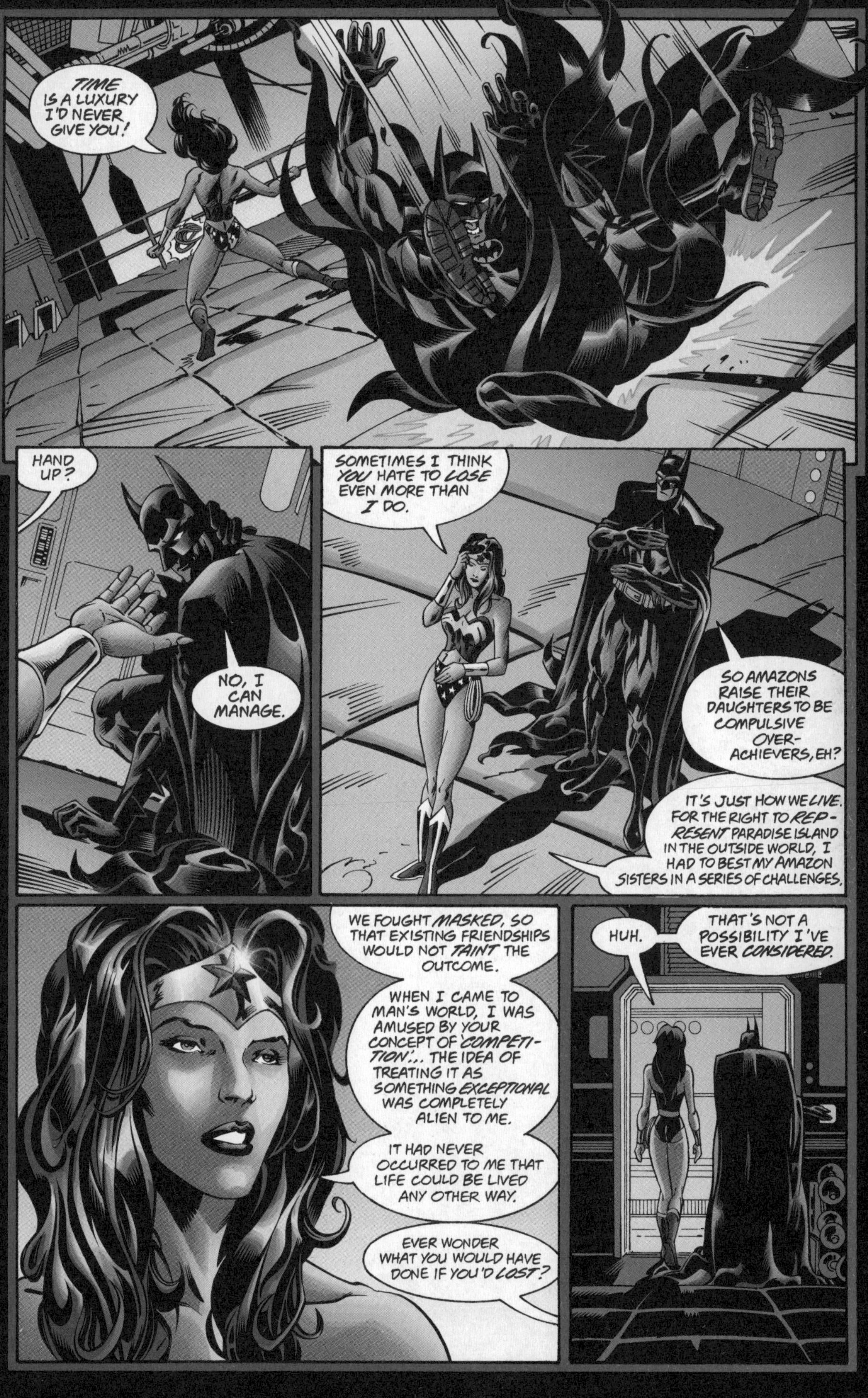

TIME IS A LUXURY I'D NEVER GIVE YOU!
HAND UP?
NO, I CAN MANAGE.
SOMETIMES I THINK YOU HATE TO LOSE EVEN MORE THAN I DO.
SO AMAZONS RAISE THEIR DAUGHTERS TO BE COMPULSIVE OVER-ACHIEVERS, EH?
IT'S JUST HOW WE LIVE. FOR THE RIGHT TO REP-RESENT PARADISE ISLAND IN THE OUTSIDE WORLD, I HAD TO BEST MY AMAZON SISTERS IN A SERIES OF CHALLENGES.
WE FOUGHT MASKED, SO THAT EXISTING FRIENDSHIPS WOULD NOT TAINT THE OUTCOME.
WHEN I CAME TO MAN'S WORLD, I WAS AMUSED BY YOUR CONCEPT OF 'COMPETITION'... THE IDEA OF TREATING IT AS SOMETHING EXCEPTIONAL WAS COMPLETELY ALIEN TO ME.
IT HAD NEVER OCCURRED TO ME THAT LIFE COULD BE LIVED ANY OTHER WAY.
EVER WONDER WHAT YOU WOULD HAVE DONE IF YOU'D LOST?
HUH.
THAT'S NOT A POSSIBILITY I'VE EVER CONSIDERED.

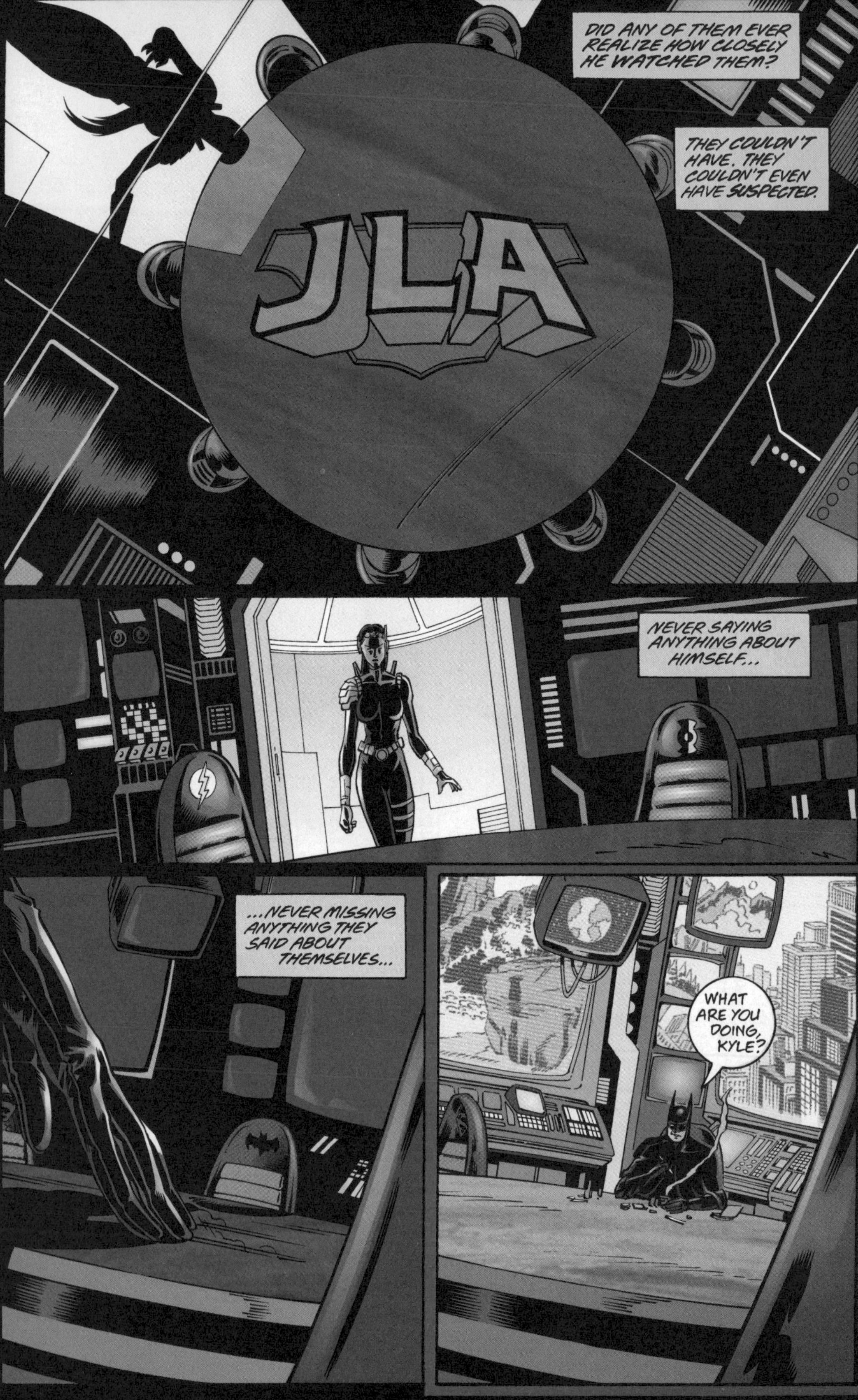
DID ANY OF THEM EVER REALIZE HOW CLOSELY HE WATCHED THEM?
THEY COULDN'T HAVE. THEY COULDN'T EVEN HAVE SUSPECTED.
JLA
NEVER SAYING ANYTHING ABOUT HIMSELF...
...NEVER MISSING ANYTHING THEY SAID ABOUT THEMSELVES...
WHAT ARE YOU DOING, KYLE?

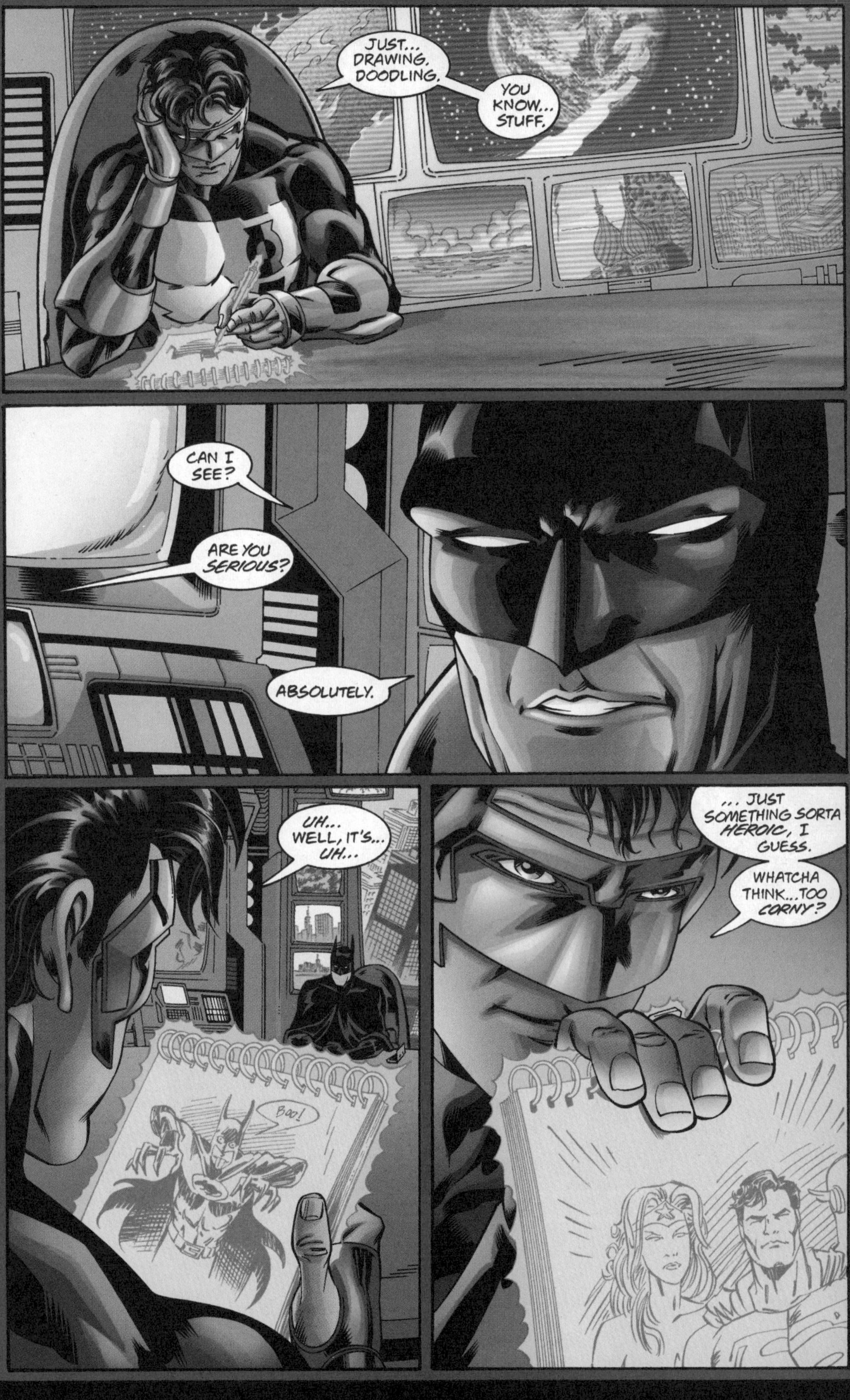
JUST... DRAWING. DOODLING.
YOU KNOW... STUFF.
CAN I SEE?
ARE YOU SERIOUS?
ABSOLUTELY.
UH... WELL, IT'S... UH...
BOO!
... JUST SOMETHING SORTA HEROIC, I GUESS.
WHATCHA THINK... TOO CORNY?

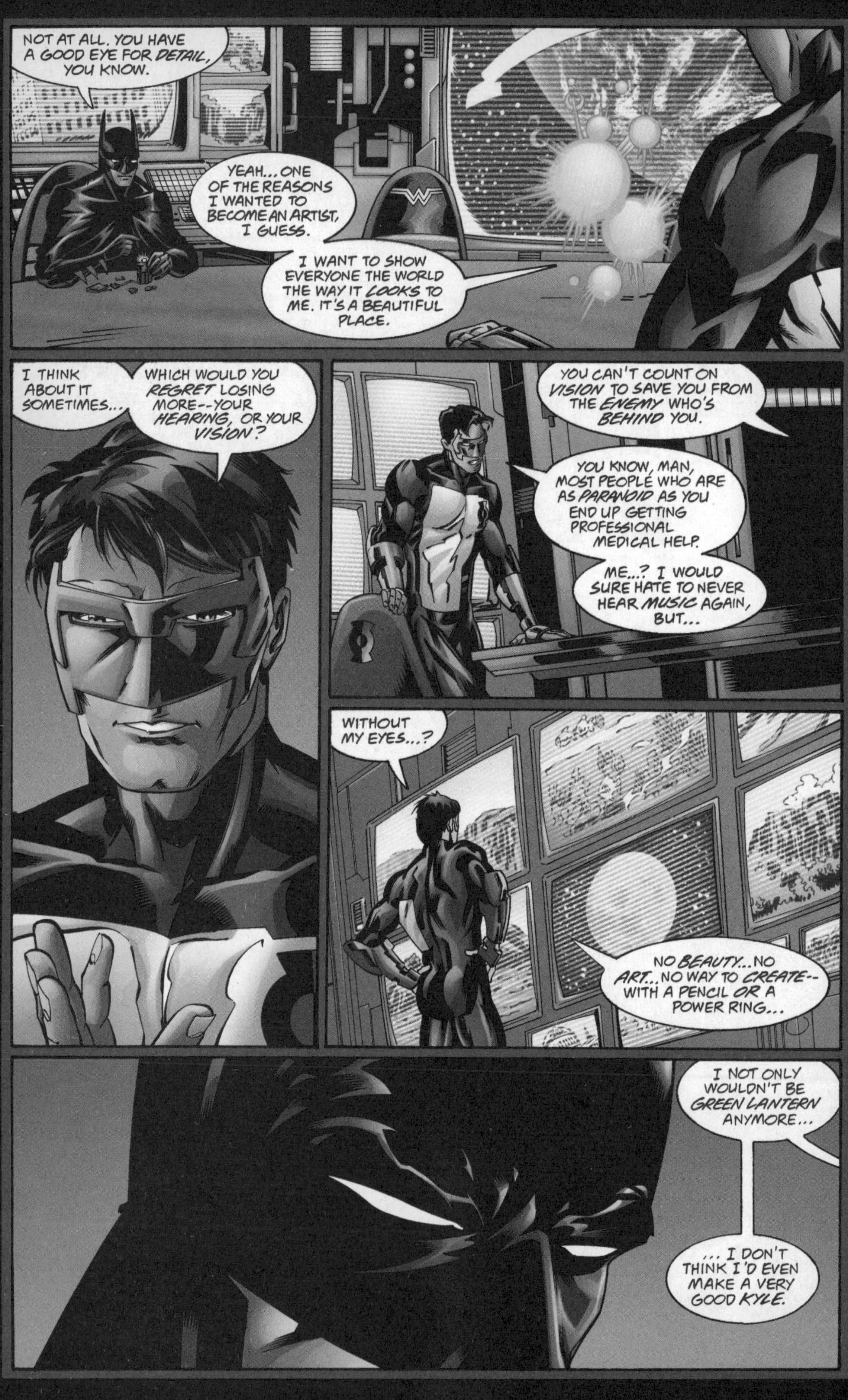
NOT AT ALL. YOU HAVE A GOOD EYE FOR DETAIL, YOU KNOW.
YEAH... ONE OF THE REASONS I WANTED TO BECOME AN ARTIST, I GUESS.
I WANT TO SHOW EVERYONE THE WORLD THE WAY IT LOOKS TO ME. IT'S A BEAUTIFUL PLACE.
I THINK ABOUT IT SOMETIMES...
WHICH WOULD YOU REGRET LOSING MORE--YOUR HEARING, OR YOUR VISION?
YOU CAN'T COUNT ON VISION TO SAVE YOU FROM THE ENEMY WHO'S BEHIND YOU.
YOU KNOW, MAN, MOST PEOPLE WHO ARE AS PARANOID AS YOU END UP GETTING PROFESSIONAL MEDICAL HELP.
ME...? I WOULD SURE HATE TO NEVER HEAR MUSIC AGAIN, BUT...
WITHOUT MY EYES...?
NO BEAUTY...NO ART...NO WAY TO CREATE-- WITH A PENCIL OR A POWER RING...
I NOT ONLY WOULDN'T BE GREEN LANTERN ANYMORE...
... I DON'T THINK I'D EVEN MAKE A VERY GOOD KYLE.

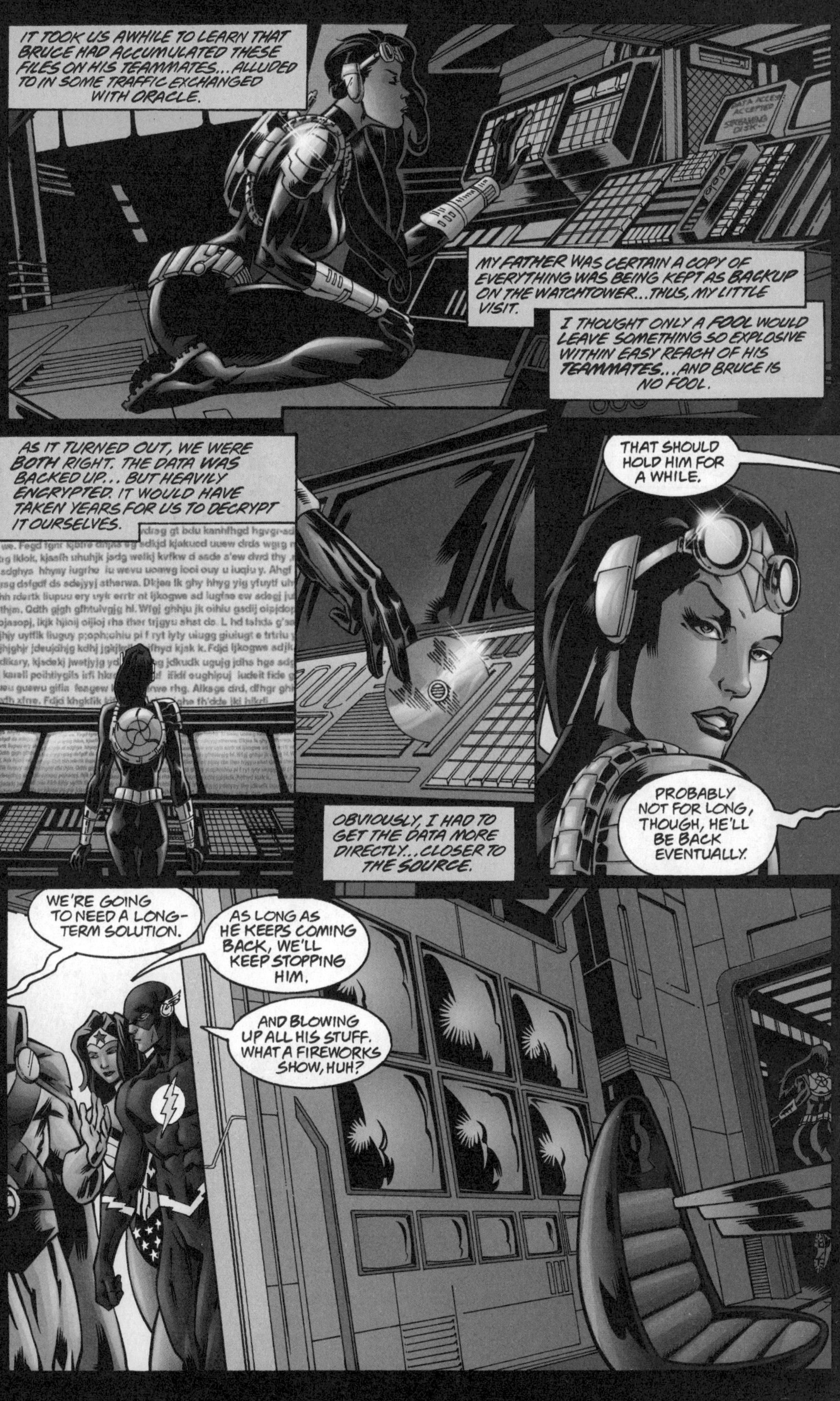
IT TOOK US AWHILE TO LEARN THAT BRUCE HAD ACCUMULATED THESE FILES ON HIS TEAMMATES... ALLUDED TO IN SOME TRAFFIC EXCHANGED WITH ORACLE.
MY FATHER WAS CERTAIN A COPY OF EVERYTHING WAS BEING KEPT AS BACKUP ON THE WATCHTOWER... THUS, MY LITTLE VISIT.
I THOUGHT ONLY A FOOL WOULD LEAVE SOMETHING SO EXPLOSIVE WITHIN EASY REACH OF HIS TEAMMATES... AND BRUCE IS NO FOOL.
AS IT TURNED OUT, WE WERE BOTH RIGHT. THE DATA WAS BACKED UP... BUT HEAVILY ENCRYPTED. IT WOULD HAVE TAKEN YEARS FOR US TO DECRYPT IT OURSELVES.
OBVIOUSLY, I HAD TO GET THE DATA MORE DIRECTLY... CLOSER TO THE SOURCE.
THAT SHOULD HOLD HIM FOR A WHILE.
PROBABLY NOT FOR LONG, THOUGH. HE'LL BE BACK EVENTUALLY.
WE'RE GOING TO NEED A LONG-TERM SOLUTION.
AS LONG AS HE KEEPS COMING BACK, WE'LL KEEP STOPPING HIM.
AND BLOWING UP ALL HIS STUFF. WHAT A FIREWORKS SHOW, HUH?

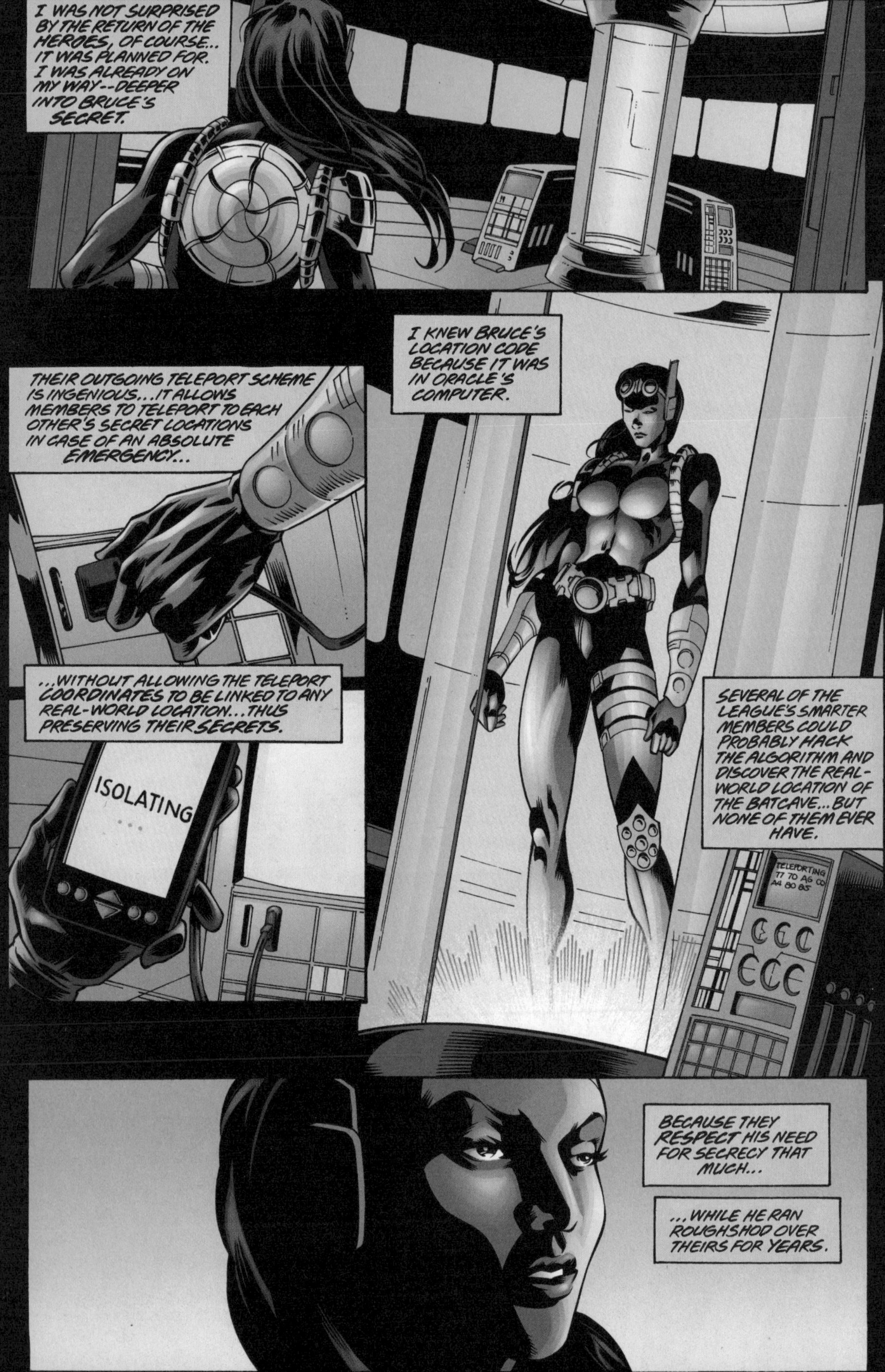
I WAS NOT SURPRISED BY THE RETURN OF THE HEROES, OF COURSE... IT WAS PLANNED FOR. I WAS ALREADY ON MY WAY--DEEPER INTO BRUCE'S SECRET.
THEIR OUTGOING TELEPORT SCHEME IS INGENIOUS...IT ALLOWS MEMBERS TO TELEPORT TO EACH OTHER'S SECRET LOCATIONS IN CASE OF AN ABSOLUTE EMERGENCY...
...WITHOUT ALLOWING THE TELEPORT COORDINATES TO BE LINKED TO ANY REAL-WORLD LOCATION...THUS PRESERVING THEIR SECRETS.
ISOLATING
I KNEW BRUCE'S LOCATION CODE BECAUSE IT WAS IN ORACLE'S COMPUTER.
SEVERAL OF THE LEAGUE'S SMARTER MEMBERS COULD PROBABLY HACK THE ALGORITHM AND DISCOVER THE REAL-WORLD LOCATION OF THE BATCAVE...BUT NONE OF THEM EVER HAVE.
TELEPORTING
77 70 A6 C0
A4 80 85
BECAUSE THEY RESPECT HIS NEED FOR SECRECY THAT MUCH...
...WHILE HE RAN ROUGHSHOD OVER THEIRS FOR YEARS.

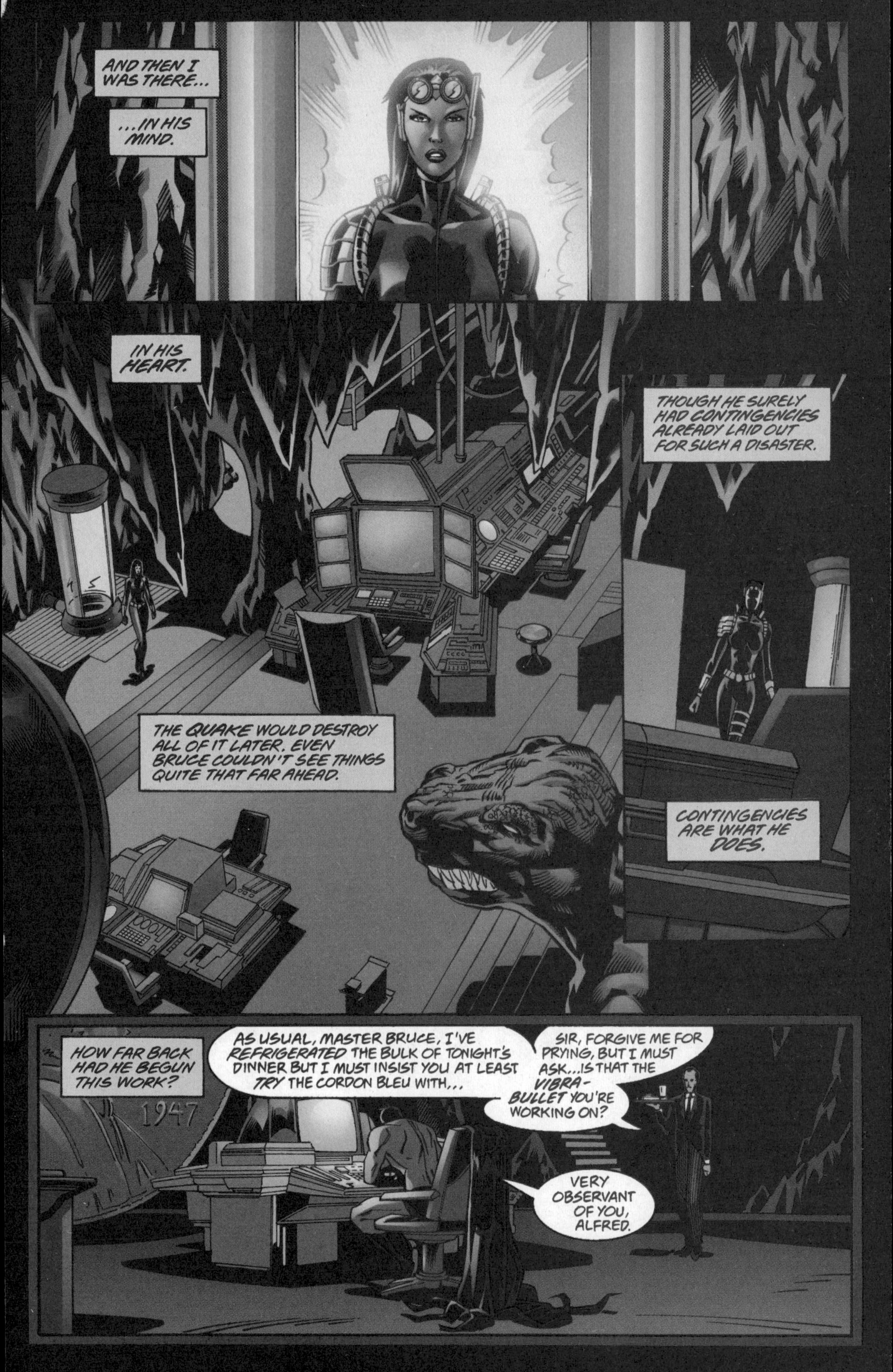
AND THEN I WAS THERE...
...IN HIS MIND.
IN HIS HEART.
THOUGH HE SURELY HAD CONTINGENCIES ALREADY LAID OUT FOR SUCH A DISASTER.
THE QUAKE WOULD DESTROY ALL OF IT LATER. EVEN BRUCE COULDN'T SEE THINGS QUITE THAT FAR AHEAD.
CONTINGENCIES ARE WHAT HE DOES.
HOW FAR BACK HAD HE BEGUN THIS WORK?
1947
AS USUAL, MASTER BRUCE, I'VE REFRIGERATED THE BULK OF TONIGHT'S DINNER BUT I MUST INSIST YOU AT LEAST TRY THE CORDON BLEU WITH...
SIR, FORGIVE ME FOR PRYING, BUT I MUST ASK...IS THAT THE VIBRA-BULLET YOU'RE WORKING ON?
VERY OBSERVANT OF YOU, ALFRED.

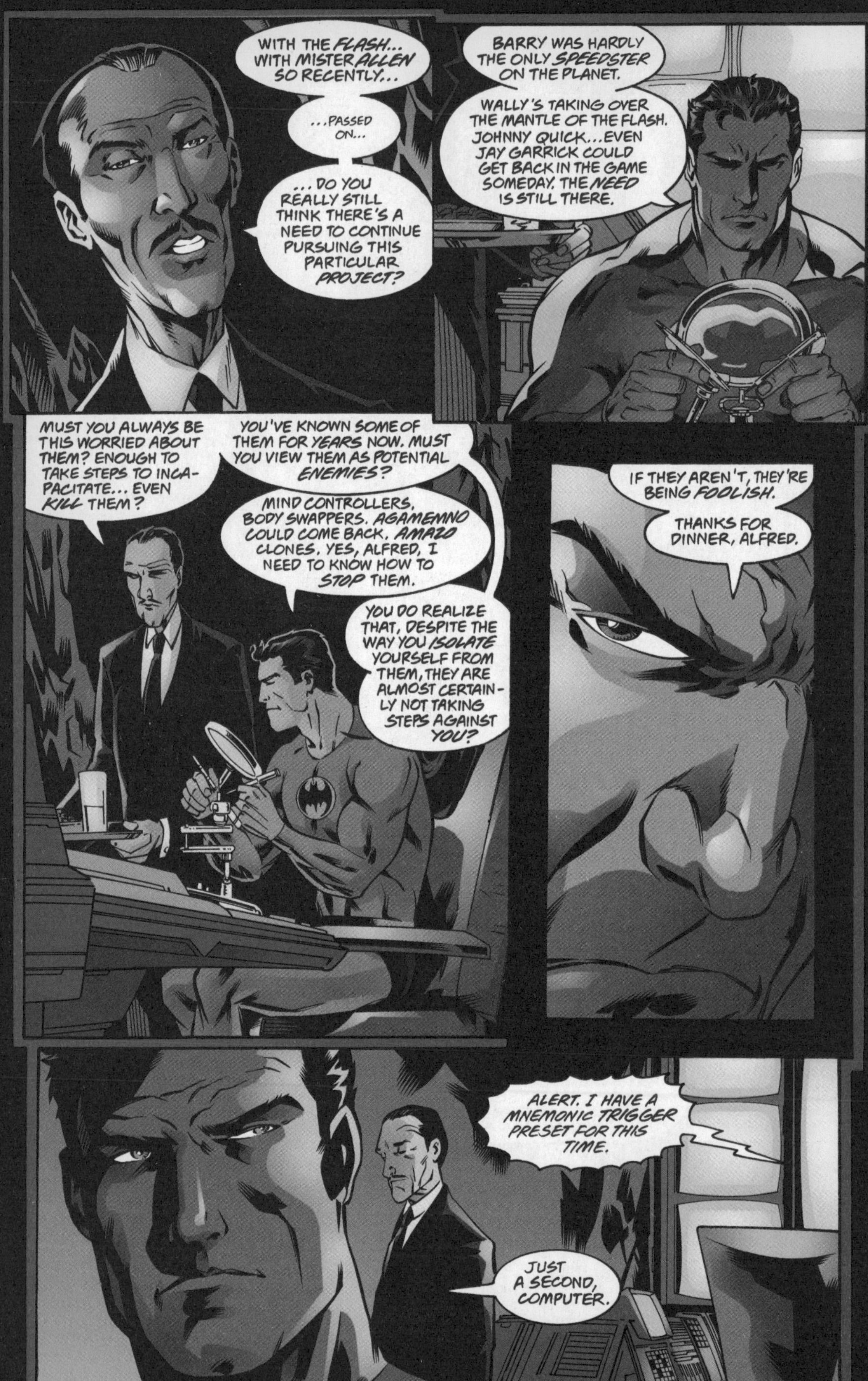
WITH THE FLASH... WITH MISTER ALLEN SO RECENTLY...
...PASSED ON...
...DO YOU REALLY STILL THINK THERE'S A NEED TO CONTINUE PURSUING THIS PARTICULAR PROJECT?
BARRY WAS HARDLY THE ONLY SPEEDSTER ON THE PLANET.
WALLY'S TAKING OVER THE MANTLE OF THE FLASH. JOHNNY QUICK... EVEN JAY GARRICK COULD GET BACK IN THE GAME SOMEDAY. THE NEED IS STILL THERE.
MUST YOU ALWAYS BE THIS WORRIED ABOUT THEM? ENOUGH TO TAKE STEPS TO INCA-PACITATE... EVEN KILL THEM?
YOU'VE KNOWN SOME OF THEM FOR YEARS NOW. MUST YOU VIEW THEM AS POTENTIAL ENEMIES?
MIND CONTROLLERS, BODY SWAPPERS. AGAMEMNO COULD COME BACK. AMAZO CLONES. YES, ALFRED, I NEED TO KNOW HOW TO STOP THEM.
YOU DO REALIZE THAT, DESPITE THE WAY YOU ISOLATE YOURSELF FROM THEM, THEY ARE ALMOST CERTAIN-LY NOT TAKING STEPS AGAINST YOU?
IF THEY AREN'T, THEY'RE BEING FOOLISH.
THANKS FOR DINNER, ALFRED.
ALERT. I HAVE A MNEMONIC TRIGGER PRESET FOR THIS TIME.
JUST A SECOND, COMPUTER.

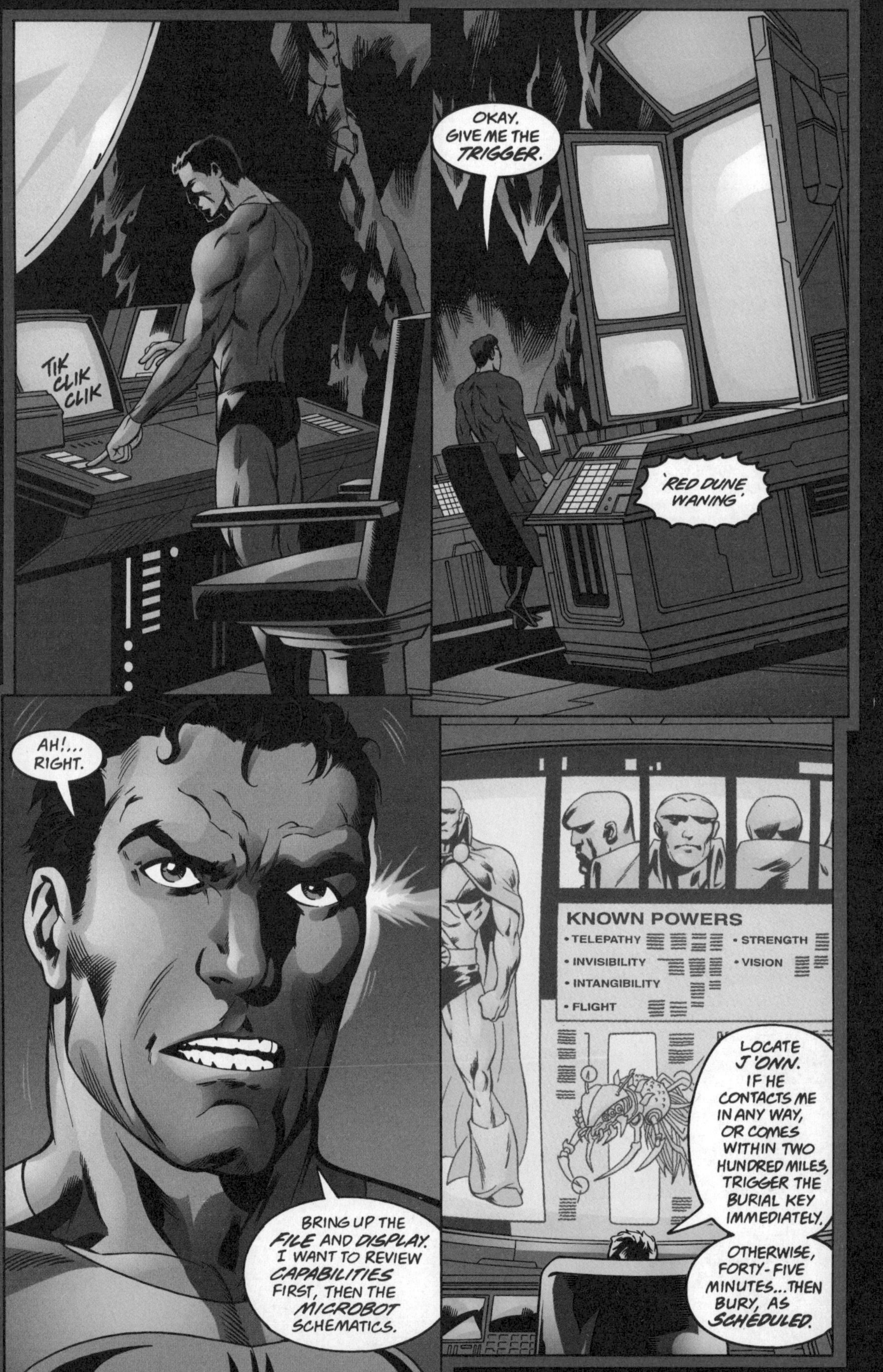
TIK
CLIK
CLIK
OKAY. GIVE ME THE TRIGGER.
'RED DUNE WANING'
AH!... RIGHT.
BRING UP THE FILE AND DISPLAY. I WANT TO REVIEW CAPABILITIES FIRST, THEN THE MICROBOT SCHEMATICS.
KNOWN POWERS
• TELEPATHY
• INVISIBILITY
• INTANGIBILITY
• FLIGHT
• STRENGTH
• VISION
LOCATE J'ONN. IF HE CONTACTS ME IN ANY WAY, OR COMES WITHIN TWO HUNDRED MILES, TRIGGER THE BURIAL KEY IMMEDIATELY.
OTHERWISE, FORTY-FIVE MINUTES...THEN BURY, AS SCHEDULED.

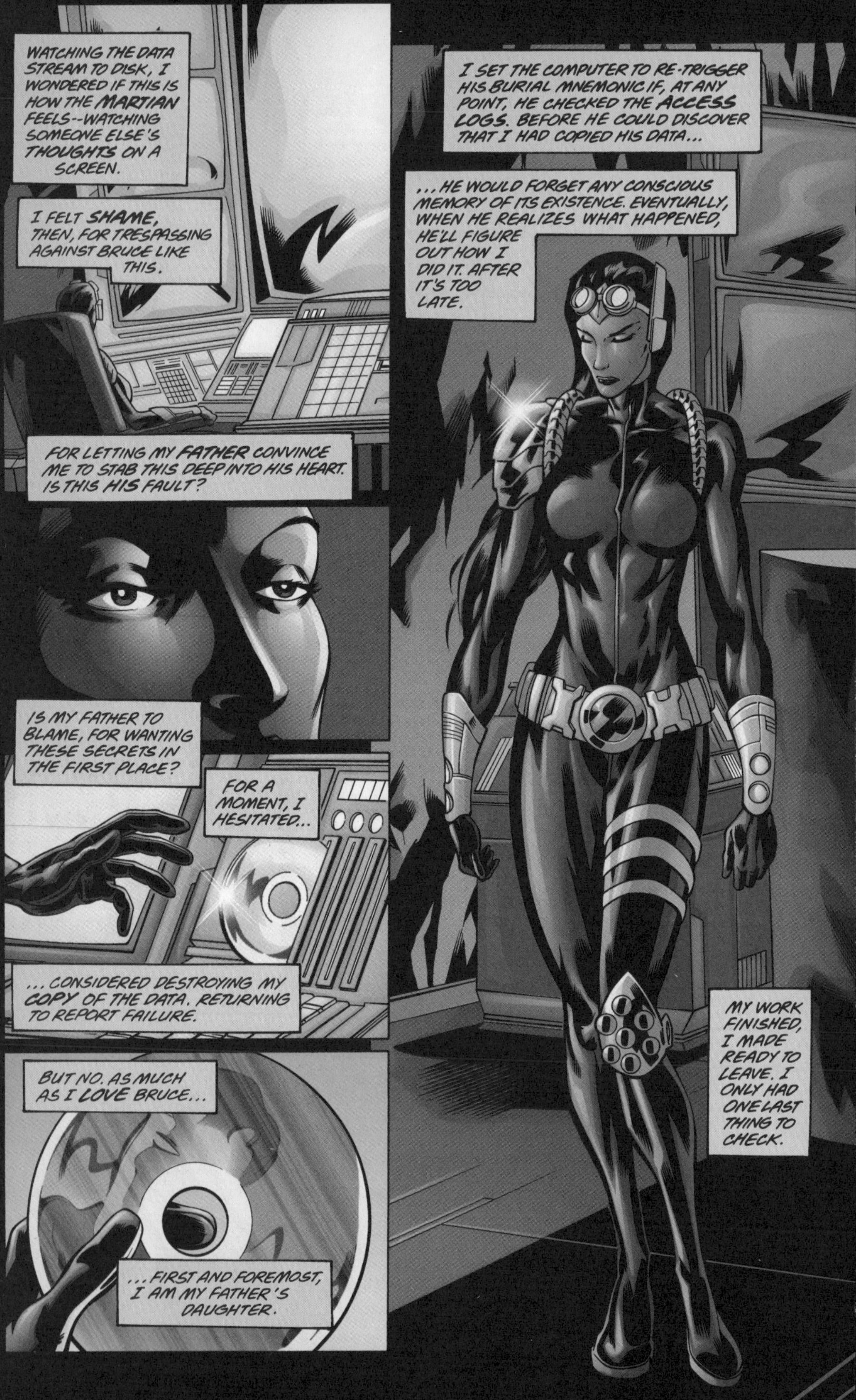
WATCHING THE DATA STREAM TO DISK, I WONDERED IF THIS IS HOW THE MARTIAN FEELS--WATCHING SOMEONE ELSE'S THOUGHTS ON A SCREEN.
I FELT SHAME, THEN, FOR TRESPASSING AGAINST BRUCE LIKE THIS.
FOR LETTING MY FATHER CONVINCE ME TO STAB THIS DEEP INTO HIS HEART. IS THIS HIS FAULT?
IS MY FATHER TO BLAME, FOR WANTING THESE SECRETS IN THE FIRST PLACE?
FOR A MOMENT, I HESITATED...
...CONSIDERED DESTROYING MY COPY OF THE DATA. RETURNING TO REPORT FAILURE.
BUT NO. AS MUCH AS I LOVE BRUCE...
...FIRST AND FOREMOST, I AM MY FATHER'S DAUGHTER.
I SET THE COMPUTER TO RE-TRIGGER HIS BURIAL MNEMONIC IF, AT ANY POINT, HE CHECKED THE ACCESS LOGS. BEFORE HE COULD DISCOVER THAT I HAD COPIED HIS DATA...
...HE WOULD FORGET ANY CONSCIOUS MEMORY OF ITS EXISTENCE. EVENTUALLY, WHEN HE REALIZES WHAT HAPPENED, HE'LL FIGURE OUT HOW I DID IT. AFTER IT'S TOO LATE.
MY WORK FINISHED, I MADE READY TO LEAVE. I ONLY HAD ONE LAST THING TO CHECK.

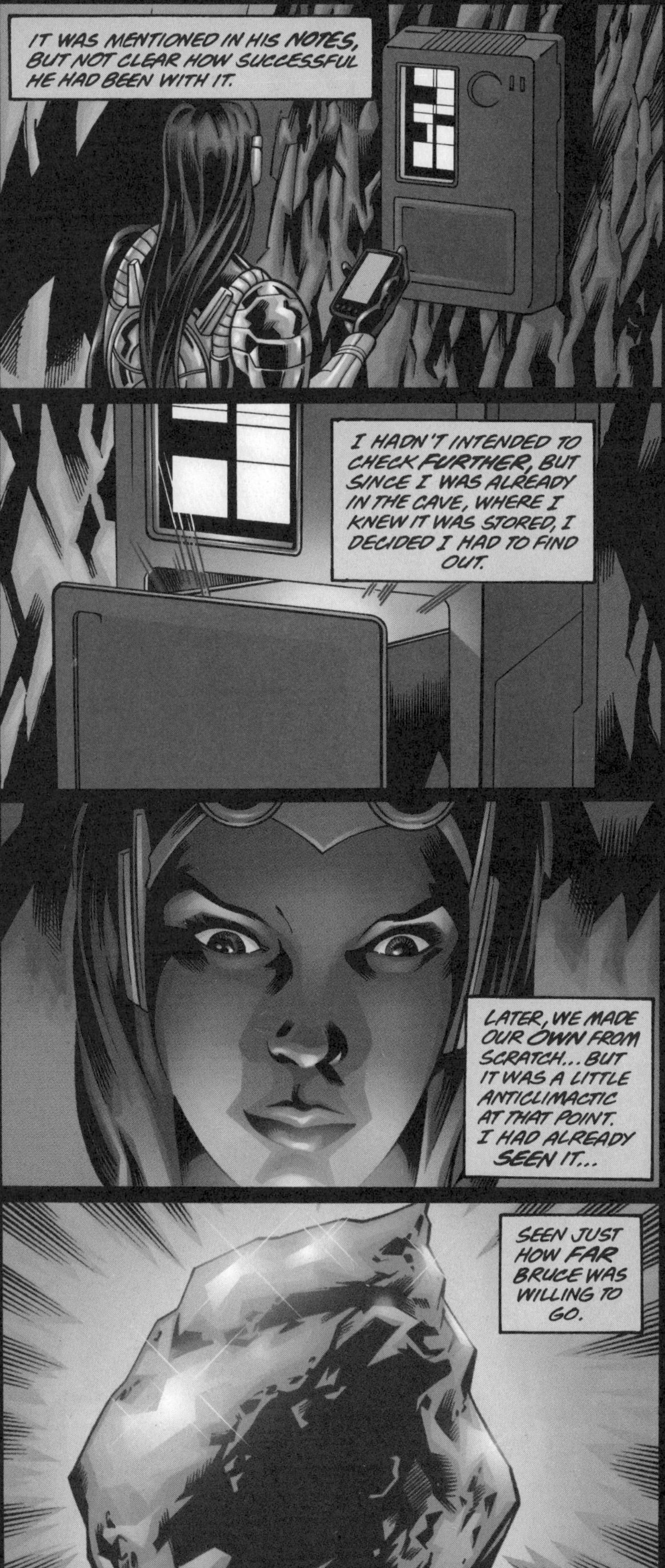
IT WAS MENTIONED IN HIS NOTES, BUT NOT CLEAR HOW SUCCESSFUL HE HAD BEEN WITH IT.
I HADN'T INTENDED TO CHECK FURTHER, BUT SINCE I WAS ALREADY IN THE CAVE, WHERE I KNEW IT WAS STORED, I DECIDED I HAD TO FIND OUT.
LATER, WE MADE OUR OWN FROM SCRATCH... BUT IT WAS A LITTLE ANTICLIMACTIC AT THAT POINT. I HAD ALREADY SEEN IT...
SEEN JUST HOW FAR BRUCE WAS WILLING TO GO.

Someday, I'm sure, it's going to come down to just him and me.
For a lot of the others, I could just wing it if I had to... but not Clark. If anyone requires a methodical and considered response, it's Superman.

If it's to the death, that's easy. I have my chunk of kryptonite. I have a pretty good idea of how it works and what it would take to synthesize more.

But what if I merely want to stop him in his tracks for a while? Interestingly enough, certain properties of kryptonite persist even when it's undergone change at the atomic level. I've found one relatively stable isotope, and there could be several others. But the effects of those isotopes... The small amount of testing I've been able to perform on Daxamite cells (the closest Kryptonian analog I have found) has created more questions than answers.

Ultimately, I would go with the red isotope. I am certain its output is weak enough not to kill Clark, and its half-life is so reduced that its effects should wear off reasonably quickly. But what will it actually do to him? I can't be sure. I know this much, though... it would certainly still be very disruptive. And probably extraordinarily painful.
When...I mean, If...the day comes that it has to be used against him, I only hope I don't have to be there to see the effects. I hope I don't have to look him in the eye when it happens.

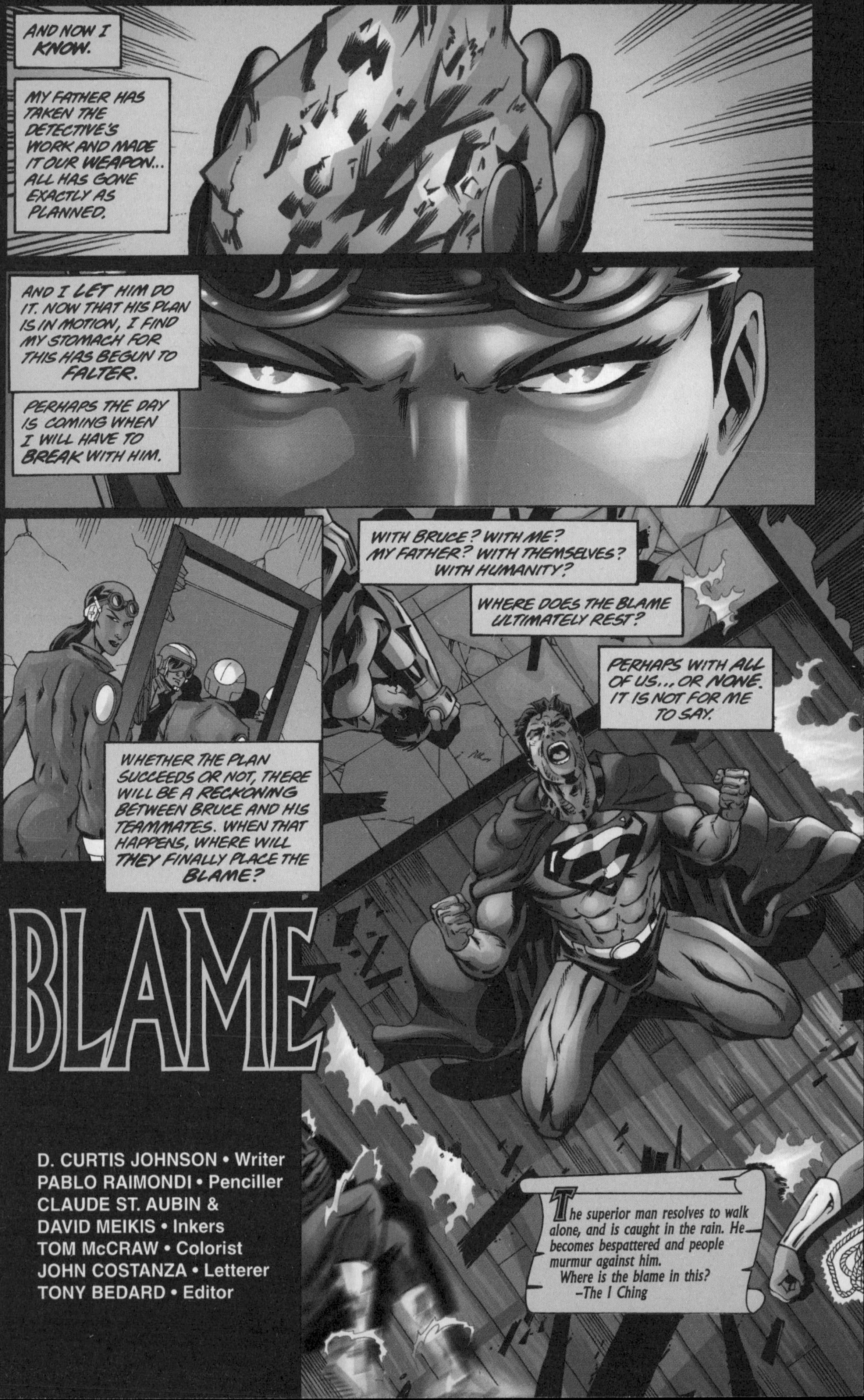
AND NOW I KNOW.
MY FATHER HAS TAKEN THE DETECTIVE'S WORK AND MADE IT OUR WEAPON... ALL HAS GONE EXACTLY AS PLANNED.
AND I LET HIM DO IT. NOW THAT HIS PLAN IS IN MOTION, I FIND MY STOMACH FOR THIS HAS BEGUN TO FALTER.
PERHAPS THE DAY IS COMING WHEN I WILL HAVE TO BREAK WITH HIM.
WHETHER THE PLAN SUCCEEDS OR NOT, THERE WILL BE A RECKONING BETWEEN BRUCE AND HIS TEAMMATES. WHEN THAT HAPPENS, WHERE WILL THEY FINALLY PLACE THE BLAME?
WITH BRUCE? WITH ME? MY FATHER? WITH THEMSELVES? WITH HUMANITY?
WHERE DOES THE BLAME ULTIMATELY REST?
PERHAPS WITH ALL OF US... OR NONE. IT IS NOT FOR ME TO SAY.
BLAME
D. CURTIS JOHNSON • Writer
PABLO RAIMONDI • Penciller
CLAUDE ST. AUBIN & DAVID MEIKIS • Inkers
TOM McCRAW • Colorist
JOHN COSTANZA • Letterer
TONY BEDARD • Editor
The superior man resolves to walk alone, and is caught in the rain. He becomes bespattered and people murmur against him.
Where is the blame in this?
–The I Ching

AT O'HARE AIRPORT, ACTING ON A TIP AND WITH TWO MINUTES TO SPARE, THE CHICAGO P.D. BOMB SQUAD HAS TRACED A PLUTONIUM EXPLOSIVE TO LOCKER 761...

...BUT THAT NUMBER MEANS NOTHING TO THEM.

ACROSS THE WORLD, A SOUTH KOREAN PLATOON ACCIDENTALLY WANDERS INTO NORTH COUNTRY THANKS TO WRITTEN ORDERS THAT ARE SUDDENLY SENSELESS.

THE RESULTANT MILITARY ACTION WILL COST HUNDREDS, PERHAPS THOUSANDS, OF LIVES.

GLOBAL ECOTERRORIST RA'S AL GHUL HAS THROWN THE EARTH INTO TURMOIL WITH HIS MODERN-DAY TOWER OF BABEL. ITS ULTRASONIC TRANSMISSIONS BLANKET THE GLOBE, SCRAMBLING THE LANGUAGE CENTERS OF THE HUMAN BRAIN.

WORLDWIDE, THE WRITTEN WORD IS NOW INCOMPREHENSIBLE--AND THINGS ARE ABOUT TO GET WORSE.

MUCH WORSE.

THE JLAERS ARE POWERLESS TO HELP. ONE BY ONE, THEY'VE BEEN PREEMPTED--CRIPPLED BY RA'S'S LEAGUE OF ASSASSINS.

GREEN LANTERN--BLINDED.

AQUAMAN--MADE PHOBIC OF THE WATER HE NEEDS TO LIVE.

FLASH--PARALYZED BY LIGHTSPEED EPILEPSY.

EACH AND EVERY LEAGUER AT THE MERCY OF THE MAN WHO DESIGNED THE TRAPS SET FOR THEM:

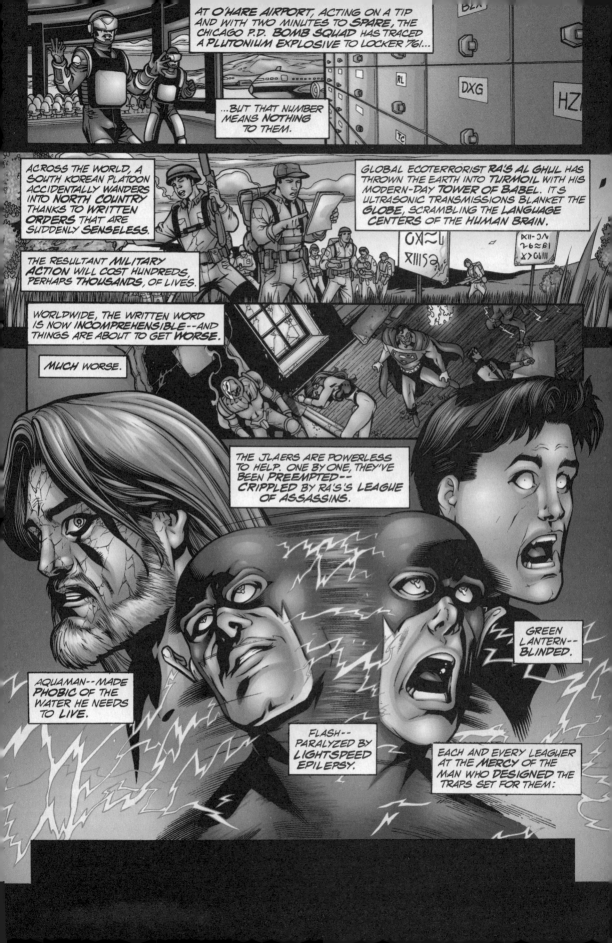

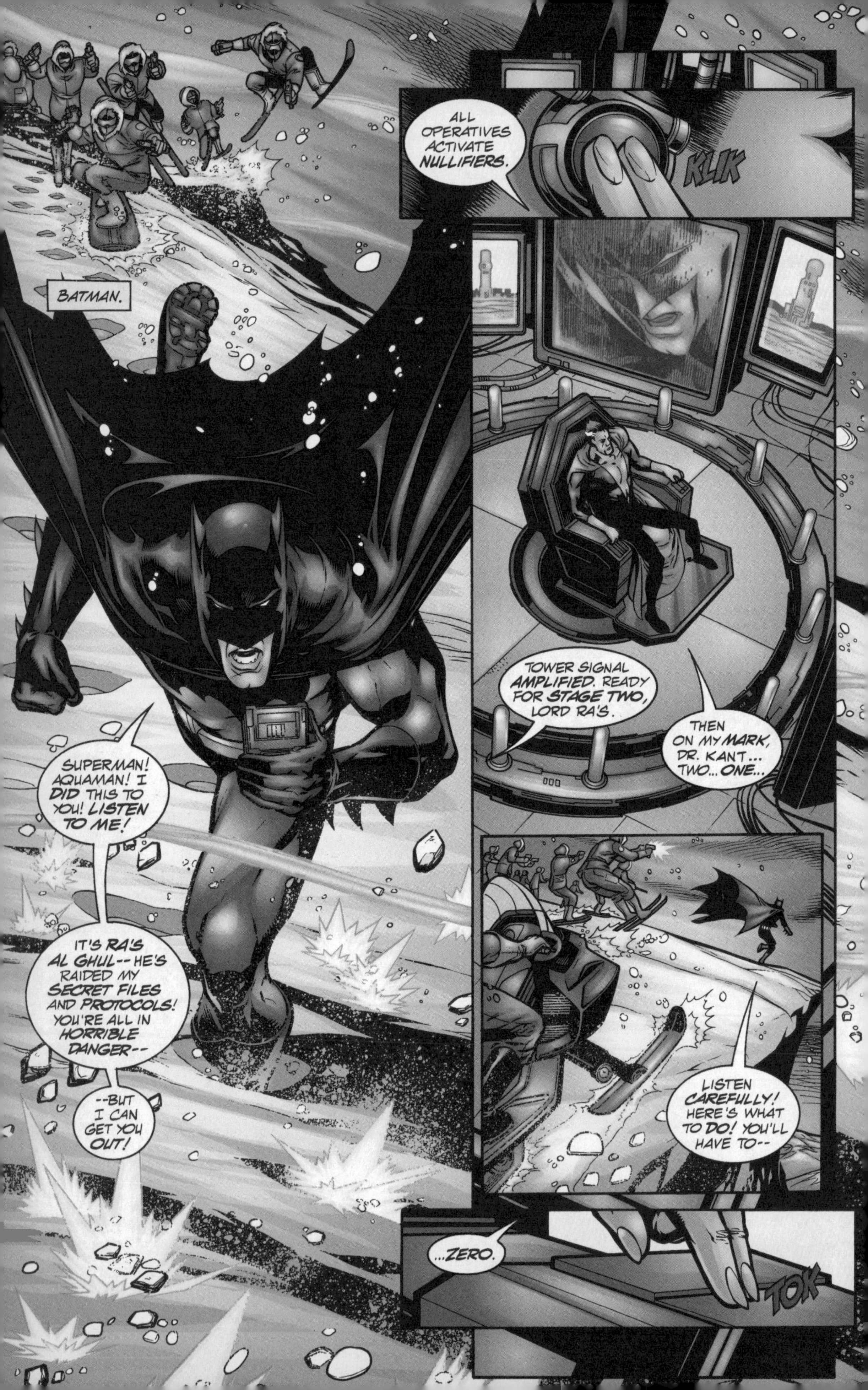
BATMAN.
ALL OPERATIVES ACTIVATE NULLIFIERS.
KLIK
SUPERMAN! AQUAMAN! I DID THIS TO YOU! LISTEN TO ME!
IT'S RA'S AL GHUL-- HE'S RAIDED MY SECRET FILES AND PROTOCOLS! YOU'RE ALL IN HORRIBLE DANGER--
--BUT I CAN GET YOU OUT!
TOWER SIGNAL AMPLIFIED. READY FOR STAGE TWO, LORD RA'S.
THEN ON MY MARK, DR. KANT... TWO... ONE...
LISTEN CAREFULLY! HERE'S WHAT TO DO! YOU'LL HAVE TO--
...ZERO.
TOK

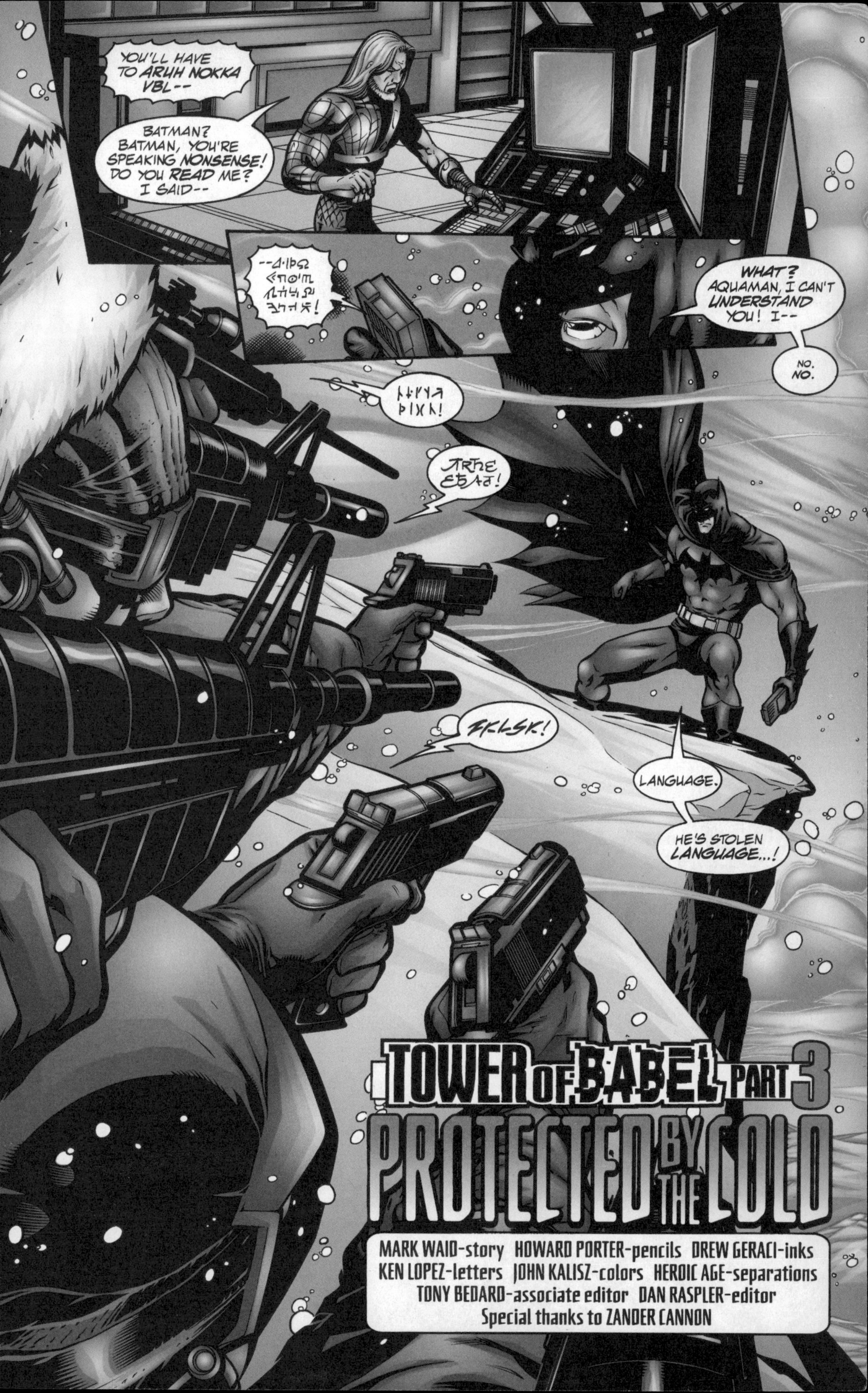
YOU'LL HAVE TO ARUH NOKKA VBL--
BATMAN? BATMAN, YOU'RE SPEAKING NONSENSE! DO YOU READ ME? I SAID--
WHAT? AQUAMAN, I CAN'T UNDERSTAND YOU! I--
NO. NO.
LANGUAGE.
HE'S STOLEN LANGUAGE...!
TOWER OF BABEL PART 3
PROTECTED BY THE COLD
MARK WAID-story HOWARD PORTER-pencils DREW GERACI-inks
KEN LOPEZ-letters JOHN KALISZ-colors HEROIC AGE-separations
TONY BEDARD-associate editor DAN RASPLER-editor
Special thanks to ZANDER CANNON

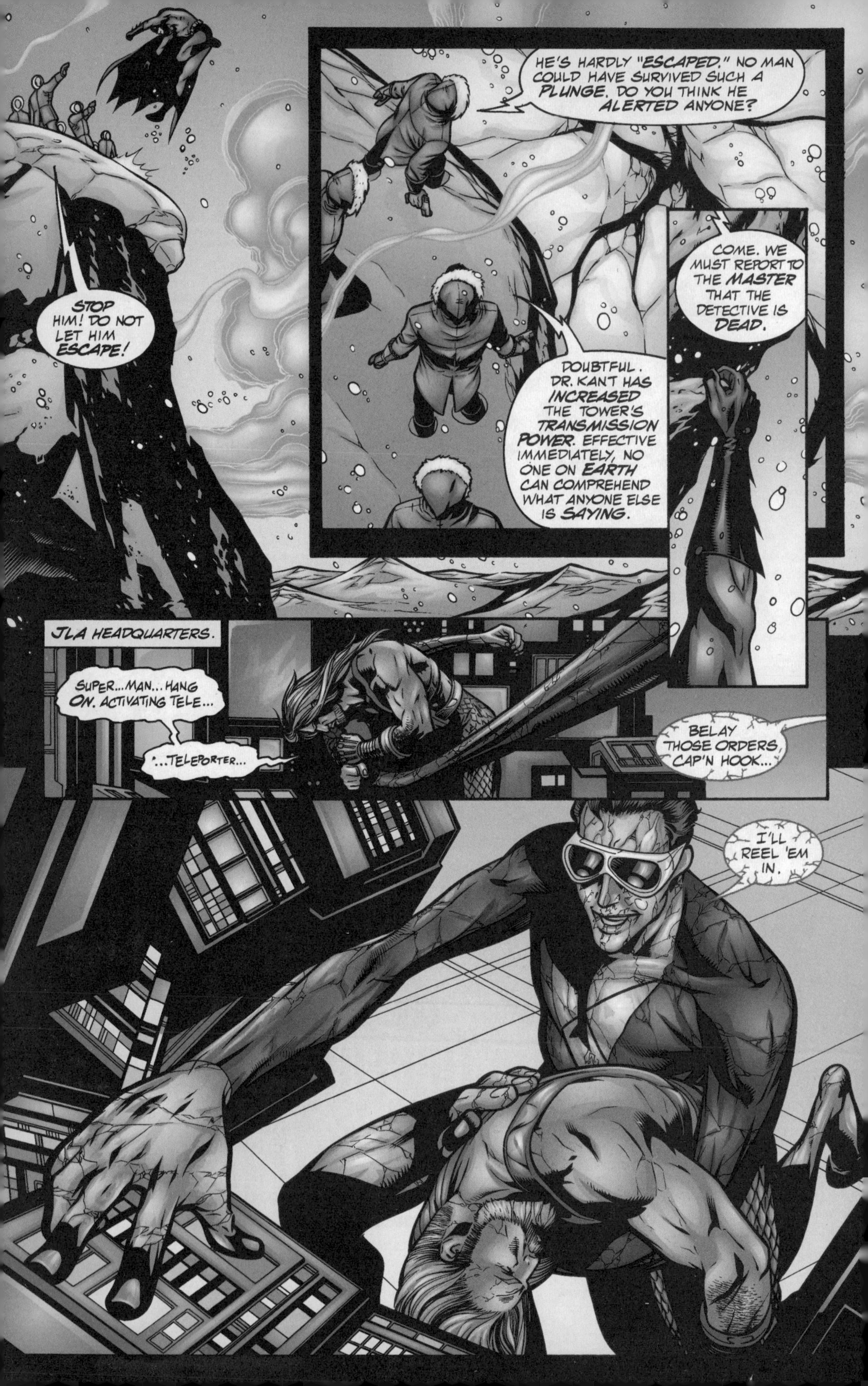
STOP HIM! DO NOT LET HIM ESCAPE!
HE'S HARDLY "ESCAPED." NO MAN COULD HAVE SURVIVED SUCH A PLUNGE. DO YOU THINK HE ALERTED ANYONE?
DOUBTFUL. DR. KANT HAS INCREASED THE TOWER'S TRANSMISSION POWER. EFFECTIVE IMMEDIATELY, NO ONE ON EARTH CAN COMPREHEND WHAT ANYONE ELSE IS SAYING.
COME. WE MUST REPORT TO THE MASTER THAT THE DETECTIVE IS DEAD.
JLA HEADQUARTERS.
SUPER...MAN...HANG ON. ACTIVATING TELE...
...TELEPORTER...
BELAY THOSE ORDERS, CAP'N HOOK...
I'LL REEL 'EM IN.

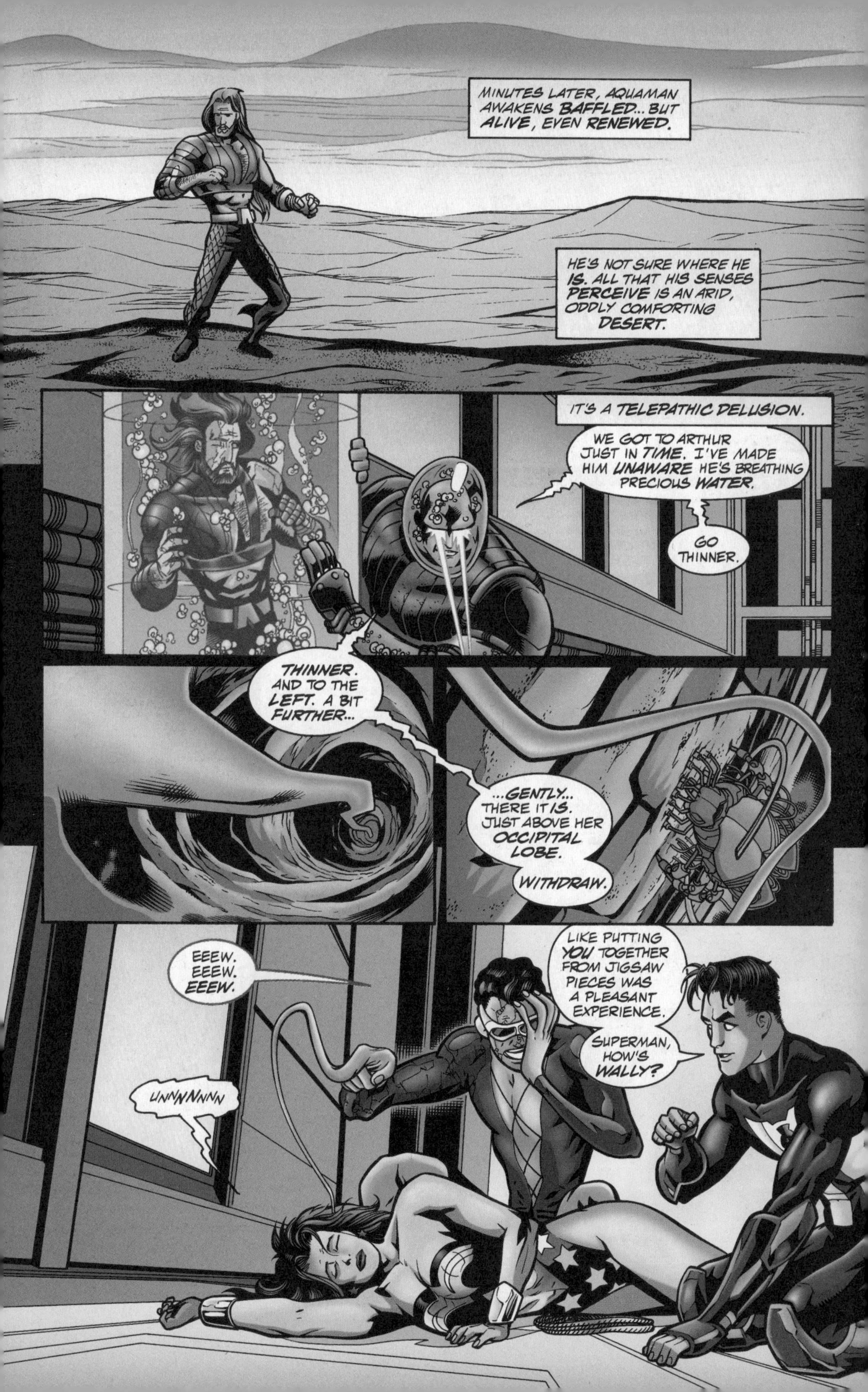

MINUTES LATER, AQUAMAN AWAKENS BAFFLED... BUT ALIVE, EVEN RENEWED.
HE'S NOT SURE WHERE HE IS. ALL THAT HIS SENSES PERCEIVE IS AN ARID, ODDLY COMFORTING DESERT.
IT'S A TELEPATHIC DELUSION.
WE GOT TO ARTHUR JUST IN TIME. I'VE MADE HIM UNAWARE HE'S BREATHING PRECIOUS WATER.
GO THINNER.
THINNER. AND TO THE LEFT. A BIT FURTHER...
...GENTLY... THERE IT IS. JUST ABOVE HER OCCIPITAL LOBE.
WITHDRAW.
EEEW. EEEW. EEEW.
LIKE PUTTING YOU TOGETHER FROM JIGSAW PIECES WAS A PLEASANT EXPERIENCE.
SUPERMAN, HOW'S WALLY?
UNNNNNNN

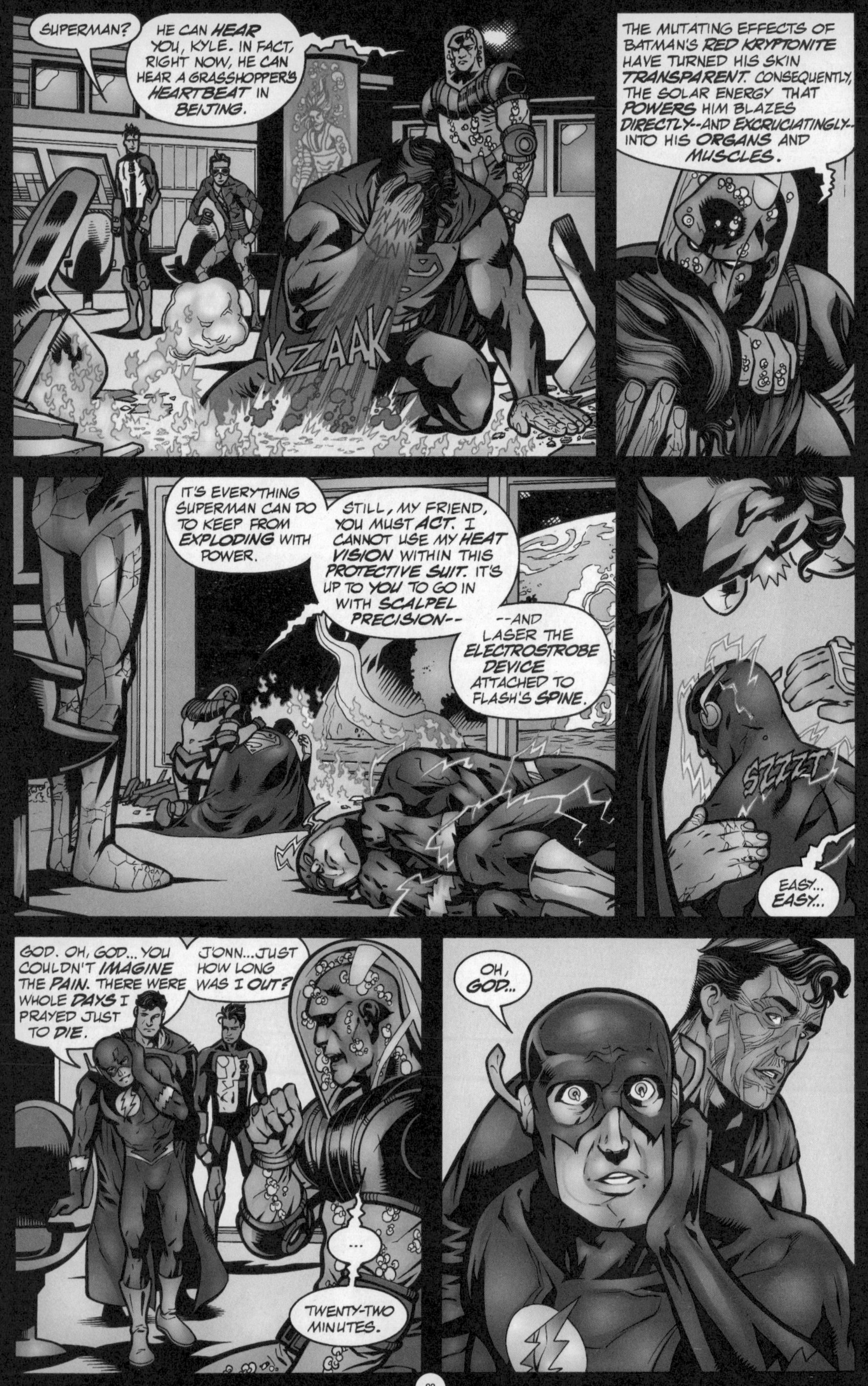
SUPERMAN?
HE CAN HEAR YOU, KYLE. IN FACT, RIGHT NOW, HE CAN HEAR A GRASSHOPPER'S HEARTBEAT IN BEIJING.
KZAAK
THE MUTATING EFFECTS OF BATMAN'S RED KRYPTONITE HAVE TURNED HIS SKIN TRANSPARENT. CONSEQUENTLY, THE SOLAR ENERGY THAT POWERS HIM BLAZES DIRECTLY--AND EXCRUCIATINGLY--INTO HIS ORGANS AND MUSCLES.
IT'S EVERYTHING SUPERMAN CAN DO TO KEEP FROM EXPLODING WITH POWER.
STILL, MY FRIEND, YOU MUST ACT. I CANNOT USE MY HEAT VISION WITHIN THIS PROTECTIVE SUIT. IT'S UP TO YOU TO GO IN WITH SCALPEL PRECISION--
--AND LASER THE ELECTROSTROBE DEVICE ATTACHED TO FLASH'S SPINE.
SZZZT
EASY... EASY...
GOD. OH, GOD... YOU COULDN'T IMAGINE THE PAIN. THERE WERE WHOLE DAYS I PRAYED JUST TO DIE.
J'ONN...JUST HOW LONG WAS I OUT?
...
TWENTY-TWO MINUTES.
OH, GOD...

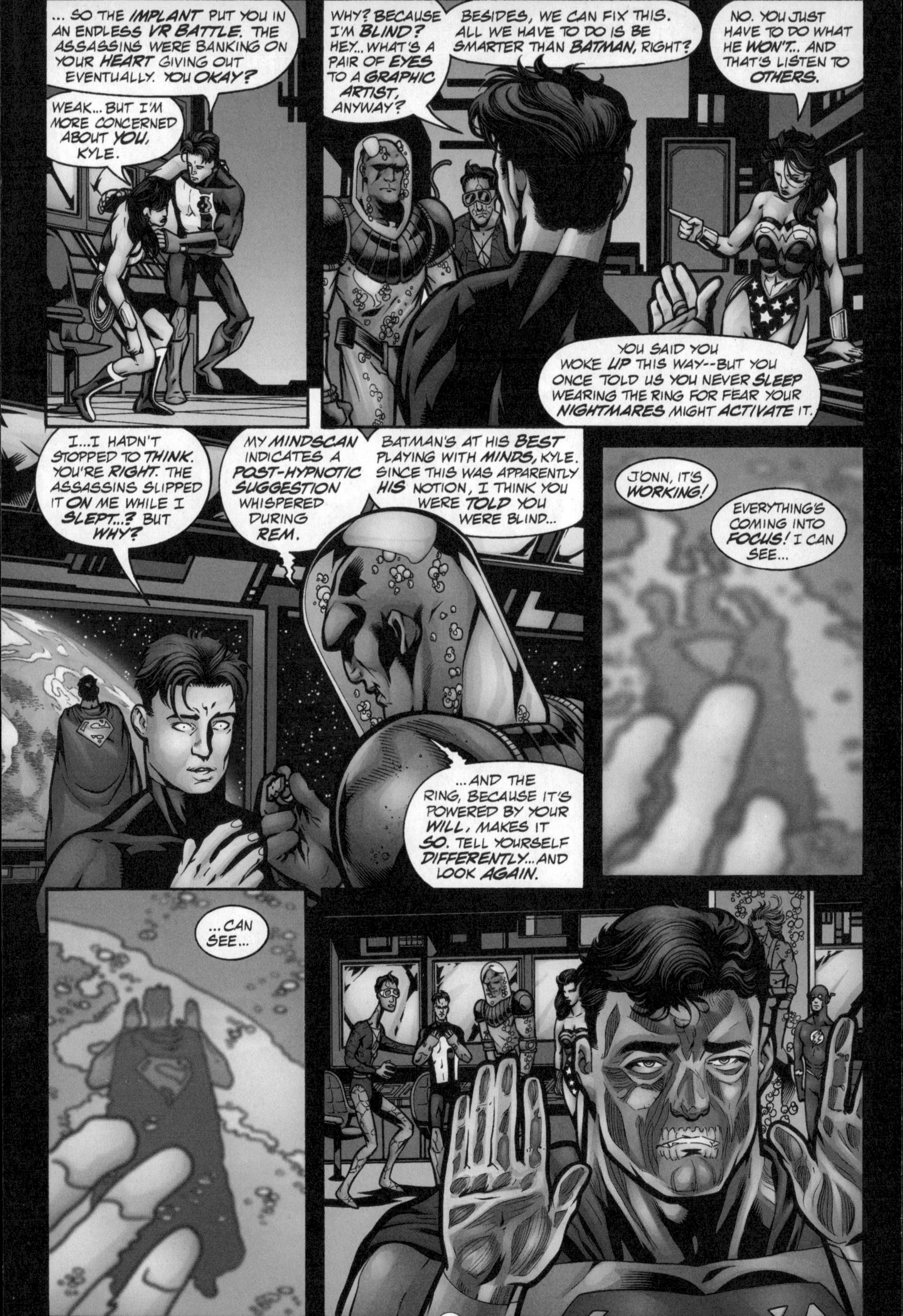
... SO THE IMPLANT PUT YOU IN AN ENDLESS VR BATTLE. THE ASSASSINS WERE BANKING ON YOUR HEART GIVING OUT EVENTUALLY. YOU OKAY?
WEAK... BUT I'M MORE CONCERNED ABOUT YOU, KYLE.
WHY? BECAUSE I'M BLIND? HEY... WHAT'S A PAIR OF EYES TO A GRAPHIC ARTIST, ANYWAY?
BESIDES, WE CAN FIX THIS. ALL WE HAVE TO DO IS BE SMARTER THAN BATMAN, RIGHT?
NO. YOU JUST HAVE TO DO WHAT HE WON'T... AND THAT'S LISTEN TO OTHERS.
YOU SAID YOU WOKE UP THIS WAY--BUT YOU ONCE TOLD US YOU NEVER SLEEP WEARING THE RING FOR FEAR YOUR NIGHTMARES MIGHT ACTIVATE IT.
I...I HADN'T STOPPED TO THINK. YOU'RE RIGHT. THE ASSASSINS SLIPPED IT ON ME WHILE I SLEPT...? BUT WHY?
MY MINDSCAN INDICATES A POST-HYPNOTIC SUGGESTION WHISPERED DURING REM.
BATMAN'S AT HIS BEST PLAYING WITH MINDS, KYLE. SINCE THIS WAS APPARENTLY HIS NOTION, I THINK YOU WERE TOLD YOU WERE BLIND...
...AND THE RING, BECAUSE IT'S POWERED BY YOUR WILL, MAKES IT SO. TELL YOURSELF DIFFERENTLY... AND LOOK AGAIN.
J'ONN, IT'S WORKING!
EVERYTHING'S COMING INTO FOCUS! I CAN SEE...
...CAN SEE...

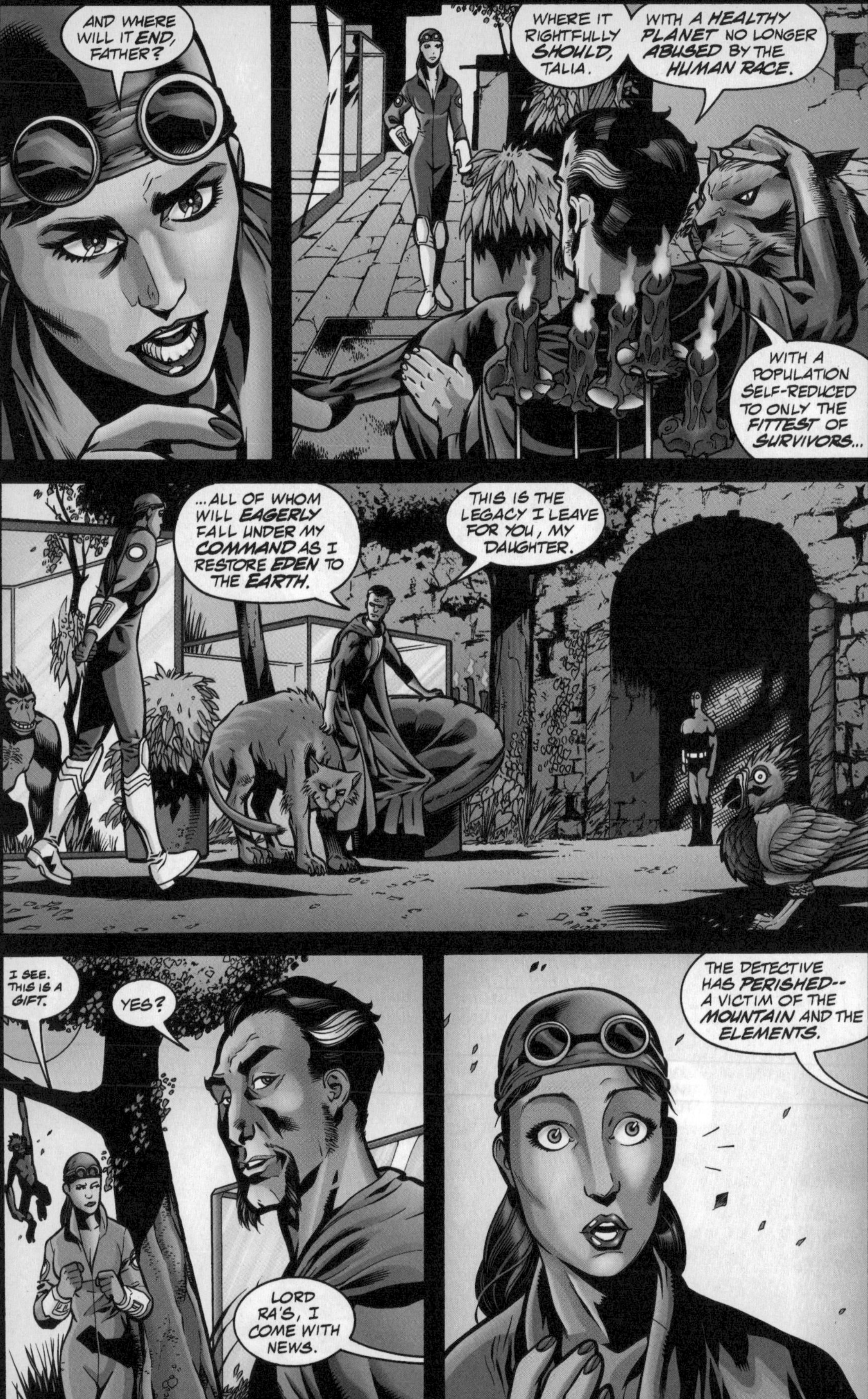
AND WHERE WILL IT END, FATHER?
WHERE IT RIGHTFULLY SHOULD, TALIA.
WITH A HEALTHY PLANET NO LONGER ABUSED BY THE HUMAN RACE.
WITH A POPULATION SELF-REDUCED TO ONLY THE FITTEST OF SURVIVORS...
...ALL OF WHOM WILL EAGERLY FALL UNDER MY COMMAND AS I RESTORE EDEN TO THE EARTH.
THIS IS THE LEGACY I LEAVE FOR YOU, MY DAUGHTER.
I SEE. THIS IS A GIFT.
YES?
LORD RA'S, I COME WITH NEWS.
THE DETECTIVE HAS PERISHED-- A VICTIM OF THE MOUNTAIN AND THE ELEMENTS.

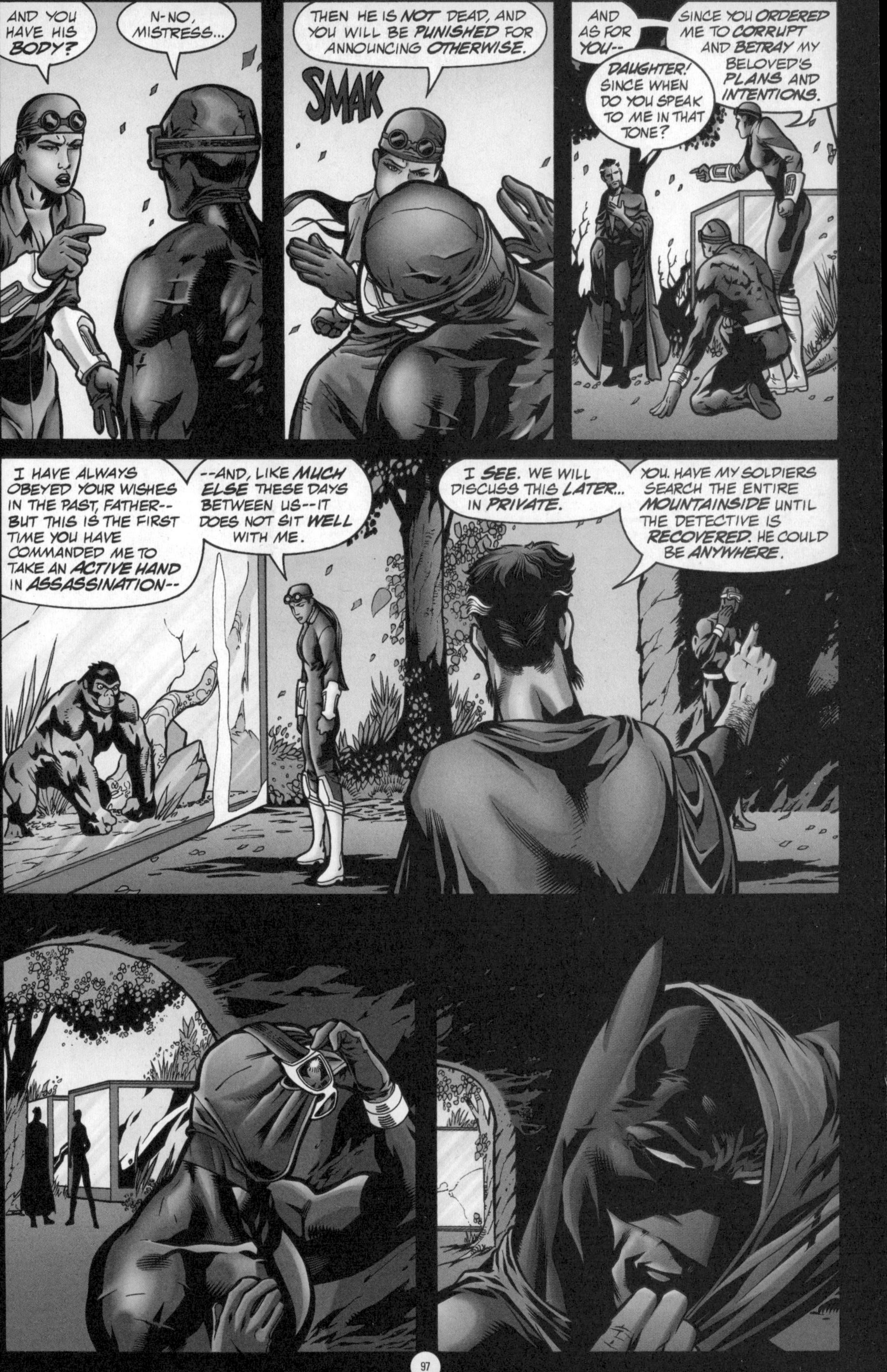

AND YOU HAVE HIS BODY?
N-NO, MISTRESS...
THEN HE IS NOT DEAD, AND YOU WILL BE PUNISHED FOR ANNOUNCING OTHERWISE.
SMAK
AND AS FOR YOU--
SINCE YOU ORDERED ME TO CORRUPT AND BETRAY MY BELOVED'S PLANS AND INTENTIONS.
DAUGHTER! SINCE WHEN DO YOU SPEAK TO ME IN THAT TONE?
I HAVE ALWAYS OBEYED YOUR WISHES IN THE PAST, FATHER-- BUT THIS IS THE FIRST TIME YOU HAVE COMMANDED ME TO TAKE AN ACTIVE HAND IN ASSASSINATION--
--AND, LIKE MUCH ELSE THESE DAYS BETWEEN US--IT DOES NOT SIT WELL WITH ME.
I SEE. WE WILL DISCUSS THIS LATER... IN PRIVATE.
YOU. HAVE MY SOLDIERS SEARCH THE ENTIRE MOUNTAINSIDE UNTIL THE DETECTIVE IS RECOVERED. HE COULD BE ANYWHERE.

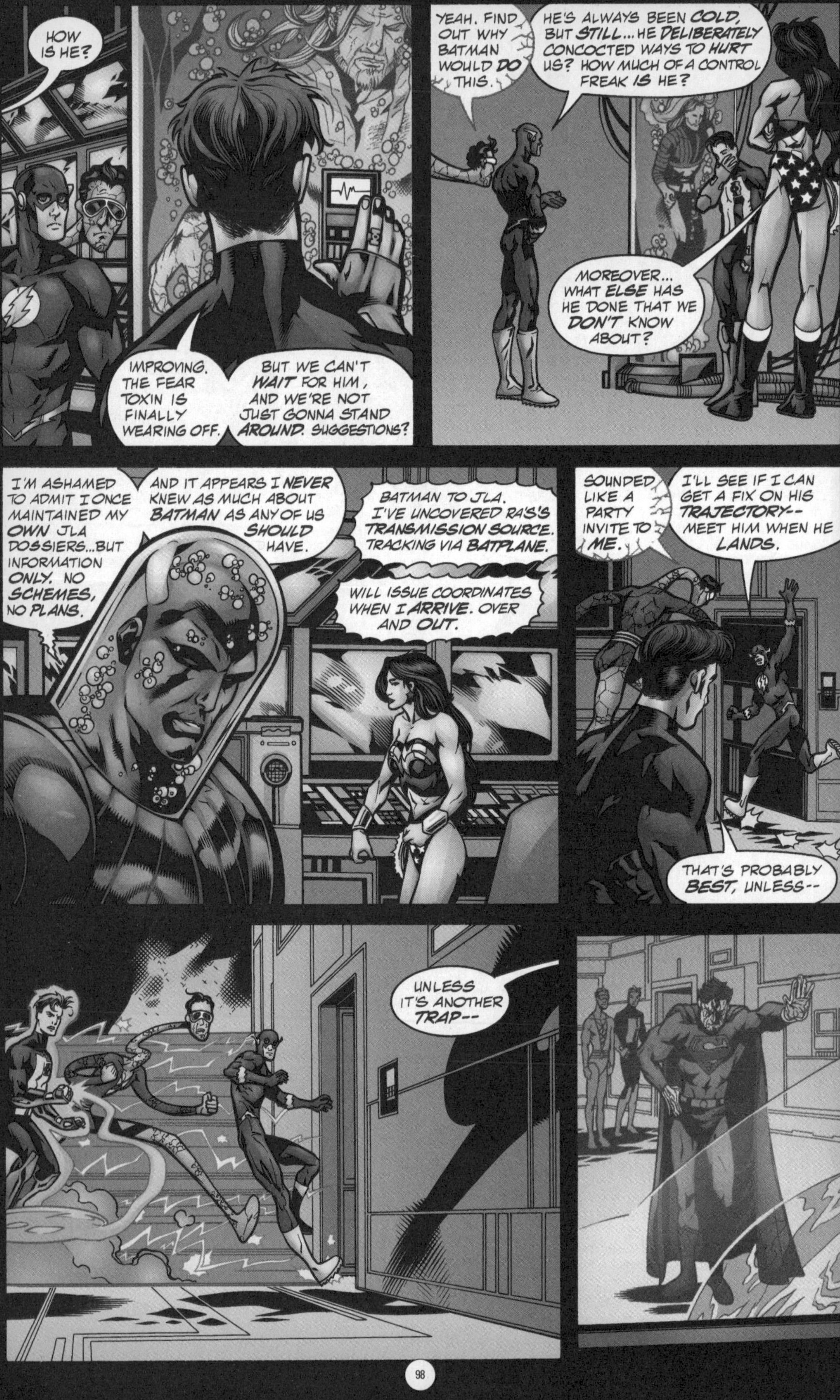
HOW IS HE?
IMPROVING. THE FEAR TOXIN IS FINALLY WEARING OFF.
BUT WE CAN'T WAIT FOR HIM, AND WE'RE NOT JUST GONNA STAND AROUND. SUGGESTIONS?
YEAH. FIND OUT WHY BATMAN WOULD DO THIS.
HE'S ALWAYS BEEN COLD, BUT STILL... HE DELIBERATELY CONCOCTED WAYS TO HURT US? HOW MUCH OF A CONTROL FREAK IS HE?
MOREOVER... WHAT ELSE HAS HE DONE THAT WE DON'T KNOW ABOUT?
I'M ASHAMED TO ADMIT I ONCE MAINTAINED MY OWN JLA DOSSIERS...BUT INFORMATION ONLY. NO SCHEMES, NO PLANS.
AND IT APPEARS I NEVER KNEW AS MUCH ABOUT BATMAN AS ANY OF US SHOULD HAVE.
BATMAN TO JLA. I'VE UNCOVERED RA'S'S TRANSMISSION SOURCE. TRACKING VIA BATPLANE.
WILL ISSUE COORDINATES WHEN I ARRIVE. OVER AND OUT.
SOUNDED LIKE A PARTY INVITE TO ME.
I'LL SEE IF I CAN GET A FIX ON HIS TRAJECTORY-- MEET HIM WHEN HE LANDS.
THAT'S PROBABLY BEST, UNLESS--
UNLESS IT'S ANOTHER TRAP--

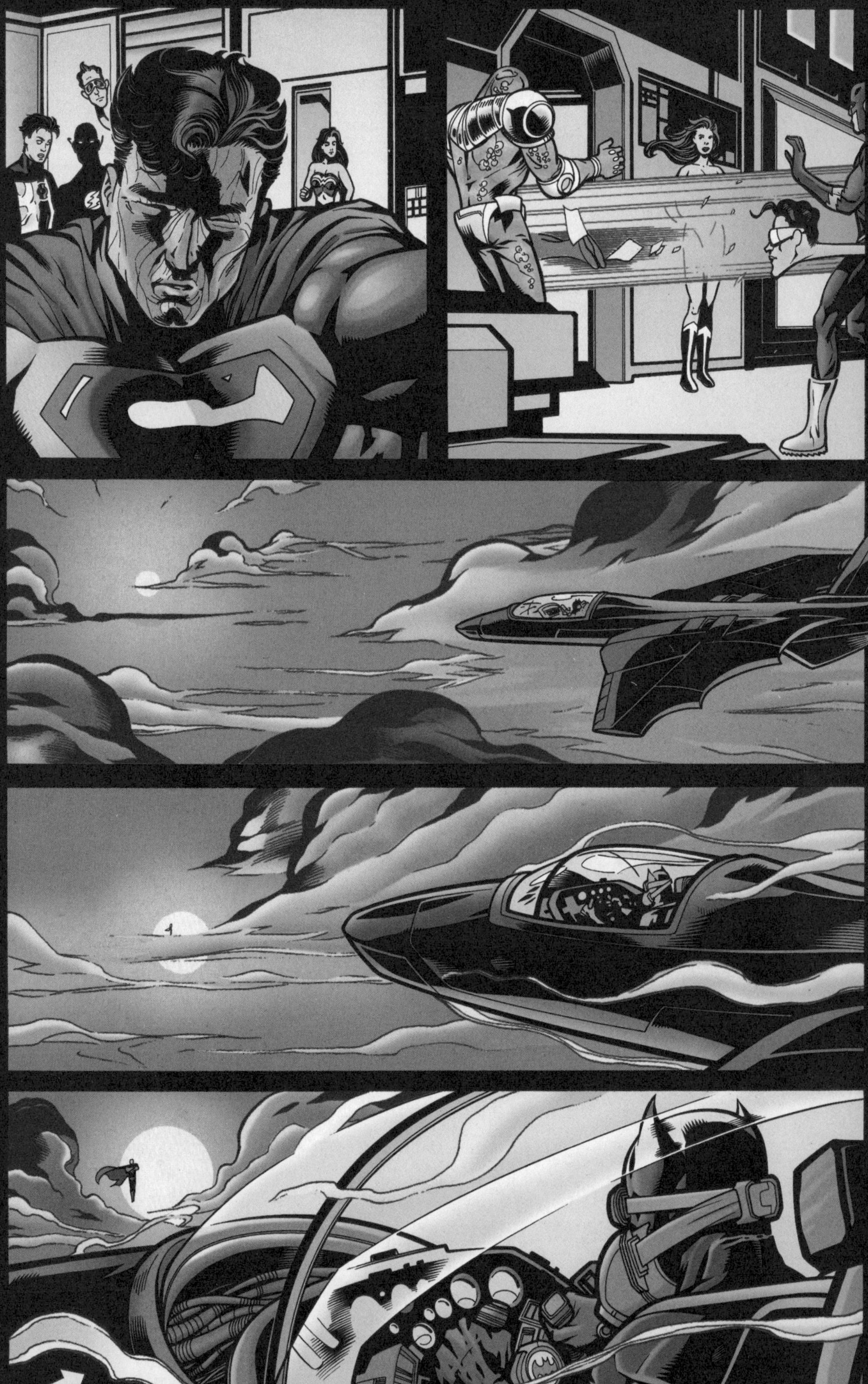

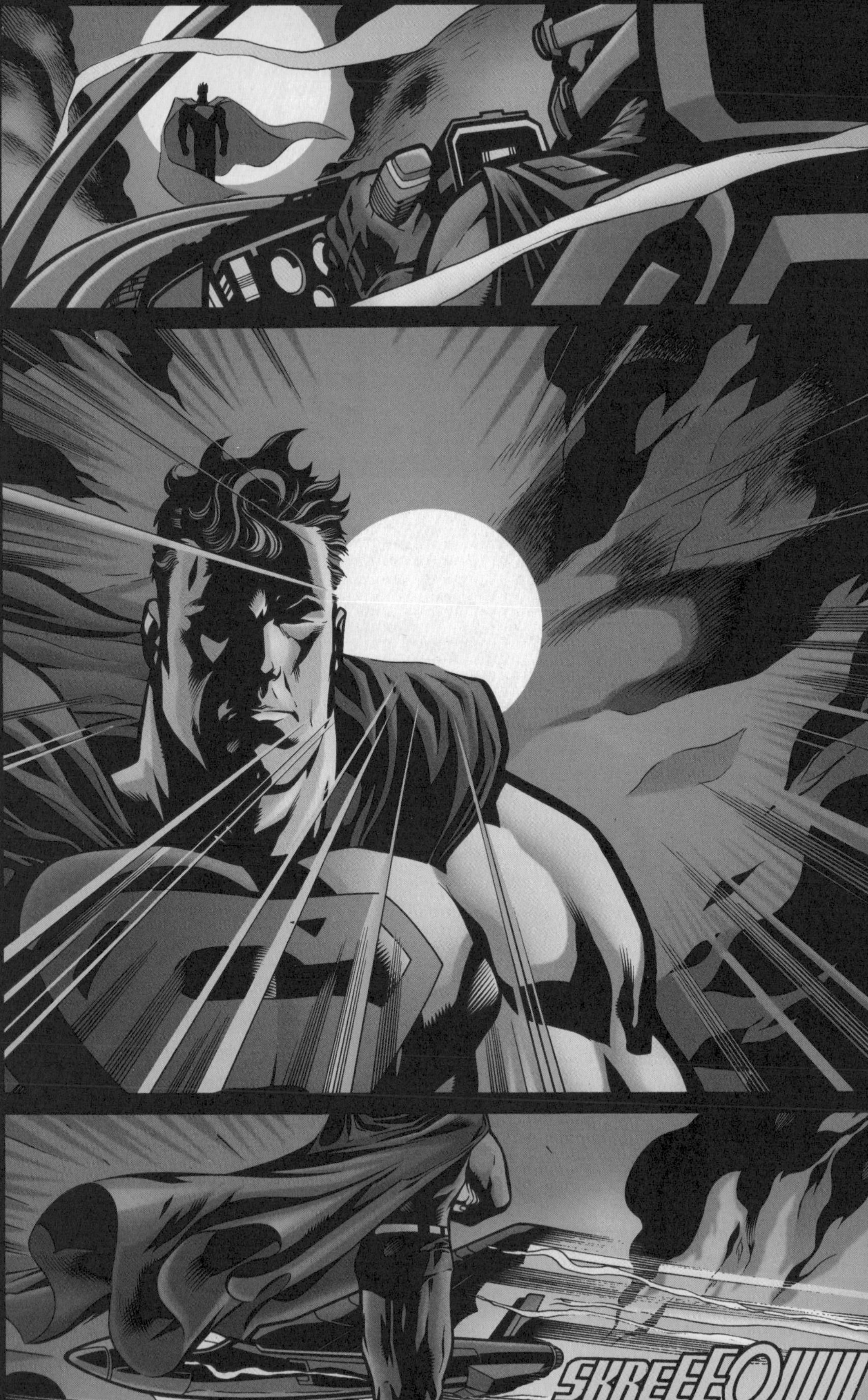
SKREEEOWW

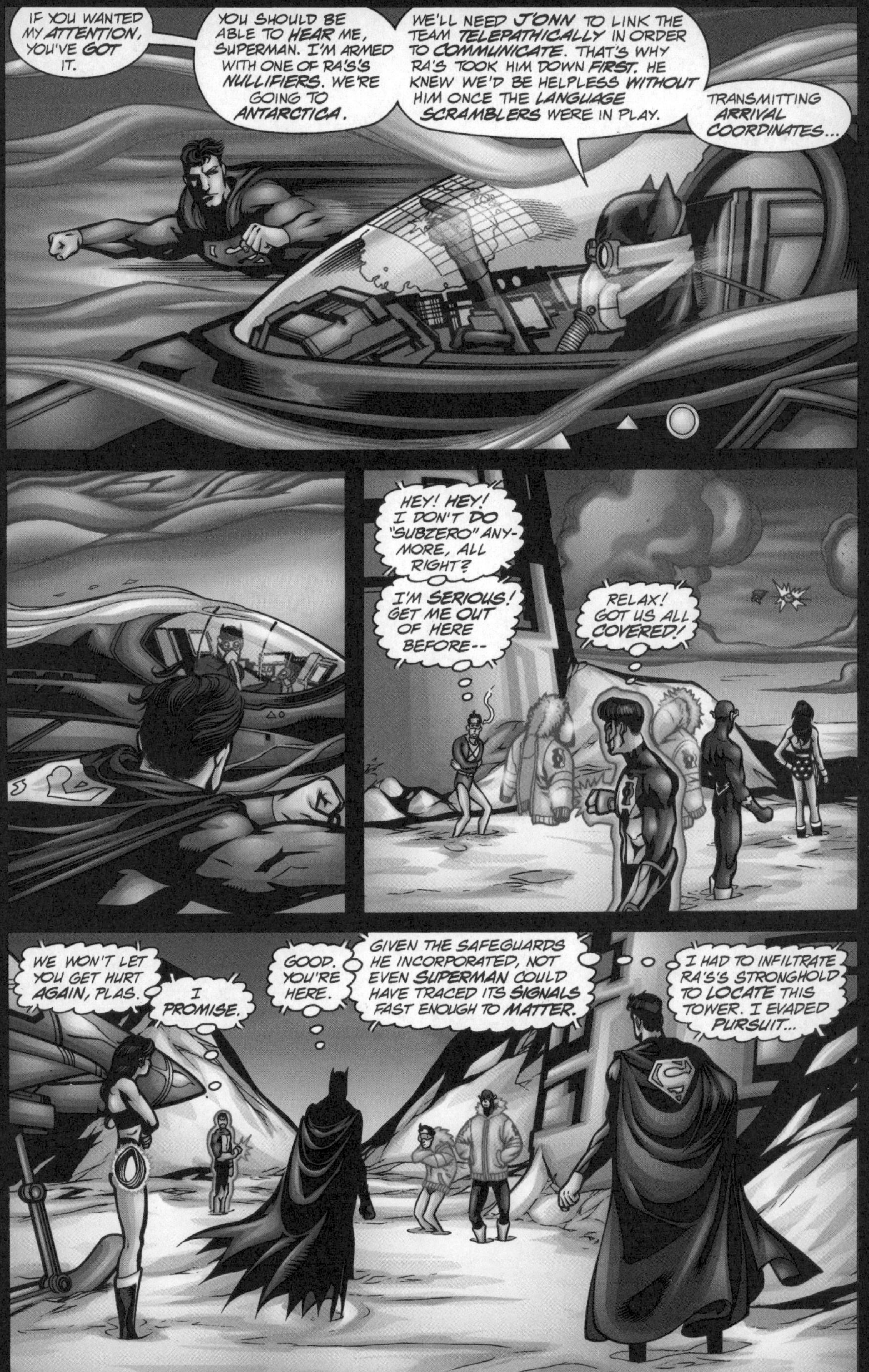
IF YOU WANTED MY ATTENTION, YOU'VE GOT IT.
YOU SHOULD BE ABLE TO HEAR ME, SUPERMAN. I'M ARMED WITH ONE OF RA'S'S NULLIFIERS. WE'RE GOING TO ANTARCTICA.
WE'LL NEED J'ONN TO LINK THE TEAM TELEPATHICALLY IN ORDER TO COMMUNICATE. THAT'S WHY RA'S TOOK HIM DOWN FIRST. HE KNEW WE'D BE HELPLESS WITHOUT HIM ONCE THE LANGUAGE SCRAMBLERS WERE IN PLAY.
TRANSMITTING ARRIVAL COORDINATES...
HEY! HEY! I DON'T DO "SUBZERO" ANYMORE, ALL RIGHT?
I'M SERIOUS! GET ME OUT OF HERE BEFORE--
RELAX! GOT US ALL COVERED!
WE WON'T LET YOU GET HURT AGAIN, PLAS.
I PROMISE.
GOOD. YOU'RE HERE.
GIVEN THE SAFEGUARDS HE INCORPORATED, NOT EVEN SUPERMAN COULD HAVE TRACED ITS SIGNALS FAST ENOUGH TO MATTER.
I HAD TO INFILTRATE RA'S'S STRONGHOLD TO LOCATE THIS TOWER. I EVADED PURSUIT...

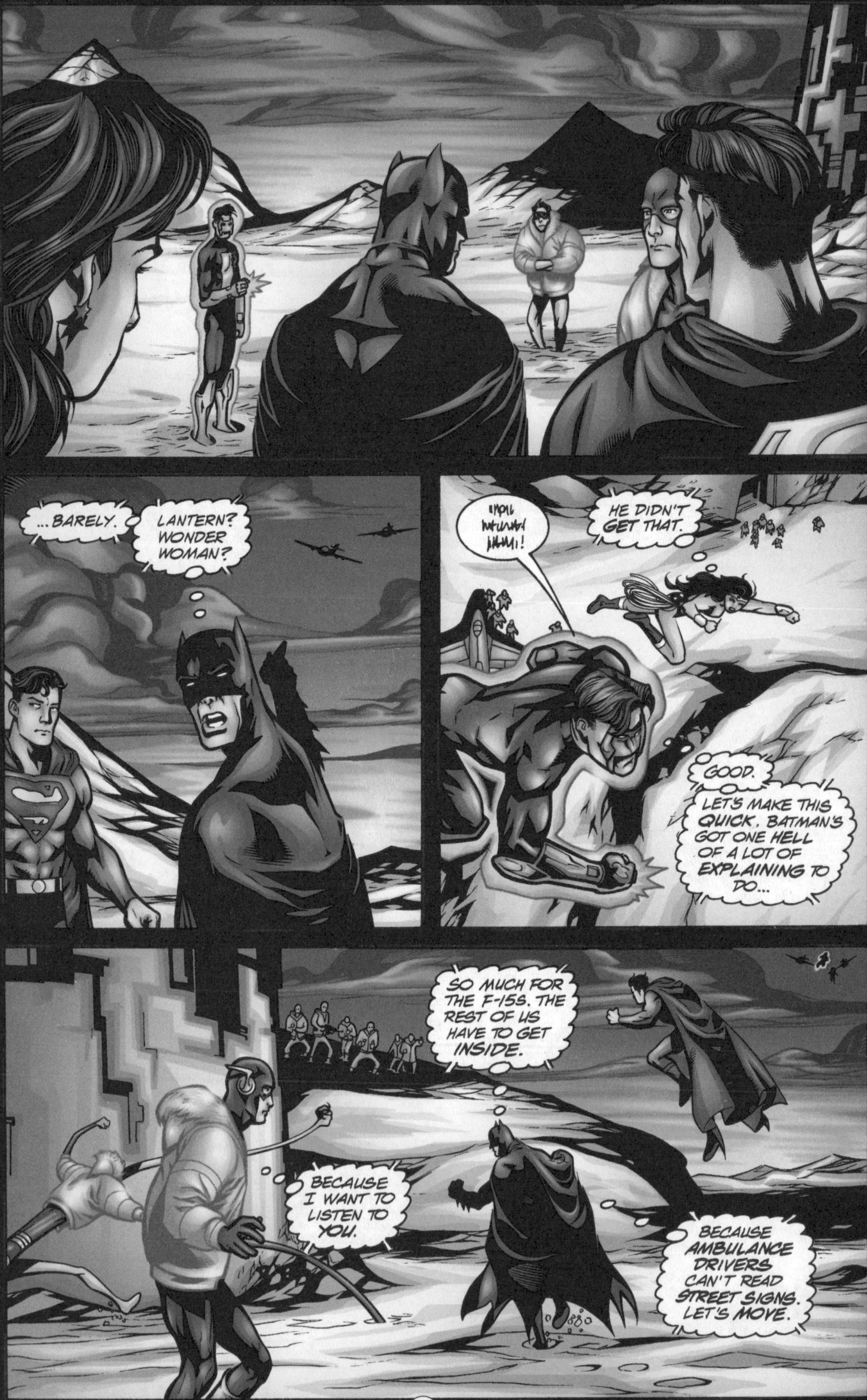
...BARELY.
LANTERN? WONDER WOMAN?
HE DIDN'T GET THAT.
GOOD.
LET'S MAKE THIS QUICK. BATMAN'S GOT ONE HELL OF A LOT OF EXPLAINING TO DO...
SO MUCH FOR THE F-15S. THE REST OF US HAVE TO GET INSIDE.
BECAUSE I WANT TO LISTEN TO YOU.
BECAUSE AMBULANCE DRIVERS CAN'T READ STREET SIGNS. LET'S MOVE.

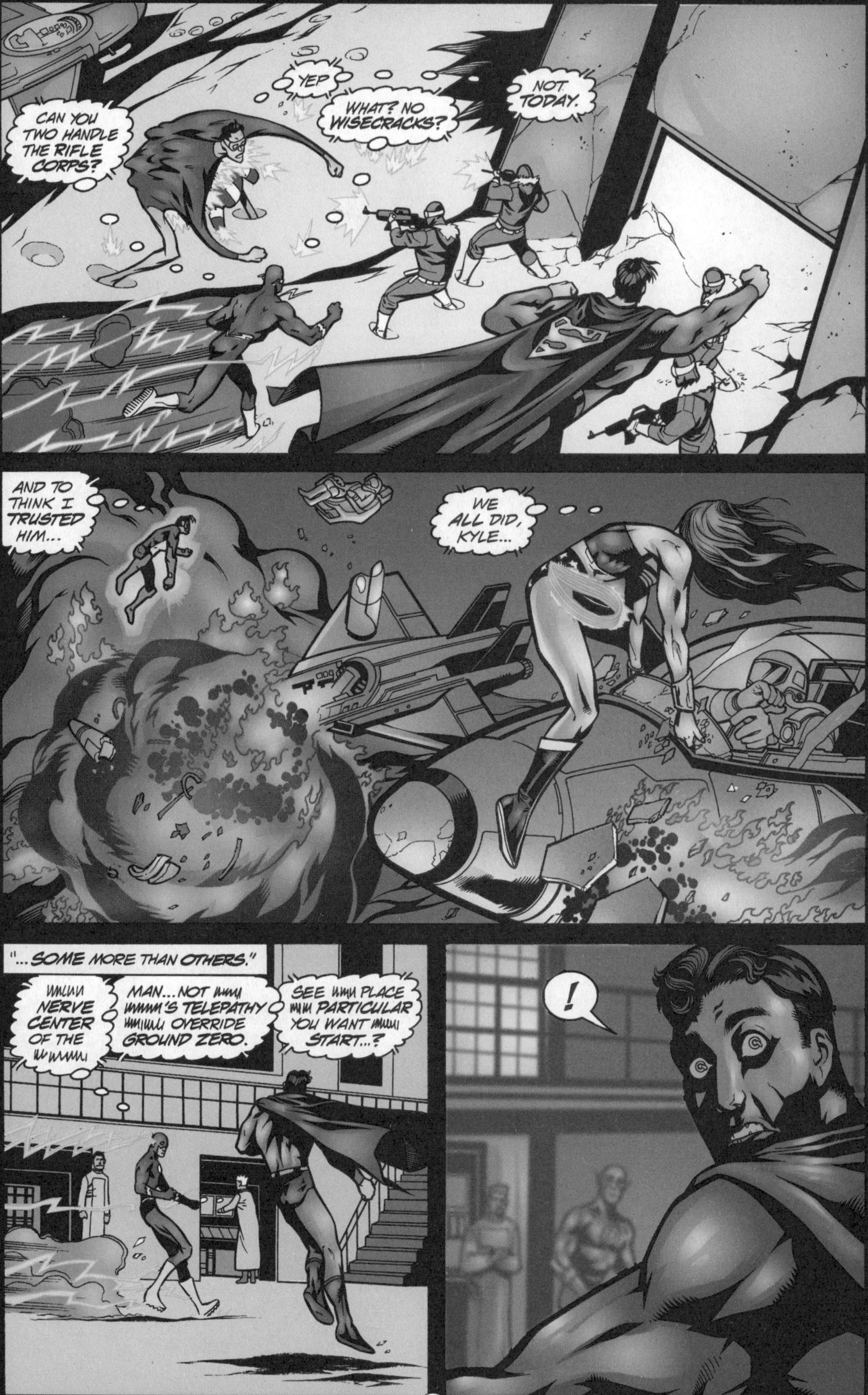

CAN YOU TWO HANDLE THE RIFLE CORPS?
YEP
WHAT? NO WISECRACKS?
NOT TODAY.
AND TO THINK I TRUSTED HIM...
WE ALL DID, KYLE...
"...SOME MORE THAN OTHERS."
NERVE CENTER OF THE
MAN... NOT 'S TELEPATHY OVERRIDE GROUND ZERO.
SEE PLACE PARTICULAR YOU WANT START...?
!

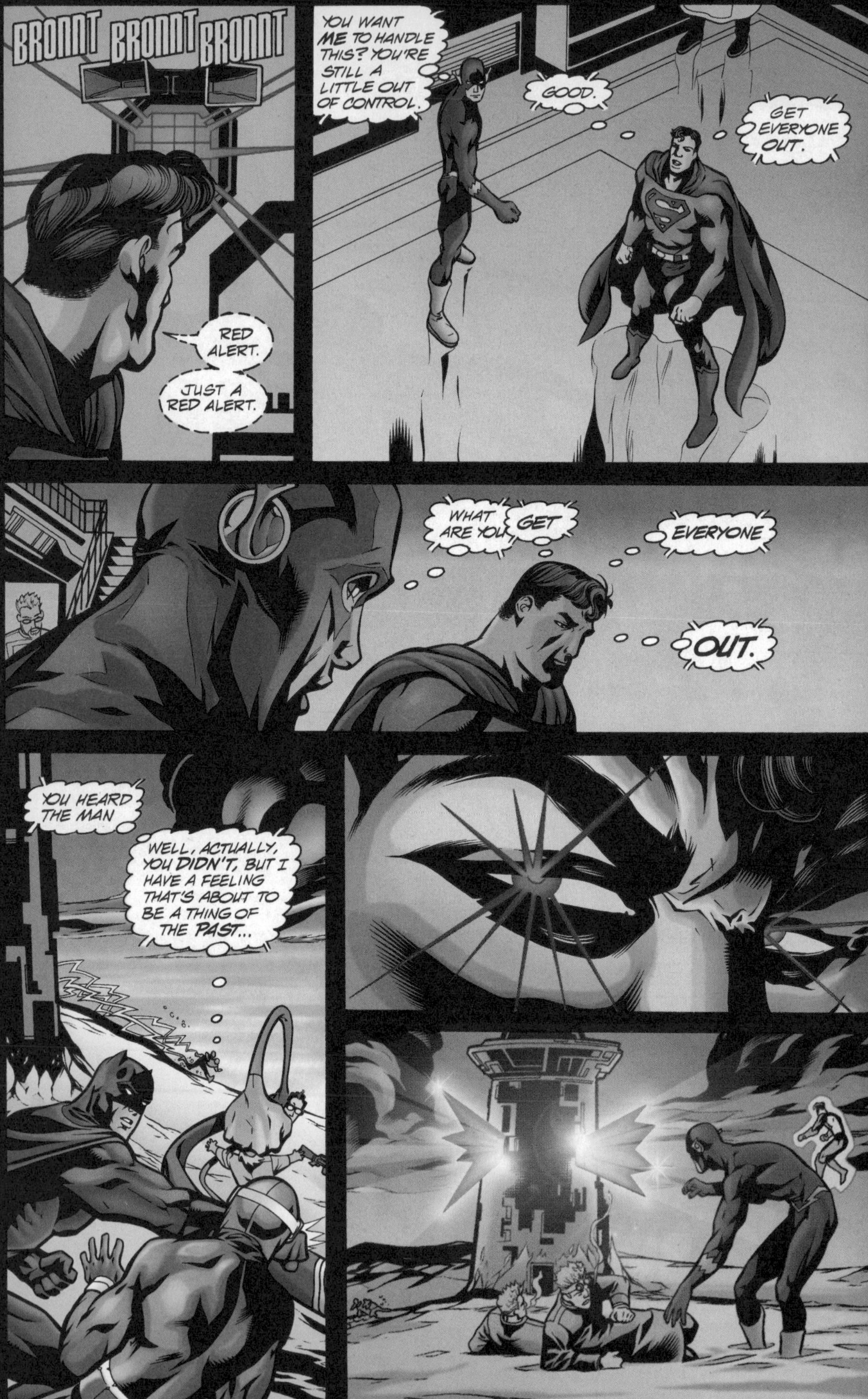
BRONNT BRONNT BRONNT
RED ALERT.
JUST A RED ALERT.
YOU WANT ME TO HANDLE THIS? YOU'RE STILL A LITTLE OUT OF CONTROL.
GOOD.
GET EVERYONE OUT.
WHAT ARE YOU
GET
EVERYONE
OUT.
YOU HEARD THE MAN
WELL, ACTUALLY, YOU DIDN'T, BUT I HAVE A FEELING THAT'S ABOUT TO BE A THING OF THE PAST...

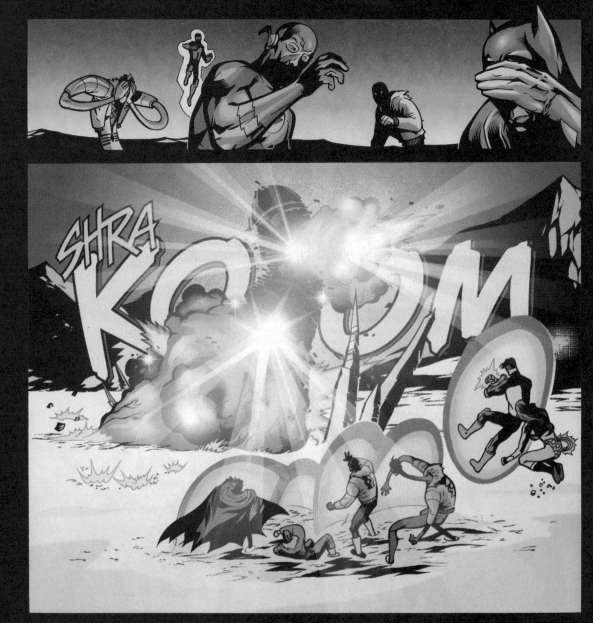

SHRA KOOM

SSSSSSS

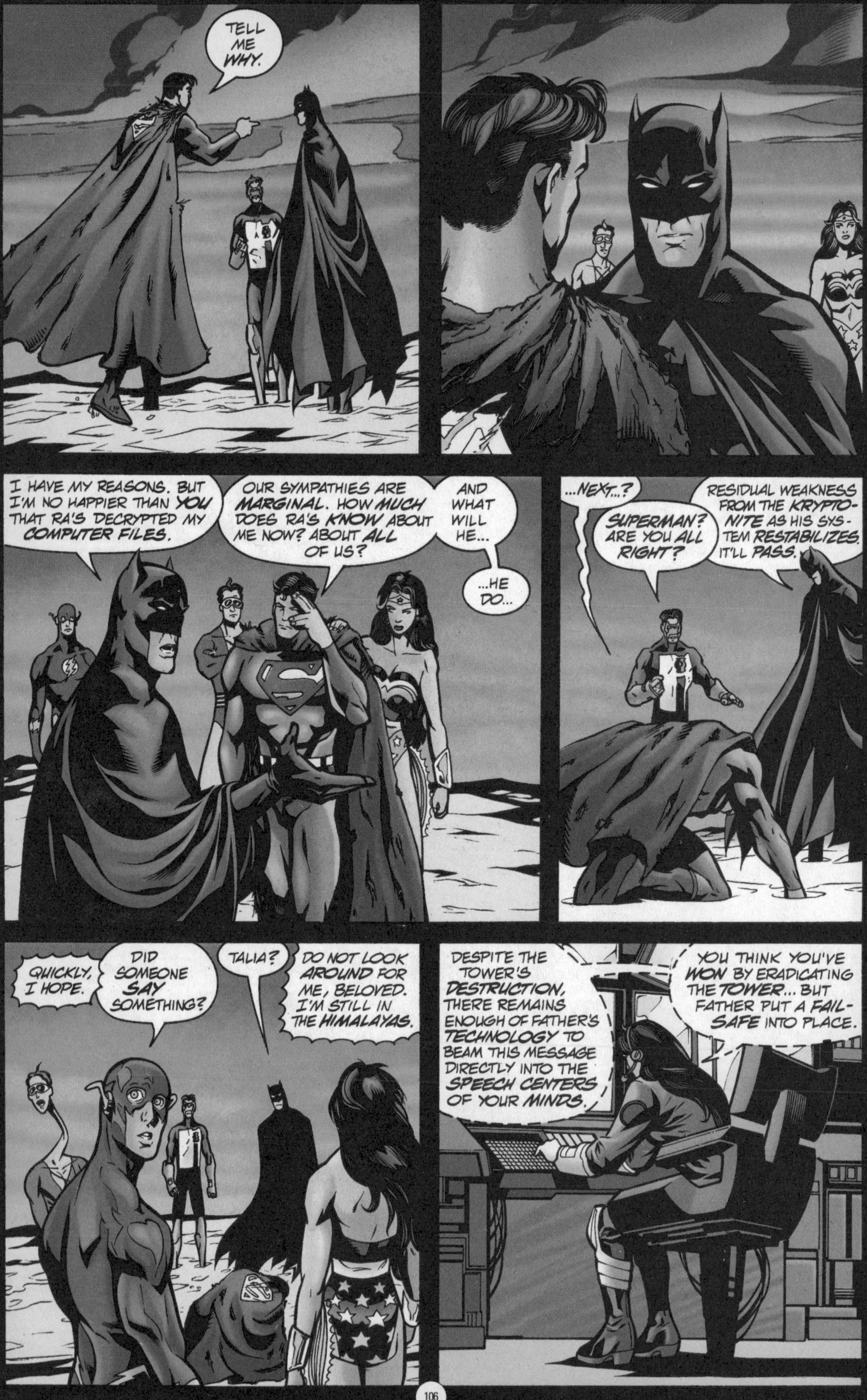
TELL ME WHY.
I HAVE MY REASONS. BUT I'M NO HAPPIER THAN YOU THAT RA'S DECRYPTED MY COMPUTER FILES.
OUR SYMPATHIES ARE MARGINAL. HOW MUCH DOES RA'S KNOW ABOUT ME NOW? ABOUT ALL OF US?
AND WHAT WILL HE...
...HE DO...
...NEXT...?
SUPERMAN? ARE YOU ALL RIGHT?
RESIDUAL WEAKNESS FROM THE KRYPTONITE AS HIS SYSTEM RESTABILIZES. IT'LL PASS.
QUICKLY, I HOPE.
DID SOMEONE SAY SOMETHING?
TALIA?
DO NOT LOOK AROUND FOR ME, BELOVED. I'M STILL IN THE HIMALAYAS.
DESPITE THE TOWER'S DESTRUCTION, THERE REMAINS ENOUGH OF FATHER'S TECHNOLOGY TO BEAM THIS MESSAGE DIRECTLY INTO THE SPEECH CENTERS OF YOUR MINDS.
YOU THINK YOU'VE WON BY ERADICATING THE TOWER... BUT FATHER PUT A FAIL-SAFE INTO PLACE.

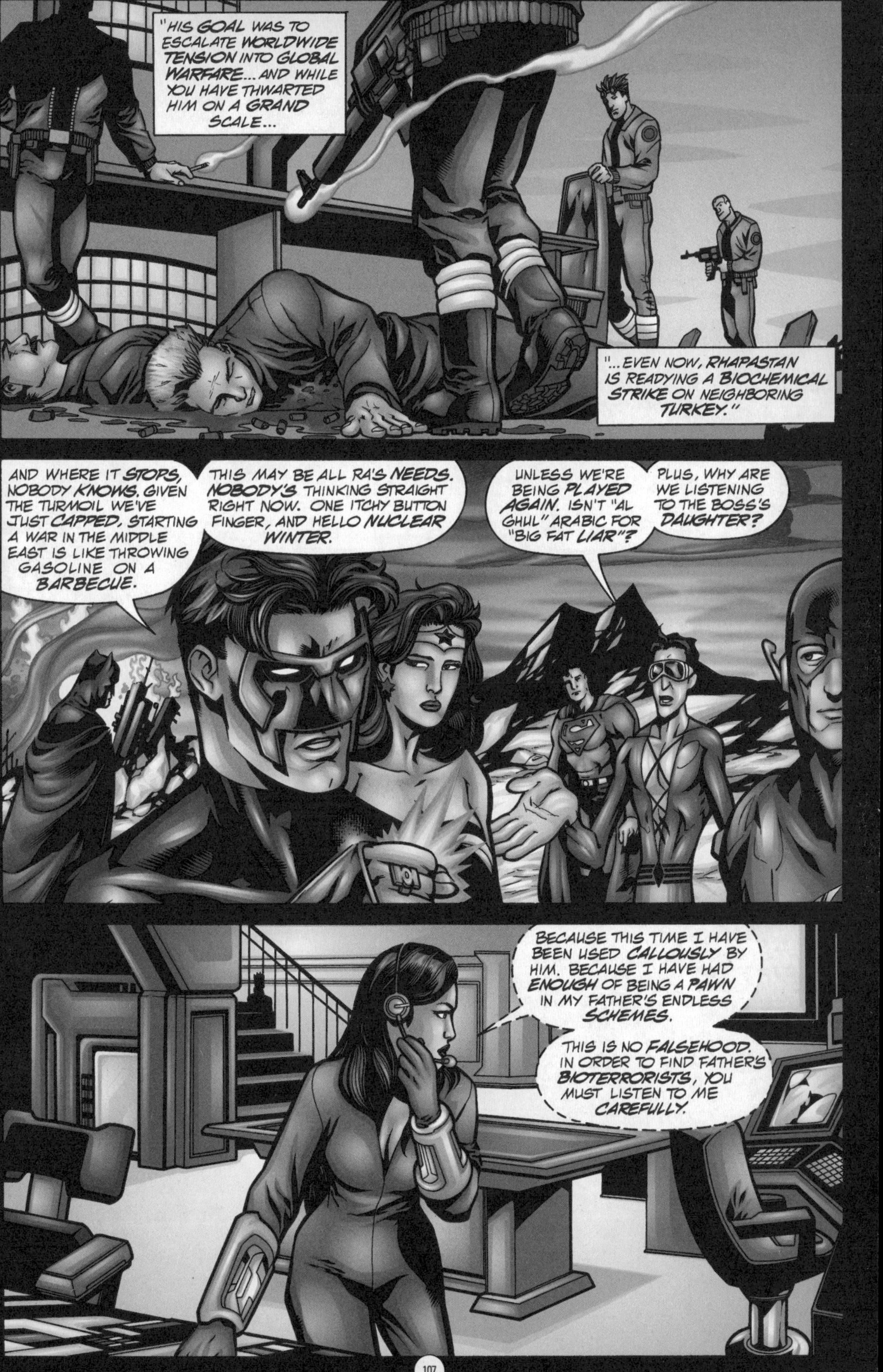
"HIS GOAL WAS TO ESCALATE WORLDWIDE TENSION INTO GLOBAL WARFARE... AND WHILE YOU HAVE THWARTED HIM ON A GRAND SCALE...
"...EVEN NOW, RHAPASTAN IS READYING A BIOCHEMICAL STRIKE ON NEIGHBORING TURKEY."
AND WHERE IT STOPS, NOBODY KNOWS. GIVEN THE TURMOIL WE'VE JUST CAPPED, STARTING A WAR IN THE MIDDLE EAST IS LIKE THROWING GASOLINE ON A BARBECUE.
THIS MAY BE ALL RA'S NEEDS. NOBODY'S THINKING STRAIGHT RIGHT NOW. ONE ITCHY BUTTON FINGER, AND HELLO NUCLEAR WINTER.
UNLESS WE'RE BEING PLAYED AGAIN. ISN'T "AL GHUL" ARABIC FOR "BIG FAT LIAR"?
PLUS, WHY ARE WE LISTENING TO THE BOSS'S DAUGHTER?
BECAUSE THIS TIME I HAVE BEEN USED CALLOUSLY BY HIM. BECAUSE I HAVE HAD ENOUGH OF BEING A PAWN IN MY FATHER'S ENDLESS SCHEMES.
THIS IS NO FALSEHOOD. IN ORDER TO FIND FATHER'S BIOTERRORISTS, YOU MUST LISTEN TO ME CAREFULLY.

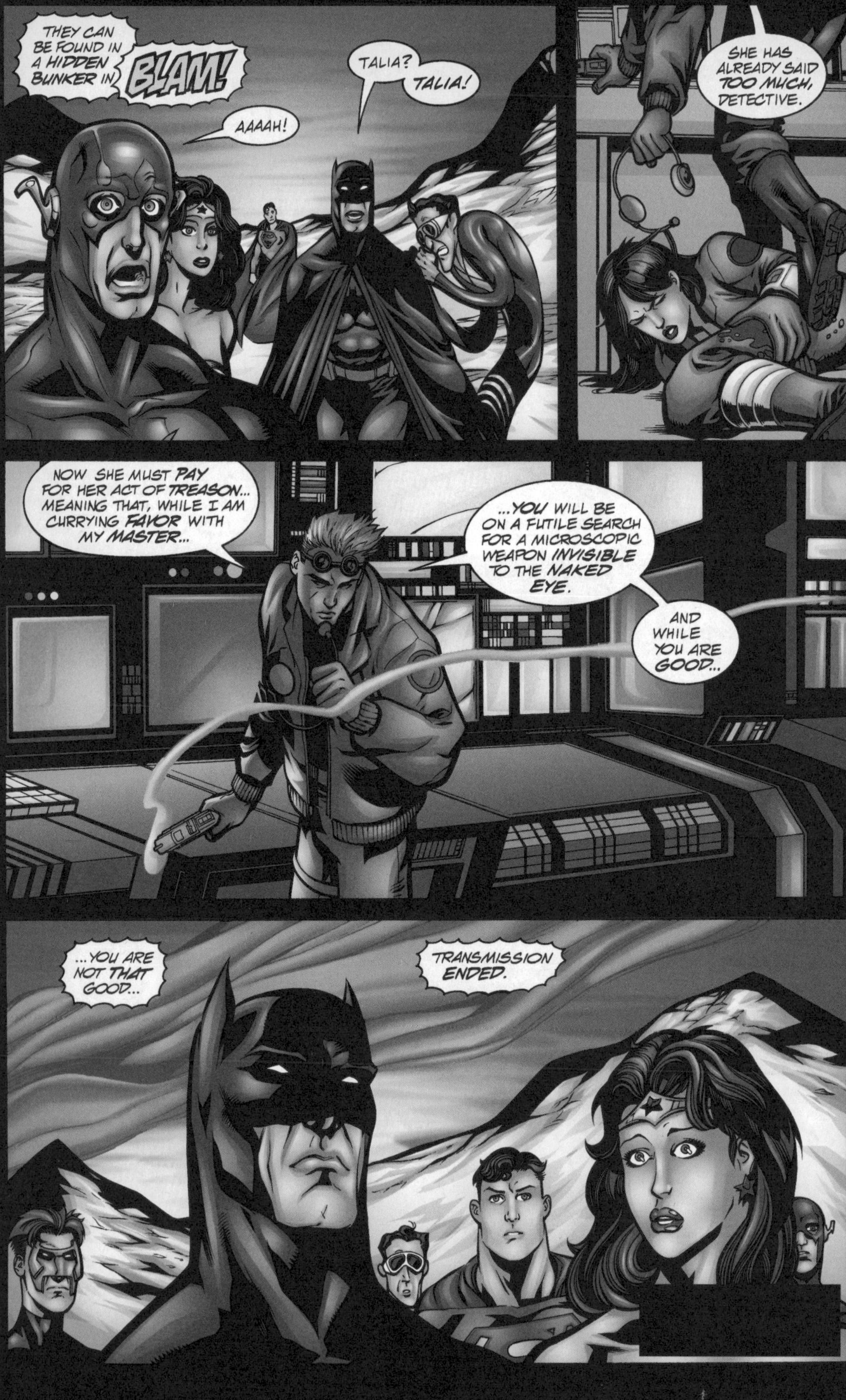
THEY CAN BE FOUND IN A HIDDEN BUNKER IN
BLAM!
AAAAH!
TALIA?
TALIA!
SHE HAS ALREADY SAID TOO MUCH, DETECTIVE.
NOW SHE MUST PAY FOR HER ACT OF TREASON... MEANING THAT, WHILE I AM CURRYING FAVOR WITH MY MASTER...
...YOU WILL BE ON A FUTILE SEARCH FOR A MICROSCOPIC WEAPON INVISIBLE TO THE NAKED EYE.
AND WHILE YOU ARE GOOD...
...YOU ARE NOT THAT GOOD...
TRANSMISSION ENDED.

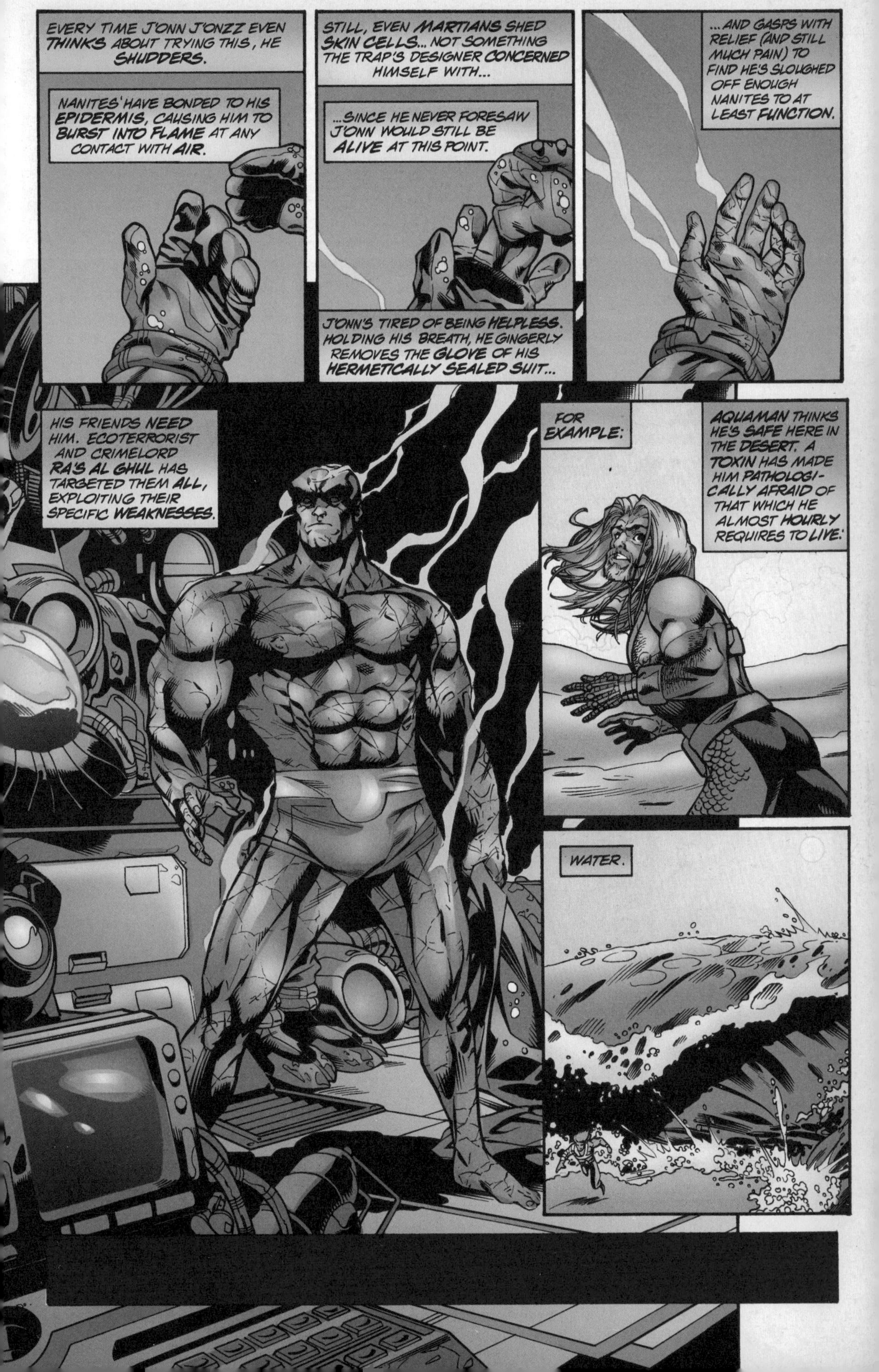
EVERY TIME J'ONN J'ONZZ EVEN THINKS ABOUT TRYING THIS, HE SHUDDERS.
NANITES' HAVE BONDED TO HIS EPIDERMIS, CAUSING HIM TO BURST INTO FLAME AT ANY CONTACT WITH AIR.
STILL, EVEN MARTIANS SHED SKIN CELLS... NOT SOMETHING THE TRAP'S DESIGNER CONCERNED HIMSELF WITH...
...SINCE HE NEVER FORESAW J'ONN WOULD STILL BE ALIVE AT THIS POINT.
J'ONN'S TIRED OF BEING HELPLESS. HOLDING HIS BREATH, HE GINGERLY REMOVES THE GLOVE OF HIS HERMETICALLY SEALED SUIT...
...AND GASPS WITH RELIEF (AND STILL MUCH PAIN) TO FIND HE'S SLOUGHED OFF ENOUGH NANITES TO AT LEAST FUNCTION.
HIS FRIENDS NEED HIM. ECOTERRORIST AND CRIMELORD RA'S AL GHUL HAS TARGETED THEM ALL, EXPLOITING THEIR SPECIFIC WEAKNESSES.
FOR EXAMPLE:
AQUAMAN THINKS HE'S SAFE HERE IN THE DESERT. A TOXIN HAS MADE HIM PATHOLOGI-CALLY AFRAID OF THAT WHICH HE ALMOST HOURLY REQUIRES TO LIVE:
WATER.

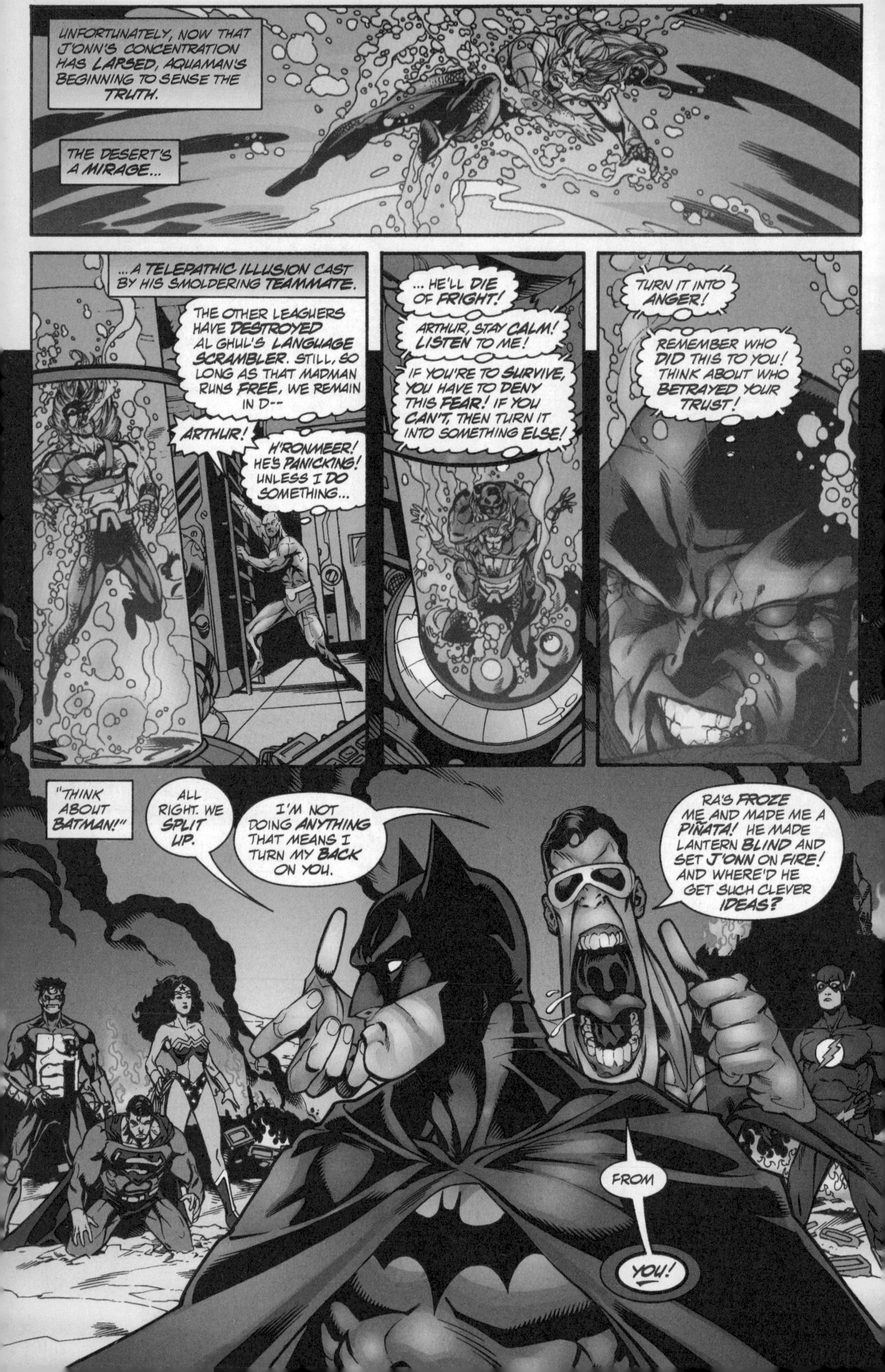

UNFORTUNATELY, NOW THAT J'ONN'S CONCENTRATION HAS LAPSED, AQUAMAN'S BEGINNING TO SENSE THE TRUTH.
THE DESERT'S A MIRAGE...
...A TELEPATHIC ILLUSION CAST BY HIS SMOLDERING TEAMMATE.
THE OTHER LEAGUERS HAVE DESTROYED AL GHUL'S LANGUAGE SCRAMBLER. STILL, SO LONG AS THAT MADMAN RUNS FREE, WE REMAIN IN D--
ARTHUR!
H'RONMEER! HE'S PANICKING! UNLESS I DO SOMETHING...
...HE'LL DIE OF FRIGHT!
ARTHUR, STAY CALM! LISTEN TO ME!
IF YOU'RE TO SURVIVE, YOU HAVE TO DENY THIS FEAR! IF YOU CAN'T, THEN TURN IT INTO SOMETHING ELSE!
TURN IT INTO ANGER!
REMEMBER WHO DID THIS TO YOU! THINK ABOUT WHO BETRAYED YOUR TRUST!
"THINK ABOUT BATMAN!"
ALL RIGHT. WE SPLIT UP.
I'M NOT DOING ANYTHING THAT MEANS I TURN MY BACK ON YOU.
RA'S FROZE ME AND MADE ME A PIÑATA! HE MADE LANTERN BLIND AND SET J'ONN ON FIRE! AND WHERE'D HE GET SUCH CLEVER IDEAS?
FROM
YOU!

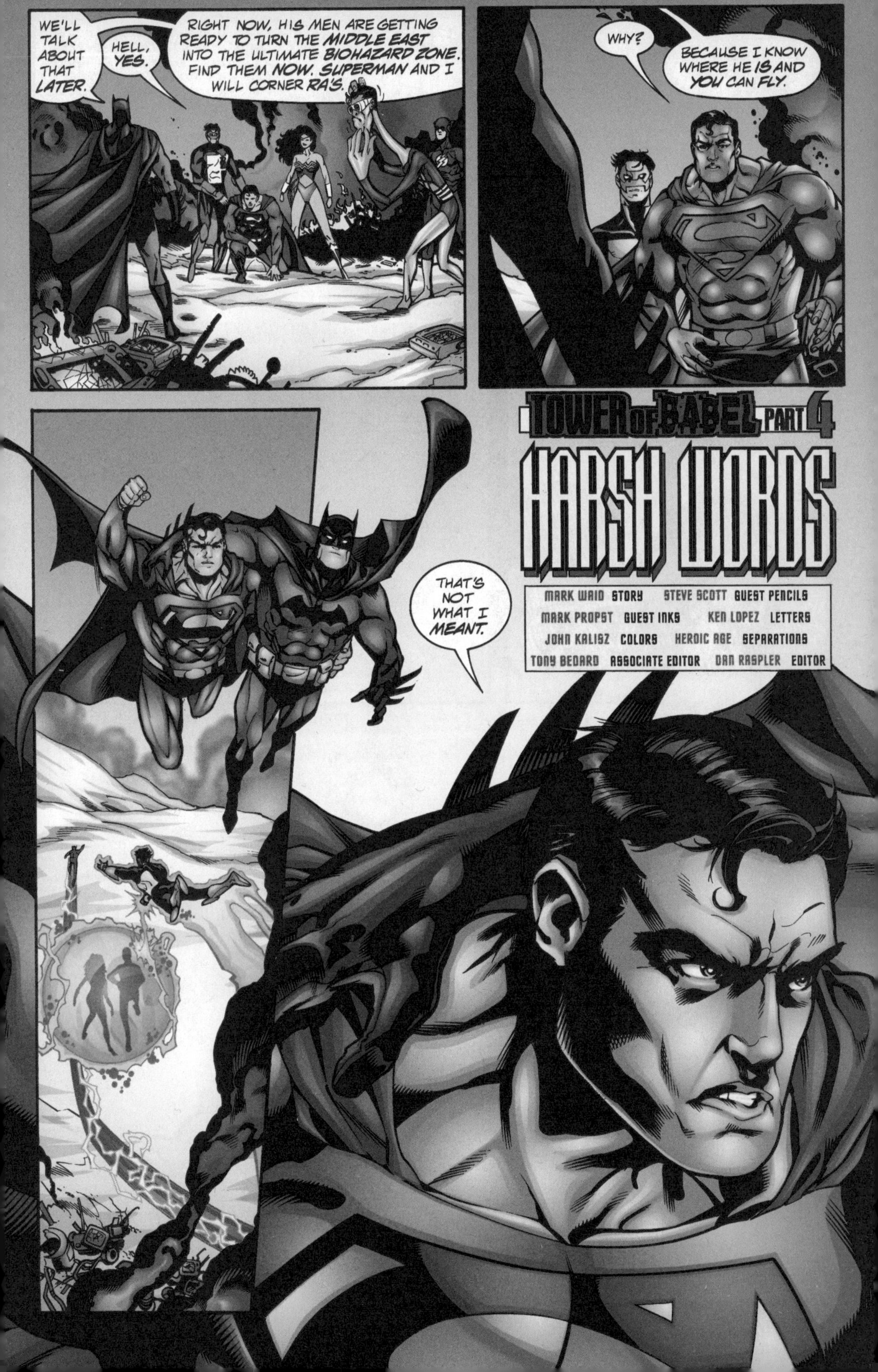
WE'LL TALK ABOUT THAT LATER.
HELL, YES.
RIGHT NOW, HIS MEN ARE GETTING READY TO TURN THE MIDDLE EAST INTO THE ULTIMATE BIOHAZARD ZONE. FIND THEM NOW. SUPERMAN AND I WILL CORNER RA'S.
WHY?
BECAUSE I KNOW WHERE HE IS AND YOU CAN FLY.
TOWER OF BABEL PART 4
HARSH WORDS
MARK WAID STORY STEVE SCOTT GUEST PENCILS
MARK PROPST GUEST INKS KEN LOPEZ LETTERS
JOHN KALISZ COLORS HEROIC AGE SEPARATIONS
TONY BEDARD ASSOCIATE EDITOR DAN RASPLER EDITOR
THAT'S NOT WHAT I MEANT.

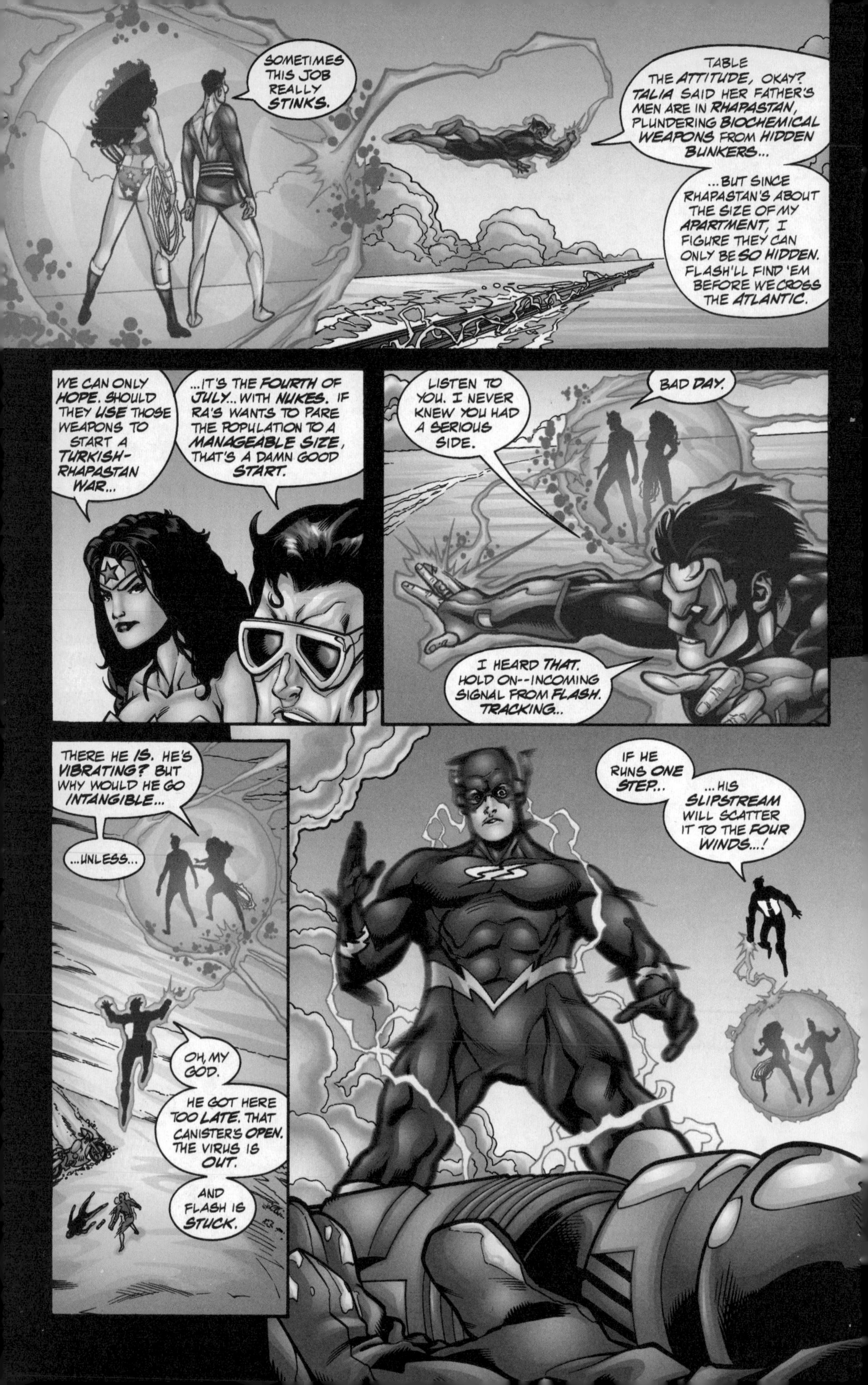
SOMETIMES THIS JOB REALLY STINKS.
TABLE THE ATTITUDE, OKAY? TALIA SAID HER FATHER'S MEN ARE IN RHAPASTAN, PLUNDERING BIOCHEMICAL WEAPONS FROM HIDDEN BUNKERS...
...BUT SINCE RHAPASTAN'S ABOUT THE SIZE OF MY APARTMENT, I FIGURE THEY CAN ONLY BE SO HIDDEN. FLASH'LL FIND 'EM BEFORE WE CROSS THE ATLANTIC.
WE CAN ONLY HOPE. SHOULD THEY USE THOSE WEAPONS TO START A TURKISH-RHAPASTAN WAR...
...IT'S THE FOURTH OF JULY... WITH NUKES. IF RA'S WANTS TO PARE THE POPULATION TO A MANAGEABLE SIZE, THAT'S A DAMN GOOD START.
LISTEN TO YOU. I NEVER KNEW YOU HAD A SERIOUS SIDE.
BAD DAY.
I HEARD THAT. HOLD ON--INCOMING SIGNAL FROM FLASH. TRACKING...
THERE HE IS. HE'S VIBRATING? BUT WHY WOULD HE GO INTANGIBLE...
...UNLESS...
OH, MY GOD.
HE GOT HERE TOO LATE. THAT CANISTER'S OPEN. THE VIRUS IS OUT.
AND FLASH IS STUCK.
IF HE RUNS ONE STEP...
...HIS SLIPSTREAM WILL SCATTER IT TO THE FOUR WINDS...!

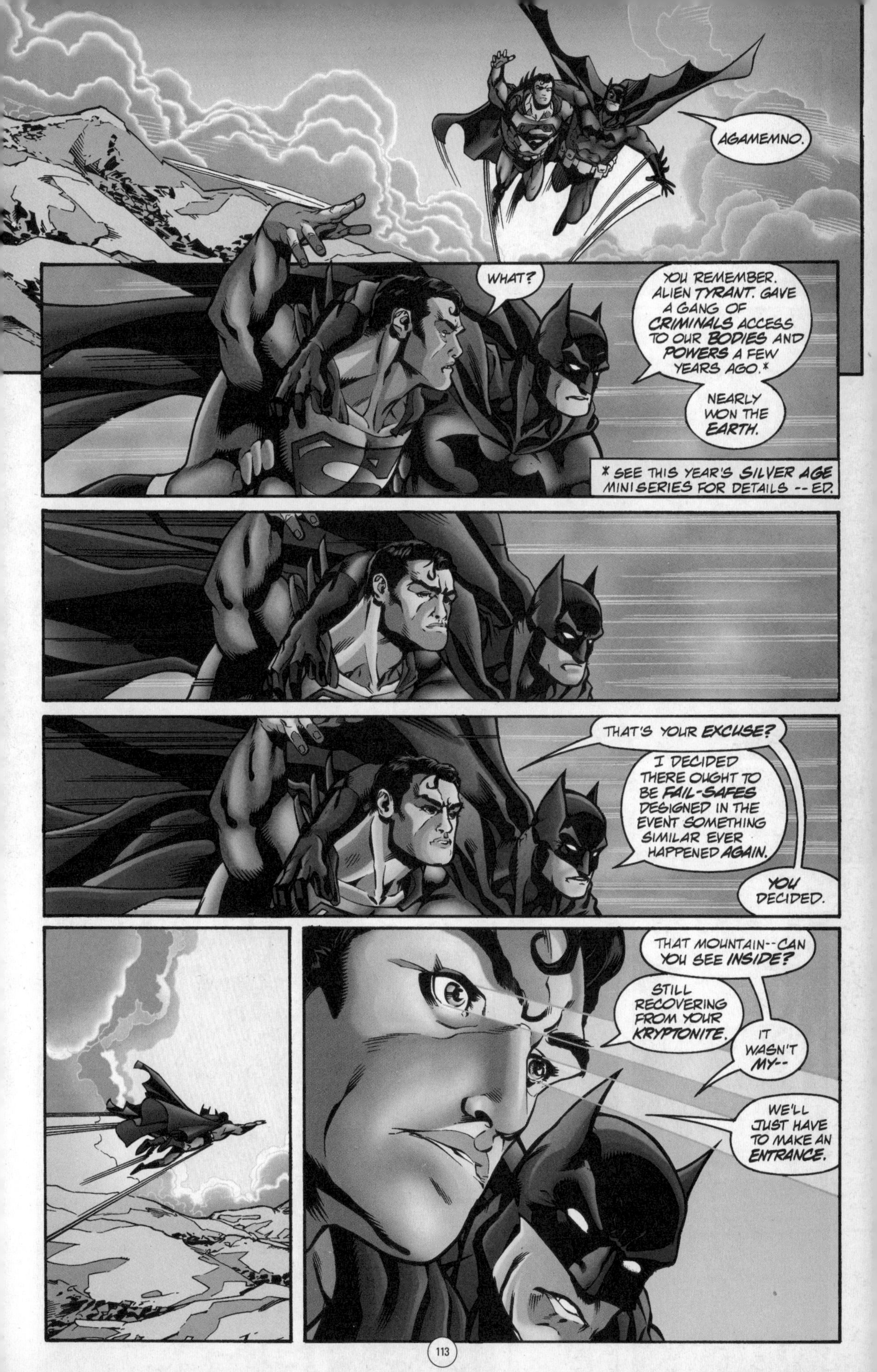
AGAMEMNO.
WHAT?
YOU REMEMBER. ALIEN TYRANT. GAVE A GANG OF CRIMINALS ACCESS TO OUR BODIES AND POWERS A FEW YEARS AGO.*
NEARLY WON THE EARTH.
* SEE THIS YEAR'S SILVER AGE MINI SERIES FOR DETAILS -- ED.
THAT'S YOUR EXCUSE?
I DECIDED THERE OUGHT TO BE FAIL-SAFES DESIGNED IN THE EVENT SOMETHING SIMILAR EVER HAPPENED AGAIN.
YOU DECIDED.
THAT MOUNTAIN--CAN YOU SEE INSIDE?
STILL RECOVERING FROM YOUR KRYPTONITE.
IT WASN'T MY--
WE'LL JUST HAVE TO MAKE AN ENTRANCE.

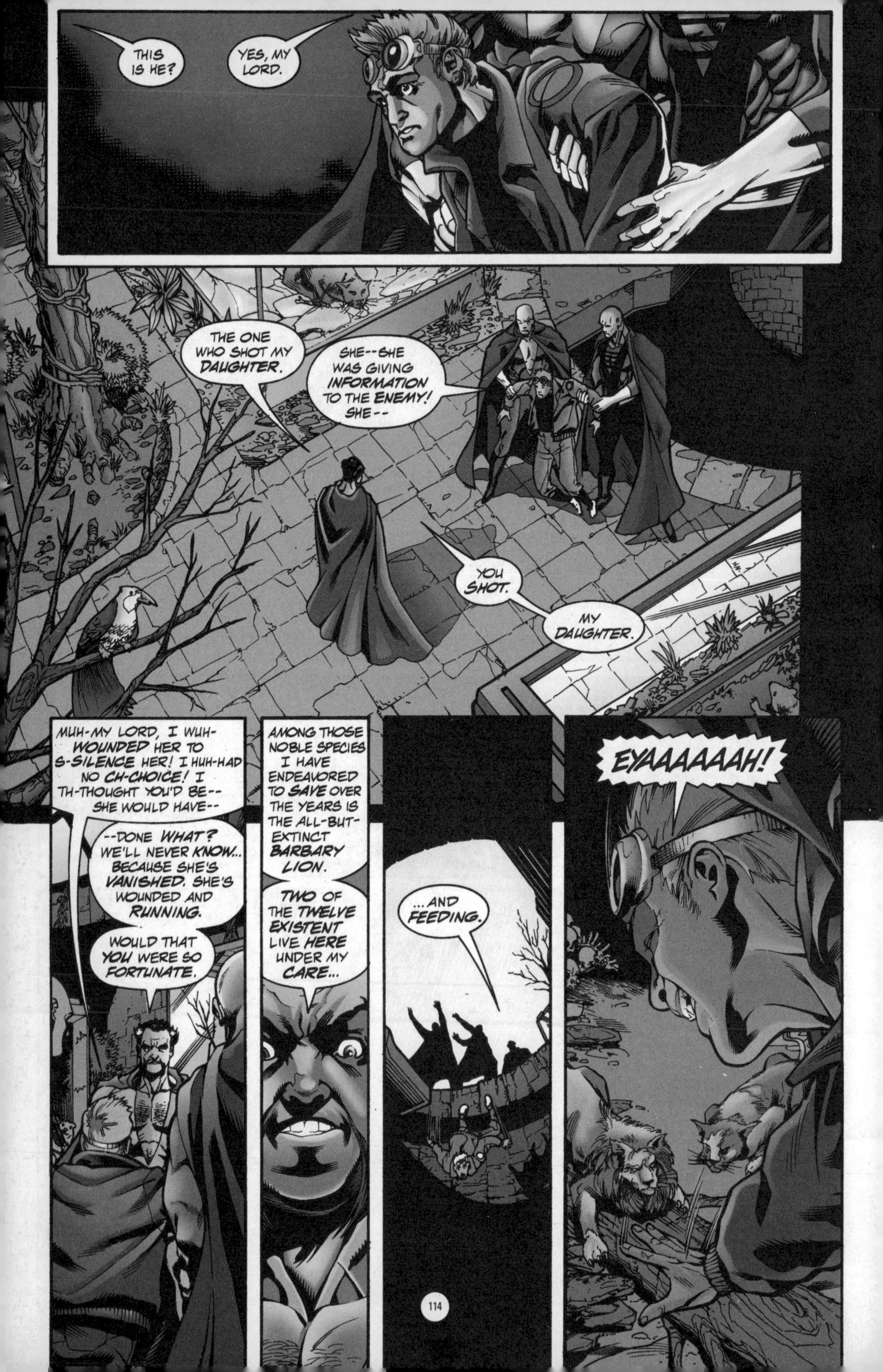
THIS IS HE?
YES, MY LORD.
THE ONE WHO SHOT MY DAUGHTER.
SHE--SHE WAS GIVING INFORMATION TO THE ENEMY! SHE--
YOU SHOT.
MY DAUGHTER.
MUH-MY LORD, I WUH-WOUNDED HER TO S-SILENCE HER! I HUH-HAD NO CH-CHOICE! I TH-THOUGHT YOU'D BE-- SHE WOULD HAVE--
--DONE WHAT? WE'LL NEVER KNOW... BECAUSE SHE'S VANISHED. SHE'S WOUNDED AND RUNNING.
WOULD THAT YOU WERE SO FORTUNATE.
AMONG THOSE NOBLE SPECIES I HAVE ENDEAVORED TO SAVE OVER THE YEARS IS THE ALL-BUT-EXTINCT BARBARY LION.
TWO OF THE TWELVE EXISTENT LIVE HERE UNDER MY CARE...
...AND FEEDING.
EYAAAAAAH!

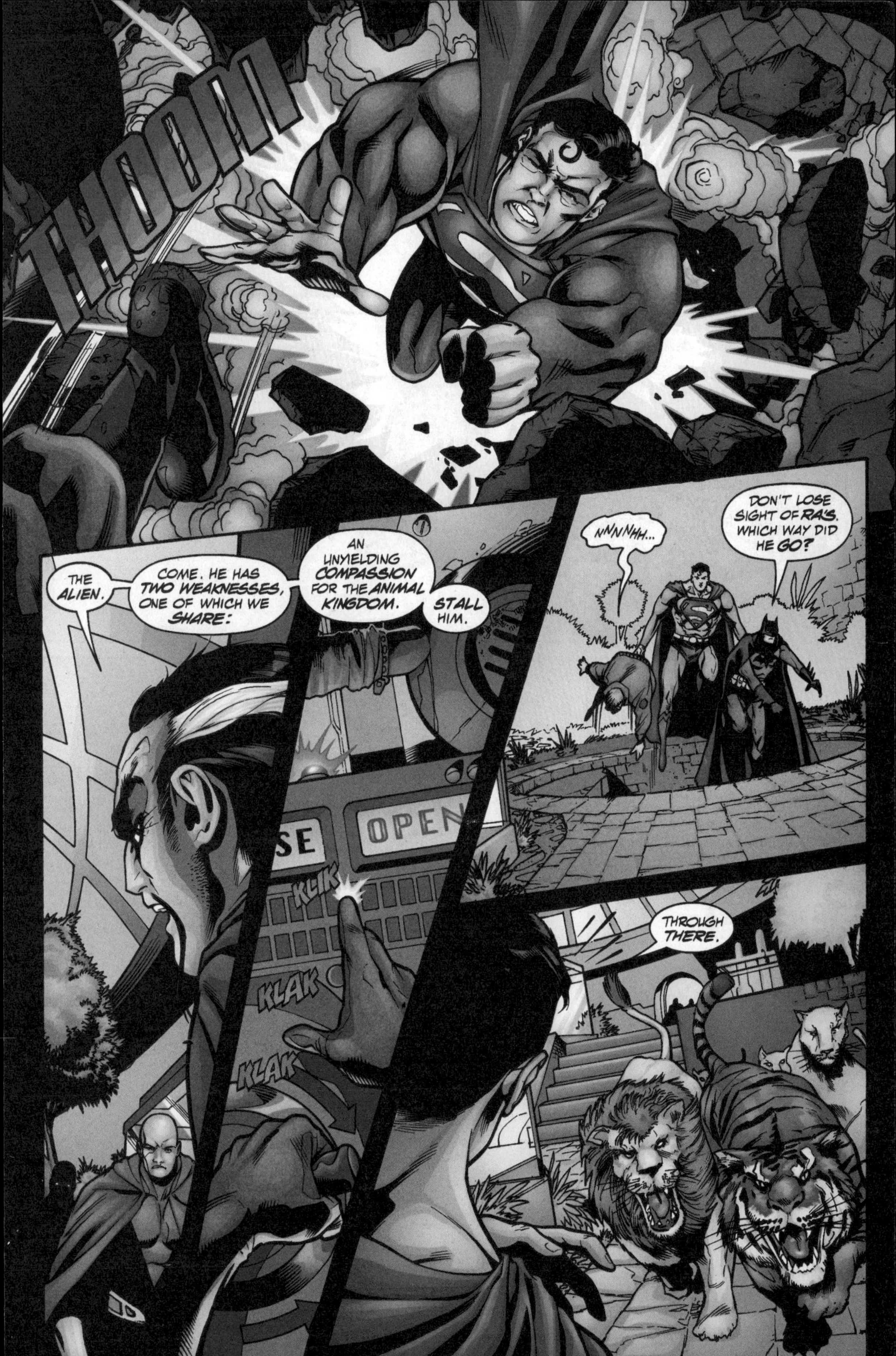
THOOM
THE ALIEN.
COME. HE HAS TWO WEAKNESSES, ONE OF WHICH WE SHARE:
AN UNYIELDING COMPASSION FOR THE ANIMAL KINGDOM.
STALL HIM.
SE
OPEN
KLIK
KLAK
KLAK
NNNNHH...
DON'T LOSE SIGHT OF RA'S. WHICH WAY DID HE GO?
THROUGH THERE.

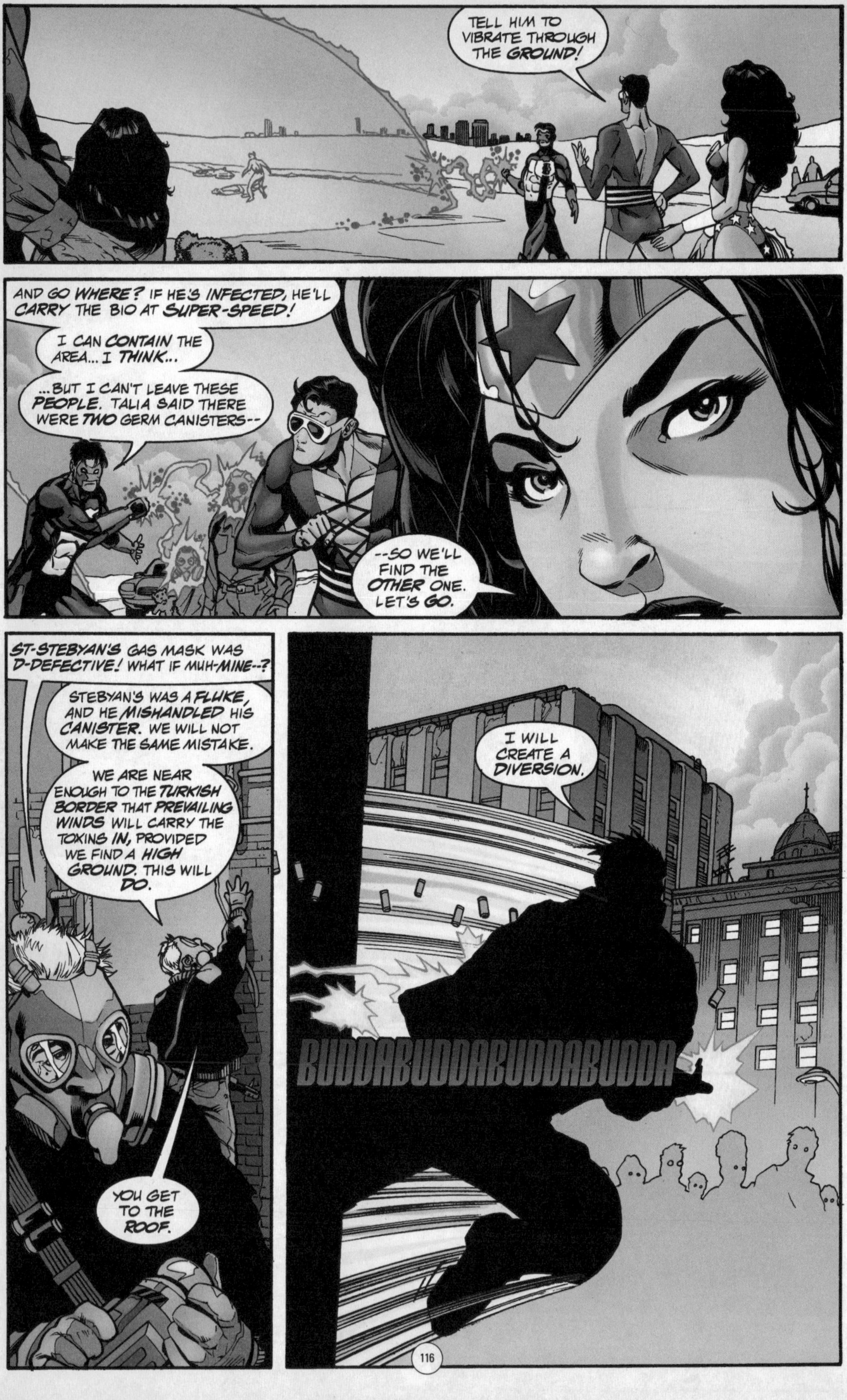

TELL HIM TO VIBRATE THROUGH THE GROUND!
AND GO WHERE? IF HE'S INFECTED, HE'LL CARRY THE BIO AT SUPER-SPEED!
I CAN CONTAIN THE AREA... I THINK...
...BUT I CAN'T LEAVE THESE PEOPLE. TALIA SAID THERE WERE TWO GERM CANISTERS--
--SO WE'LL FIND THE OTHER ONE. LET'S GO.
ST-STEBYAN'S GAS MASK WAS D-DEFECTIVE! WHAT IF MUH-MINE--?
STEBYAN'S WAS A FLUKE, AND HE MISHANDLED HIS CANISTER. WE WILL NOT MAKE THE SAME MISTAKE.
WE ARE NEAR ENOUGH TO THE TURKISH BORDER THAT PREVAILING WINDS WILL CARRY THE TOXINS IN, PROVIDED WE FIND A HIGH GROUND. THIS WILL DO.
YOU GET TO THE ROOF.
I WILL CREATE A DIVERSION.
BUDDABUDDABUDDABUDDA

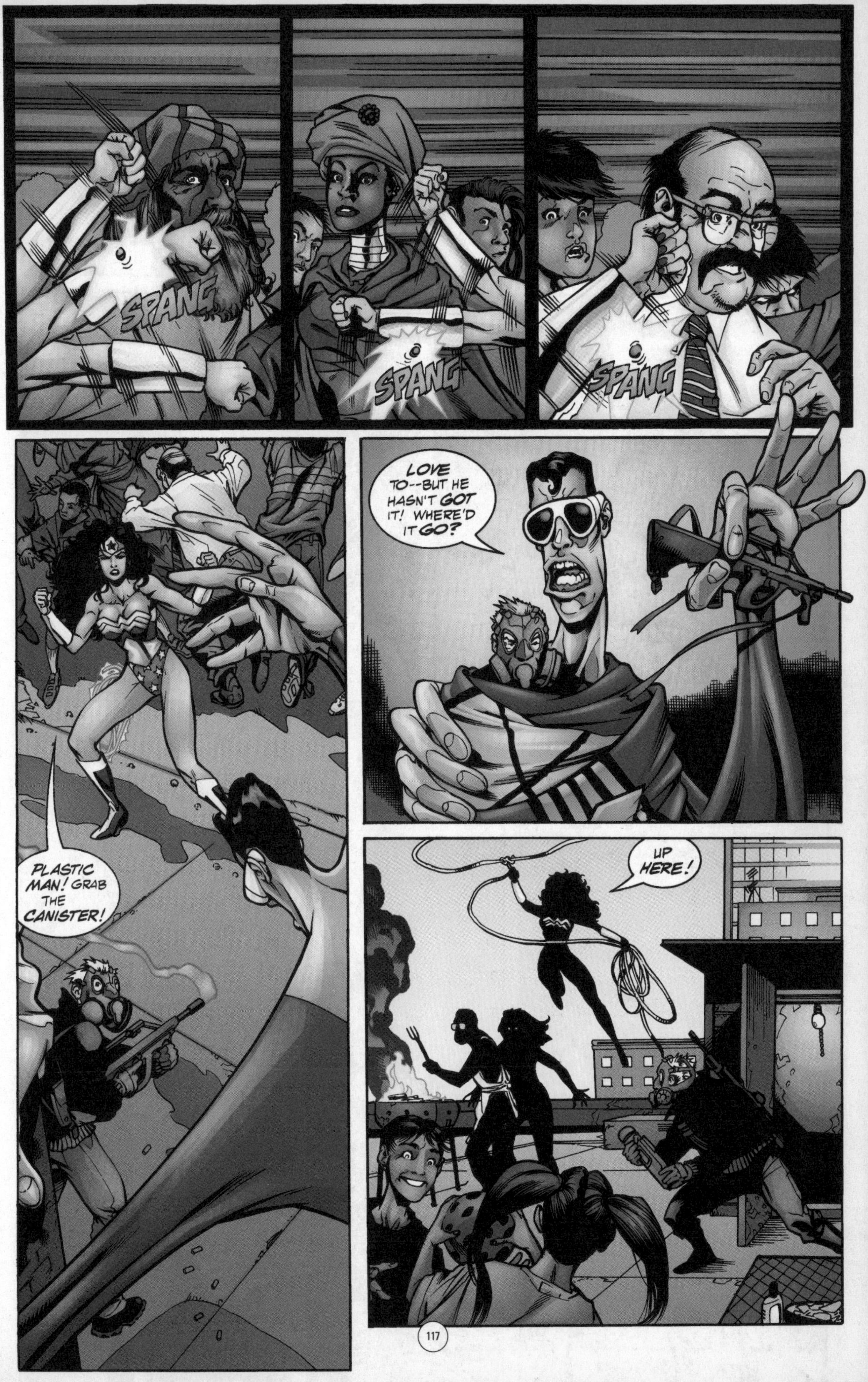
SPANG
SPANG
SPANG
PLASTIC MAN! GRAB THE CANISTER!
LOVE TO--BUT HE HASN'T GOT IT! WHERE'D IT GO?
UP HERE!

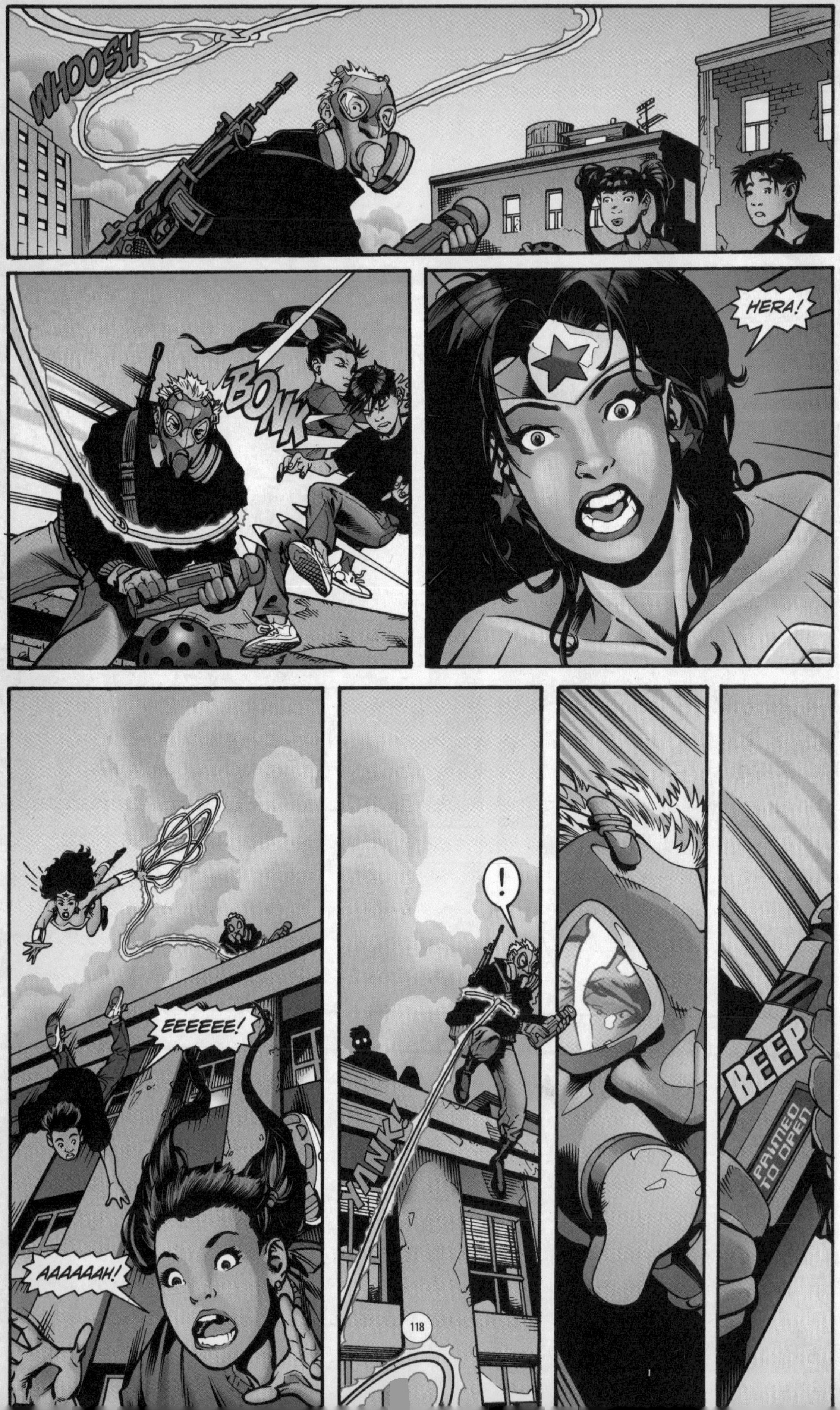
WHOOSH
BONK
HERA!
EEEEEE!
AAAAAAH!
!
YANK
BEEP
ARMED TO OPEN

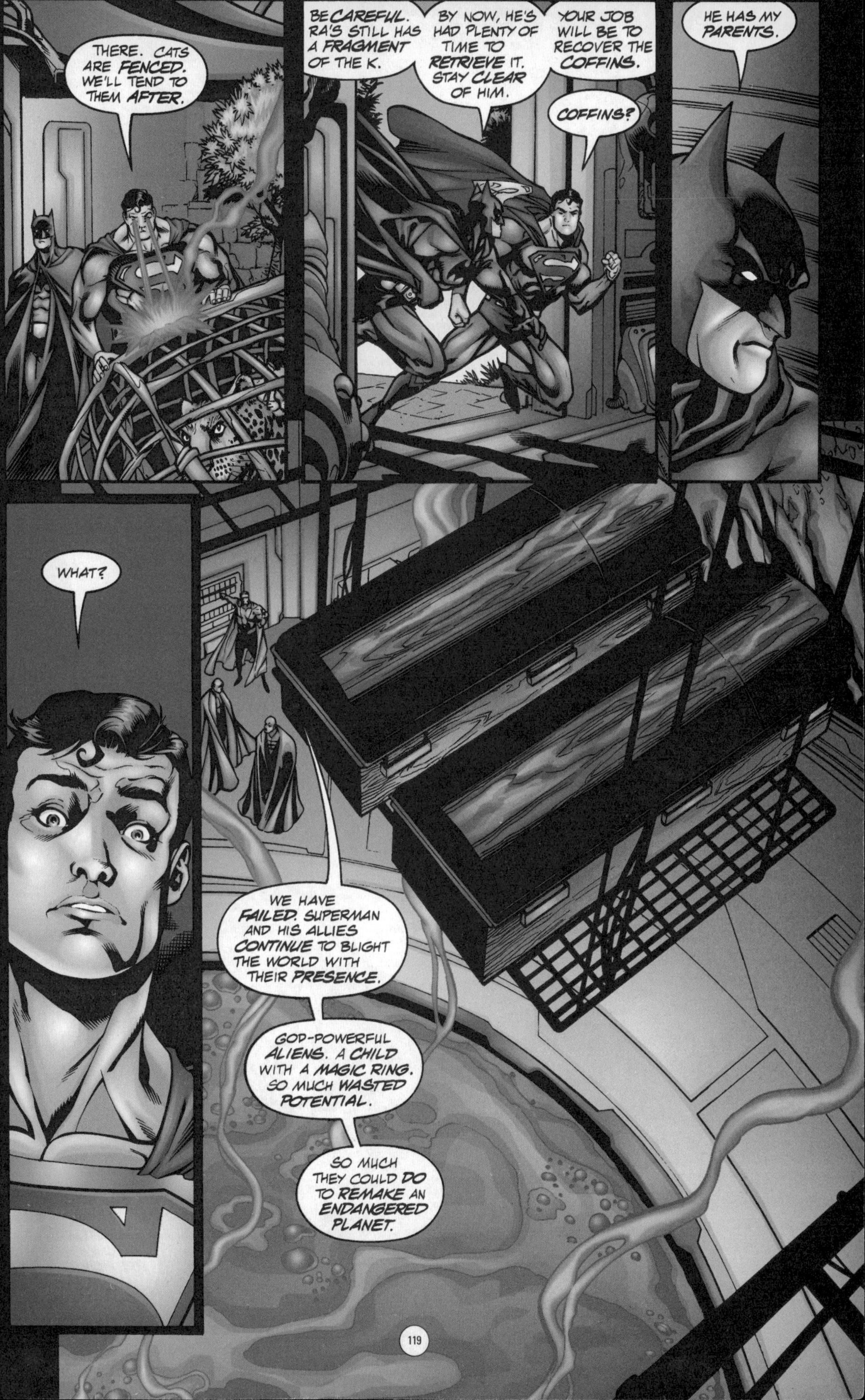

THERE. CATS ARE FENCED. WE'LL TEND TO THEM AFTER.
BE CAREFUL. RA'S STILL HAS A FRAGMENT OF THE K.
BY NOW, HE'S HAD PLENTY OF TIME TO RETRIEVE IT. STAY CLEAR OF HIM.
YOUR JOB WILL BE TO RECOVER THE COFFINS.
COFFINS?
HE HAS MY PARENTS.
WHAT?
WE HAVE FAILED. SUPERMAN AND HIS ALLIES CONTINUE TO BLIGHT THE WORLD WITH THEIR PRESENCE.
GOD-POWERFUL ALIENS. A CHILD WITH A MAGIC RING. SO MUCH WASTED POTENTIAL.
SO MUCH THEY COULD DO TO REMAKE AN ENDANGERED PLANET.

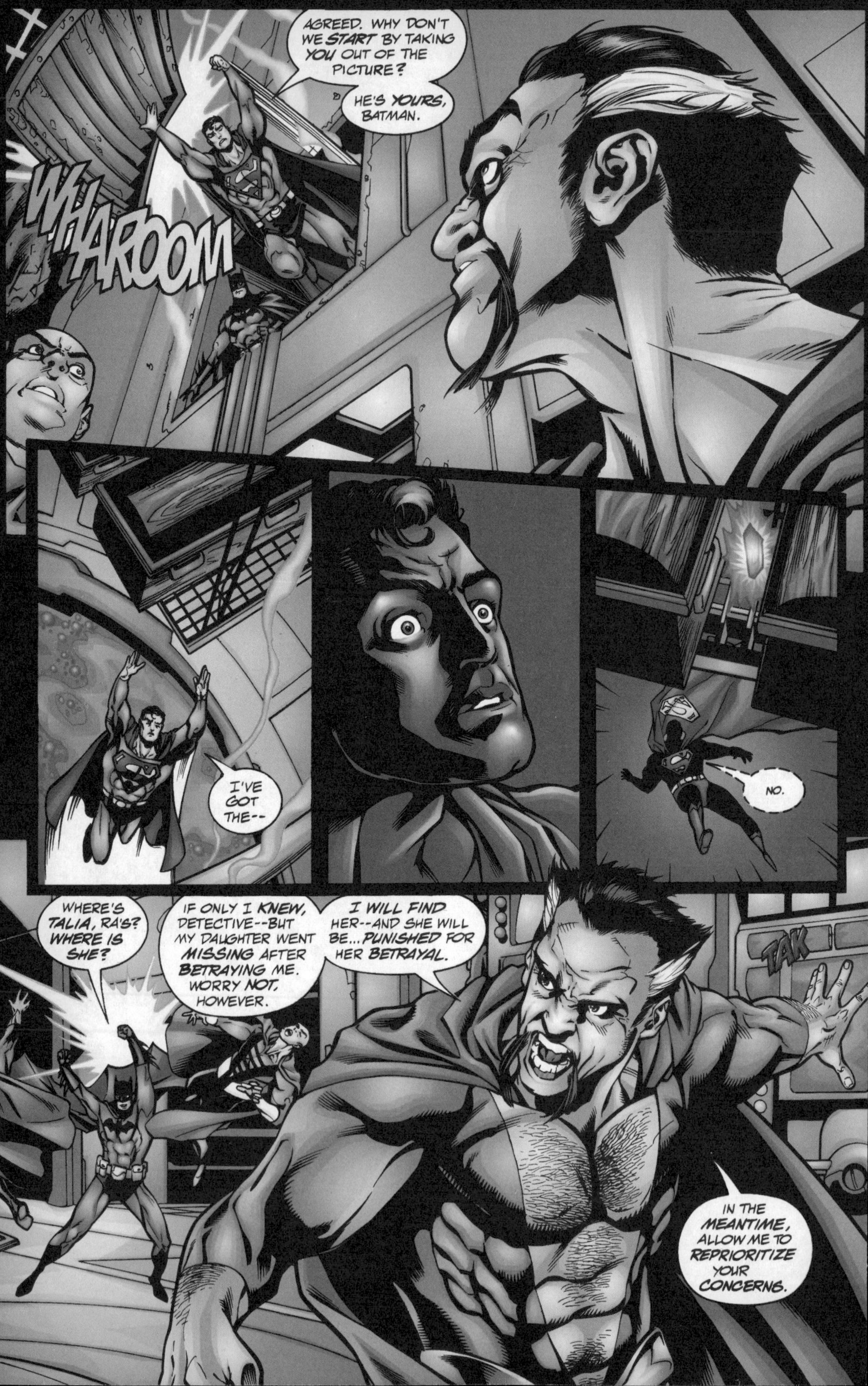
AGREED. WHY DON'T WE START BY TAKING YOU OUT OF THE PICTURE?
HE'S YOURS, BATMAN.
WHAROOM
I'VE GOT THE--
NO.
WHERE'S TALIA, RA'S? WHERE IS SHE?
IF ONLY I KNEW, DETECTIVE--BUT MY DAUGHTER WENT MISSING AFTER BETRAYING ME. WORRY NOT, HOWEVER.
I WILL FIND HER--AND SHE WILL BE...PUNISHED FOR HER BETRAYAL.
TAK
IN THE MEANTIME, ALLOW ME TO REPRIORITIZE YOUR CONCERNS.

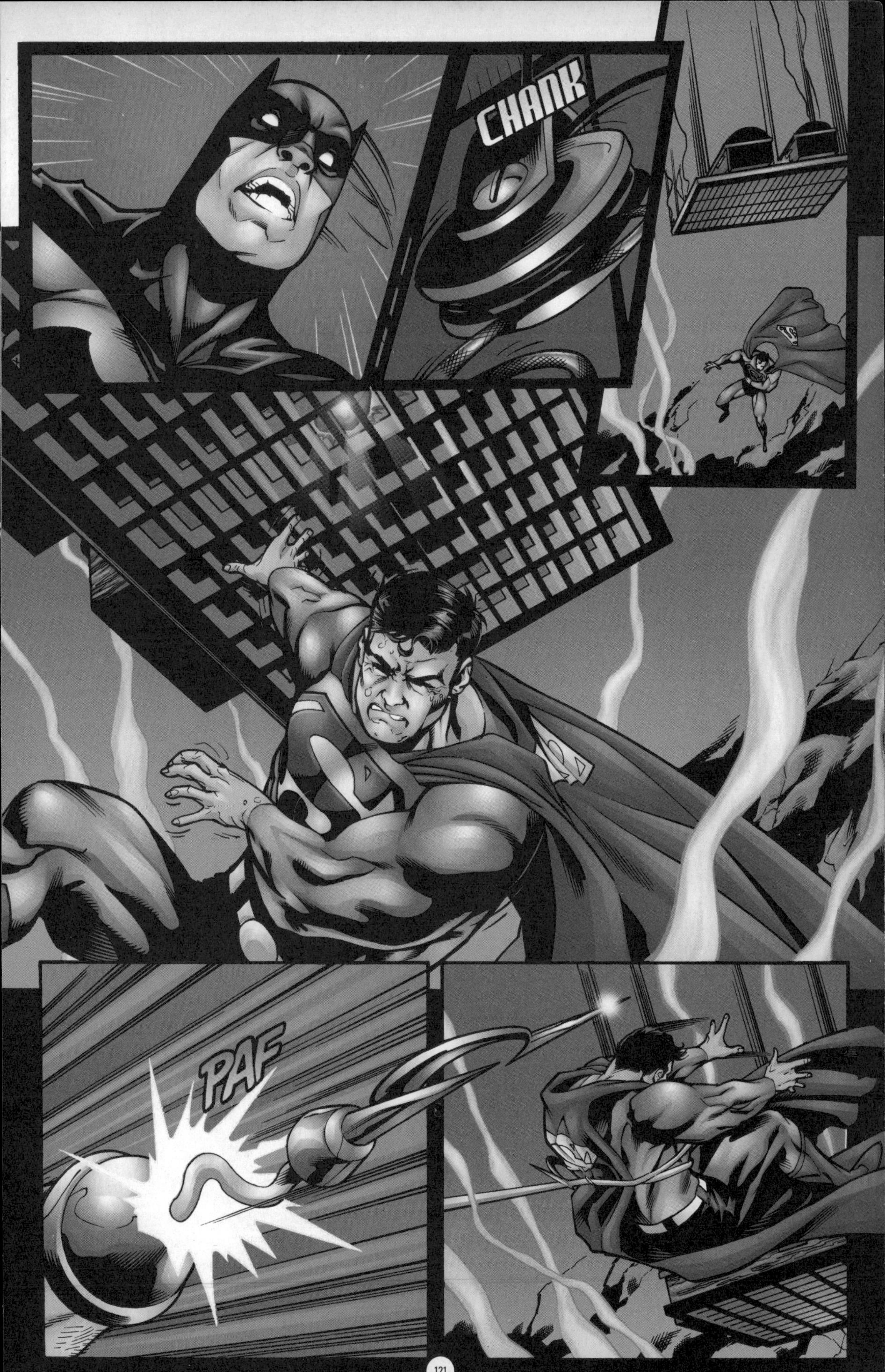
CHANK
PAF

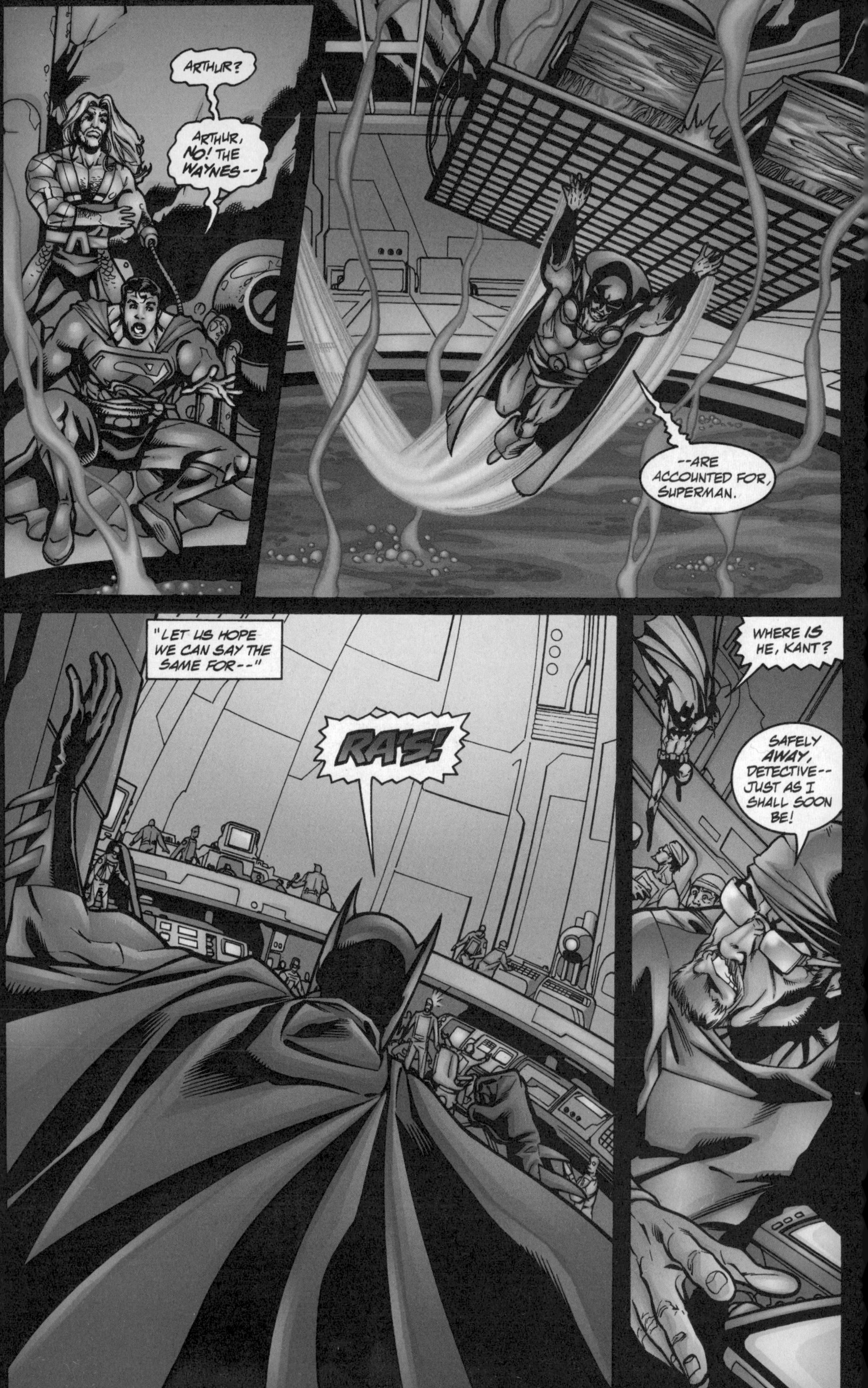
ARTHUR?
ARTHUR, NO! THE WAYNES--
--ARE ACCOUNTED FOR, SUPERMAN.
"LET US HOPE WE CAN SAY THE SAME FOR--"
RA'S!
WHERE IS HE, KANT?
SAFELY AWAY, DETECTIVE-- JUST AS I SHALL SOON BE!

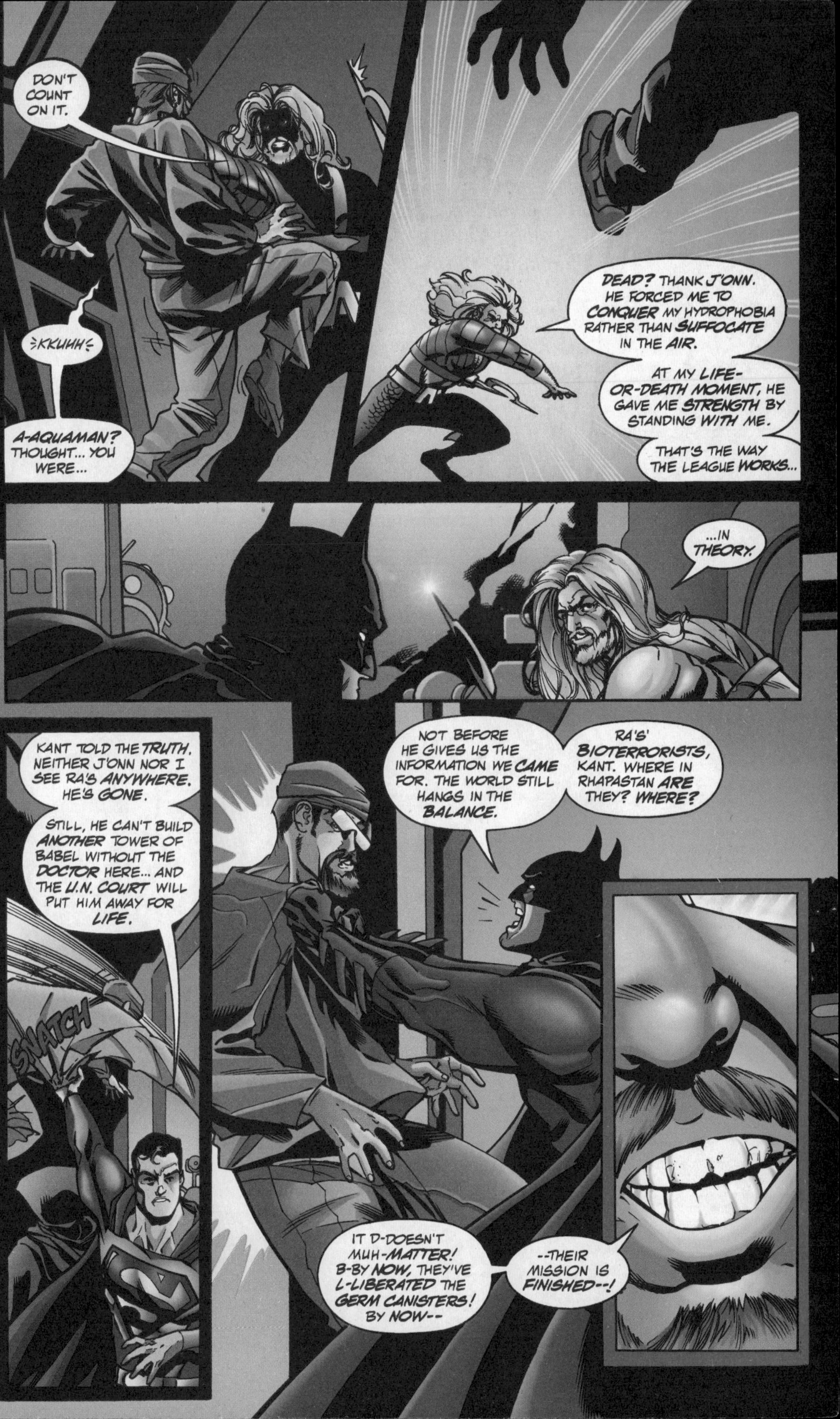
DON'T COUNT ON IT.
KKUHH
A-AQUAMAN? THOUGHT... YOU WERE...
DEAD? THANK J'ONN. HE FORCED ME TO CONQUER MY HYDROPHOBIA RATHER THAN SUFFOCATE IN THE AIR.
AT MY LIFE-OR-DEATH MOMENT, HE GAVE ME STRENGTH BY STANDING WITH ME.
THAT'S THE WAY THE LEAGUE WORKS...
...IN THEORY.
KANT TOLD THE TRUTH. NEITHER J'ONN NOR I SEE RA'S ANYWHERE. HE'S GONE.
STILL, HE CAN'T BUILD ANOTHER TOWER OF BABEL WITHOUT THE DOCTOR HERE... AND THE U.N. COURT WILL PUT HIM AWAY FOR LIFE.
NOT BEFORE HE GIVES US THE INFORMATION WE CAME FOR. THE WORLD STILL HANGS IN THE BALANCE.
RA'S' BIOTERRORISTS, KANT. WHERE IN RHAPASTAN ARE THEY? WHERE?
SNATCH
IT D-DOESN'T MUH-MATTER! B-BY NOW, THEY'VE L-LIBERATED THE GERM CANISTERS! BY NOW--
--THEIR MISSION IS FINISHED--!

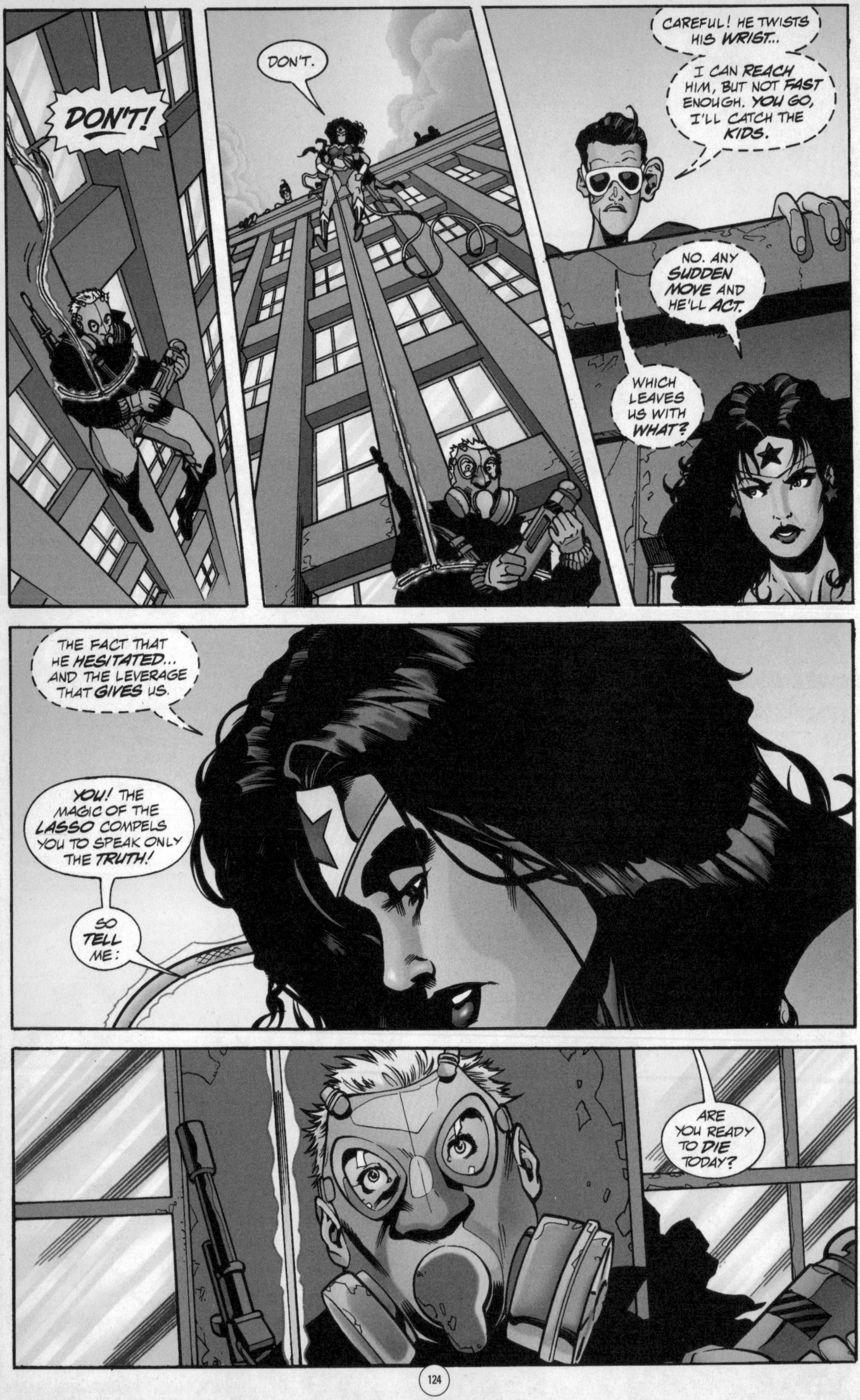
DON'T!
DON'T.
CAREFUL! HE TWISTS HIS WRIST...
I CAN REACH HIM, BUT NOT FAST ENOUGH. YOU GO, I'LL CATCH THE KIDS.
NO. ANY SUDDEN MOVE AND HE'LL ACT.
WHICH LEAVES US WITH WHAT?
THE FACT THAT HE HESITATED... AND THE LEVERAGE THAT GIVES US.
YOU! THE MAGIC OF THE LASSO COMPELS YOU TO SPEAK ONLY THE TRUTH!
SO TELL ME:
ARE YOU READY TO DIE TODAY?

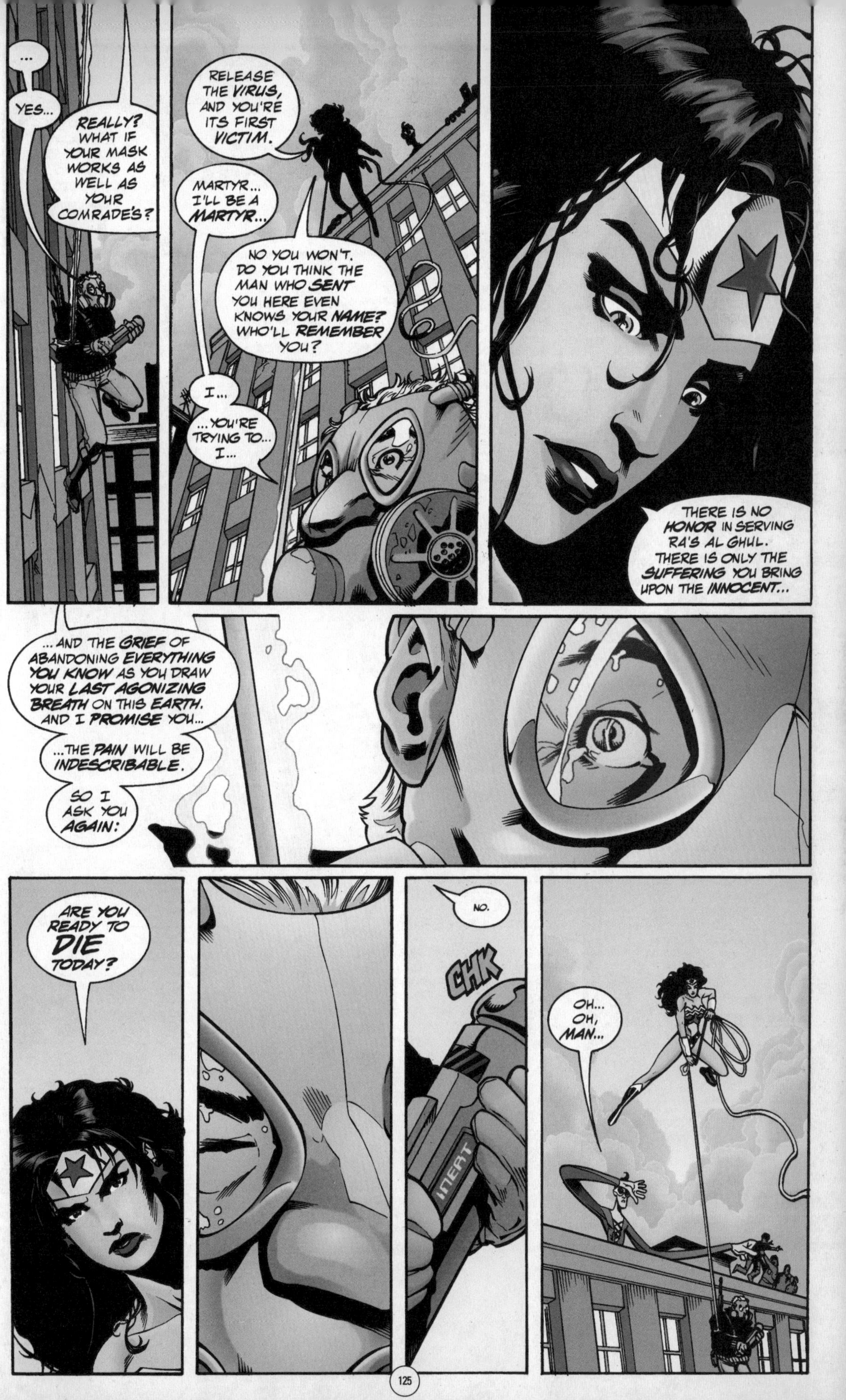
...
YES...
REALLY? WHAT IF YOUR MASK WORKS AS WELL AS YOUR COMRADE'S?
RELEASE THE VIRUS, AND YOU'RE ITS FIRST VICTIM.
MARTYR... I'LL BE A MARTYR...
NO YOU WON'T. DO YOU THINK THE MAN WHO SENT YOU HERE EVEN KNOWS YOUR NAME? WHO'LL REMEMBER YOU?
I...
...YOU'RE TRYING TO... I...
THERE IS NO HONOR IN SERVING RA'S AL GHUL. THERE IS ONLY THE SUFFERING YOU BRING UPON THE INNOCENT...
...AND THE GRIEF OF ABANDONING EVERYTHING YOU KNOW AS YOU DRAW YOUR LAST AGONIZING BREATH ON THIS EARTH. AND I PROMISE YOU...
...THE PAIN WILL BE INDESCRIBABLE.
SO I ASK YOU AGAIN:
ARE YOU READY TO DIE TODAY?
NO.
CHK
INERT
OH... OH, MAN...

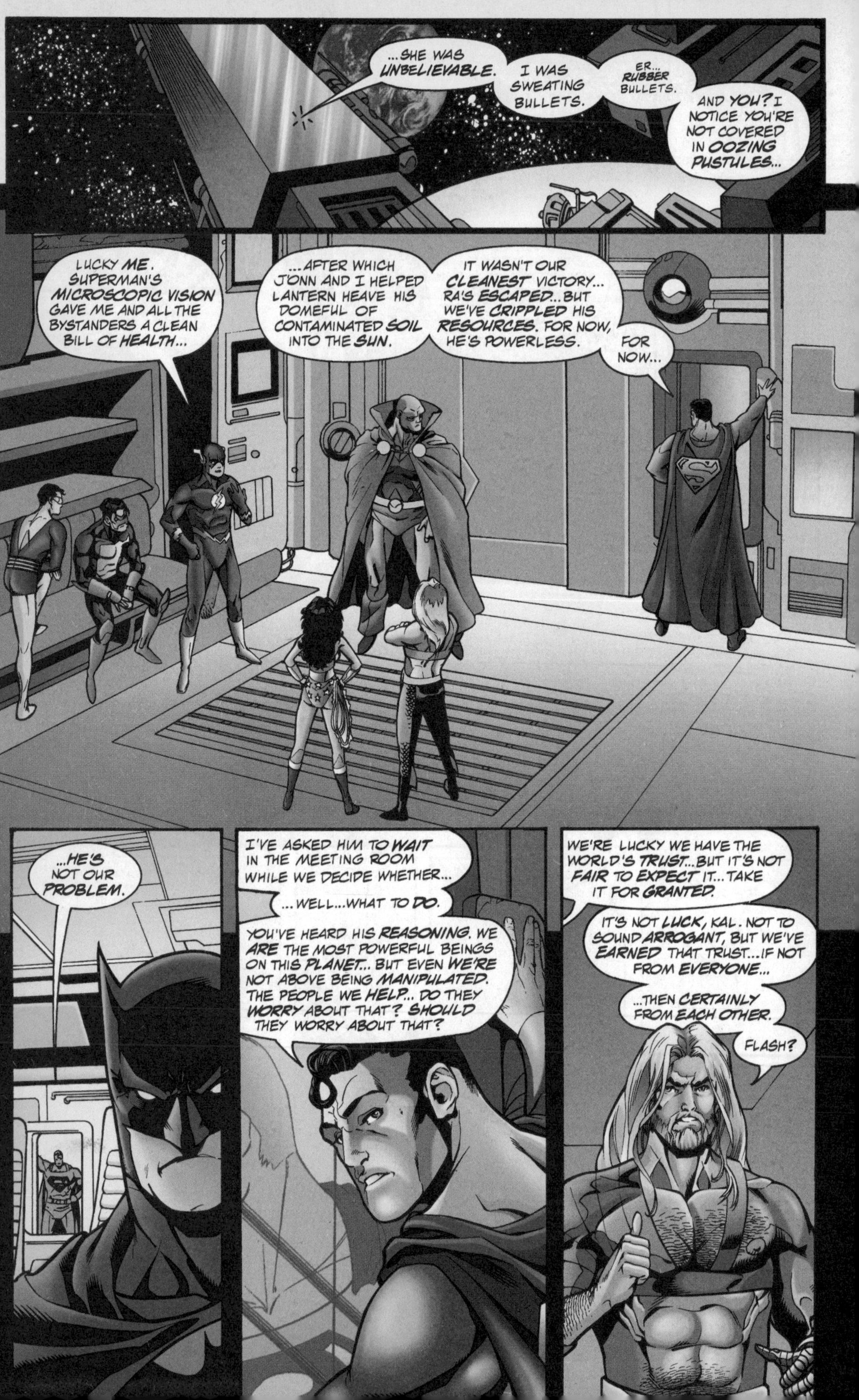
...SHE WAS UNBELIEVABLE.
I WAS SWEATING BULLETS.
ER... RUBBER BULLETS.
AND YOU? I NOTICE YOU'RE NOT COVERED IN OOZING PUSTULES...
LUCKY ME. SUPERMAN'S MICROSCOPIC VISION GAVE ME AND ALL THE BYSTANDERS A CLEAN BILL OF HEALTH...
...AFTER WHICH J'ONN AND I HELPED LANTERN HEAVE HIS DOMEFUL OF CONTAMINATED SOIL INTO THE SUN.
IT WASN'T OUR CLEANEST VICTORY... RA'S ESCAPED... BUT WE'VE CRIPPLED HIS RESOURCES. FOR NOW, HE'S POWERLESS.
FOR NOW...
...HE'S NOT OUR PROBLEM.
I'VE ASKED HIM TO WAIT IN THE MEETING ROOM WHILE WE DECIDE WHETHER...
...WELL...WHAT TO DO.
YOU'VE HEARD HIS REASONING. WE ARE THE MOST POWERFUL BEINGS ON THIS PLANET... BUT EVEN WE'RE NOT ABOVE BEING MANIPULATED. THE PEOPLE WE HELP... DO THEY WORRY ABOUT THAT? SHOULD THEY WORRY ABOUT THAT?
WE'RE LUCKY WE HAVE THE WORLD'S TRUST... BUT IT'S NOT FAIR TO EXPECT IT... TAKE IT FOR GRANTED.
IT'S NOT LUCK, KAL. NOT TO SOUND ARROGANT, BUT WE'VE EARNED THAT TRUST... IF NOT FROM EVERYONE...
...THEN CERTAINLY FROM EACH OTHER.
FLASH?

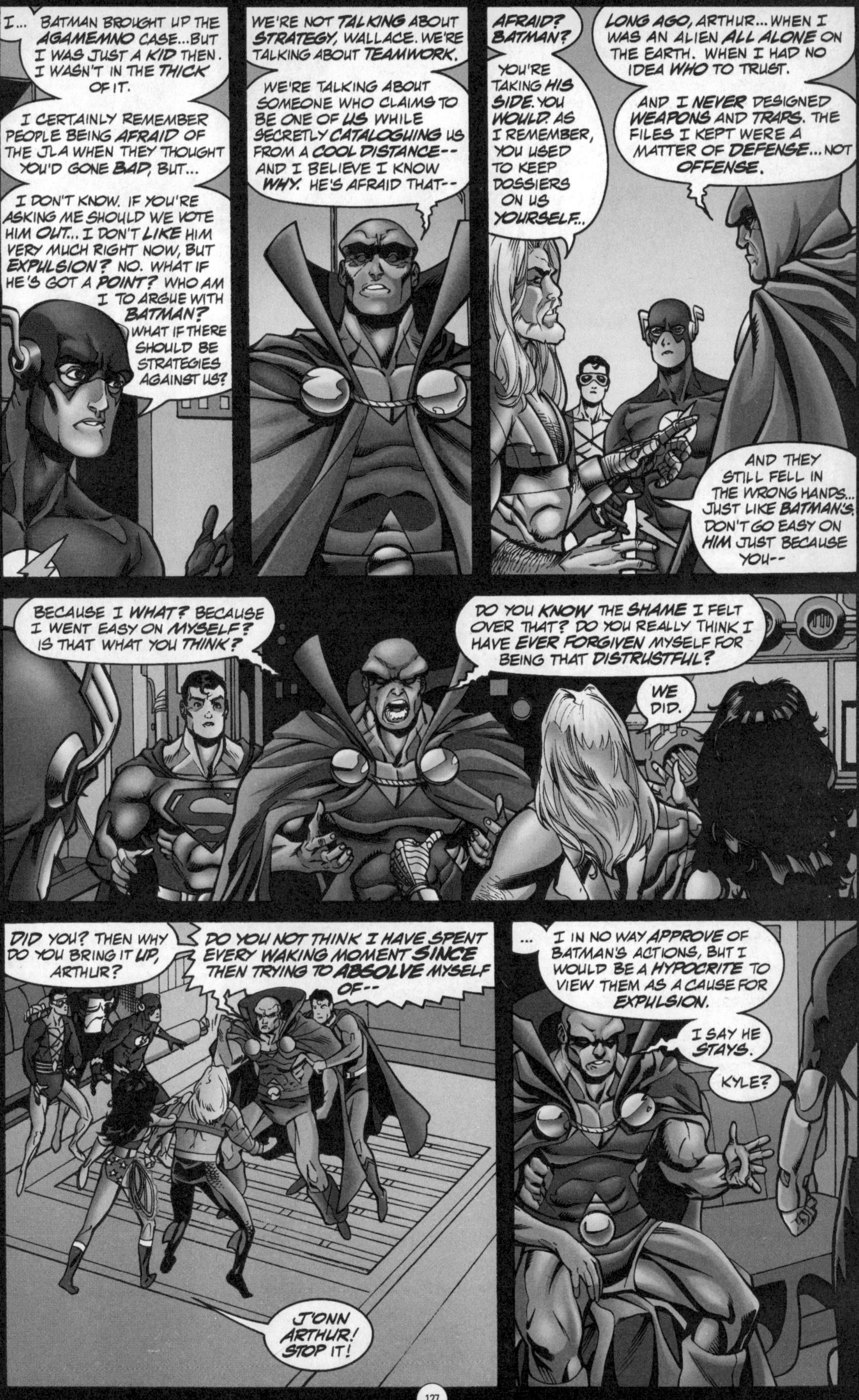
I... BATMAN BROUGHT UP THE AGAMEMNO CASE...BUT I WAS JUST A KID THEN. I WASN'T IN THE THICK OF IT.
I CERTAINLY REMEMBER PEOPLE BEING AFRAID OF THE JLA WHEN THEY THOUGHT YOU'D GONE BAD, BUT...
I DON'T KNOW. IF YOU'RE ASKING ME SHOULD WE VOTE HIM OUT... I DON'T LIKE HIM VERY MUCH RIGHT NOW, BUT EXPULSION? NO. WHAT IF HE'S GOT A POINT? WHO AM I TO ARGUE WITH BATMAN?
WHAT IF THERE SHOULD BE STRATEGIES AGAINST US?
WE'RE NOT TALKING ABOUT STRATEGY, WALLACE. WE'RE TALKING ABOUT TEAMWORK.
WE'RE TALKING ABOUT SOMEONE WHO CLAIMS TO BE ONE OF US WHILE SECRETLY CATALOGUING US FROM A COOL DISTANCE-- AND I BELIEVE I KNOW WHY. HE'S AFRAID THAT--
AFRAID? BATMAN?
YOU'RE TAKING HIS SIDE. YOU WOULD. AS I REMEMBER, YOU USED TO KEEP DOSSIERS ON US YOURSELF...
LONG AGO, ARTHUR... WHEN I WAS AN ALIEN ALL ALONE ON THE EARTH. WHEN I HAD NO IDEA WHO TO TRUST.
AND I NEVER DESIGNED WEAPONS AND TRAPS. THE FILES I KEPT WERE A MATTER OF DEFENSE... NOT OFFENSE.
AND THEY STILL FELL IN THE WRONG HANDS... JUST LIKE BATMAN'S. DON'T GO EASY ON HIM JUST BECAUSE YOU--
BECAUSE I WHAT? BECAUSE I WENT EASY ON MYSELF? IS THAT WHAT YOU THINK?
DO YOU KNOW THE SHAME I FELT OVER THAT? DO YOU REALLY THINK I HAVE EVER FORGIVEN MYSELF FOR BEING THAT DISTRUSTFUL?
WE DID.
DID YOU? THEN WHY DO YOU BRING IT UP, ARTHUR?
DO YOU NOT THINK I HAVE SPENT EVERY WAKING MOMENT SINCE THEN TRYING TO ABSOLVE MYSELF OF--
J'ONN ARTHUR! STOP IT!
... I IN NO WAY APPROVE OF BATMAN'S ACTIONS, BUT I WOULD BE A HYPOCRITE TO VIEW THEM AS A CAUSE FOR EXPULSION.
I SAY HE STAYS.
KYLE?

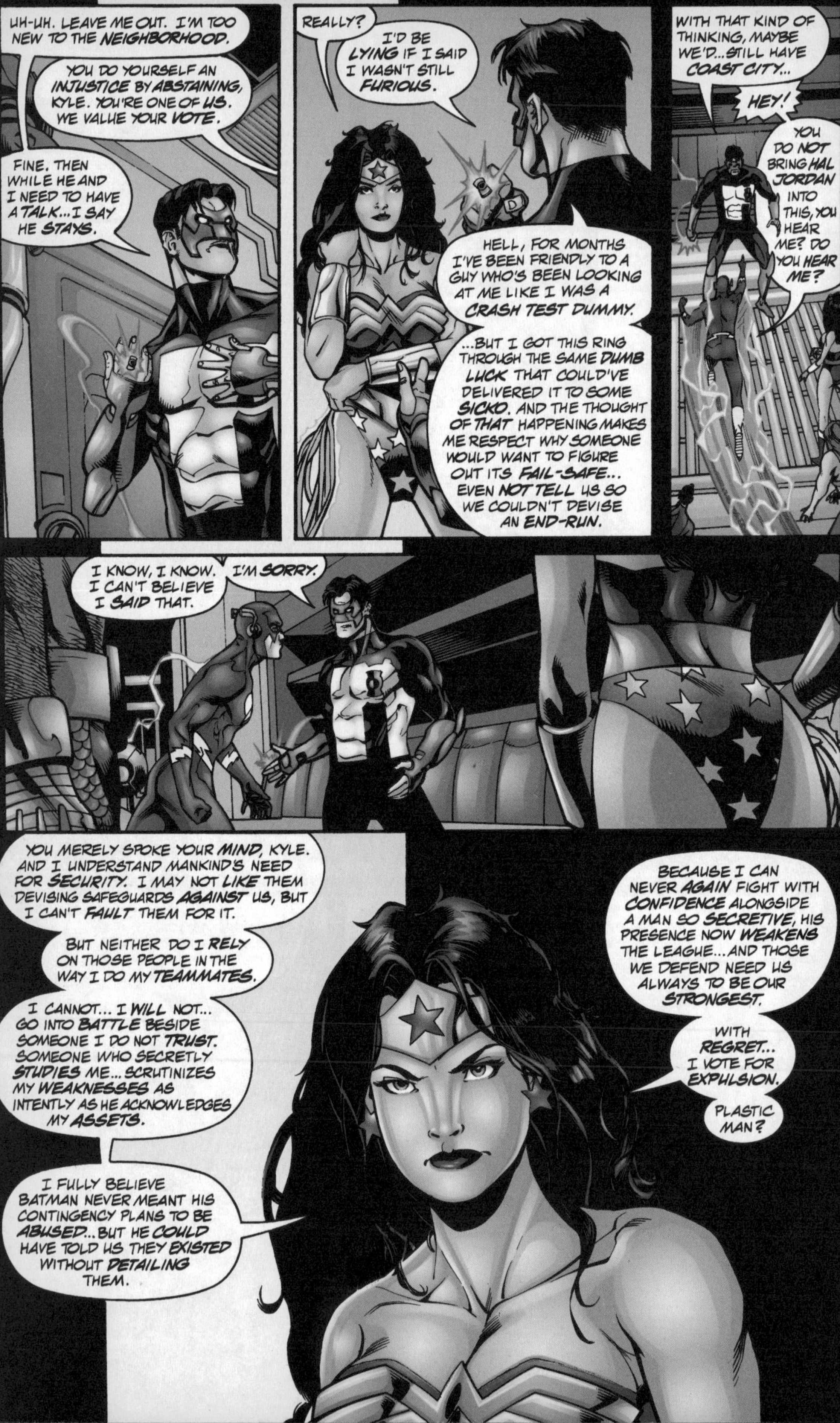
UH-UH. LEAVE ME OUT. I'M TOO NEW TO THE NEIGHBORHOOD.
YOU DO YOURSELF AN INJUSTICE BY ABSTAINING, KYLE. YOU'RE ONE OF US. WE VALUE YOUR VOTE.
FINE. THEN WHILE HE AND I NEED TO HAVE A TALK... I SAY HE STAYS.
REALLY?
I'D BE LYING IF I SAID I WASN'T STILL FURIOUS.
HELL, FOR MONTHS I'VE BEEN FRIENDLY TO A GUY WHO'S BEEN LOOKING AT ME LIKE I WAS A CRASH TEST DUMMY.
...BUT I GOT THIS RING THROUGH THE SAME DUMB LUCK THAT COULD'VE DELIVERED IT TO SOME SICKO. AND THE THOUGHT OF THAT HAPPENING MAKES ME RESPECT WHY SOMEONE WOULD WANT TO FIGURE OUT ITS FAIL-SAFE... EVEN NOT TELL US SO WE COULDN'T DEVISE AN END-RUN.
WITH THAT KIND OF THINKING, MAYBE WE'D... STILL HAVE COAST CITY...
HEY!
YOU DO NOT BRING HAL JORDAN INTO THIS, YOU HEAR ME? DO YOU HEAR ME?
I KNOW, I KNOW. I CAN'T BELIEVE I SAID THAT.
I'M SORRY.
YOU MERELY SPOKE YOUR MIND, KYLE. AND I UNDERSTAND MANKIND'S NEED FOR SECURITY. I MAY NOT LIKE THEM DEVISING SAFEGUARDS AGAINST US, BUT I CAN'T FAULT THEM FOR IT.
BUT NEITHER DO I RELY ON THOSE PEOPLE IN THE WAY I DO MY TEAMMATES.
I CANNOT... I WILL NOT... GO INTO BATTLE BESIDE SOMEONE I DO NOT TRUST. SOMEONE WHO SECRETLY STUDIES ME... SCRUTINIZES MY WEAKNESSES AS INTENTLY AS HE ACKNOWLEDGES MY ASSETS.
I FULLY BELIEVE BATMAN NEVER MEANT HIS CONTINGENCY PLANS TO BE ABUSED... BUT HE COULD HAVE TOLD US THEY EXISTED WITHOUT DETAILING THEM.
BECAUSE I CAN NEVER AGAIN FIGHT WITH CONFIDENCE ALONGSIDE A MAN SO SECRETIVE, HIS PRESENCE NOW WEAKENS THE LEAGUE... AND THOSE WE DEFEND NEED US ALWAYS TO BE OUR STRONGEST.
WITH REGRET... I VOTE FOR EXPULSION.
PLASTIC MAN?

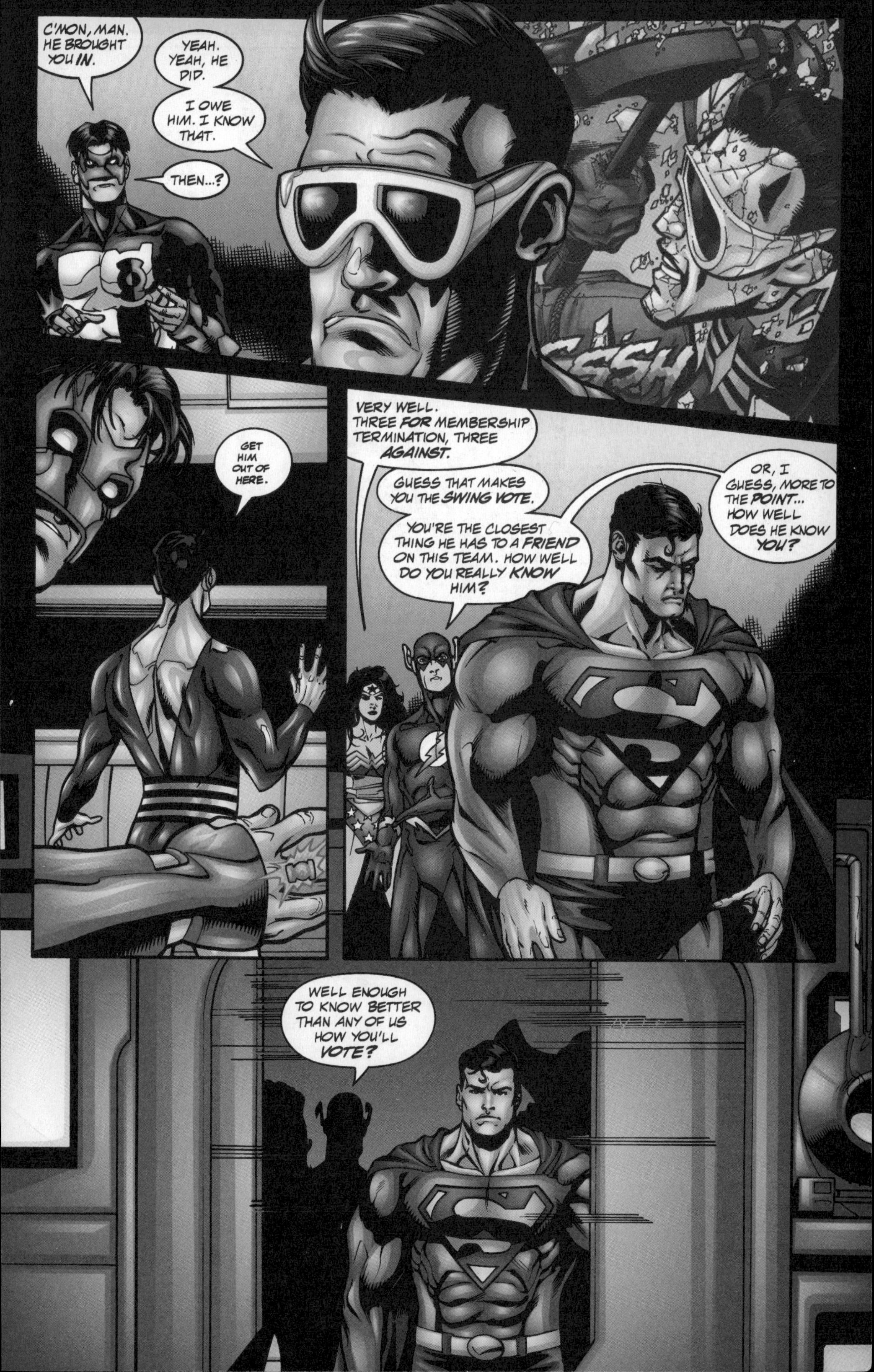
C'MON, MAN. HE BROUGHT YOU IN.
YEAH. YEAH, HE DID.
I OWE HIM. I KNOW THAT.
THEN...?
CSSH
GET HIM OUT OF HERE.
VERY WELL. THREE FOR MEMBERSHIP TERMINATION, THREE AGAINST.
GUESS THAT MAKES YOU THE SWING VOTE.
YOU'RE THE CLOSEST THING HE HAS TO A FRIEND ON THIS TEAM. HOW WELL DO YOU REALLY KNOW HIM?
OR, I GUESS, MORE TO THE POINT... HOW WELL DOES HE KNOW YOU?
WELL ENOUGH TO KNOW BETTER THAN ANY OF US HOW YOU'LL VOTE?

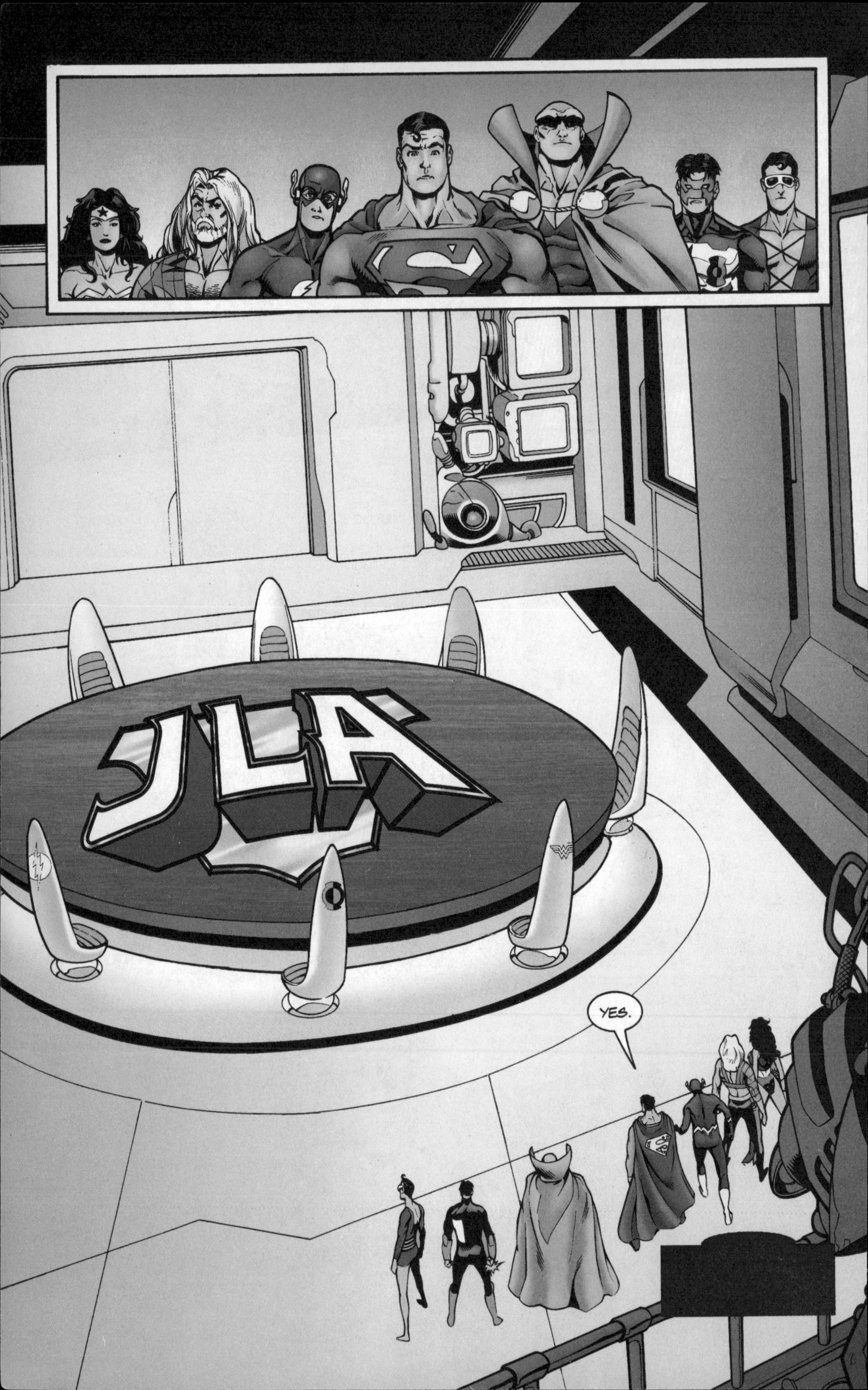
JLA
YES.

EPILOGUE

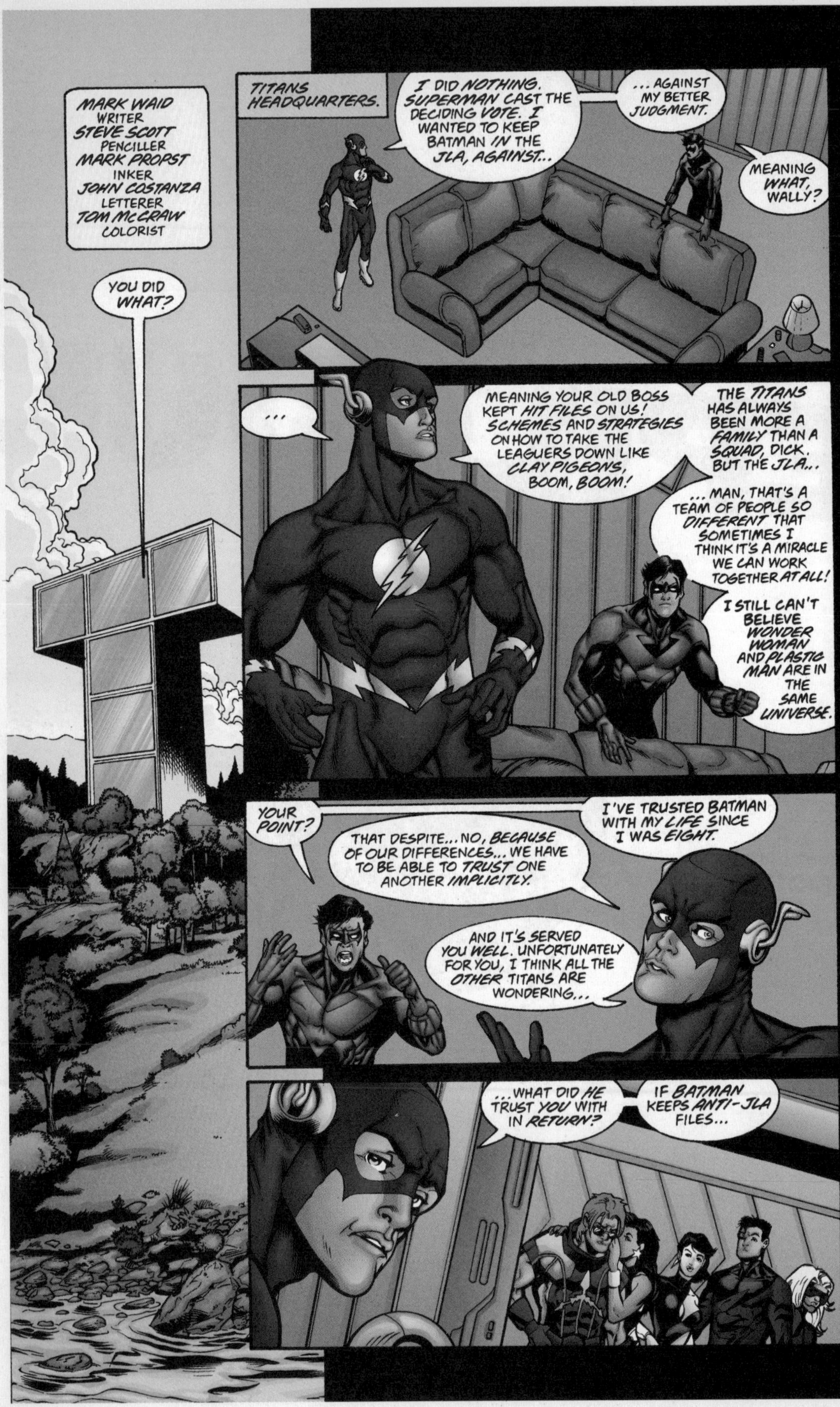
MARK WAID
WRITER
STEVE SCOTT
PENCILLER
MARK PROPST
INKER
JOHN COSTANZA
LETTERER
TOM McCRAW
COLORIST
YOU DID WHAT?
TITANS HEADQUARTERS.
I DID NOTHING. SUPERMAN CAST THE DECIDING VOTE. I WANTED TO KEEP BATMAN IN THE JLA, AGAINST...
...AGAINST MY BETTER JUDGMENT.
MEANING WHAT, WALLY?
...
MEANING YOUR OLD BOSS KEPT HIT FILES ON US! SCHEMES AND STRATEGIES ON HOW TO TAKE THE LEAGUERS DOWN LIKE CLAY PIGEONS, BOOM, BOOM!
THE TITANS HAS ALWAYS BEEN MORE A FAMILY THAN A SQUAD, DICK. BUT THE JLA...
...MAN, THAT'S A TEAM OF PEOPLE SO DIFFERENT THAT SOMETIMES I THINK IT'S A MIRACLE WE CAN WORK TOGETHER AT ALL!
I STILL CAN'T BELIEVE WONDER WOMAN AND PLASTIC MAN ARE IN THE SAME UNIVERSE.
YOUR POINT?
THAT DESPITE... NO, BECAUSE OF OUR DIFFERENCES... WE HAVE TO BE ABLE TO TRUST ONE ANOTHER IMPLICITLY.
I'VE TRUSTED BATMAN WITH MY LIFE SINCE I WAS EIGHT.
AND IT'S SERVED YOU WELL. UNFORTUNATELY FOR YOU, I THINK ALL THE OTHER TITANS ARE WONDERING...
...WHAT DID HE TRUST YOU WITH IN RETURN?
IF BATMAN KEEPS ANTI-JLA FILES...

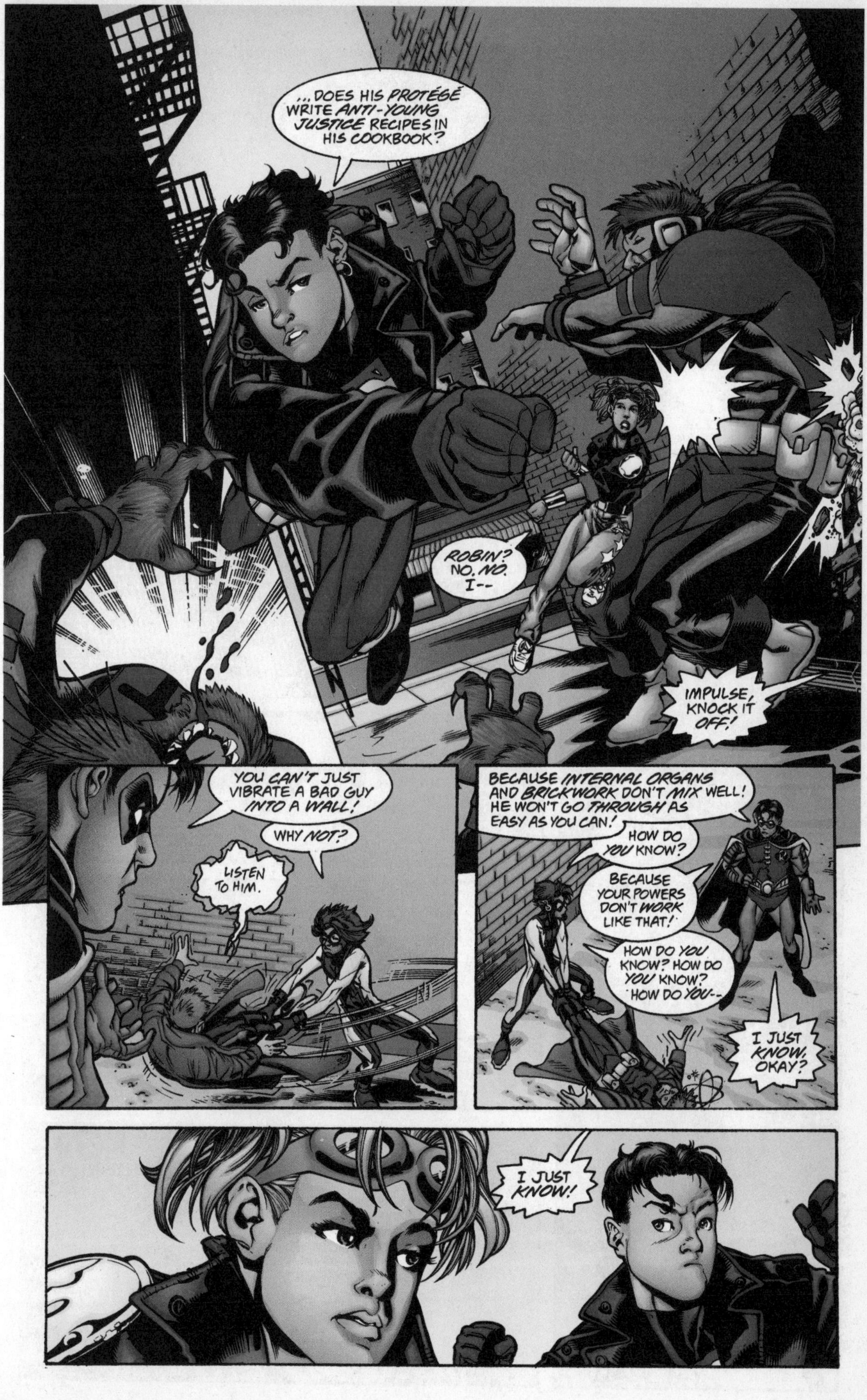
...DOES HIS PROTÉGÉ WRITE ANTI-YOUNG JUSTICE RECIPES IN HIS COOKBOOK?
ROBIN? NO. NO. I--
IMPULSE, KNOCK IT OFF!
YOU CAN'T JUST VIBRATE A BAD GUY INTO A WALL!
WHY NOT?
LISTEN TO HIM.
BECAUSE INTERNAL ORGANS AND BRICKWORK DON'T MIX WELL! HE WON'T GO THROUGH AS EASY AS YOU CAN!
HOW DO YOU KNOW?
BECAUSE YOUR POWERS DON'T WORK LIKE THAT!
HOW DO YOU KNOW? HOW DO YOU KNOW? HOW DO YOU--
I JUST KNOW, OKAY?
I JUST KNOW!

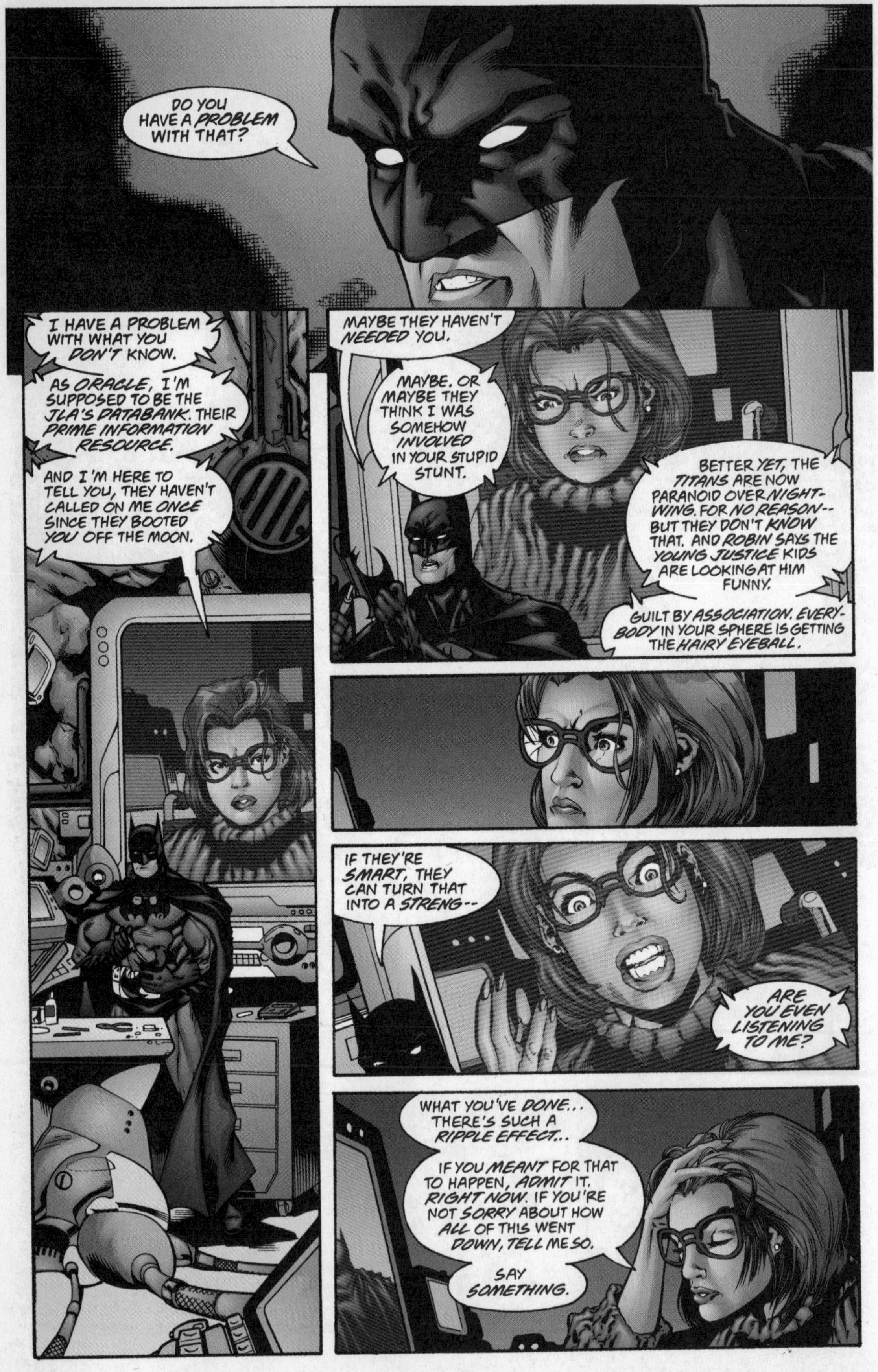
DO YOU HAVE A PROBLEM WITH THAT?
I HAVE A PROBLEM WITH WHAT YOU DON'T KNOW.
AS ORACLE, I'M SUPPOSED TO BE THE JLA'S DATABANK. THEIR PRIME INFORMATION RESOURCE.
AND I'M HERE TO TELL YOU, THEY HAVEN'T CALLED ON ME ONCE SINCE THEY BOOTED YOU OFF THE MOON.
MAYBE THEY HAVEN'T NEEDED YOU.
MAYBE. OR MAYBE THEY THINK I WAS SOMEHOW INVOLVED IN YOUR STUPID STUNT.
BETTER YET, THE TITANS ARE NOW PARANOID OVER NIGHT-WING. FOR NO REASON-- BUT THEY DON'T KNOW THAT. AND ROBIN SAYS THE YOUNG JUSTICE KIDS ARE LOOKING AT HIM FUNNY.
GUILT BY ASSOCIATION. EVERY-BODY IN YOUR SPHERE IS GETTING THE HAIRY EYEBALL.
IF THEY'RE SMART, THEY CAN TURN THAT INTO A STRENG--
ARE YOU EVEN LISTENING TO ME?
WHAT YOU'VE DONE... THERE'S SUCH A RIPPLE EFFECT...
IF YOU MEANT FOR THAT TO HAPPEN, ADMIT IT. RIGHT NOW. IF YOU'RE NOT SORRY ABOUT HOW ALL OF THIS WENT DOWN, TELL ME SO.
SAY SOMETHING.

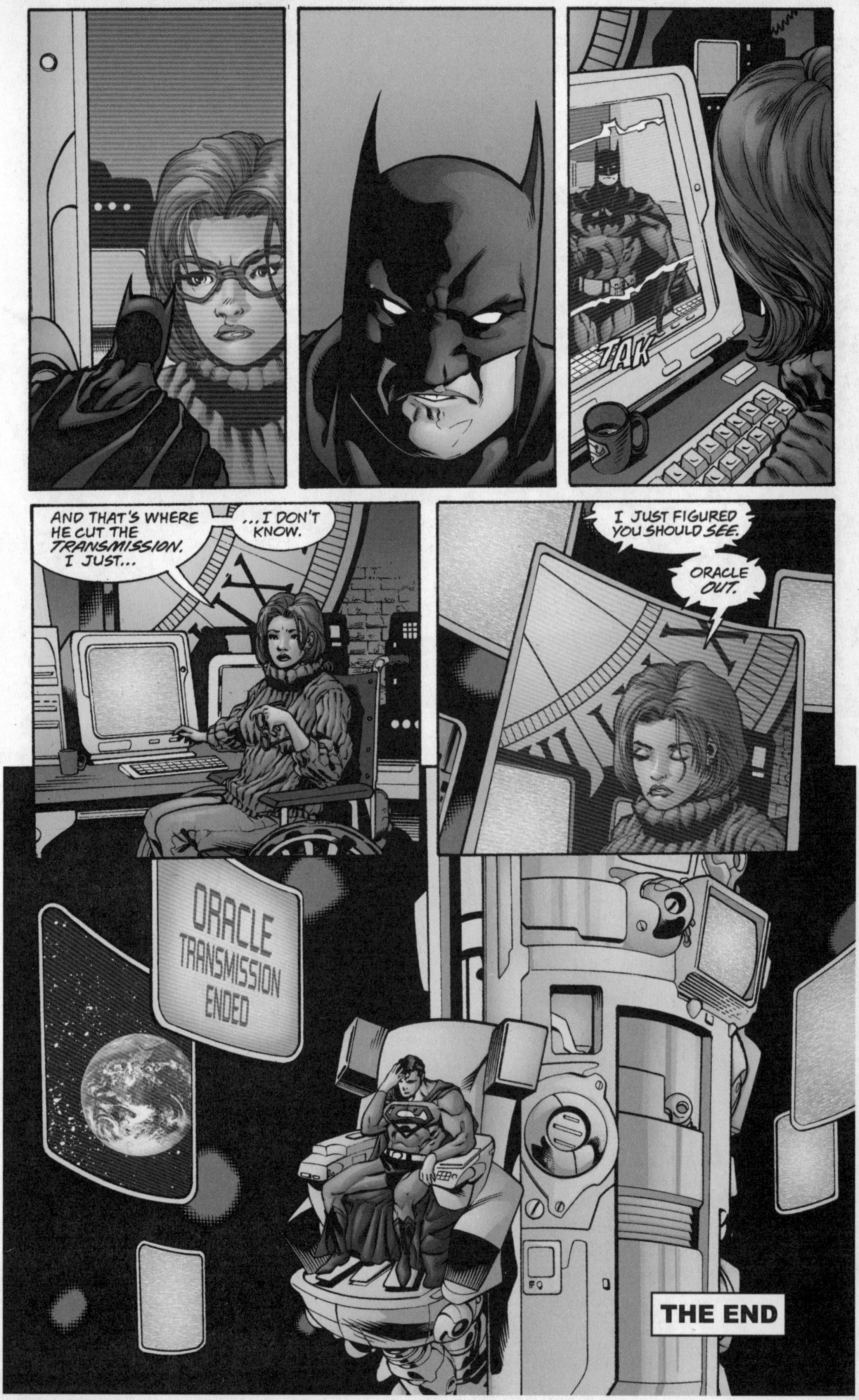
TAK
AND THAT'S WHERE HE CUT THE TRANSMISSION. I JUST...
...I DON'T KNOW.
I JUST FIGURED YOU SHOULD SEE.
ORACLE OUT.
ORACLE TRANSMISSION ENDED
THE END

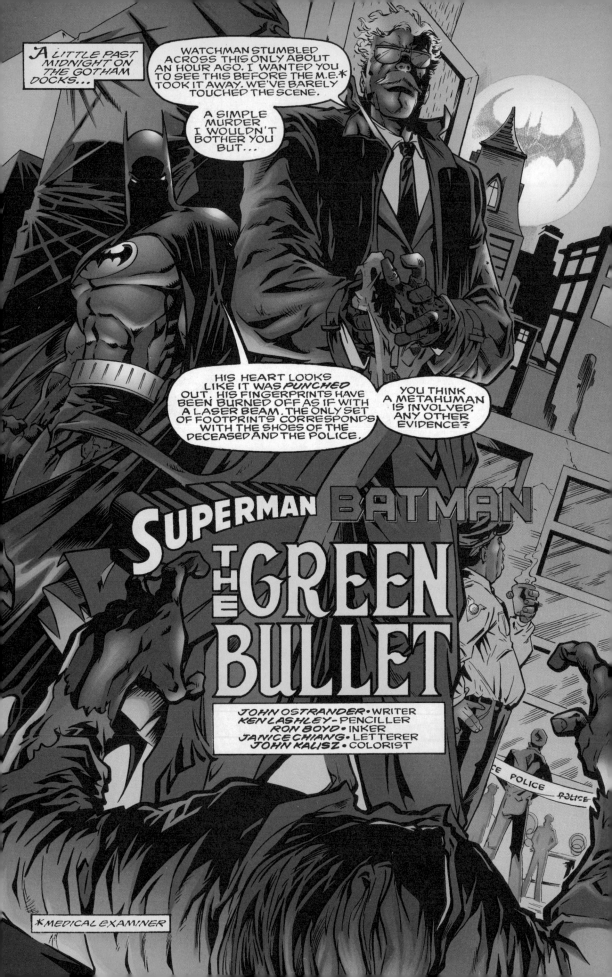

A LITTLE PAST MIDNIGHT ON THE GOTHAM DOCKS...

WATCHMAN STUMBLED ACROSS THIS ONLY ABOUT AN HOUR AGO. I WANTED YOU TO SEE THIS BEFORE THE M.E.* TOOK IT AWAY. WE'VE BARELY TOUCHED THE SCENE.

A SIMPLE MURDER I WOULDN'T BOTHER YOU BUT...

HIS HEART LOOKS LIKE IT WAS *PUNCHED* OUT. HIS FINGERPRINTS HAVE BEEN BURNED OFF AS IF WITH A LASER BEAM. THE ONLY SET OF FOOTPRINTS CORRESPONDS WITH THE SHOES OF THE DECEASED AND THE POLICE.

YOU THINK A METAHUMAN IS INVOLVED. ANY OTHER EVIDENCE?

SUPERMAN BATMAN
THE GREEN BULLET

JOHN OSTRANDER • WRITER
KEN LASHLEY • PENCILLER
RON BOYD • INKER
JANICE CHIANG • LETTERER
JOHN KALISZ • COLORIST

*MEDICAL EXAMINER

THE WATCHMAN SAYS HE HEARD VOICES AND FELT A RUSH OF AIR AS HE CAME UP.

CRIME SCENE BOYS SAY THE BODY WAS STILL WARM WHEN THEY GOT THERE SO THE MURDER MUST HAVE JUST HAPPENED WHEN THE WATCHMAN WANDERED BY.

Hm. MIGHT EXPLAIN WHY THE DECEASED'S JAW IS INTACT. WHY DESTROY THE FINGERPRINTS WHEN DENTAL RECORDS CAN ALSO MAKE AN I.D.? WE'RE ASSUMING, OF COURSE, THAT THE MURDERER WAS INTERRUPTED.

ANYTHING ELSE?

THIS POUCH WAS FOUND IN THE DEAD MAN'S UPPER COAT POCKET. IT'S LEAD-LINED.

THIS WAS INSIDE.

I DON'T KNOW WHAT THE GREEN BULLET MEANS, BUT ALL THE EVIDENCE SEEMS TO SUGGEST OUR PRIME SUSPECT SHOULD BE... *SUPERMAN.*

YOU CAN SEE THE PROBLEM. IF WORD GETS OUT AND SUPERMAN *DIDN'T* DO IT, HIS CREDIBILITY IS RUINED. IF HE *DID* DO IT...

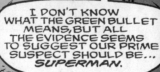

I'LL BE IN TOUCH.

BATMAN?

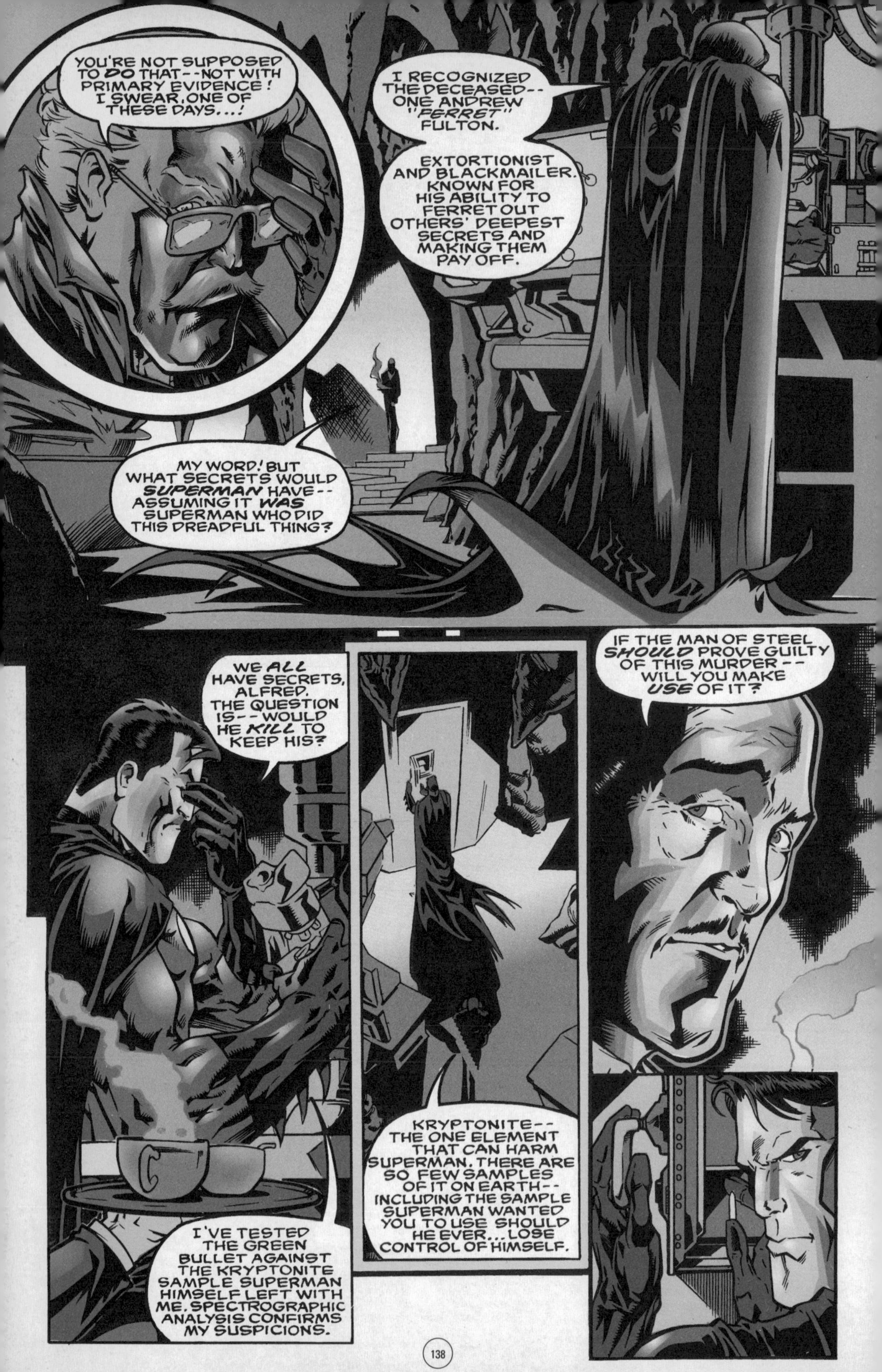
YOU'RE NOT SUPPOSED TO DO THAT--NOT WITH PRIMARY EVIDENCE! I SWEAR, ONE OF THESE DAYS...!
I RECOGNIZED THE DECEASED-- ONE ANDREW "FERRET" FULTON.
EXTORTIONIST AND BLACKMAILER. KNOWN FOR HIS ABILITY TO FERRET OUT OTHERS' DEEPEST SECRETS AND MAKING THEM PAY OFF.
MY WORD! BUT WHAT SECRETS WOULD SUPERMAN HAVE-- ASSUMING IT WAS SUPERMAN WHO DID THIS DREADFUL THING?
WE ALL HAVE SECRETS, ALFRED. THE QUESTION IS-- WOULD HE KILL TO KEEP HIS?
I'VE TESTED THE GREEN BULLET AGAINST THE KRYPTONITE SAMPLE SUPERMAN HIMSELF LEFT WITH ME. SPECTROGRAPHIC ANALYSIS CONFIRMS MY SUSPICIONS.
KRYPTONITE-- THE ONE ELEMENT THAT CAN HARM SUPERMAN. THERE ARE SO FEW SAMPLES OF IT ON EARTH-- INCLUDING THE SAMPLE SUPERMAN WANTED YOU TO USE SHOULD HE EVER... LOSE CONTROL OF HIMSELF.
IF THE MAN OF STEEL SHOULD PROVE GUILTY OF THIS MURDER-- WILL YOU MAKE USE OF IT?

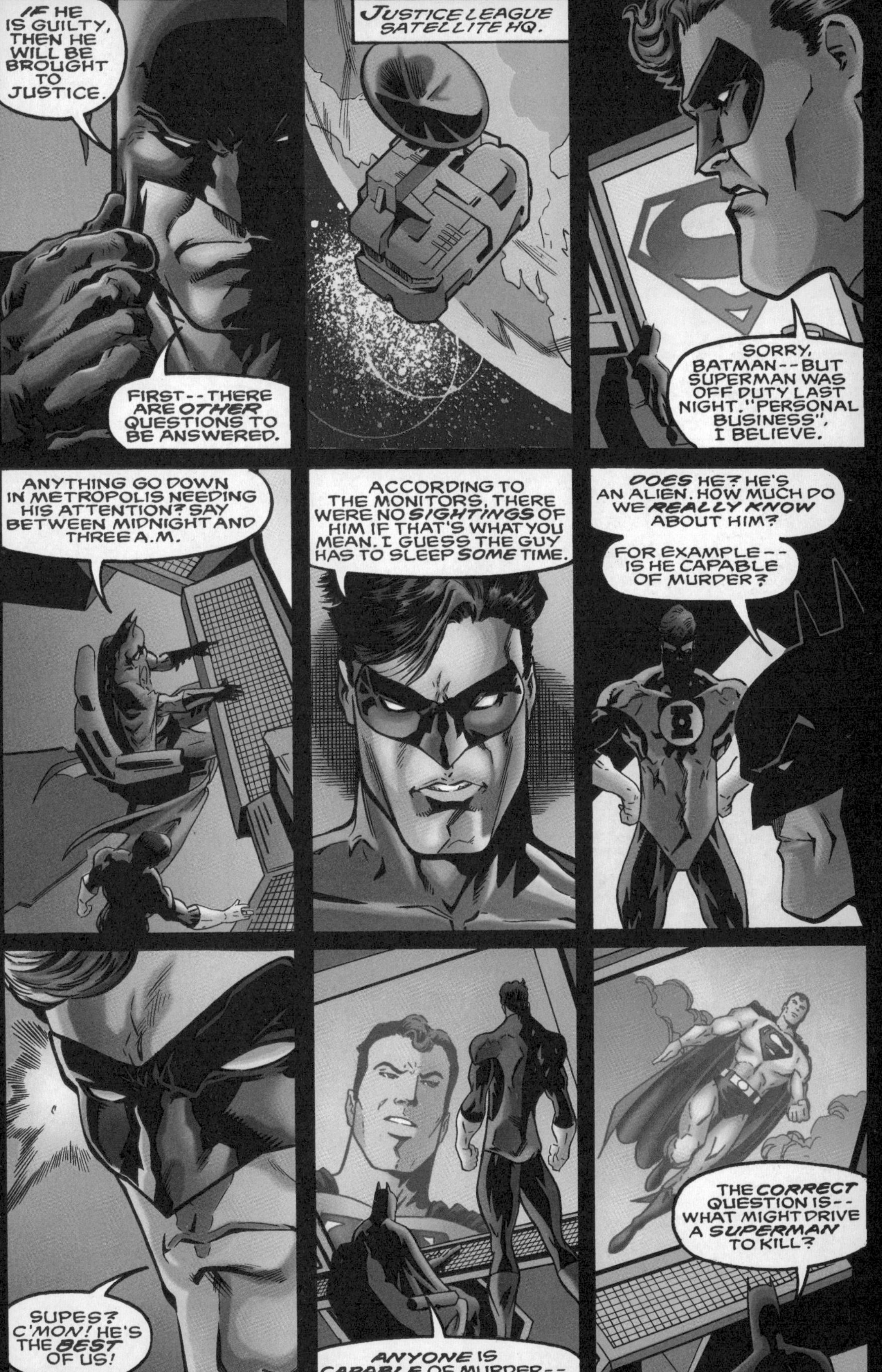
IF HE IS GUILTY, THEN HE WILL BE BROUGHT TO JUSTICE.
FIRST--THERE ARE OTHER QUESTIONS TO BE ANSWERED.
JUSTICE LEAGUE SATELLITE HQ.
SORRY, BATMAN--BUT SUPERMAN WAS OFF DUTY LAST NIGHT. "PERSONAL BUSINESS", I BELIEVE.
ANYTHING GO DOWN IN METROPOLIS NEEDING HIS ATTENTION? SAY BETWEEN MIDNIGHT AND THREE A.M.
ACCORDING TO THE MONITORS, THERE WERE NO SIGHTINGS OF HIM IF THAT'S WHAT YOU MEAN. I GUESS THE GUY HAS TO SLEEP SOMETIME.
DOES HE? HE'S AN ALIEN. HOW MUCH DO WE REALLY KNOW ABOUT HIM?
FOR EXAMPLE--IS HE CAPABLE OF MURDER?
SUPES? C'MON! HE'S THE BEST OF US!
ANYONE IS CAPABLE OF MURDER--IF THE CIRCUMSTANCES ARE RIGHT.
THE CORRECT QUESTION IS--WHAT MIGHT DRIVE A SUPERMAN TO KILL?

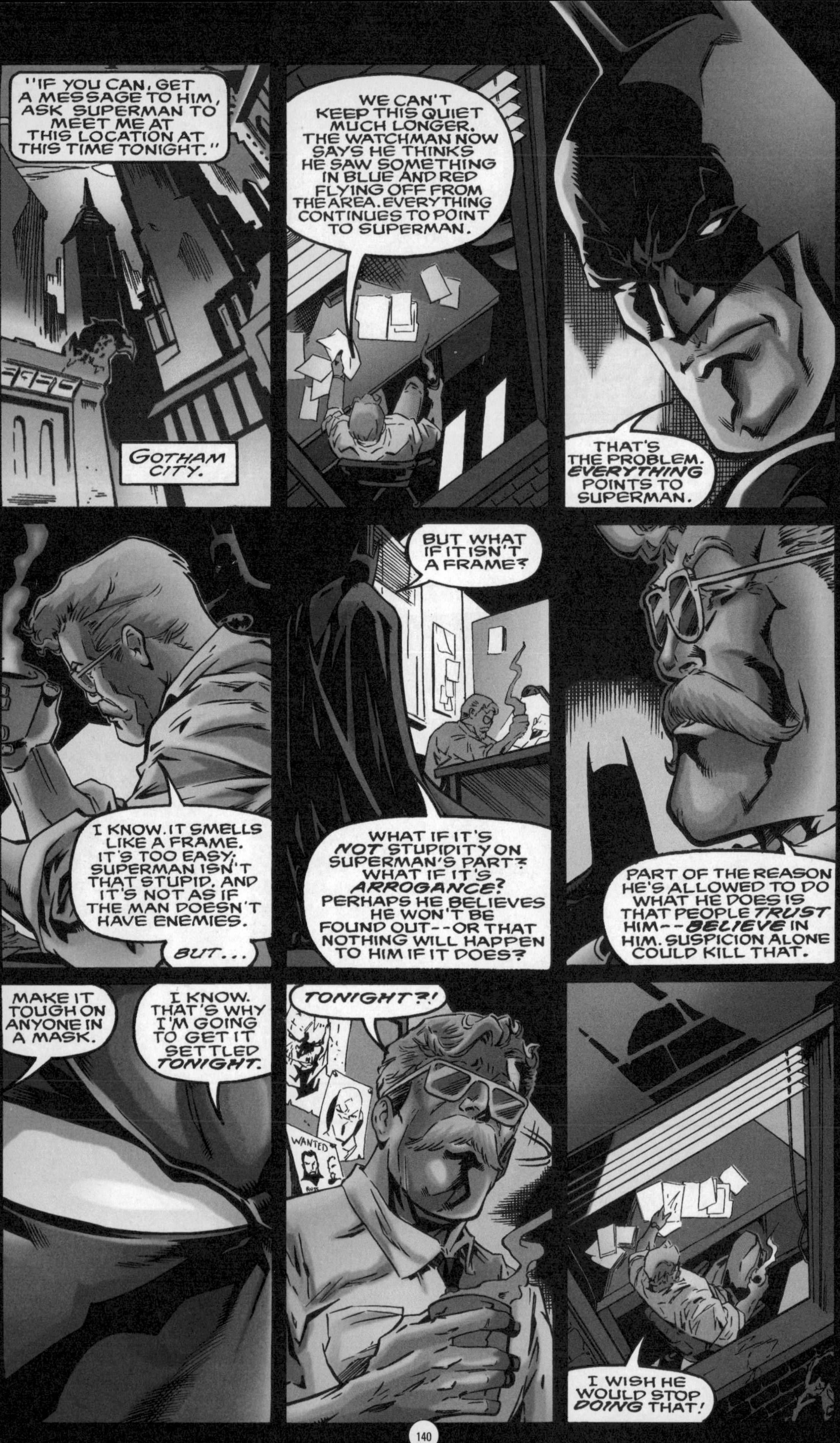
"IF YOU CAN, GET A MESSAGE TO HIM, ASK SUPERMAN TO MEET ME AT THIS LOCATION AT THIS TIME TONIGHT."
GOTHAM CITY.
WE CAN'T KEEP THIS QUIET MUCH LONGER. THE WATCHMAN NOW SAYS HE THINKS HE SAW SOMETHING IN BLUE AND RED FLYING OFF FROM THE AREA. EVERYTHING CONTINUES TO POINT TO SUPERMAN.
THAT'S THE PROBLEM. EVERYTHING POINTS TO SUPERMAN.
I KNOW. IT SMELLS LIKE A FRAME. IT'S TOO EASY; SUPERMAN ISN'T THAT STUPID. AND IT'S NOT AS IF THE MAN DOESN'T HAVE ENEMIES.
BUT...
BUT WHAT IF IT ISN'T A FRAME?
WHAT IF IT'S NOT STUPIDITY ON SUPERMAN'S PART? WHAT IF IT'S ARROGANCE? PERHAPS HE BELIEVES HE WON'T BE FOUND OUT--OR THAT NOTHING WILL HAPPEN TO HIM IF IT DOES?
PART OF THE REASON HE'S ALLOWED TO DO WHAT HE DOES IS THAT PEOPLE TRUST HIM--BELIEVE IN HIM. SUSPICION ALONE COULD KILL THAT.
MAKE IT TOUGH ON ANYONE IN A MASK.
I KNOW. THAT'S WHY I'M GOING TO GET IT SETTLED TONIGHT.
TONIGHT?!
WANTED
I WISH HE WOULD STOP DOING THAT!

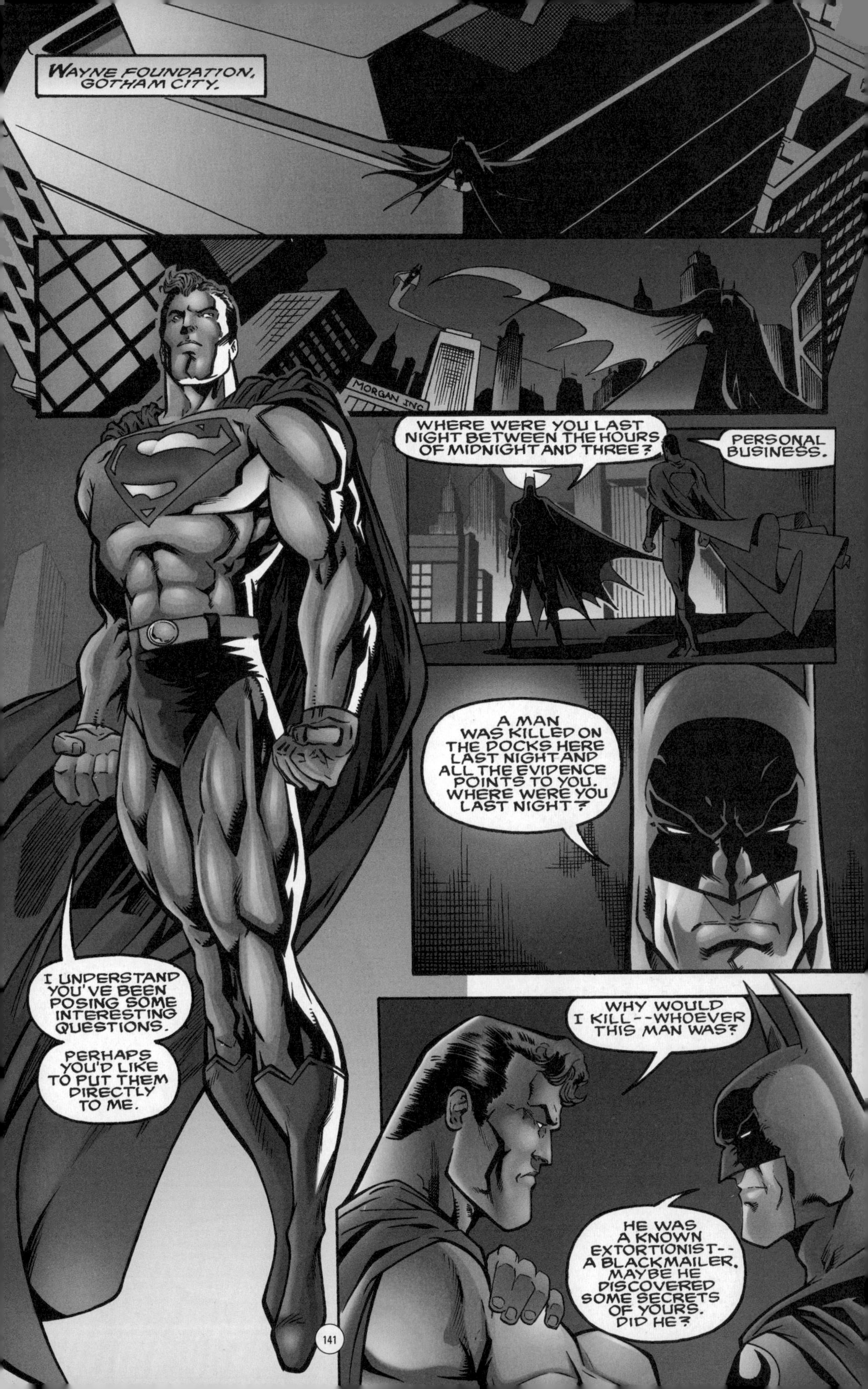
WAYNE FOUNDATION, GOTHAM CITY.
MORGAN INC
I UNDERSTAND YOU'VE BEEN POSING SOME INTERESTING QUESTIONS.
PERHAPS YOU'D LIKE TO PUT THEM DIRECTLY TO ME.
WHERE WERE YOU LAST NIGHT BETWEEN THE HOURS OF MIDNIGHT AND THREE?
PERSONAL BUSINESS.
A MAN WAS KILLED ON THE DOCKS HERE LAST NIGHT AND ALL THE EVIDENCE POINTS TO YOU. WHERE WERE YOU LAST NIGHT?
WHY WOULD I KILL--WHOEVER THIS MAN WAS?
HE WAS A KNOWN EXTORTIONIST--A BLACKMAILER. MAYBE HE DISCOVERED SOME SECRETS OF YOURS. DID HE?

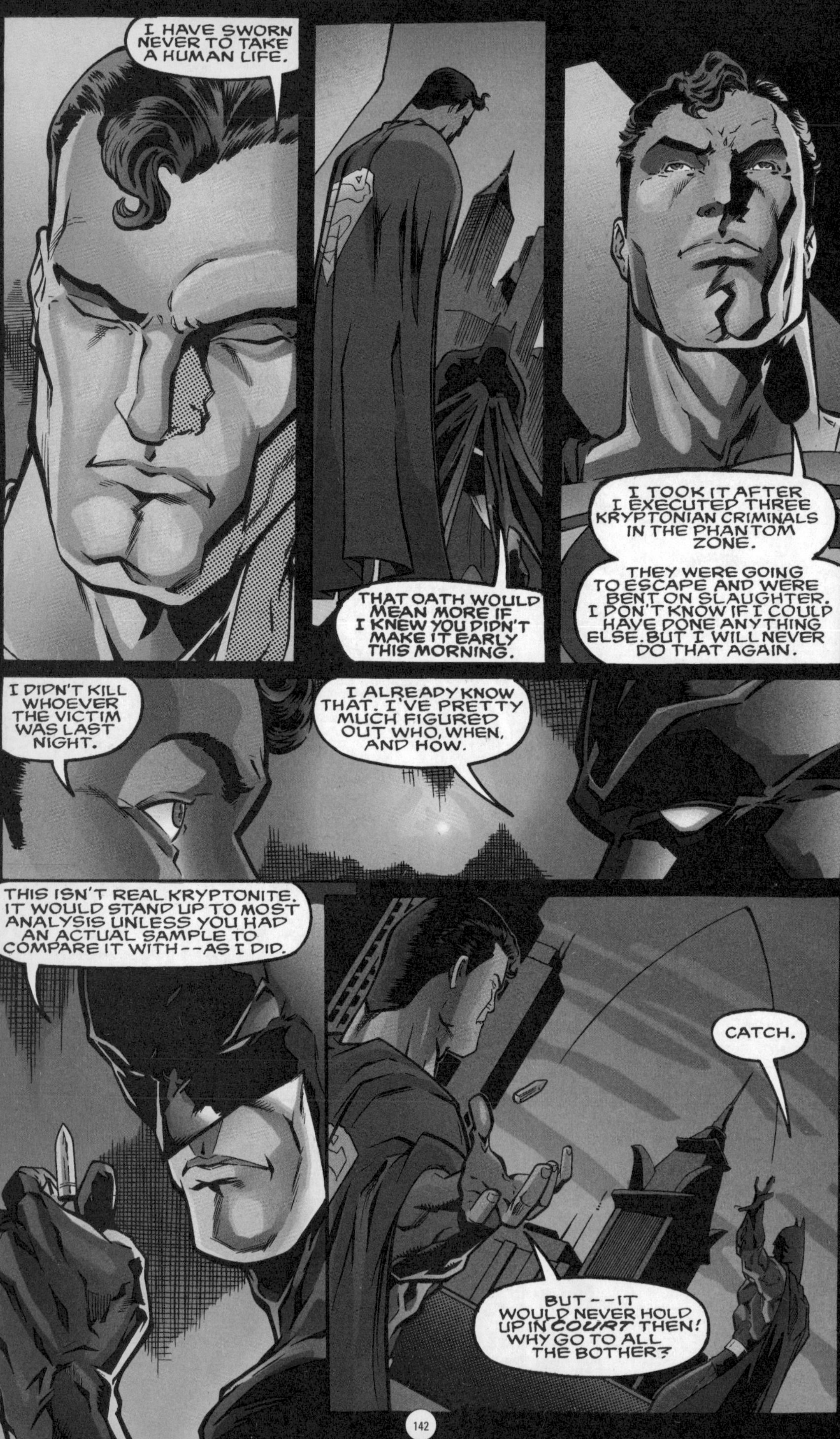
I HAVE SWORN NEVER TO TAKE A HUMAN LIFE.
THAT OATH WOULD MEAN MORE IF I KNEW YOU DIDN'T MAKE IT EARLY THIS MORNING.
I TOOK IT AFTER I EXECUTED THREE KRYPTONIAN CRIMINALS IN THE PHANTOM ZONE.
THEY WERE GOING TO ESCAPE AND WERE BENT ON SLAUGHTER. I DON'T KNOW IF I COULD HAVE DONE ANYTHING ELSE. BUT I WILL NEVER DO THAT AGAIN.
I DIDN'T KILL WHOEVER THE VICTIM WAS LAST NIGHT.
I ALREADY KNOW THAT. I'VE PRETTY MUCH FIGURED OUT WHO, WHEN, AND HOW.
THIS ISN'T REAL KRYPTONITE. IT WOULD STAND UP TO MOST ANALYSIS UNLESS YOU HAD AN ACTUAL SAMPLE TO COMPARE IT WITH--AS I DID.
CATCH.
BUT--IT WOULD NEVER HOLD UP IN COURT THEN! WHY GO TO ALL THE BOTHER?

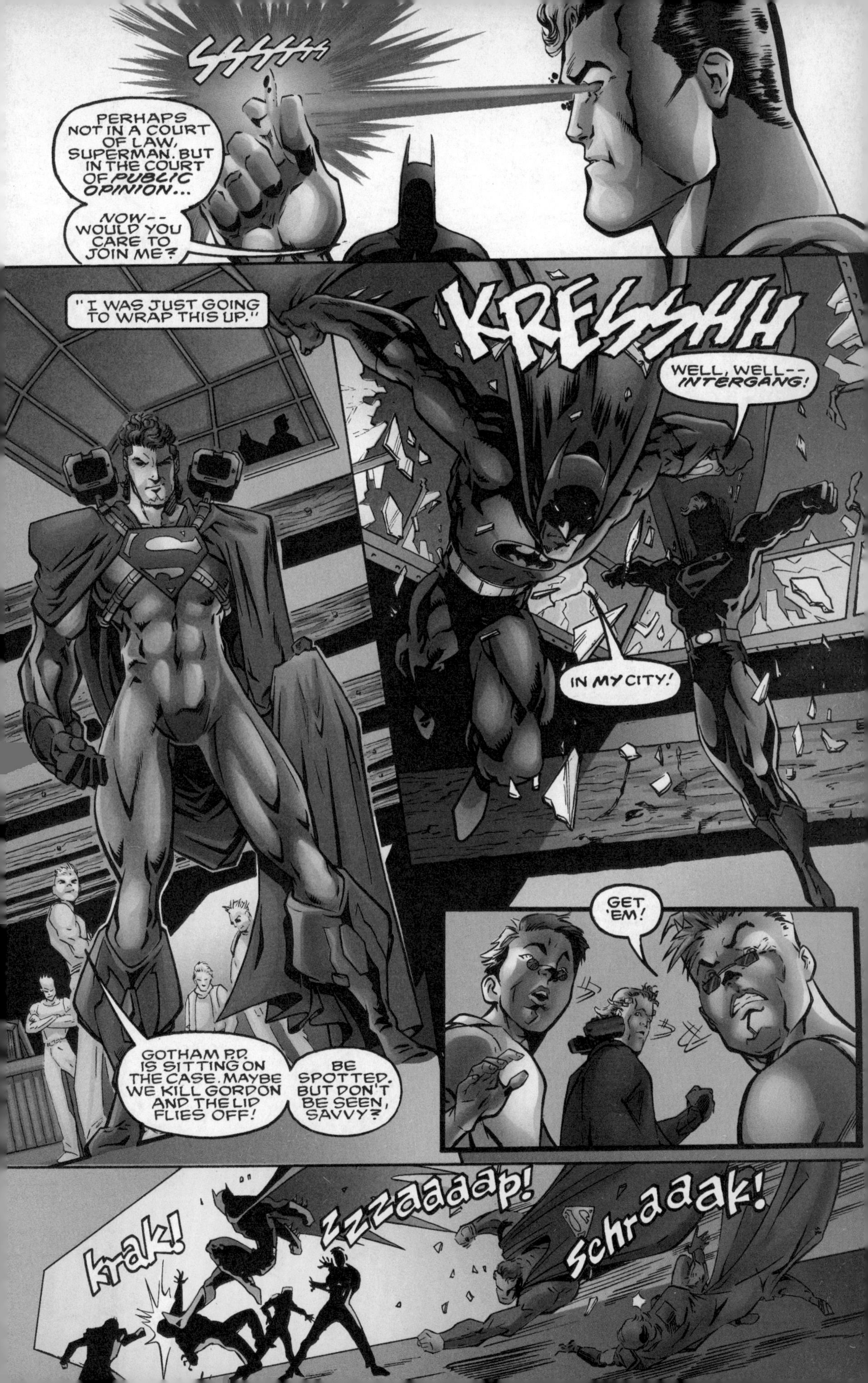
SSSSSSS
PERHAPS NOT IN A COURT OF LAW, SUPERMAN. BUT IN THE COURT OF *PUBLIC OPINION*...
NOW-- WOULD YOU CARE TO JOIN ME?
"I WAS JUST GOING TO WRAP THIS UP."
KRESSHH
WELL, WELL-- *INTERGANG!*
IN MY CITY!
GET 'EM!
GOTHAM P.D. IS SITTING ON THE CASE. MAYBE WE KILL GORDON AND THE LID FLIES OFF!
BE SPOTTED. BUT DON'T BE SEEN, SAVVY?
krak!
Zzzaaaaap!
Schraaak!

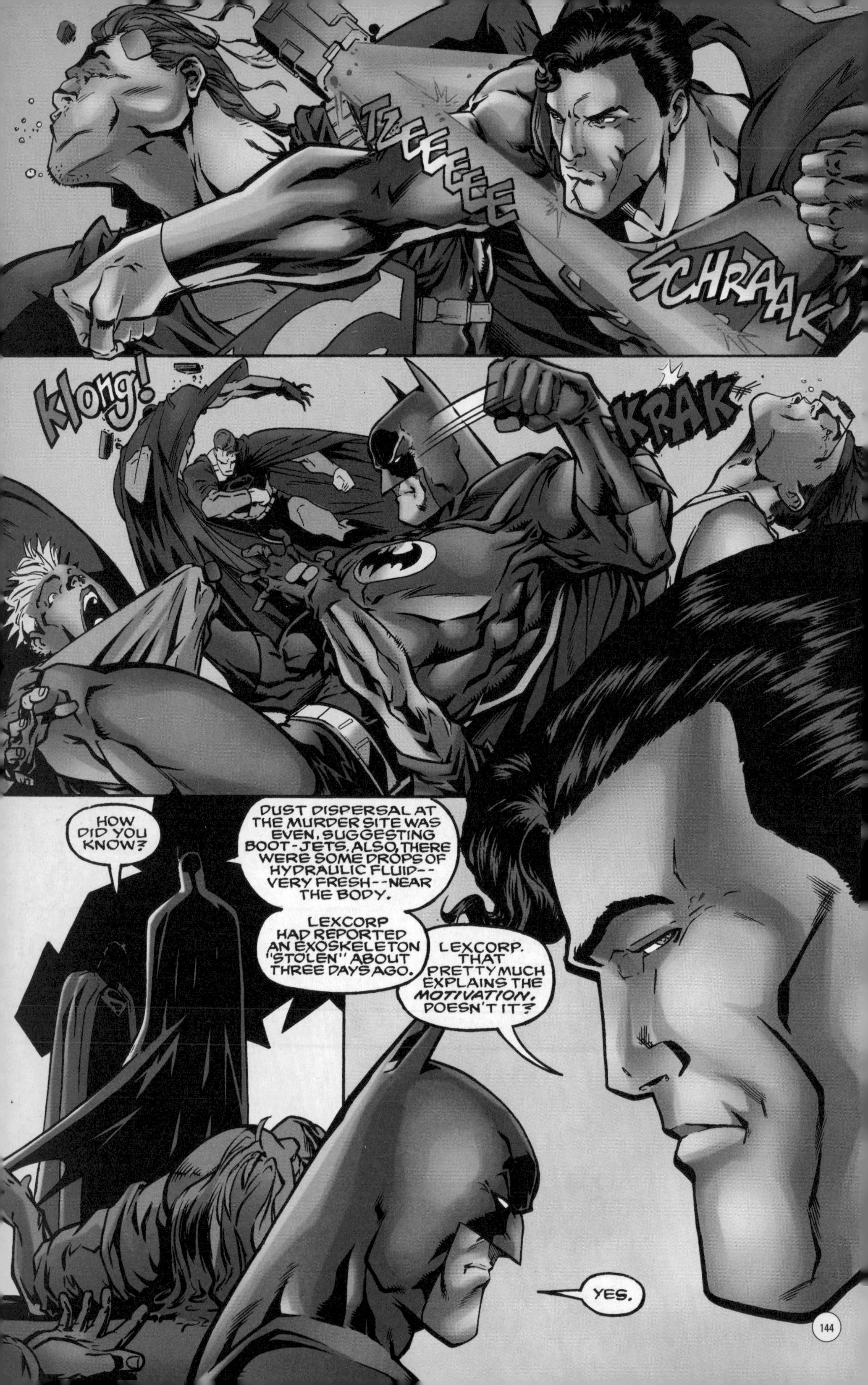
TZEEEEEE
SCHRAAK!
KLONG!
KRAK
HOW DID YOU KNOW?
DUST DISPERSAL AT THE MURDER SITE WAS EVEN, SUGGESTING BOOT-JETS. ALSO, THERE WERE SOME DROPS OF HYDRAULIC FLUID-- VERY FRESH--NEAR THE BODY.
LEXCORP HAD REPORTED AN EXOSKELETON "STOLEN" ABOUT THREE DAYS AGO.
LEXCORP. THAT PRETTY MUCH EXPLAINS THE *MOTIVATION*, DOESN'T IT?
YES.

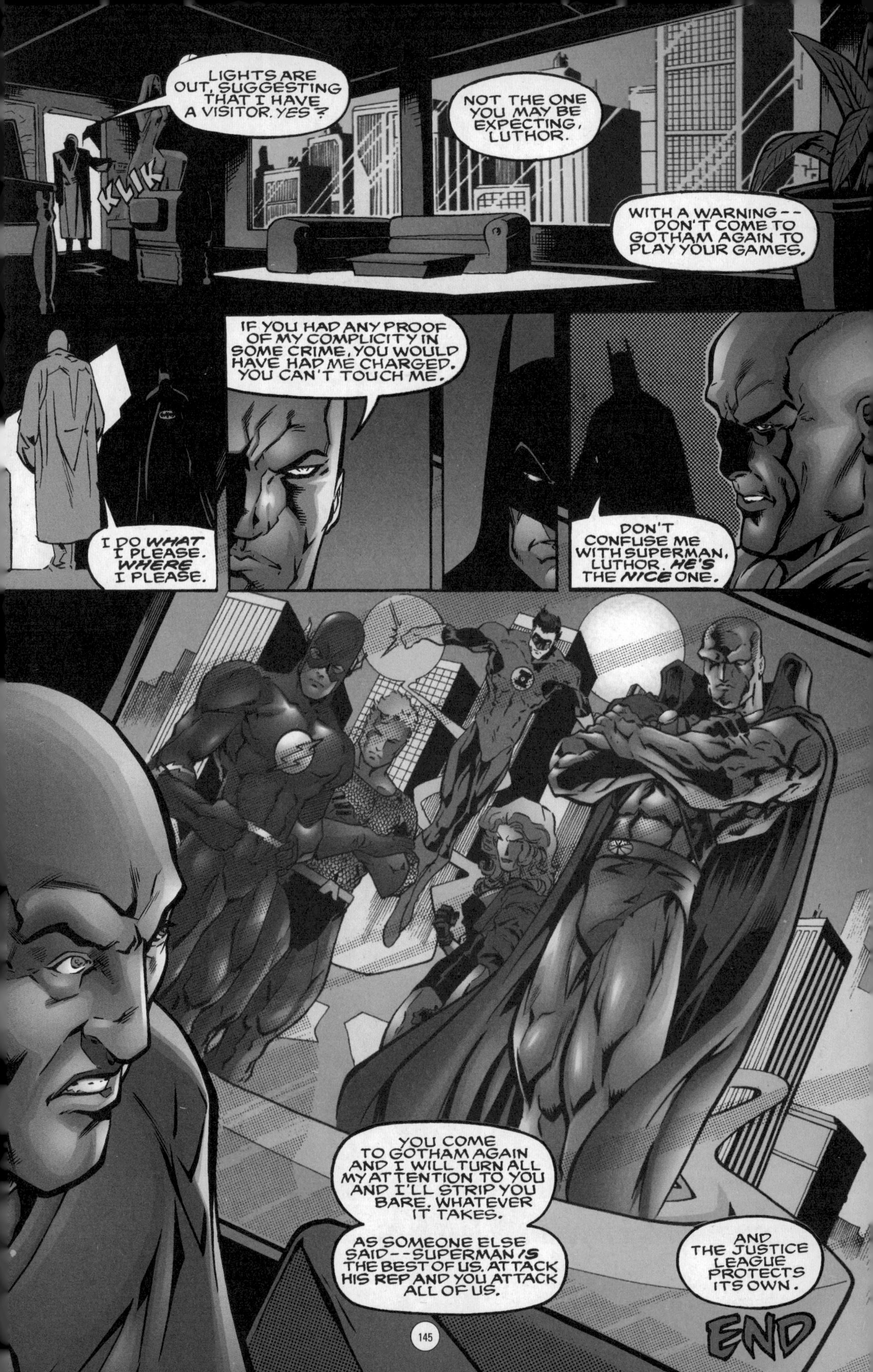
LIGHTS ARE OUT, SUGGESTING THAT I HAVE A VISITOR. YES?
KLIK
NOT THE ONE YOU MAY BE EXPECTING, LUTHOR.
WITH A WARNING-- DON'T COME TO GOTHAM AGAIN TO PLAY YOUR GAMES.
I DO WHAT I PLEASE. WHERE I PLEASE.
IF YOU HAD ANY PROOF OF MY COMPLICITY IN SOME CRIME, YOU WOULD HAVE HAD ME CHARGED. YOU CAN'T TOUCH ME.
DON'T CONFUSE ME WITH SUPERMAN, LUTHOR. HE'S THE NICE ONE.
YOU COME TO GOTHAM AGAIN AND I WILL TURN ALL MY ATTENTION TO YOU AND I'LL STRIP YOU BARE. WHATEVER IT TAKES.
AS SOMEONE ELSE SAID--SUPERMAN IS THE BEST OF US. ATTACK HIS REP AND YOU ATTACK ALL OF US.
AND THE JUSTICE LEAGUE PROTECTS ITS OWN.
END

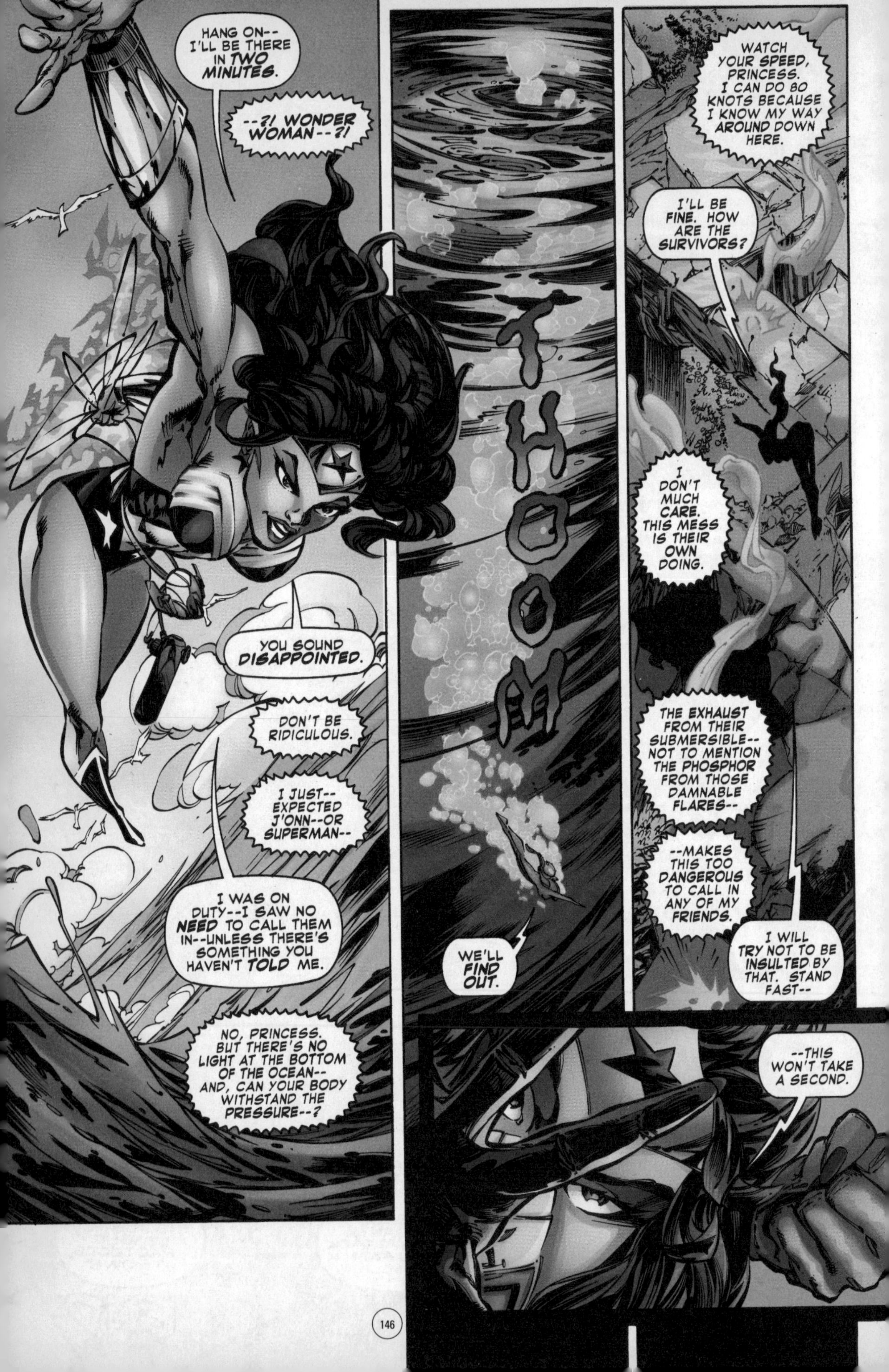
HANG ON-- I'LL BE THERE IN TWO MINUTES.
--?! WONDER WOMAN--?!
YOU SOUND DISAPPOINTED.
DON'T BE RIDICULOUS.
I JUST-- EXPECTED J'ONN--OR SUPERMAN--
I WAS ON DUTY--I SAW NO NEED TO CALL THEM IN--UNLESS THERE'S SOMETHING YOU HAVEN'T TOLD ME.
NO, PRINCESS. BUT THERE'S NO LIGHT AT THE BOTTOM OF THE OCEAN-- AND, CAN YOUR BODY WITHSTAND THE PRESSURE--?
THOOM
WE'LL FIND OUT.
WATCH YOUR SPEED, PRINCESS. I CAN DO 80 KNOTS BECAUSE I KNOW MY WAY AROUND DOWN HERE.
I'LL BE FINE. HOW ARE THE SURVIVORS?
I DON'T MUCH CARE. THIS MESS IS THEIR OWN DOING.
THE EXHAUST FROM THEIR SUBMERSIBLE-- NOT TO MENTION THE PHOSPHOR FROM THOSE DAMNABLE FLARES--
--MAKES THIS TOO DANGEROUS TO CALL IN ANY OF MY FRIENDS.
I WILL TRY NOT TO BE INSULTED BY THAT. STAND FAST--
--THIS WON'T TAKE A SECOND.

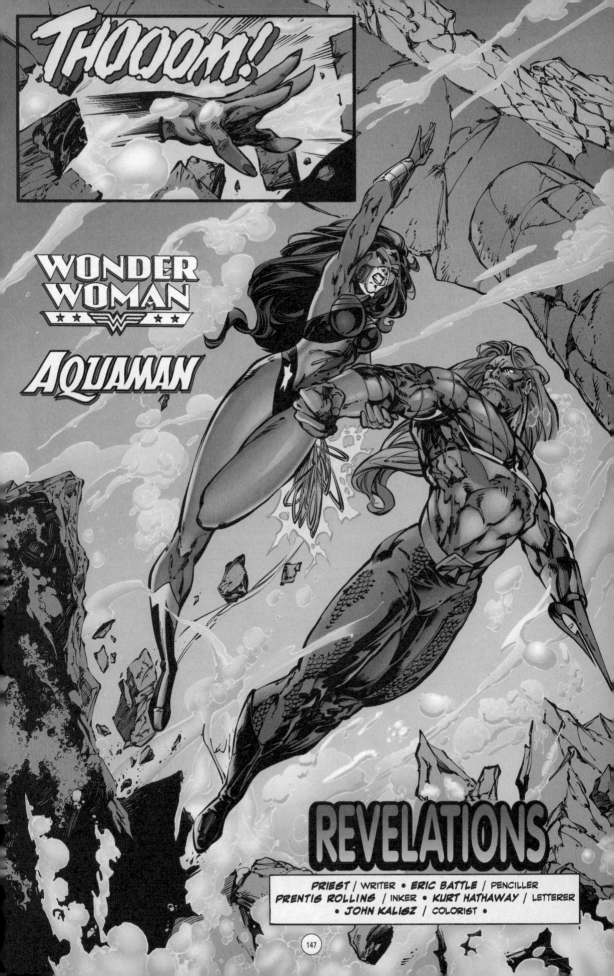

THOOOM!

WONDER WOMAN

AQUAMAN

REVELATIONS

PRIEST / WRITER • ERIC BATTLE / PENCILLER
PRENTIS ROLLINS / INKER • KURT HATHAWAY / LETTERER
• JOHN KALISZ / COLORIST •

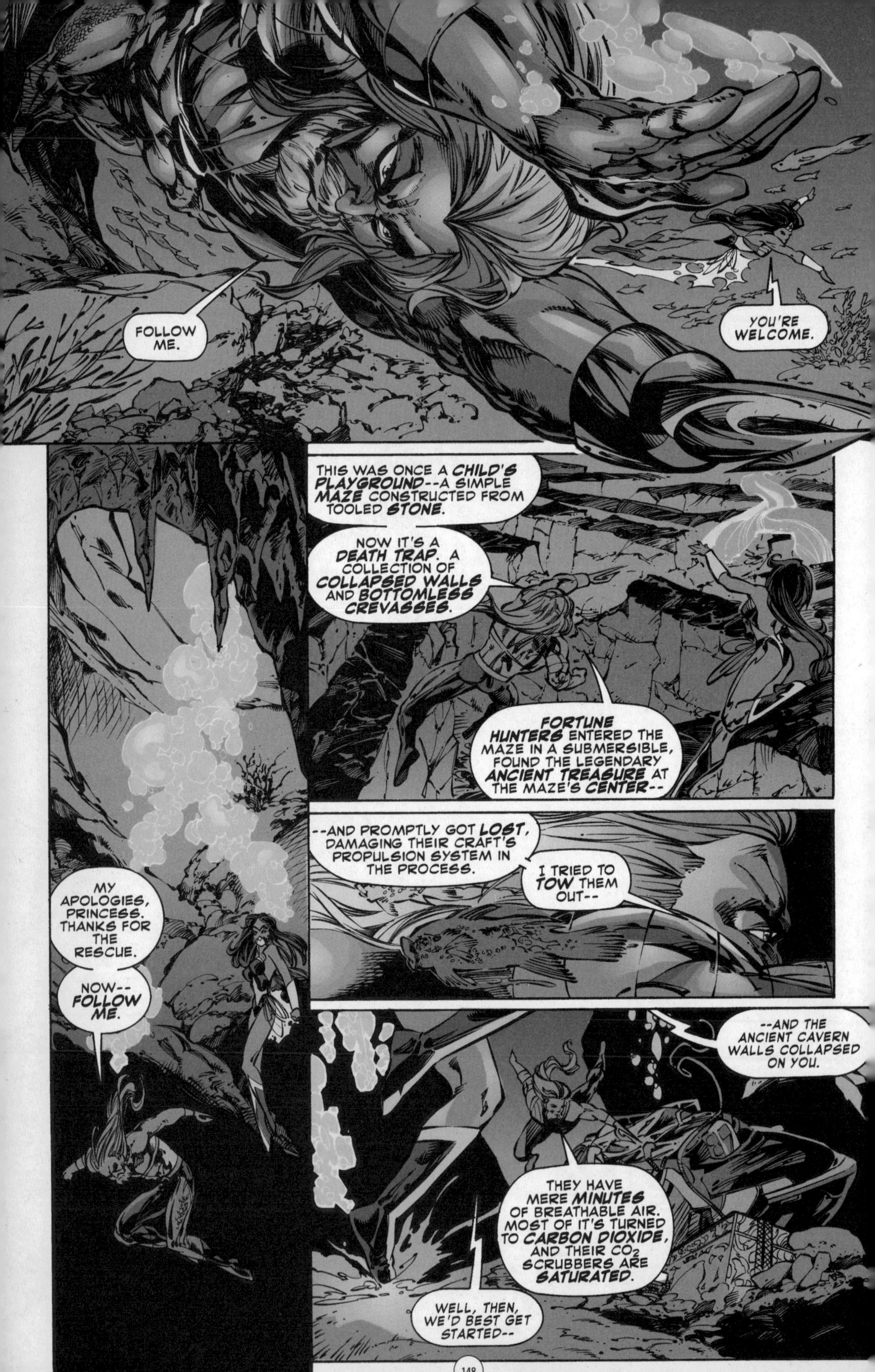
FOLLOW ME.
YOU'RE WELCOME.
MY APOLOGIES, PRINCESS. THANKS FOR THE RESCUE.
NOW-- FOLLOW ME.
THIS WAS ONCE A CHILD'S PLAYGROUND--A SIMPLE MAZE CONSTRUCTED FROM TOOLED STONE.
NOW IT'S A DEATH TRAP. A COLLECTION OF COLLAPSED WALLS AND BOTTOMLESS CREVASSES.
FORTUNE HUNTERS ENTERED THE MAZE IN A SUBMERSIBLE, FOUND THE LEGENDARY ANCIENT TREASURE AT THE MAZE'S CENTER--
--AND PROMPTLY GOT LOST, DAMAGING THEIR CRAFT'S PROPULSION SYSTEM IN THE PROCESS.
I TRIED TO TOW THEM OUT--
--AND THE ANCIENT CAVERN WALLS COLLAPSED ON YOU.
THEY HAVE MERE MINUTES OF BREATHABLE AIR. MOST OF IT'S TURNED TO CARBON DIOXIDE, AND THEIR CO_2 SCRUBBERS ARE SATURATED.
WELL, THEN, WE'D BEST GET STARTED--

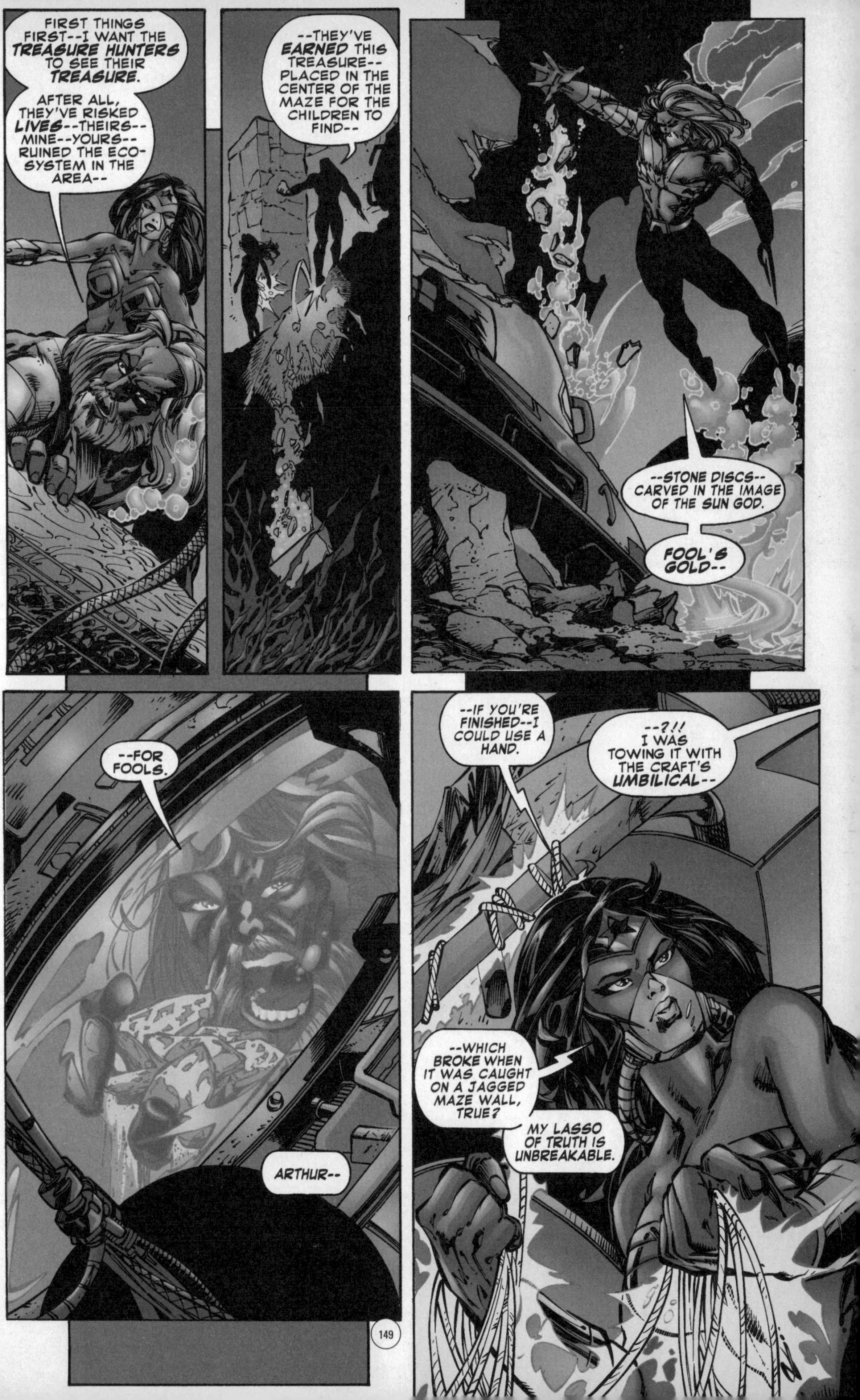
FIRST THINGS FIRST--I WANT THE TREASURE HUNTERS TO SEE THEIR TREASURE.
AFTER ALL, THEY'VE RISKED LIVES--THEIRS--MINE--YOURS--RUINED THE ECO-SYSTEM IN THE AREA--
--THEY'VE EARNED THIS TREASURE--PLACED IN THE CENTER OF THE MAZE FOR THE CHILDREN TO FIND--
--STONE DISCS--CARVED IN THE IMAGE OF THE SUN GOD.
FOOL'S GOLD--
--FOR FOOLS.
ARTHUR--
--IF YOU'RE FINISHED--I COULD USE A HAND.
--?!! I WAS TOWING IT WITH THE CRAFT'S UMBILICAL--
--WHICH BROKE WHEN IT WAS CAUGHT ON A JAGGED MAZE WALL, TRUE?
MY LASSO OF TRUTH IS UNBREAKABLE.

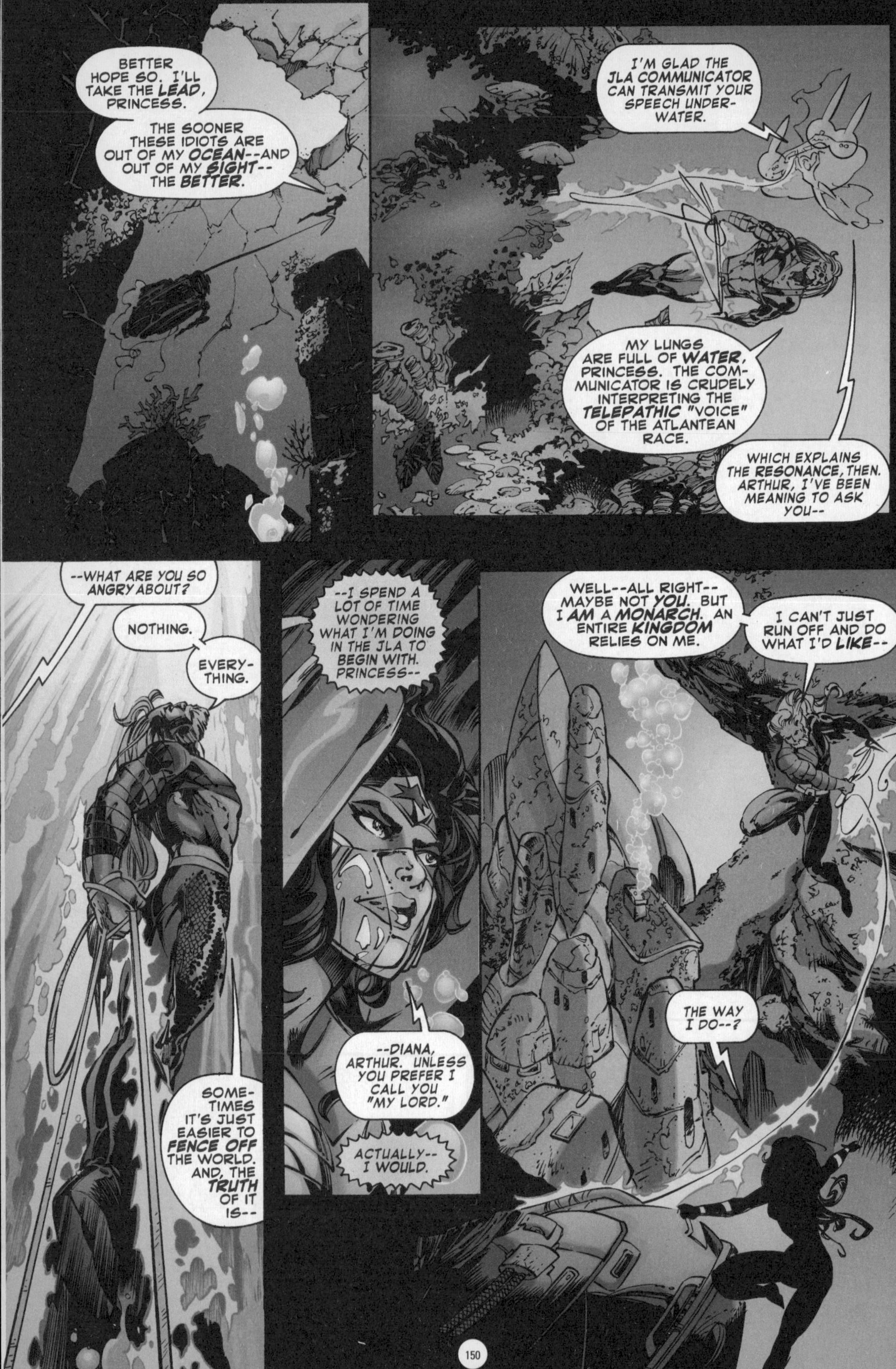
BETTER HOPE SO. I'LL TAKE THE LEAD, PRINCESS.
THE SOONER THESE IDIOTS ARE OUT OF MY OCEAN--AND OUT OF MY SIGHT--THE BETTER.
I'M GLAD THE JLA COMMUNICATOR CAN TRANSMIT YOUR SPEECH UNDER-WATER.
MY LUNGS ARE FULL OF WATER, PRINCESS. THE COM-MUNICATOR IS CRUDELY INTERPRETING THE TELEPATHIC "VOICE" OF THE ATLANTEAN RACE.
WHICH EXPLAINS THE RESONANCE, THEN. ARTHUR, I'VE BEEN MEANING TO ASK YOU--
--WHAT ARE YOU SO ANGRY ABOUT?
NOTHING.
EVERY-THING.
SOME-TIMES IT'S JUST EASIER TO FENCE OFF THE WORLD. AND, THE TRUTH OF IT IS--
--I SPEND A LOT OF TIME WONDERING WHAT I'M DOING IN THE JLA TO BEGIN WITH. PRINCESS--
--DIANA, ARTHUR. UNLESS YOU PREFER I CALL YOU "MY LORD."
ACTUALLY--I WOULD.
WELL--ALL RIGHT--MAYBE NOT YOU. BUT I AM A MONARCH. AN ENTIRE KINGDOM RELIES ON ME.
I CAN'T JUST RUN OFF AND DO WHAT I'D LIKE--
THE WAY I DO--?

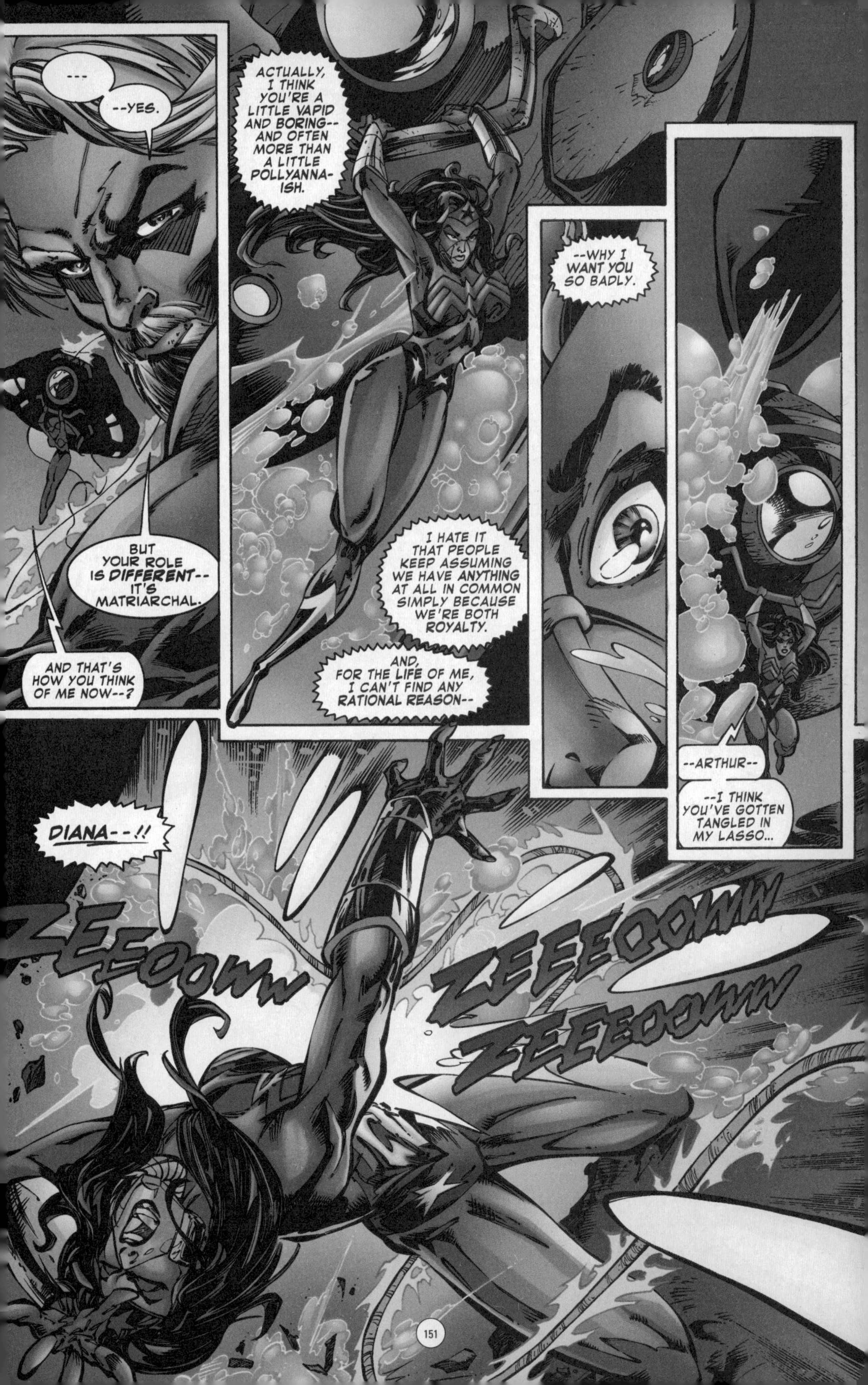

--YES.
ACTUALLY, I THINK YOU'RE A LITTLE VAPID AND BORING--AND OFTEN MORE THAN A LITTLE POLLYANNA-ISH.
BUT YOUR ROLE IS DIFFERENT--IT'S MATRIARCHAL.
AND THAT'S HOW YOU THINK OF ME NOW--?
I HATE IT THAT PEOPLE KEEP ASSUMING WE HAVE ANYTHING AT ALL IN COMMON SIMPLY BECAUSE WE'RE BOTH ROYALTY.
AND, FOR THE LIFE OF ME, I CAN'T FIND ANY RATIONAL REASON--
--WHY I WANT YOU SO BADLY.
--ARTHUR--
--I THINK YOU'VE GOTTEN TANGLED IN MY LASSO...
DIANA--!!
ZEEEOOWW
ZEEEOOWW
ZEEEOOWW

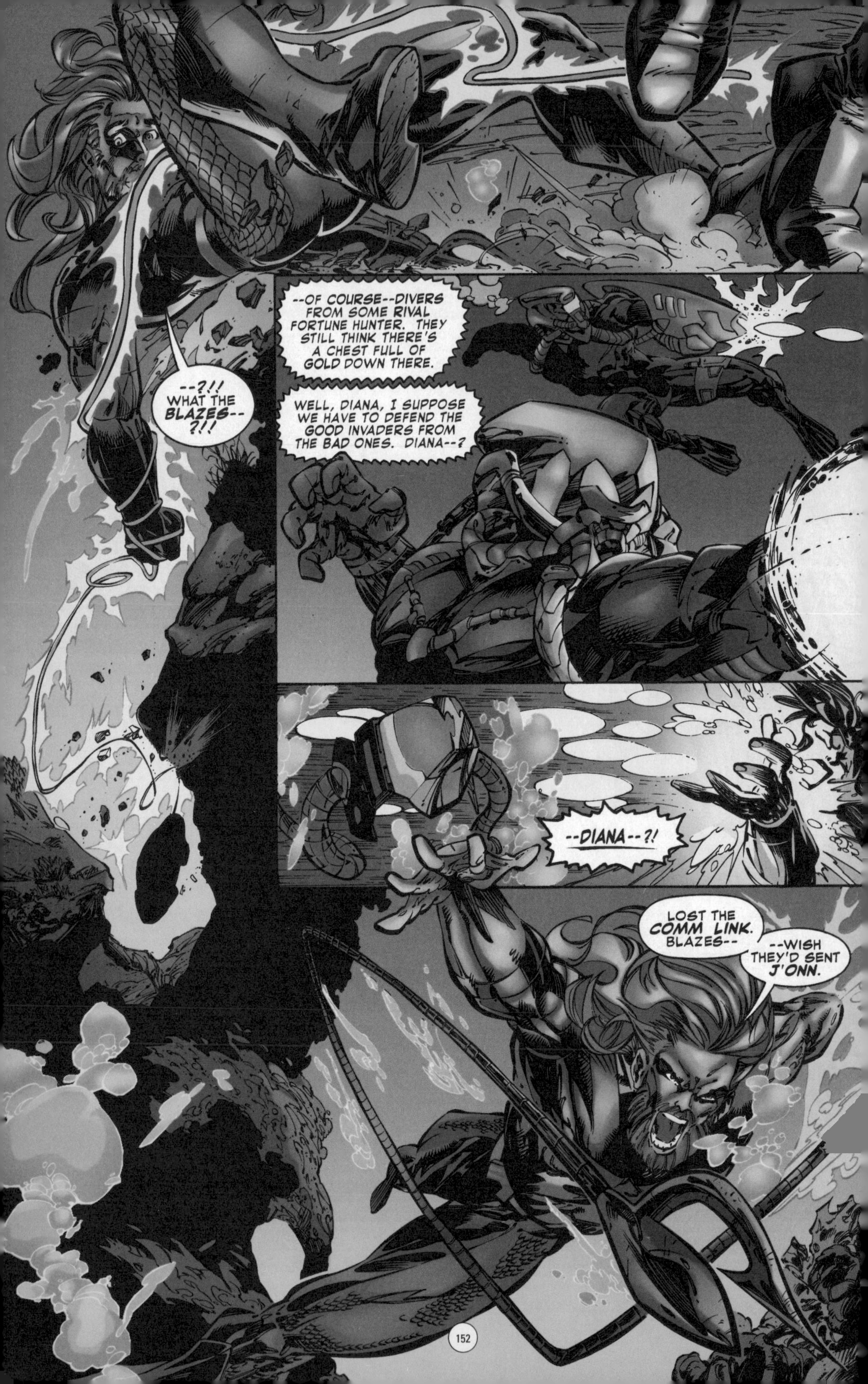
--?!! WHAT THE BLAZES-- ?!!
--OF COURSE--DIVERS FROM SOME RIVAL FORTUNE HUNTER. THEY STILL THINK THERE'S A CHEST FULL OF GOLD DOWN THERE.
WELL, DIANA, I SUPPOSE WE HAVE TO DEFEND THE GOOD INVADERS FROM THE BAD ONES. DIANA--?
--DIANA--?!
LOST THE COMM LINK. BLAZES--
--WISH THEY'D SENT J'ONN.

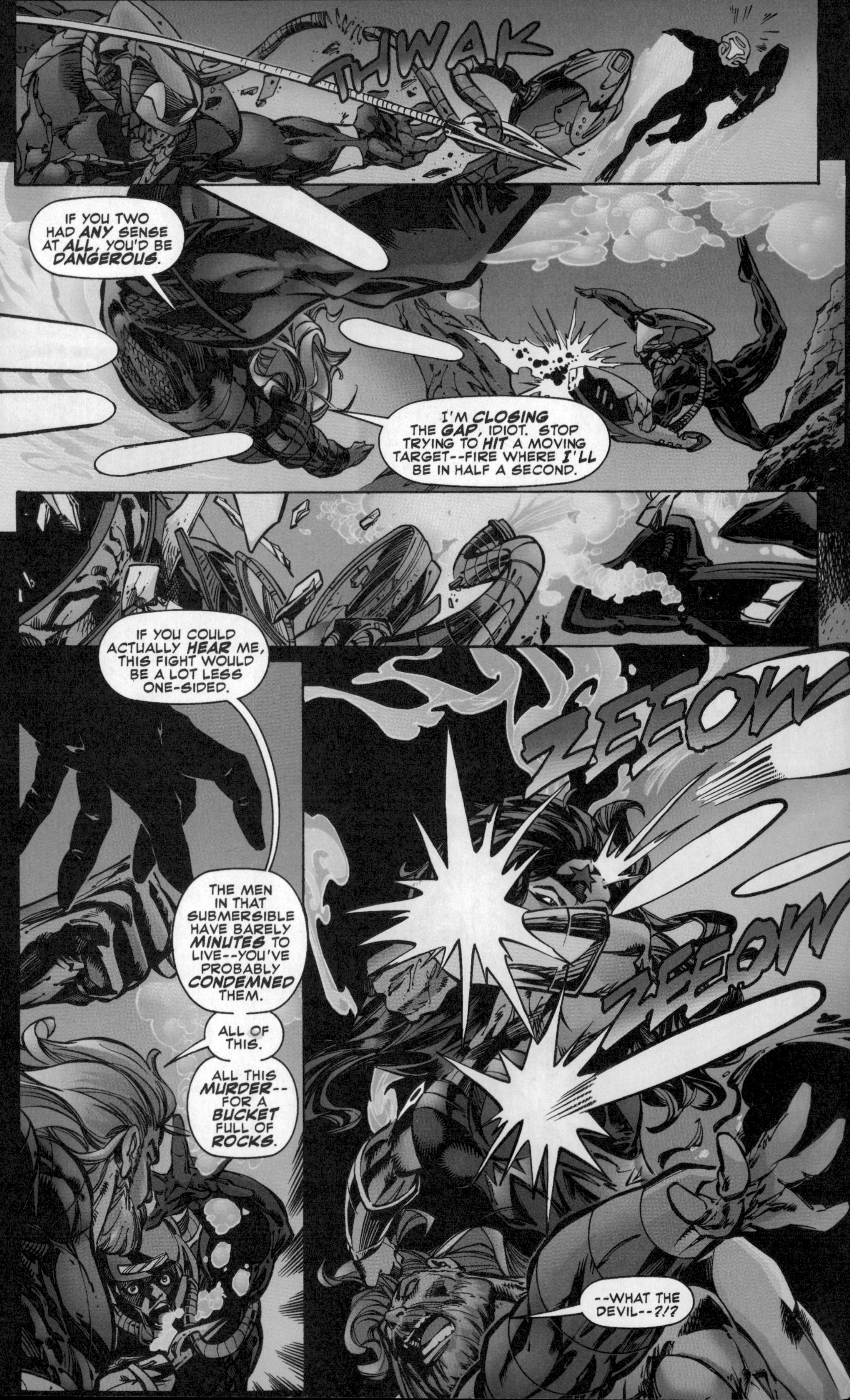
THWAK
IF YOU TWO HAD ANY SENSE AT ALL, YOU'D BE DANGEROUS.
I'M CLOSING THE GAP, IDIOT. STOP TRYING TO HIT A MOVING TARGET--FIRE WHERE I'LL BE IN HALF A SECOND.
IF YOU COULD ACTUALLY HEAR ME, THIS FIGHT WOULD BE A LOT LESS ONE-SIDED.
ZEEOW
THE MEN IN THAT SUBMERSIBLE HAVE BARELY MINUTES TO LIVE--YOU'VE PROBABLY CONDEMNED THEM.
ZEEOW
ALL OF THIS.
ALL THIS MURDER--FOR A BUCKET FULL OF ROCKS.
--WHAT THE DEVIL--?!?

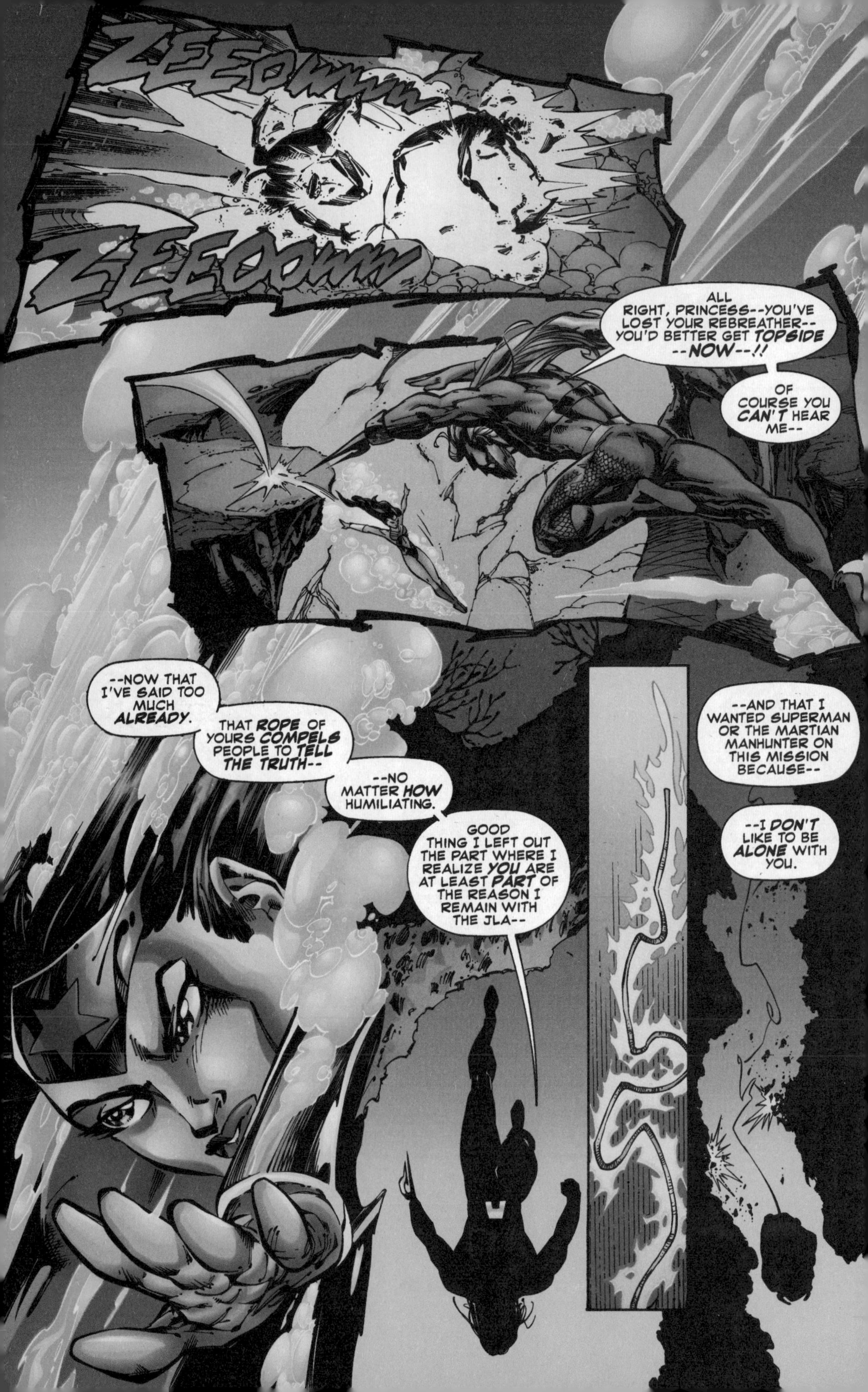

ZEEOWWWW
ZEEOOWWW
ALL RIGHT, PRINCESS--YOU'VE LOST YOUR REBREATHER--YOU'D BETTER GET TOPSIDE --NOW--!!
OF COURSE YOU CAN'T HEAR ME--
--NOW THAT I'VE SAID TOO MUCH ALREADY.
THAT ROPE OF YOURS COMPELS PEOPLE TO TELL THE TRUTH--
--NO MATTER HOW HUMILIATING.
GOOD THING I LEFT OUT THE PART WHERE I REALIZE YOU ARE AT LEAST PART OF THE REASON I REMAIN WITH THE JLA--
--AND THAT I WANTED SUPERMAN OR THE MARTIAN MANHUNTER ON THIS MISSION BECAUSE--
--I DON'T LIKE TO BE ALONE WITH YOU.

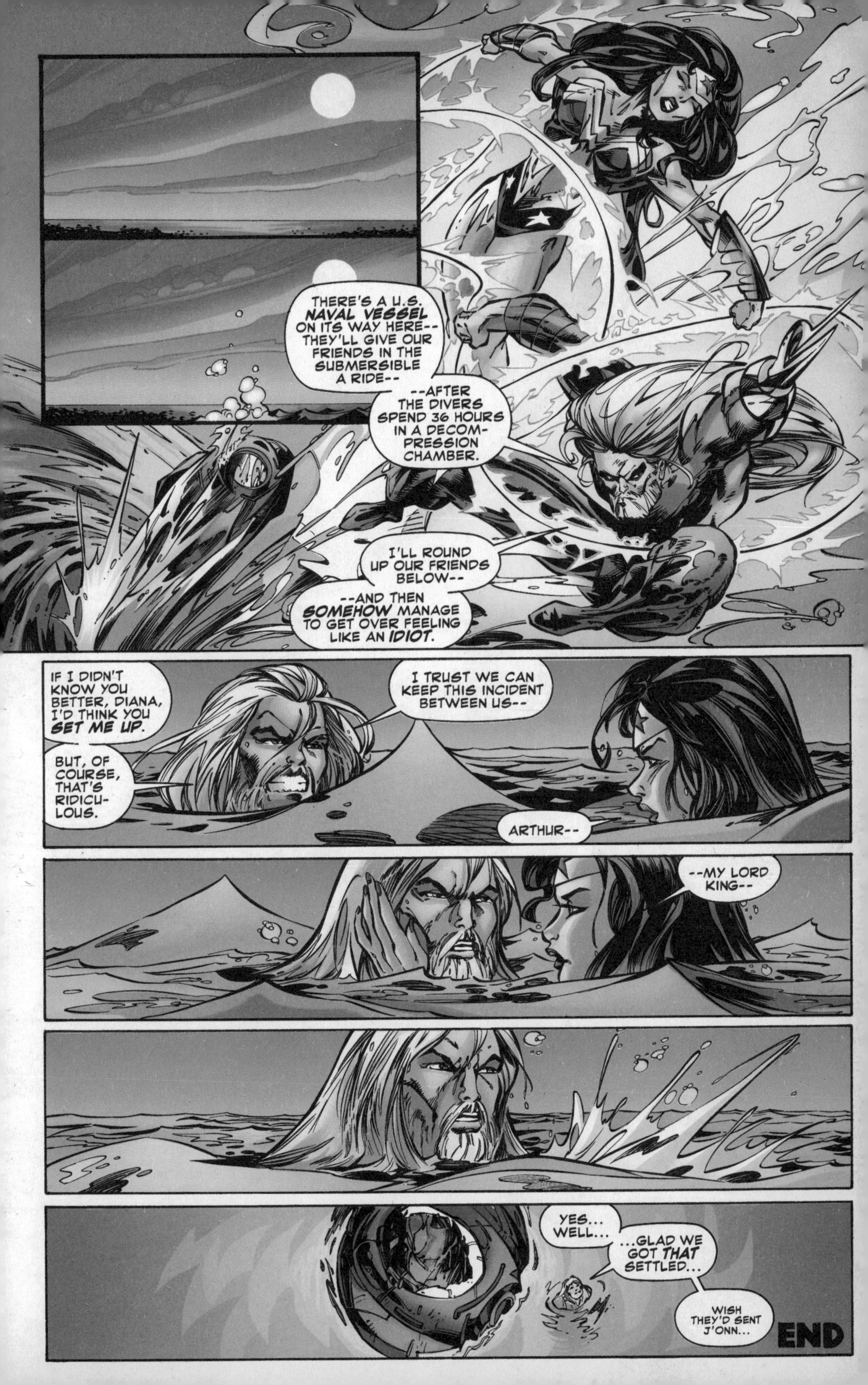
THERE'S A U.S. NAVAL VESSEL ON ITS WAY HERE-- THEY'LL GIVE OUR FRIENDS IN THE SUBMERSIBLE A RIDE--
--AFTER THE DIVERS SPEND 36 HOURS IN A DECOMPRESSION CHAMBER.
I'LL ROUND UP OUR FRIENDS BELOW--
--AND THEN SOMEHOW MANAGE TO GET OVER FEELING LIKE AN IDIOT.
IF I DIDN'T KNOW YOU BETTER, DIANA, I'D THINK YOU SET ME UP.
BUT, OF COURSE, THAT'S RIDICULOUS.
I TRUST WE CAN KEEP THIS INCIDENT BETWEEN US--
ARTHUR--
--MY LORD KING--
YES... WELL...
...GLAD WE GOT THAT SETTLED...
WISH THEY'D SENT J'ONN...
END

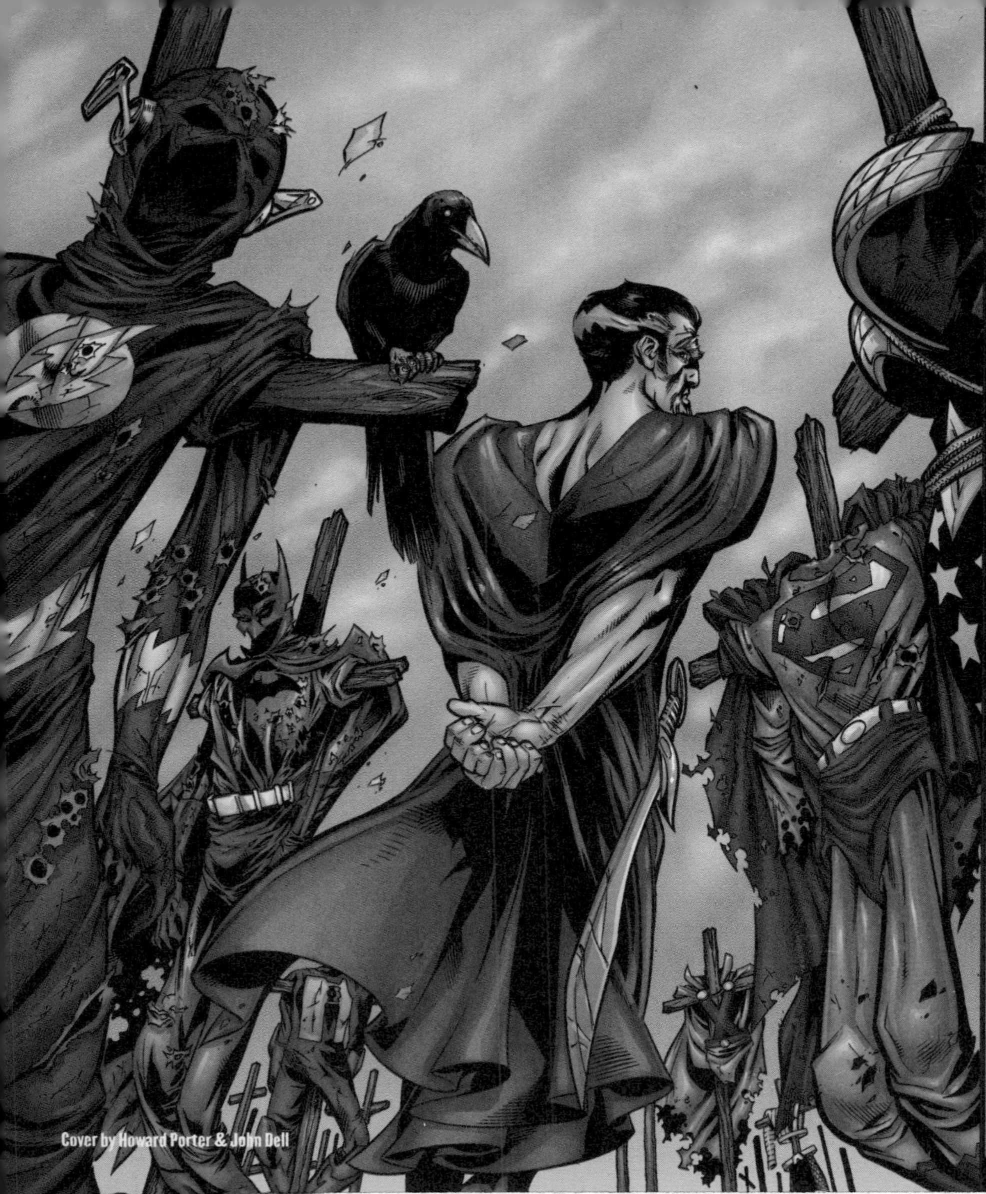
Cover by Howard Porter & John Dell

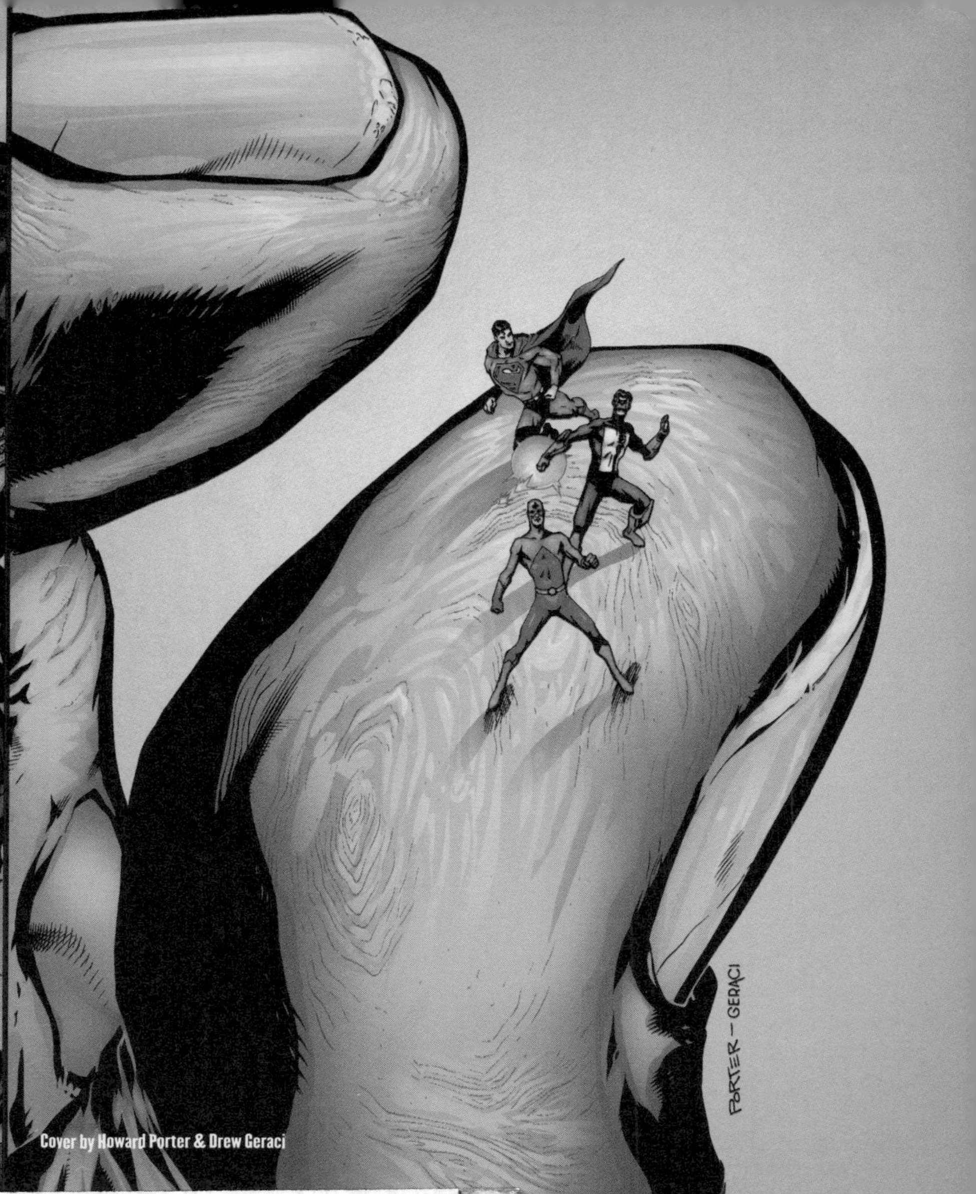
PORTER – GERACI
Cover by Howard Porter & Drew Geraci

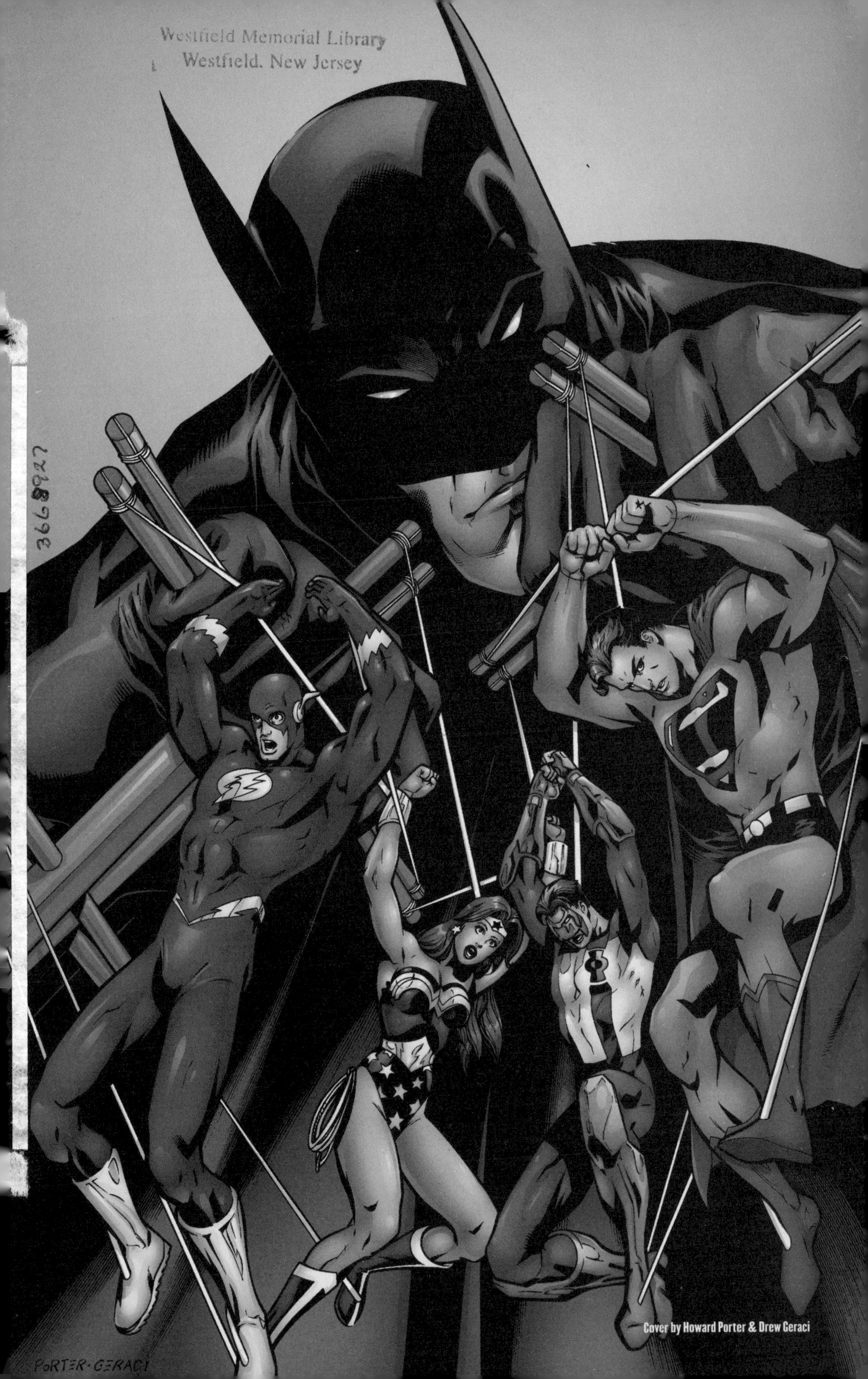
PORTER·GERACI

Cover by Howard Porter & Drew Geraci

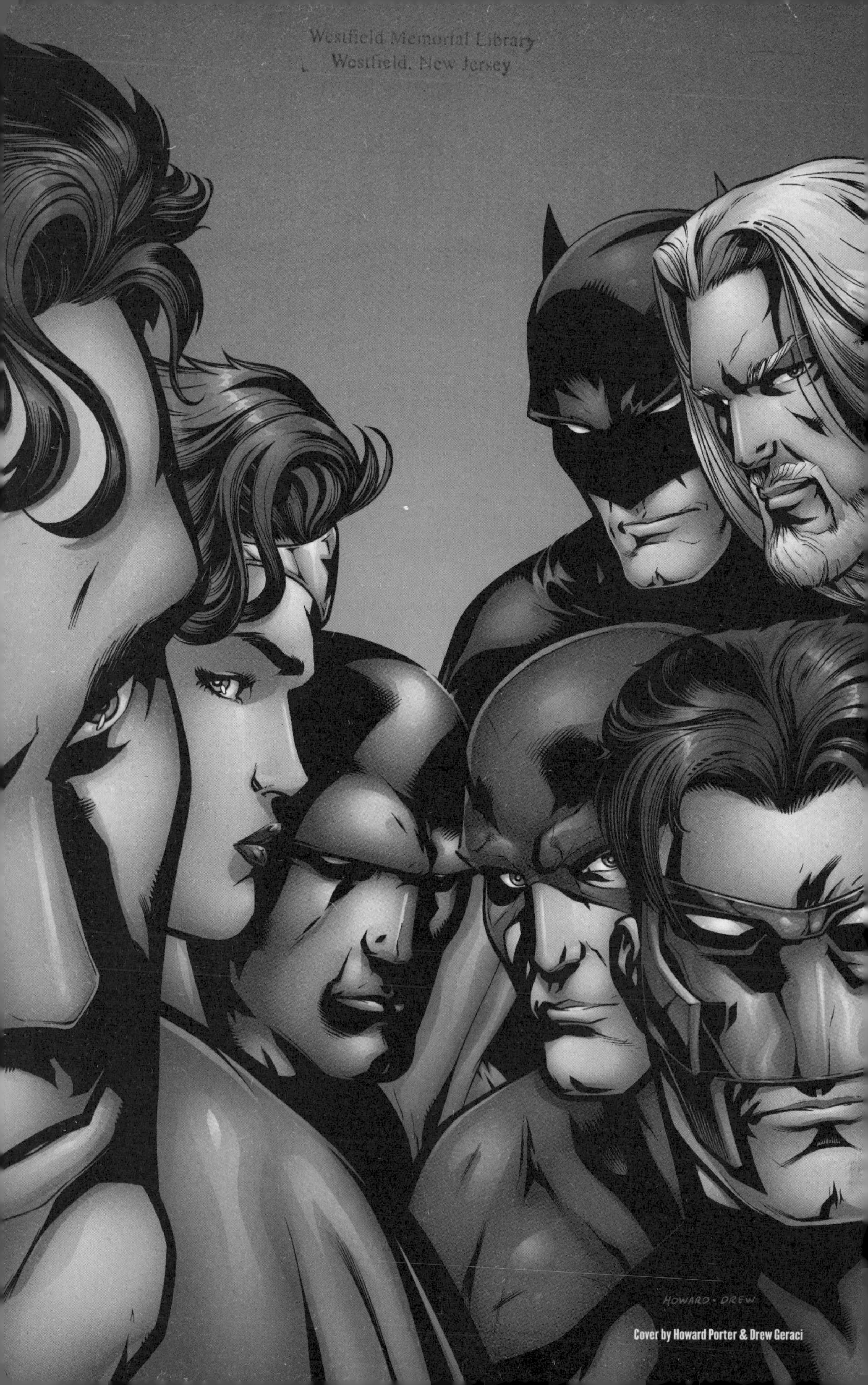
HOWARD • DREW

Cover by Howard Porter & Drew Geraci